CAPE: A Multidimensional Model of Fan Interest

CAPE: A Multidimensional Model of Fan Interest

Courtney N. Plante
Bishop's University

Stephen Reysen
Texas A&M University-Commerce

Thomas R. Brooks
New Mexico Highlands University

Daniel Chadborn
New Mexico Highlands University

CAPE Model Research Team
Commerce, Texas, USA

ISBN: 978-0997628821

Acknowledgments

We would like to thank long time collaborators Dr. Sharon Roberts and Dr. Kathleen Gerbasi for aid in collecting data for furries and anime fans and Grace Packard for collecting data for *Star Wars* fans.

Contents

Introduction

Allow us to start this book with a bold prediction: You're probably a fan of something. Be it a sport, television show, music group, or hobby, chances are reasonably good that you enthusiastically and ardently engage in at least one interest (Reysen & Branscombe, 2010).

Unimpressed by our prophetic ability? It's probably because you know, whether intuitively or through research, that fans are a ubiquitous part of modern culture. The U.S. sport industry alone brings in more than 70 billion dollars annually (Kim, Qian, et al., 2020; Yousaf et al., 2017), while global competitions like the Olympics or the World Cup are among the most-viewed events on the planet. Whether we're talking about sport fans or binge-watchers of a new Netflix original series, fans the world over spend a significant portion of their valuable free time engaging in fan-related activities. One study found that U.S. adults spend an average of 20 and 38 hours per week on their leisure activities (Ruggeri, 2020) while, on the other side of the globe, Chinese college students spend upwards of 9 hours per day on leisure (Chen & Liu, 2020). People, rather paradoxically, take their leisure activities, very seriously.

Given the amount of time and money people spend on their interests, it was inevitable that marketers and academics alike would show an interest in fans. Part of this endeavor includes efforts to categorize fans into types or taxonomies. To those in marketing, segmenting the market this way allows companies to target products and advertising directly to the most interested potential customers (Hunt et al., 1999). To academics, this sort of categorization allows researchers to better understand the important dimensions and mechanisms driving fan behavior.

In this book we're building off the work of both of these groups. Specifically, we'll be looking at the variables used to distinguish between different "types" of fans. Before we do, however, we should briefly review some of the different taxonomic and typological approaches used by those studying fans, including categorizing fans based on...

1. The nature of their identification with their fan interest.
2. Their engagement in specific fan-related behaviors.
3. The motivations underlying their fan interest.
4. A stage-like progression through their interest.

We should also mention, before we begin, two important caveats. First, despite our treatment of these categorizations as conceptually distinct, there may be associations between them. For example, fans who engage in one type of fan behavior (e.g., attending fan conventions) may be differently motivated (e.g., by social needs) than fans who engage in a different type of behavior (e.g., writing fanfiction for reasons of self-expression). In this case, categorization based on specific behaviors overlaps at least somewhat with categorization based on motivation. This doesn't detract from the utility of these categorizations, but rather illustrates the complex interplay of dimensions driving differences between any two fans.

The second caveat is that our summary of these different theoretical approaches to organizing the academic literature on fans is far from exhaustive. There are many more "types" of fans and fan engagement than what we cover here, including distinguishing fans from non-fans and anti-fans (Gray, 2003), enjoyment and appreciation (Oliver & Bartsch, 2011), harmonious and obsessive passion (Vallerand et al., 2003), subcultures within fandoms (e.g., creators, critics, collectors, joiners, and spectators, Hanna et al., 2011), utilitarian and authentic (Wallace et al., 2014), and the related phenomenon of parasocial connections with fictional characters and celebrities (e.g., Eyal & Cohen, 2006). As you read the rest of this introduction and the chapters which follow, keep this in mind: Our goal is to review the most influential or theoretically-central dimensions of fans, not to catalogue every typology and dimension ever created.

Categorizing Fans Based on Identification

The extent to which fans identify as fans of their fan interest is arguably the dimension most widely used to differentiate fans from one another. Those who identify more strongly with facets of their fan interest are "bigger fans," and contrasted against those who identify less strongly. The particular facet being identified with will vary from study to study as researchers focus on different aspects of the interest. For example, one researcher may study identification with the fan interest itself (e.g., "I strongly identify with anime"), a construct referred to as "fanship." Another researcher may assess identification with other fans who share the same interest (e.g., "I strongly identify with other fans in the anime community"), a construct referred to as "fandom."

At first glance, you might think that the distinction between "fanship" and "fandom" is an exercise in theoretical hair-splitting. After all, people who identify with other fans probably also identify with the interest itself, right? As it turns out, while the two constructs are highly correlated, they are far from perfectly correlated and can be shown to be empirically distinct (Reysen & Branscombe, 2010). For instance, fanship and fandom predict different fan behaviors (e.g., Edwards et al., 2019). This being the case, a study which only assesses fanship while ignoring fandom will necessarily get an incomplete picture of the factors which predict fan behavior. Nevertheless, most fan studies assessing fanship do not also assess fandom—a trend which, fortunately, has been changing over time.

We'll continue to discus the constructs of fanship (see Chapter 15) and fandom (see Chapter 7) later in this book. For now, we'll shift our focus to some of the ways fanship and fandom have been assessed to give the reader a feel for how scholars empirically distinguish highly-identified fans from less-identified ones.

In their approach to measuring fan identity, Daniel Wann and Nyla Branscombe (1993) drew upon the social identity perspective, which posits that the groups to which we belong—from our national identity down to the sport teams we cheer for—impact our self-esteem (Tajfel & Turner, 1979; Turner et al., 1987). They construed an eight-item measure to assess the extent to which their participants identified with a sport team, using a scale ranging from *not important* to *very important* to answer questions like "How important is being a fan of [insert team] to you?" This Sport Spectator Identification Scale (SSIS) is the most frequently-used measure of team identification in psychology, although it's not without its drawbacks. For one thing, the measure was designed with sport fans in mind, meaning that some of the items were inapplicable for other types of fans, like media fans (e.g., "How important is it to you that the team wins?"). In response to these concerns, researchers would later develop fandom-general measures of fanship inspired by the SSIS (Reysen & Branscombe, 2010).

The SSIS is not the only measure of fan identification to be derived from, or applied to, sport fans in particular. Trail et al. (2003) based their points of attachment scale on the idea that varsity sport fans may identify with different aspect of a sport beyond the team. Their measure assesses:

- identification with players (e.g., "I am a big fan of specific players more than I am a fan of the team")
- identification with teams (e.g., "Being a fan of [insert team name] is very important to me")
- identification with coaches (e.g., "I am a big fan of Coach [insert name]")
- identification with the sport itself ("[insert sport] is my favorite sport"), the university (e.g., "I identify with the university rather than with any specific university team")
- identification with the level of the sport (e.g., "I am a fan of college [insert sport] regardless of who is playing")

One notable flaw with the scale is its failure to assess identification with other fans (i.e., fandom) despite assessing fan identification with so many other facets of their interest.

Heere and James (2007) developed a different measure of sport team identification grounded in the social identity perspective. Their measure includes six subscales assessing:

- how the participant's team is viewed by the general public (e.g., "Overall, my college football team is viewed positively by others")
- how participants privately feel about their team (e.g., "I feel good about my college football team)
- the participant's connection to their team (e.g., "I have a strong sense of belonging to my college football team")
- feelings of interdependence with a team (e.g., "My destiny is tied to the destiny of the college football team")
- fan-related behavior (e.g., "I am active in organizations that include mostly fans of my college football team")
- team-related thoughts and knowledge (e.g., "I am aware of the tradition and history of my college football team")

All six subscales were positively associated with fans' psychological commitment to their team, illustrating how the construct of fanship can itself be broken down into its constituent parts.

More recently, Vinney et al. (2019) developed a measure of fan identity in a sample of media fans rather than sport fans. Their analyses revealed three dimensions or aspects of fans:

- extent of enthusiasm (e.g., "How passionate are you about your favorite television show or movie?")
- deeper appreciation of the interest (e.g., "Has helped me grow as a person")
- interaction with other fans (e.g., "I often talk about my favorite television show or movie with a friend").

While identification as a fan was one of the variables assessed in their study, neither fanship nor fandom were present among the three dimensions of their model.

Finally, we wrap up this section on fan identification by considering measures of fandom, or felt connection to one's fan group. Unlike many of the fanship scales above, these scales were not designed in the context of fan groups. Instead, they were adapted from studies of other groups (e.g., racial groups) for use in fan studies. Such measures include unidimensional measures, such as Doosje et al.'s (1995) four-item measure (e.g., "I see myself as a [insert group]"), and multidimensional measures, such as Leach et al.'s (2008) five-dimensional measure assessing:

- solidarity (e.g., "I feel committed to [insert group]")

- satisfaction (e.g., "It is pleasant to be [insert group]")
- centrality (e.g., "I often think about the fact that I am [insert group]")
- individual self-stereotyping (e.g., "I have a lot in common with the average [insert group] person")
- ingroup homogeneity (e.g., "[insert group] people have a lot in common with each other")

In longer studies, where survey space is at a premium, researchers have also used single-item measures of fan group identification ("I strongly identify with other fans in the [insert group] community") which have proven to be fairly valid (Postmes et al., 2013; Reysen et al., 2013).

The scales we've reviewed in this section illustrate one approach researchers have taken to meaningfully distinguishing fans from one another: Measuring differences in the magnitude of their felt connection to their fan interest (or to other fans). We'll see these measures return in later chapters, but for now we turn our attention to another means of differentiating fans: Measuring differences in their tendency to engage in particular fan behaviors.

Categorizing Fans Based on Behavior

In a 1997 paper, Sutton et al. proposed a model of sport fans to help teams ensure fan loyalty through rising ticket prices and losing streaks. The model itself builds upon Wann's conceptualization of fan identity by categorizing fans based on whether they engaged in behaviors indicative of low, medium, and high levels of identification. Low-identification fans tend to spend little money on the team and are not especially involved in fan activities while medium-identification fans are the most likely to bandwagon (like a team only when it's doing well) and interact with other fans. High-identification fans, in contrast, are loyal during the team's more difficult stretches and spending much of their free time following the team's exploits. The model ultimately categorized fans based on their behavior despite labeling these behaviors as indicative of their degree of team identification.

A few years later, Tapp (2004) proposed a model which similarly distinguished sport fans based on their attitudinal and behavioral loyalty to their team. The football fans in their study rated how loyal they considered themselves to be (an attitude) and indicated how many games they had attended (behavior). Based on the interaction of these two variables, Tapp proposed four types of fans:

- "carefree casuals" who scored low in both and for whom football was mere entertainment
- "committed casuals" who scored high only in loyal attitudes but did not attend many games

- "repertoire fans" who were low in loyal attitudes but who frequently attended games of their own team as well as other teams
- "fanatics" who scored high on both indices of loyalty and were avid collectors of team-related memorabilia.

In this model, fan behavior was thus used to not only categorize fans, but also to predict behaviors that franchise owners and investors would consider to be practically useful (e.g., fans' purchasing of team-related merchandise).

Taking a slightly different approach, Collins and Murphy (2018) proposed a folk taxonomy based on three key variables: knowledge about the interest and its history, socializing with others in the context of the object (e.g., talking about it with others), and passion for the interest, sometimes to an irrational extent. The authors posited six "types" of fans based on these variables:
- "geeks," obsessive consumers who share knowledge about the interest with others
- "mavens," who know more than geeks, but try to appear impartial when talking about their interest
- "alphas," popular opinion leaders
- "evangelists," who actively seek to promote their interest
- "fanboys," who have an irrational passion for their interest
- "haters," who intensely dislike the object of interest

The model is intuitively appealing and uses the language of fans themselves, although it suffers from a clear description of how, quantitatively, the three variables themselves contribute to the six types of fans.

In a final example of a behavior-centered fan typology, Hunt et al. (1999) developed a model which recognizes five types of sport fans based on the extremity of their behavior:
- "temporary fans" who don't identify as a fan but who show interest for a short period of time (e.g., during a winning season)
- "local fans" who happen to live in close proximity to the team
- "devoted fans" who feel connected to the team (i.e., the team is part of their self-concept) and who will attend games and buy merchandise
- "fanatical fans" who are connected to the team but maintain important other connections (e.g., family) and who attend games while painting themselves in their team colors
- "dysfunctional fans" who are wholly consumed with the team and may engage in extreme behaviors (e.g., violence to defend the team against insult or threat)

Hunt and colleagues argue that this typology is a product of both behavior and motivation, although the above categorization seems far more heavily based on behavior than on motivation. Despite the straightforwardness of the categories, Samra and Wos (2014) would later streamline the typology down to just three categories: temporary, devoted, and fanatical fans. It's also worth noting that that much of this work has been theoretical in nature, with minimal empirical evidence to validate the existence and distinctiveness of these categories.

Categorizing Fans Based on Motivation

The previous model attempted to categorize fans on the basis of the motivations underlying their fan interest, although it's debatable how strong a role fan motivation played in the distinction. A model which directly differentiates fans on the basis of their underlying motivation was developed by Wann (1995), whose 23-item measure considered eight different motivations of sport fans:

- eustress, the extent to which watching sports provides fans with enjoyable stimulation
- self-esteem
- escape or reprieve from daily hassles
- entertainment
- economic benefits such as gambling
- aesthetic or artistic beauty
- group affiliation
- belongingness with other fans
- the opportunity to socialize with one's family

American sport fans given the scale rated entertainment, eustress, group affiliation, self-esteem, and aesthetics as the strongest motivators, respectively. The resilience of these findings was more recently demonstrated in a sample of South African soccer and rugby fans who scored similarly high on the same motivators (Wiid & Cant, 2015).

Others have similarly attempted to differentiate fans on the basis of their underlying motivation. For instance, Kahle et al. (1996) proposed a model that would predict fan attendance at a sporting event based on fans' underlying motivations. The model suffered from operationalization and interpretation difficulties, however. For instance, the variable labeled "compliance" more closely reflected the concept of friendship or belonging, the variable labeled "camaraderie" more closely reflected entertainment, the variable labeled "self-defining experience" was perhaps better construed as achievement, and "self-expressive experience" could more accurately be described as a desire to watch games live. Nevertheless, it was an attempt to do as Wann had done and meaningfully distinguish fans based on their underlying motivations.

Milne and McDonald (1999) would later propose their own set of 16 motivations which included, among other motivations, stress release, self-esteem, social needs, mental well-being needs, aesthetics, and achievement. Some of these variables overlapped with Wann's own motivations. Others included variables posited by Kahle and colleagues. Still others were entirely novel. The model itself failed to gain much traction, however.

Rhein (2000) likewise constructed a 12-item measure assessing different facets of German music fans, some of which tapped into fan motivation. The items included:
- Considering the music to be exciting
- Having knowledge about the music
- Being motivated by escapism
- Feeling that being a fan facilitates talking with others
- Seeing fan activities as a social activity
- Commitment to the fan interest
- Romantic attraction as a result of the fan interest
- Admiration for the interest and those involve in it
- Feeling distinct as a result of the interest
- Feeling a sense of achievement
- Feeling that the interest has changed one's life
- Feelings of belongingness

A cluster analysis revealed three types of fans based on how high or low they scored on the scale. As one might predict, fans who score higher on the scale (and thus were more motivated, or had a wider base of motivations) are more likely to consume and engage with the music (e.g., memorize lyrics) and to interact with others who also like the music. While not the purest test of this association, the results can be framed as evidence that fan motivation can predict fan behavior.

In a more direct measure of fan motivation, Trail and James (2001) asked 203 U.S. baseball season ticket holders about their underlying motivations. The measure ultimately assessed nine different motivations driving fanship:
- the desire for achievement (e.g., "I feel like I have won when the team wins")
- knowledge (e.g., "I read the box scores and team statistics regularly")
- aesthetics (e.g., "There is a certain natural beauty to the game")
- drama (e.g., "I enjoy the drama of a "one run" game")
- escape (e.g., "Games represent an escape for me from my day-to-day activities")
- family (e.g., "I like going to games with my children")

- physical attraction (e.g., "I enjoy watching players who are physically attractive")
- physical skills (e.g., "I enjoy a skillful performance by the team")
- social (e.g., "Games are great opportunities to socialize with other people")

Astute readers will note that many of these items overlap with Wann's original set, although new variables (e.g., physical skills) were also proposed.

A few years later, Funk and colleagues (2004) proposed a different measure which looked at 18 antecedents or motivations underlying sport fans' involvement with women's basketball:

- interest in basketball (e.g., "My interest in basketball sparked my interest in the team")
- interest in players (e.g., "The main reason why I attend is to cheer for my favorite player")
- bonding with friends (e.g., "Attending games gives me a chance to bond with my friends")
- socialization (e.g., "I like to talk with other people sitting near me at games")
- drama (e.g., "I like games where the outcome is uncertain")
- the team (e.g., "I am a fan of the entire team")
- community pride (e.g., "My connection to the community is why I like the team")
- support of women (e.g., "I attend games because I think it is important to support women's sport")
- role models (e.g., "Players provide inspiration for girls and boys")
- bonding with family (e.g., "Attending games gives me a chance to bond with my family")
- style of play (e.g., "The WNBA style of basketball is a more pure form of basketball compared to the NBA's style")
- customer service (e.g., "I feel like customer satisfaction is important to the game day staff")
- excitement (e.g., "The games provide affordable entertainment")
- knowledge (e.g., "Knowing the rules of basketball helps me to enjoy the games")
- vicarious achievement (e.g., "I feel like I have won when the team wins")
- wholesome environment (e.g., "There is a friendly, family atmosphere at the games")

- escape (e.g., "I like attending games because they provide me with a distraction from my daily life for a while")

While the scale contains more motivations than we've seen in any model so far, there is also notable conceptual overlap between some of the subscales (e.g., socializing / bonding with friends/ family, interest in basketball / interest in players / interest in the team). Some of the variables also seem unrelated or only tangentially related to the fan interest (e.g., customer service). Later analyses suggest that these variables load onto a smaller number of higher-order factors: attraction, risk, centrality, and self-expression.

Chadborn et al. (2017) constructed a different 14-item measure assessing fan motivation, this one emphasizing the functions that one's fan interest provides for them. The results revealed three dimensions representing the extent to which one's fan interest provides them with:

- a sense of purpose in life (e.g., "Provides me with a focus or sense of purpose")
- a sense of escapism (e.g., "Provides me with a break from life's stresses")
- social connections (e.g., "Provides me with a chance to expand my circle of friends")

The researchers used the scales to test a mediation model wherein the fandom's ability to fulfill social needs mediates the link between fans' fanship scores and specific fan behaviors (e.g., displaying group symbols). Studies such as these go beyond merely cataloguing different fan motivations and illustrate the utility of distinguishing between fans on the basis of their underlying motivations. The studies also hint at fan motivation as a potentially important mechanism driving some of the psychological effects previously observed in fans.

At the risk of belaboring the point, one final model by Todd and Soule (2018) suggests that three different groups ultimately coalesce around a fan interest: the fandom itself, the brand community, and the brand public. Importantly, the authors propose that motivation was one of two variables that influence this distinction, such that those in the fandom are motivated by creativity, affiliation, and self-expression, those in the brand community are motived by admiration and sharing information, and those in the brand public are motivated by imitation and signaling their interest in uncreative and largely unsocial ways. In short, alongside the previous study by Chadborn et al. (2017), recent studies such as these which look at motivation-based typologies demonstrate the necessity of considering fan motivation in any model attempting to meaningfully compare fans.

Categorizing Fans Based on Stage of Fanship

One final way to distinguish between different types of fans involves conceptualizing fans as dynamic, rather than static. This means recognizing that, over time, fans can become increasingly involved in their fan interest and change in how they engage with it. Such changes may be both theoretically interesting to researchers and of practical significance to those in marketing or with a vested interest in fan consumption behaviors (e.g., artists).

Based on the idea that fans can change over time in a predictable fashion and that fans can be distinguished on the basis of where they are in this transition, Funk and James (2001) propose a psychological continuum model. In the model, sport fans' are expected to increase in the connection they feel with a particular sport or team over time. The first stage along this continuum—*awareness*—reflects fans' initial discovery of a team or sport. Next, fans become *attracted* to the team or sport, which gradually gives way to *attachment* to the team, where the team has become meaningful and important to the fan. Finally, at the far end of the spectrum, fans develop a sense of intrinsic *allegiance* or loyalty to their team. The researchers posit that fans at different points in this continuum differ significantly from one another with respect to the motivations driving their behavior, the behaviors they engage in, and in the situational factors that are most impactful to them. For example, Wu et al. (2018) documents how Apple fans, like sport fans, moved through analogous stages with respect to their interest in Steve Jobs: Initial exposure to his story, fascination with his personality, a sense of emotional connection to him, and eventual worship. Along the way, their motivation and consumption of Apple products shifted to reflect their movement along the continuum from awareness to allegiance.

Jia et al. (2018) took a somewhat different approach to this progression approach in their work on fans of singer/actor Wallace Chung. The authors created a hierarchy of progression that was based more on maturation and the passage of time than on the extremeness of the fan's interest over time. The model starts with causal fans motivated by an interest in play and with little cognitive or emotional investment. These casual fans become fascinated fans that gather information and build their knowledge of the fan interest over time. Fascinated fans may eventually become devoted fans, shifting from fanship into fandom by joining clubs and communities of like-minded others while gaining a sense of belonging. The next stage includes dysfunctional fans who excessively idolize the object of their interest and try to boost the object's popularity in extreme or irrational ways. The final step, one which doesn't reflect an increase in extremeness or devotion, instead involves maturation and gaining a sense of perspective when it comes to one's fan interest, recognizing the importance of avoiding dysfunctional fan behavior (e.g., eschewing extreme parasocial connection in favor of instead seeing the celebrity as a faraway friend.) As with many of the intuitively appealing models described in this chapter, the model raises several important questions, such as whether all fans must necessarily go through a dysfunctional stage before becoming self-reflecting and maturing in their interests.

This Book

We've considered four different approaches fan scholars have adopted to categorize and meaningfully distinguish between different fans: how or what fans identify with (and to what extent), the behaviors fans engage in, fan motivations, and progression through stages of maturation or devotion as a fan.

As we mentioned earlier, this review should not be taken as a systematic look at all of the different ways scholars have studied fan groups. Instead, we consider it to be a testament to the dizzying amount of time and effort scholars have put into the task of organizing what is known about fans in a way that allows us to meaningfully compare and contrast fans of all interests. In the chapters that follow, we will attempt to do justice to this massive body of work by detailing some of the theory and research behind 28 constructs related to fan interest, each of which can be thought of as a plausible dimension on which to differentiate fans. We'll consider some of the ways these dimensions have been assessed, research on the utility of these constructs for predicting important fan outcomes, and places where theory on these constructs overlaps, given the much broader problem in science of researchers inadequately talking to one another and comparing notes, leading to countless instances of reinventing the wheel.

In the final chapters of this book, we then attempt to move beyond a review of what has been done to what we believe is a plausible next step for the field. We describe a series of studies designed to empirically derive and validate a model that simultaneously takes many of these different dimensions into account. In doing so, we hope to not only integrate and improve the state of the discourse in the field through a common model and vernacular, but also to highlight numerous areas of potentially fruitful research that may be going unnoticed while avoiding all of the wheel-reinventing that so-commonly occurs in especially interdisciplinary fields like fan research.

Chapter 1
Magnitude

Fan interests are as diverse as fans themselves. As such, the prospect of finding dimensions on which to meaningfully compare groups as diverse as sport fans and model train enthusiasts is a bit daunting. An easily solution is to consider a dimension so basic that it can easily be applied regardless of what one is a fan of. In this spirit, we devote the first chapter of this book to the question of magnitude: Just how big a fan is someone?

Before we begin, let's quickly note that we're distinguishing (at least somewhat) the magnitude of one's fan interest from their sense of fanship—the extent to which they explicitly identify as a fan. In reality, these two constructs are quite highly correlated with one another. After all, those with a strong interest in something are probably the people most likely to identify with that same interest. Nevertheless, as these constructs have been investigated independent of one another in prior research, we'll consider them separately.

We begin by reviewing the related psychological construct of fan involvement and its theoretical underpinnings, given that magnitude may be another way of assessing how involved someone is with their fan interest. We then review examples of studies where different measures of involvement have been adapted to the context of fans. Finally, we present some of our own work in which we take a different approach to assessing the magnitude of a fan's interest, namely asking participants whether different magnitude-related labels (e.g., avid, devout) describe the nature of their fan interest.

Involvement

Zaichkowsky (1985, p. 342) defines involvement as "a person's perceived relevance of the object based on inherent needs, values, and interests" (for an in-depth review of the topic in the context of marathon runners see Beaton et al., 2011). In other words, the extent to which the object has become a part of a person's life. And while a definition from the 1980s may seem a bit dated, theorizing on the topic can be traced back much further. In fact, modern theorizing on involvement stems from at least two lines of inquiry put forth decades ago by the renowned researchers Gordon Allport and Muzafer Sherif. According to Allport, people become involved in activities that have both hedonic and symbolic value and which become central to their life. This approach to psychological involvement has proven fruitful in other, non-fan domains. As Beaton et al. note, however, fan and leisure researchers tend to rely more on Sherif's conceptualization of ego-involvement.

Sherif and Cantril (1947) argued that the ego is neither innate nor a personality, but rather is a collection of attitudes connected to the self and determined by the situations people find themselves in. As they put it, "when any stimulus or situation is consciously or unconsciously related to them by the individual, we can say there is "ego-involvement"" (p. 117). Or, to put it simply, the more psychologically connected we are to a thing (e.g., group, attitude), the more ego-involvement there can be said to be. As an illustrative example, moviegoers can be said to be exhibiting greater ego-involvement with a film's characters when the characters are similar to themselves, as they can more easily imagine that they are those characters.

While modern fan researchers rarely trace their roots this far back, various measures have been developed which assess fan involvement, largely as conceptualized by Sherif and Cantril. Of note, nearly all of these measures have assessed fan involvement in the context of sport fans and their involvement with a particular team. For example, as we mentioned in the introduction, Funk et al. (2004) put forth a measure assessing 18 different motivations to be a sport fan. Many of these variables loaded onto factors like attraction, centrality, and self-expression—factors which might be considered "ego-involving" or relevant to the self. Some researchers have, like Funk and their colleagues, similarly attempted to study fan involvement via multidimensional scales. Others chose to more directly assess fan involvement as a single dimension. What follows is a brief review of both types of scales and some of the findings from research employing them.

Consumer Involvement Profile

Building on research looking at consumer involvement profiles (Laurent & Kapferer, 1985), Havitz and Howard (1995) examined the stability of an involvement measure across several seasons for fans of different recreational activities (windsurfing, skiing, golf). Their measure assessed four subscales of involvement:

- attraction/importance of the activity (e.g., "Golf interests me")
- the activity as an informative sign (e.g., "You can tell about a person by whether or not they golf")
- consequences of risks related to the activity (e.g., "If my choice proved to be poor, I would be upset")
- risk probability (e.g., "I always feel at a loss when choosing golf courses")

In addition to finding support for the scale's four-factor structure, the results of the study found that, indeed, involvement scores were relatively stable across seasons. Others using the same scale, however, found a different factor structure.

Laurent and Kapferer (1985), for example, found evidence for a five-dimension structure, while Kyle et al. (2002) observed three factors. In a study of women's basketball fans, Kerstetter and Kovich (1997) found that the items only loaded onto two factors.

Despite concerns about the reliability of the scale's factor structure, however, the measure itself and variants thereof have been used across a variety of studies to assess the association between fan involvement and other important variables. In a sample of tennis fans involvement was positively correlated with resistance to change, psychological commitment, fan attraction toward tennis, and behavioral loyalty (Bee & Havitz, 2010). In another study, involvement predicted flow experiences and enjoyment of leisure activities (Havitz & Mannell, 2005). In a sample of Turkish birdwatchers, involvement was positively related to the centrality of the hobby (e.g., "I would rather go birding than do most anything else") and well as dedication to it (e.g., "I find that a lot of my life is organized around birding;" Çakici & Harman, 2007). And, lest you think the applicability of this study's findings was limited only to Turkish birdwatchers, a study of American birdwatchers found that subscales of the involvement scale were positively related to commitment, consumptive behavior, attendance at birdwatching events, and even the ability to correctly identify birds (Kim et al., 1997).

Personal Involvement Inventory

Somewhat analogous to Havitz and Howard, who adapted their measure of involvement from research on consumer profiles, Shank and Beasley took a measure of consumer involvement with specific products and adapted it for use in fan research. The scale in question was developed by Zaichkowsky (1985) and asked participants to rate products on a series of bipolar adjectives such as "relevant/irrelevant" or "desirable/undesirable." This measure of participants' involvement with the products was found to predict consumer behavior (e.g., the desire to seek out and read information about the product.) Zaichkowsky (1994) later revised the measure to include two both an affective component and a cognitive component.

It was this revised, two-dimensional measure that Shank and Beasley (1998) validated for use as a measure of fan involvement in U.S. sport fans. The measure was streamlined down to eight items which loaded onto the same affective (e.g., "exciting") and cognitive (e.g., "relevant") dimensions proposed by Zaichkowsky. The authors found that greater involvement across these two dimensions was associated with greater fan-related consumption among their sample of sport fans.

Now called the personal involvement inventory, the scale has since been used in a variety of sport fan studies worldwide, proving itself useful as a predictor of theoretically and practically important variables. Notable examples of the personal involvement inventory's use include:

- In a sample of fans at a U.S. woman's basketball game, involvement scores predicted fan satisfaction, salience of fan identity, felt attachment to the team, and frequency of game attendance (Laverie & Arnett, 2000)
- Fantasy football fans' involvement scores predicted loyalty to their favorite team (Dwyer, 2011) and to team identity salience (Larkin & Fink, 2016)
- In a sample of NASCAR fans, involvement was positively associated with fans' identification with the sport itself, repeat purchases, and consumption of NASCAR-related media (Goldsmith & Walker, 2015)
- Involvement was positively correlated with loyalty, fan identification, and frequency of sport consumption in a sample of Australian rugby fans (Stevens & Rosenberger, 2012)
- Involvement scores were predicted by perceptions of a team's sophistication and credibility in Greek sport fans (Tsiotsou, 2010)

Enduring Involvement Index

In 1986, Bloch et al. constructed the enduring involvement index which measures a person's (1) interest in a product, (2) frequency thinking about a product, and (3) importance of a product to themselves. Research with this scale revealed that those who were more involved with a product ultimately had a greater interest in seeking out information about the product. As a real-world example, someone in the market for a new computer (i.e., highly-involved) might seek out more information about the computer (e.g., reading articles, browsing stores) and even enjoy the search itself.

Bennett et al. (2009) gave the measure to a sample of participants at a sporting event sponsored by the beverage Mountain Dew. The authors found that scores on the measure of enduring involvement predicted fan spectatorship (e.g., consuming more media about action sports), behavioral involvement (e.g., talking to others about action sports), sport-related consumption (e.g., purchasing action sports apparel), and brand use (e.g., drinking Mountain Dew). The same measure of involvement has also proven effective in predicting future game attendance in a sample of Australian rugby fans (Hill & Green, 2000).

Product Enduring Involvement Scale

Akin to several of the measures we've already reviewed, Higie and Feick (1989) developed a scale to asses participants' involvement with a product. The scale asked participants to rate items using a series of bipolar continuums (e.g., "fun – not fun," "tells me about a person – shows nothing"). The result was a two-factor structure consisting of a hedonic component and a self-expression component, both of which contributed to a person's involvement with a product. Those who scored higher on the scale spent more time seeking out information about the product, talking about the product with others, and trying to influencing the purchasing decisions of their friends with respect to the product.

As we've seen with other measures, fan researchers would adopt the measure for use with fans, sport and non-sport alike. In a sample of fans attending a women's basketball game, involvement scores were positively correlated with feeling satisfied about the game, fan identity salience, attachment to the team, and frequency of game attendance (Laverie & Arnett, 2000). In a sample of Japanese comics fans, Katsumata and Ichikohji (2014) similarly found that fan involvement was positively related to purchasing and consuming comics. This same study also revealed that the associations differed depending on the nature of fan themselves, whether they were artists who made comics for their own enjoyment or produced comics for profit.

Recreation Involvement

In these last two sections we'll consider measures that weren't developed in the context of consumer research. The first, developed by McIntyre and Pigram (1992), was constructed specifically to measure peoples' involvement in recreational activities across three dimensions:

- attraction to the recreational activity (e.g., "Camping is one of the most satisfying things I do")
- self-expression through the activity (e.g., "Camping says a lot about who I am")
- centrality of the activity to one's life (e.g., "I find that a lot of my life is organized around camping")

When the scale was given to people hiking the Appalachian trail, their involvement scores predicted identification with the location of the recreational activity (e.g., "This trail means a lot to me") as well as feelings of dependence on the location (e.g., "Hiking here is more important than hiking in another place:" Kyle et al., 2003). Similar results were found for individuals sampled in Cleveland metroparks (Kyle & Mowen, 2005).

Kyle et al. (2007) later added two dimensions to the measure: a social bonding subscale (e.g., "I enjoy discussing [insert activity] with my friends") and an identity affirmation subscale (e.g., "When I participate in [insert activity], I can really be myself"). When given to samples of campers and fishers in South Carolina, the five involvement dimensions predicted like satisfaction and frequency of camping and fishing.

Since then, the measure has seen extensive use worldwide and has been found to be associated with numerous fan-relevant thoughts, attitudes, and behaviors:

- In a sample of Taiwanese baseball fans, involvement was positively related to team identification, knowledge of the team, and intention to watch games (Gau et al., 2019)
- Hargrove (2011) surveyed women in an outdoor recreation program and found that involvement predicted activity involvement, frequency of participation, and satisfaction
- In a sample of Greek tennis club members, subscales of recreational involvement predicted intrinsic motivation to play recreational tennis (Alexandris, 2012)
- Japanese participants' involvement with a Korean celebrity was positively related to intention to visit South Korea (Lee et al., 2008), a finding similarly found in a sample of Taiwanese participants (Yen & Teng, 2015)
- In a study of Busan International Film Festival attendees (South Korea), recreational involvement scores were positively associated with identity salience, psychological commitment, and loyalty to the festival (Lee et al., 2016)
- Recreational involvement was associated with purchasing intentions (Nassis et al., 2012) and with commitment to the team (Tachis & Tzetzis, 2015) in Greek football fans, with word of mouth advertising in Greek basketball fans (Nassis et al., 2014), and with frequency of consuming sport-related media in Greek volleyball fans (Zetou et al., 2013)
- Taiwanese baseball fans showed a positive relationship between recreational involvement and well-being (Pan et al., 2018)

Sport Team Involvement

In this final section on fan involvement we review a study by Shuv-Ami et al. (2015), who assessed fans' commitment to a sport team with a measure that included three items assessing involvement ("I connected and am emotionally involved with my basketball team," "My basketball team is important for me," "I am involved and interested in my basketball team"). The measure, which also included subscales related to loyalty, satisfaction, and performance, was positively associated with positive attitudes toward the team, recommending the team to others, and intention to consume. Subsequent research using the scale similarly found that involvement with a sport team positively correlated with fandom identification, fan satisfaction, optimism, and behavioral loyalty (Shuv-Ami & Alon, 2020) and with love for one's team, hate for a rival team, identification with the sport, team loyalty, and willingness to pay a premium price to watch one's favorite team (Shuv-Ami et al., 2020).

Magnitude Labels

So far we've reviewed a sizable body of research which shows the importance of involvement when it comes to predicting fan attitudes and behavior regardless of the specific measure used, the region where the study is being conducted, or whether the study involves sport fans or non-sport fans. This chapter, however, is about magnitude of fan interest. While involvement can be argued to be an imperfect, proxy measure of magnitude, the two concepts are arguably not one and the same. To this end, we'll finish this chapter by considering converging evidence looking at another approach to assessing magnitude of fan interest: the extent to which fans identify as a big fan of something.

We begin with research by Vinney et al. (2019), who constructed a measure of fan identity in two samples of media fans. The measure included three dimensions, enthusiasm, appreciation, and social interaction, the first of which is the most presently relevant. Fan enthusiasm consists of three items asking fans how much they love a particular television show, how passionate they are about the show, and how big of a fan they are of the show. Scoring high in fan enthusiasm (magnitude) was ultimately related to the extent to which fans liked a show and reported being passionate about it.

In a 2017 study of Greek football fans, Yannopoulos (2017) attempted to meaningfully segment the market of football fans. The author argued that there are three types of fans:

- ardent fans (e.g., "Football is like a religion to me")
- rational fans (e.g., "The cost of the game affects my attendance")
- casual fans (e.g., "I like all types of sports")

Subsequent cluster analysis on additional data (e.g., fan motivation) found that the ardent fan label was strongly associated with fanatical behavior, including consuming more sports and generally being more engaged and committed fans than those who identified with the "rational" or "casual" fan labels. In short, like fan involvement, higher-magnitude fans engage in more fan behaviors and are more passionate, committed fans.

We'll finish up this section by describing the results of two studies we conducted to assess magnitude of fan interest using a novel, single-item measure. The item is based on fans' willingness to identifying with labels related to the magnitude of their fan interest. In the first study, we asked U.S. college students (N = 2,525, 73.6% female; M_{age} = 22.49, SD = 7.14) to list their favorite fan interest before completing measures related to that interest. Among those measures was the single-item magnitude scale which asked fans to pick one of five options, increasing in magnitude, which best described them:

- "I have a LOW LEVEL of fan interest or involvement"
- "I am SOMEWHAT of a "fan"
- "I would describe myself as a MODERATE fan"
- "I regard myself as a DEVOUT fan, as this fandom is important to me"
- "I regard myself as an AVID fan, as this fandom plays a central role in my life"

We also next asked participants about the frequency with which they engaged in specific fan-related behaviors on a 5-point scale (from 1 = *not at all* to 5 = *very frequently*), including:

- Purchasing merchandise ("I purchase and/or wear/display items associated or identified with the fandom (dvd, toys, clothing, etc.)")
- Attending gatherings ("I attend meetings, meet-ups, concerts, games, conventions, or any other gathering associated with the fandom")
- Talking with ingroup members ("I talk and share with other members of the fandom")
- Producing fan-made works ("I find creative inspiration to produce music, art, fanfiction, or other works based on the fandom")
- Talking with non-ingroup members ("I share my experiences and/or fan interest with non-members of the fandom (non-fans)")

As shown in Table 1.1, the most common label fans applied to themselves was "devout" (39.8%), followed closely by "moderate" (34.8%) and then by "avid" (15.5%).

Also shown in Table 1.1, those who used higher-magnitude fan identity labels engaged in more fan-related behavior. Specifically, those identifying with the "low" and "somewhat" labels tended to be comparable to one another while "moderate," "devout," and "avid" fans tended to significantly differ from one another, becoming increasingly involved in fan-related behavior with each jump in magnitude.

We also examined participants' scores on a measure of fanship (Reysen & Branscombe, 2010; see Chapter 15) and fandom identification (Obst et al., 2002a, 2002b; see Chapter 7) using a 5-point scale from 1 = *strongly disagree* to 5 = *strongly agree*. Again, fans identifying with the "low" and "somewhat" labels tended to be similar while "moderate," "devout," and "avid" fans were significantly different from one another in a linear fashion, with higher fanship and fandom scores for higher-magnitude fans.

Table 1.1

Mean Differences in Degree of Magnitude of Being a Fan

Variable	Low	Somewhat	Moderate	Devout	Avid
n	72	179	879	1004	391
Purchase Merchandise	1.78_a	1.99_a	2.49_b	3.34_c	4.04_d
Attend Gatherings	1.65_a	1.74_a	1.89_a	2.51_b	3.28_c
Talk with Ingroup	1.71_a	2.01_{ab}	2.16_b	2.78_c	3.60_d
Produce Fan Art	2.13_a	2.77_b	3.34_c	4.14_d	4.57_e
Talk with Non-Ingroup	2.06_a	2.47_b	3.02_c	3.64_d	4.03_e
Fanship	2.05_a	2.36_b	2.81_c	3.56_d	4.16_e
Belonging	3.11_a	3.31_b	3.69_c	4.19_d	4.40_e
Shared Values	3.00_a	3.04_a	3.28_b	3.67_c	3.91_d
Emotional Connection	2.91_a	2.78_a	2.98_a	3.41_b	3.68_c
Influence	2.36_a	2.47_a	2.39_{ab}	2.66_b	3.07_c
Conscious Identification	2.38_a	2.49_a	2.56_a	3.21_b	3.85_c
Global Sense Community	3.04_a	3.20_a	3.50_b	4.02_c	4.32_d

Note. Means with different subscripts are significantly different ($p < .05$).

Finally, to disambiguate the association between magnitude and these other conceptually similar variables, we conducted a factor analysis which included the 11 fanship items, five items from the sense of community fandom identification subscale, and the single magnitude item. As expected, the fanship and fandom items loaded on separate dimensions, in line with prior research suggesting that while fanship and fandom are related, they are empirically distinct constructs (i.e., Reysen & Branscombe, 2010). More importantly, the magnitude item loaded more strongly onto the fanship dimension than it did the fandom dimension. This finding is in line with what we suggested at the start of this chapter, that the concepts of magnitude and fanship are conceptually very similar to one another.

The results of our first study suggest that those using higher-magnitude labels are more likely to score higher on measures of fanship and fandom. These findings also suggest that assessing magnitude of fan interest using a single item, while not ideal, is valid and useful, particularly in circumstances when it is difficult to use a longer measure (e.g., on longer surveys).

In a follow-up study of U.S. undergraduates ($N = 896$, 71.5% women; $M_{age} = 20.72$, $SD = 5.21$) we administered the same single-item magnitude measure along with measures of specific fan behaviors. The measures tapped into constructs including:

- Consuming official content (e.g., "I often watch, read, listen, or otherwise engage with my fan interest")
- Consuming fan made content (e.g., "I engage (e.g., watch, read) fan made material related to my fan interest almost everyday")
- Buying official merchandise (e.g., "I purchase officially licensed items associated or identified with my fan interest")
- Buying fan made products (e.g., "I purchase fan produced products related to my fan interest")
- Communicating with other fans in person (e.g., "I often communicate with other fans of my interest in person")
- Communicating with other fans online (e.g., "I talk with other members of the fan community online (e.g., social media)")
- Creating fan-made content (e.g., "I spend time creating or working on videos, music, art or other material involving my fan interest")
- Attending gatherings (e.g., "I often attend meetings or conventions involving my fan interest")
- Word-of-mouth transmission of fan interest to others (e.g., "I mention this fan interest to others quite frequently"; adapted from Harrison-Walker, 2001)

Table 1.2

Mean Differences in Behaviors by Degree of Magnitude of Being a Fan

Variable	Low	Somewhat	Moderate	Devout	Avid
n	15	55	371	297	158
Consume Official Content	3.12_a	3.89_b	4.24_b	5.14_c	6.08_d
Consume Fan Content	2.39_a	3.13_a	3.20_{ab}	4.09_b	5.45_c
Buy Official Products	3.11_a	3.09_a	3.74_{ab}	4.74_{bc}	5.67_c
Buy Fan Products	2.53_a	2.64_a	2.79_a	3.47_{ab}	4.48_b
Talk Face-to-Face	3.40_a	4.00_a	3.96_a	4.93_b	5.65_b
Talk Online	2.31_a	3.21_{ab}	3.16_{ab}	3.97_b	5.08_c
Create Fan Content	2.32_a	2.77_a	2.45_a	3.09_a	4.35_b
Attend Gatherings	2.37_a	2.84_a	2.62_a	3.12_a	4.32_b
Word of Mouth	2.92_a	3.60_{ab}	3.97_b	4.99_c	5.85_d

Note. Means with different subscripts are significantly different ($p < .05$). 7-point scale from 1 = *strongly disagree* to 7 = *strongly agree.*

As shown in Table 1.2, the pattern of results were almost identical to those in the previous study. Specifically, fans labeling themselves as "low" or "somewhat" in the magnitude of their fan interest tended to be similar to one another, alongside "moderate" fans. In contrast, "avid" fans scored distinctly high on most of the behavioral outcomes. The study thus shows that there is a robust linear relationship between the magnitude of one's fan interest and their tendency to engage in fan-related behavior.

Conclusion

In this chapter we reviewed research on the first fan-related dimension from our list, magnitude. It's clear from the work reviewed that fan scholars and marketers alike have been interested since at least the 1980s in devising ways to measure magnitude of someone's fan interest. The measures devised include measures of involvement, scales derived for other purposes (e.g., consumer behavior), and questions asking fans to indicate which magnitude-related label most applies to them.

We've seen that the magnitude of one's fan interest is strongly associated with the way fans think, feel, and behave, with higher-magnitude fans consuming more, identifying more strongly with, and being more engaged with the broader fan community. We'll see this similar trends for many of the other dimensions in this book, with higher scores predicting stronger fan thoughts, feelings, and behaviors. Few other dimensions match the simply and intuitiveness of magnitude, however, which, when you boil it down, is just asking someone how big a fan they are of something.

Chapter 2
Participation

In the previous chapter we reviewed the literature on magnitude of fan interest, not only because a significant body of research shows that magnitude predicts important outcome variables, but also because the distinction between high- and low-magnitude fans can be easily recognized across fan groups, regardless of the interest itself.

In the present chapter, we introduce fan participation, another seemingly intuitive and obvious variable that lends itself to easy study across fan interests. Fans participate in their fan interests in a variety of ways, including attending events, reading and writing fanfiction, creating art, cosplaying, making music and music videos, hosting local gatherings, and contributing to online forums. An obvious way to differentiate fans from one another would be to compare those who engage in some of these behaviors to those who engage in other behaviors (e.g., fanfiction writers versus cosplayers). Alternatively, one could focus their attention on a particularly diagnostic or high-impact fan behavior to better understand the differences between fans who engage in more or less of that behavior. In fact, it is difficult to whittle down the body of research on fan participation precisely because so much of the existing fan research does exactly this, examining similarities and differences between different fan behaviors and their antecedents and outcomes. Speaking to this point, Kim et al. (2019) conducted a meta-analysis on a sizable body of sport fan research dedicated solely to the topic of sport fan game attendance, a single type of fan behavior.[1]

Since nearly every other chapter in this book examines specific fan behaviors as an outcome, we've decided to approach this chapter in a slightly different way. Rather than trying to synthesize and condense all of the relevant research on this topic—an endeavor which would balloon this chapter's length and cause it to overlap with nearly every other chapter—we'll instead start by briefly describing a psychological theory used to predict specific fan behaviors. We'll then present some of our own research on the subject which, rather surprisingly, shows that specific fan behaviors are not as useful as one might think when it comes to understanding what it means to be a fan.

---

[1] It's understandable that so much research has focused specifically on fans' consumptive behaviors (e.g., game attendance), given that marketers have a vested interest in predicting and increasing fan spending.

The Theory of Planned Behavior

Icek Ajzen's theory of planned behavior (1985, 1991) was not designed with fan groups in mind. Nevertheless, the theory has been instrumental in helping psychologists better understand and predict fan behavior. In a nutshell, the theory of planned behavior posits that most day-to-day behaviors are volitional in nature, usually preceded by a behavioral intention. Such intentions are predicted by three key variables:

• Attitude toward the behavior: The extent to which your impression of the target behavior is positive

• Subjective norms about the behavior: The perception that there is societal pressure to engage in the behavior

• Perceived control over the behavior: The perceived ease or difficulty of engaging in the behavior.

To better understand the theory, let's apply it to the prediction of a specific behavior: donating to charity. If one has a positive attitude toward the behavior (e.g., giving to charity is good), if they perceive social norms as being favorable to the behavior (e.g., their friends and family think giving to charity is good), and if they perceive that it's within their ability to engage in the behavior (e.g., they have the money to spare for a donation), then they are likely to form an intention to do the behavior (e.g., they intend to give to charity). Ajzen recognized that these are far from the only variables which can predict a given behavior, but notes that these three variables are fairly consistently important. The model has been well-supported empirically, even as researchers continue to search for additional variables to add to the model's ability to predict behavioral intentions (e.g., Ulker-Demirel & Ciftci, 2020).

The theory of planned behavior has been used to predict behaviors as diverse as riding the bus (Heath & Gifford, 2002) and illegally parking in emergency lanes (Zheng et al., 2018). It also lends itself quite readily to predicting all manner of volitional behavior, including specific fan behavior. Even so, the theory of planned behavior has only rarely been applied to the prediction of fan behavior. When it has, however, it's proven rather fruitful. For example, researchers have found that measuring attitudes, subjective norms, and perceived control can allow researchers to predict participants' intention to revisit a festival in subsequent years (Alonso et al., 2015; Horng et al., 2013). Others have used the same variables to predict consumption behavior, including attending a sporting event (Cunningham & Kwon, 2003; Lu et al., 2011), going to a fan convention (Reysen, Chadborn, & Plante, 2018), or purchasing merchandise from a celebrity (Chiou et al., 2005).

In short, those studies which have applied the theory of planned behavior to fans have shown that fans' attitudes, perceptions of subjective norms, and perceived behavioral control can predict the intent to engage in fan-related behaviors. But if it's true that psychological variables can tell us something about fan behavior, can those specific fan behaviors, in turn, be used to tell us something meaningful and significant about the psychology of the fans who engage in them?

True Fans

Fans, almost by definition, take the objects of their interest quite seriously. As such, gauging the authenticity of a self-proclaimed fan's interest is important to many fans (e.g., see Plante et al., 2020 for a review). It's the reason why bandwagon fans of a team are held in low regard by lifelong fans and why gamers often decry "fake gamer girls" as a threat to their fandom.

Given the importance of establishing authenticity for fans, as well as the possibility that fans may rely on behavioral credentials to establish their authenticity, we conducted a set of studies examining whether certain behaviors are perceived by fans as differentiating "true" fans from casual, bandwagon, or "wannabe" fans. Participants in the study ($N = 219$, 78.1% women; $M_{age} = 23.21$, $SD = 8.22$) were U.S. undergraduate students. At the beginning of the semester they completed a prescreening measure assessing whether they identified as a fan of sport ($n = 53$), music ($n = 49$), media ($n = 74$), or a particular hobby ($n = 43$). Participants were later asked to rate the extent to which 22 specific traits and behaviors were seen as representative of true fans (see Table 2.1 for the list of items). Responses were made on a 7-point Likert-type scale from 1 = *unimportant* to 7 = *important*.

As shown in Table 2.1, participants scored above the scale's midpoint (i.e., 4) on 11 of the items. In other words participants' felt that these 11 traits and behaviors in particular were especially indicative of what it means to be a true fan. Rather tellingly, most of these higher-scoring items were traits, not specific behaviors. In fact, many specific behaviors like club membership and spending money on one's interest were below the midpoint of the scale, indicating that they were seen as not especially important as an indicator of being a true fan.

We next examined whether these traits and behaviors held together as indicators of true fan status by conducting a principal components analysis with an oblimin rotation. The eigenvalues and scree plot suggested that there were four factors:

- Participation in the fan interest (items 7, 11, 12, 13, 14, 15, 16)
- Passionate commitment to the interest (items 1, 2, 3, 4, 5)
- Knowledge and evangelism about the interest (items 6, 8, 9, 10)

• Willingness to sacrifice for the interest (items 17, 18, 19, 20, 21, 22)

Table 2.1

Means (Standard Deviation) of Important Characteristics of a "True Fan"

Item	Mean (*SD*)
Item 1. Enthusiastic	6.41 (1.02)
Item 2. Loyal	6.21 (1.24)
Item 3. Passionate	6.19 (1.32)
Item 4. Committed	6.15 (1.24)
Item 5. Devoted	6.07 (1.34)
Item 6. Know a great deal of information about the fan interest	5.11 (1.83)
Item 7. Emotionally connected with fan interest	5.09 (1.76)
Item 8. Try to get other friends to also like fan interest	4.69 (1.87)
Item 9. Spend large amounts of time on fan interest	4.48 (2.02)
Item 10. Spend a number of years as a fan of the interest	4.26 (2.11)
Item 11. Obsessed	4.25 (1.99)
Item 12. Attendance at conventions	3.89 (2.03)
Item 13. Member of fan club (in person)	3.80 (2.05)
Item 14. Member of fan club (online)	3.78 (2.04)
Item 15. Create fan artifacts (e.g., art, stories)	3.41 (1.98)
Item 16. Write fan mail	3.34 (2.04)
Item 17. Willingness to spend large amounts of money on fan interest	3.16 (2.08)
Item 18. Critique and write about the fan interest (e.g., online blogs)	3.09 (2.07)
Item 19. Willingness to skip work to engage in fan interest	3.06 (2.06)
Item 20. Willingness to give up relationships to engage in fan interest	2.55 (1.96)
Item 21. Only have friends that are also fans of the same interest	2.51 (1.98)
Item 22. Willingness to incur bodily harm for the fan interest	2.34 (1.99)

Note. 7-point Likert-type scale from 1 = *unimportant* to 7 = *important*.

Finally, we conducted a MANOVA with participants' type of fan interest (i.e., sports, music, media, hobby) as the independent variable and the four factors (i.e., participation, passionate commitment, knowledge/evangelism, and sacrifice) from the principal components analysis as the dependent variables. The analysis revealed that scores on the four factors did not differ by the type of fan interest the participant had. To put it another way, what it means to be a true fan is similar across fan interests—and appears to have less to do with specific behaviors than it does with the traits or personality of the fan themselves.

In a follow-up study, we asked U.S. undergraduates ($N = 209$, 74.6% women; $M_{age} = 23.20$, $SD = 6.74$) to rate the same items from the previous study, but to do so with respect to themselves, rather than for fans in general (e.g., "Regarding my favorite fan interest, I would say..." "I am devoted," "I write fan mail," "I am obsessed"). Participants again indicated their interest in sport ($n = 52$), music ($n = 43$), media ($n = 87$), or a hobby ($n = 27$), and, again, these groups did not substantively differ with respect to the four "true fans" factors. Similar to the previous study, even when rating themselves and their own fan behaviors, passionate commitment ($M = 5.45$) and knowledge and evangelism ($M = 4.50$) were seen as stronger indicators of being a true fan than participating in specific fan behaviors ($M = 3.29$) or being willing to sacrifice ($M = 2.78$).

In a final study, we asked another sample of U.S. undergraduates ($N = 896$, 71.5% women; $M_{age} = 20.72$, $SD = 5.21$) to indicate their favorite fan interest and to complete a variety of measures related to their engagement in fan activities. Like in the previous studies, participants completed a measure assessing indicators of being a true fan, which again found that passionate commitment ($M = 5.24$) and knowledge and evangelism ($M = 4.20$) were more important than participating in specific fan behaviors ($M = 3.34$), and willingness to sacrifice ($M = 2.47$) when it comes to what participants feel makes them a "true fan."

We also administered a short, 10-item measure of participants' motivations for being a fan (Schroy et al., 2016). Following the prompt "I am a fan of this interest because of...", participants rated the extent to which 10 different motivations explained their fan interest (e.g., "Belongingness (social reasons)," "Eustress (positive stress)," "sexual attraction"). These motivations were based on Wann's (1995) motivations (discussed in the introduction chapter) with two additions: attention and sexual attraction. To examine which motivations uniquely predict the four true fan dimensions, we conducted a series of four regressions. In each regression we allowed the 10 motivations to simultaneously predict one of the four true fan dimensions. As shown in Table 2.2, the strongest unique predictors of participating in specific fan behaviors were the need for belongingness, economic benefits, and a desire for self-esteem.

Finally, we examined the association between the true fan dimensions and positive and negative fantasy engagement. Plante, Reysen, Groves et al. (2017) developed the fantasy engagement scale to distinguish between positive, healthy ways of engaging in fantasy activities (e.g., "Fantasizing about this makes me more creative") and more maladaptive, pathological ways of engaging in fantasy (e.g., "My fantasies about this have been the source of a lot of problems in my life"). Most presently relevant, both positive fantasy engagement ($\beta = .32$, $p < .001$) and negative fantasy engagement ($\beta = .35$, $p < .001$) were positively predicted by participation scores, suggesting that fan behavior is neither inherently positive or maladaptive, at least when it comes to the occasional flight of fantasy associated with particular fan interests (e.g., fictional media, gaming).

Table 2.2
Regressions of Motivations Predicting True Fan Dimensions

Variable	Factor 1	Factor 2	Factor 3	Factor 4
Belongingness	.16**	.15**	.15**	.14**
Family	.02	.06	.04	.05
Aesthetics	.07*	.06	.11**	.02
Self-Esteem	.15**	.10*	.03	.10*
Economic	.16**	.04	.02	.18**
Eustress	.10*	.12**	.08*	.08*
Escape	.05	.12**	.17**	-.01
Entertainment	-.04	.23**	.08*	-.15**
Attention	.07*	.01	-.02	.09*
Sexual Attraction	.09**	.02	.07*	.11**

Note. Factor 1 = participation in fan interest, Factor 2 = passionate commitment, Factor 3 = knowledge and evangelism, and Factor 4 = willingness to sacrifice. * $p < .05$, ** $p < .01$.

Conclusion

Given that most of the other chapters in this book directly or indirectly assess participation in specific fan behaviors as predictors or outcomes of other fan-relevant variables, we focused this chapter instead on reviewing a representative, if somewhat underutilized, theory predicting fans' intention to engage in fan-related behavior as a product of their own attitudes, perceived social norms, and perceptions of ability to engage in the behavior itself. We also looked at fans' perceptions of what constitutes being a "true fan" and the extent to which this judgment is grounded in fans' participation in fan-related behaviors. Somewhat surprisingly, participating in specific fan behaviors does not seem to be the defining feature of what it means to be a true fan, both when it comes to judging other fans as well as when it comes to judging one's own fan interest. This stands in stark contrast to what an outsider looking into a given fan interest might expect, like a non-fan expecting *Star Trek* fans to be defined by their attending *Star Trek* conventions, watching *Star Trek* religiously, and wearing *Star Trek* costumes.

While most fans probably engage in fan-related behaviors, sometimes in-line with stereotypes about these fan groups, these behaviors may not be the defining, necessary, or important indicators of fan identity that we might think they are. While it's true that we can predict such behaviors from fans' attitudes and a fandom's social norms, these behaviors themselves do not appear to make the fan. Even so, as we'll see throughout this book, differences in fans' tendency to engage in these behaviors may nevertheless provide researchers with hints about the nature of that fan's interest, and should thus not be overlooked as a potential source of useful information, albeit one taken with a grain of salt.

Chapter 3
Recreation

Recreational activities are the things we do outside of work or our other obligations. While they may seem like fruitless endeavors destined to waste the off-time between our more productive work periods, it's thought that recreational activities serve a number of important functions – not the least of which is to provide people with positive emotions, psychological resilience, social interaction, and the opportunity for personal growth. When described this way, fan activities seem to fit the bill as a recreational activity, being activities that we do of our own volition rather than for survival[1] and, at least for most of us, being done because they bring us enjoyment (Davidson, 2018).

Having said this, not all fans are created equal; the manner or extent to which fans derive enjoyment from their fan interest may vary considerably from person to person. "Casual" fans may watch a favorite TV series for fun but derive little enjoyment from learning trivia about the show, discussing the show with other fans, or attending fan conventions. Others may derive more enjoyment from the fandom and its social activities than they do from the interest itself. Regardless of how fans engage with their fan interest however (or whether they even identify with the label of "fan" itself), most people consider their fan-related activities to be a desirable way to spend their free time—even if highly-identified fans derive more enjoyment from their fan activities (e.g., Raney, 2013).

In the present chapter we review the literature on recreation and consider whether knowing how and why fans derive enjoyment from their fan-related activities can tell us something important about their psychology. We'll cover the topic in three sections, starting with a review of the research on recreation and casual leisure more broadly. Next, we'll consider media consumption and the enjoyment we derive from the media we consume. We'll finish up by looking at recreation as a motivational factor driving fan identification in the most-studied group of fans there is: sport fans.

Casual Leisure

We begin with a look at Stebbins (1982), who made an important theoretical distinction between serious leisure and casual leisure that we'll continue to reference throughout this book. Conceptualized thusly, serious and casual

---

[1] As an exception to this, those who make their living through their fan activities (e.g., artists, writers, backstage workers at concerts) could well say that their fandom-related activities contribute to their ability to sustain themselves financially.

leisure can be thought of as opposite ends of a continuum describing a given leisure activity. Where people fall on this continuum is a product of their level of involvement in the activity. On the one end, Stebbins (2001, p. 53) defines causal leisure as an "immediately, intrinsically rewarding, relatively short-lived pleasurable activity requiring little to no special training to enjoy it." On the opposite end of the continuum, serious leisure is the systematic pursuit of a leisure activity that involves special skills, experience, or knowledge and which can become like a career, significant and fulfilling for the person involved (Stebbins, 1992).

When it comes to casual leisure, Stebbins (1997) initially suggested that there are six distinct types of casual leisure, although he would later include two additional types (Stebbins, 2007). Any casual leisure activity can be described as a combination of one or more of these types:

- Play, or carefree suspension of the activity's consequences
- Relaxation, including letting go of stress or tension
- Entertainment, passively taking in a pleasurable experience
- Active entertainment, which involves the participant's direct input (e.g., a puzzle or board game)
- Sociable conversation, talking with others with the primarily purpose of socializing
- Sensory stimulation, such as viewing aesthetically beautiful things or pleasures such as eating and sex
- Casual volunteering
- Aerobic activity

Stebbins argues that, at their core, casual leisure activities are hedonic activities; that is, they're activities which elicit pleasure and enjoyment in and of themselves. For example, college students often frequent bars and drink for fun and to socialize (McDonald et al., 2008), which would make this activity an example of casual leisure, since engaging in the activity itself is enjoyable (Shinew & Parry, 2005). This does not mean that those involved in serious leisure are unable to derive pleasure from their activities, to be sure. Instead, serious leisure is driven by something more than pleasure, or is pleasurable for reasons beyond the immediate enjoyment of the activity itself.

In recent years researchers have sought to empirically distinguish casual leisure activity from more serious leisure activities. Shen and Yarnal (2010), for example, examined the casual-serious leisure continuum in a sample of women from the Red Hat Society, an organization seeking personal growth and empowerment for women through the organization's social events. The researchers coded responses to an open-ended question about participants' meaningful experiences with the society and extracted 13 themes (e.g., identity, fun/enjoyment, social support). Socialization and enjoyment emerged as the most frequently mentioned themes, themes that are, themselves, markers of casual leisure. In another study, Derom and Taks (2011) also attempted to distinguish causal leisure from serious leisure by giving a survey to attendees at national and international sporting events. Characteristics of serious leisure (e.g., seeking mastery, fan as part of one's identity) were observed for participants in international events, while casual leisure characteristics (social and escape motivation) were more prominent among those at national events. Both studies suggest the importance of socialization and relaxation as key variables distinguishing casual leisure from serious leisure.

While we've focused so far on Stebbins' work, other scholars have similarly attempted to distinguish different ways of leisure engagement. Kerins et al. (2007), for example, proposed a measure that includes three dimensions: behavior (e.g., time spent on activity), skill (e.g., perception of skills), and commitment (e.g., importance of activity, desire to engage in activity over other potential activities). In a sample of ultimate Frisbee players, the authors noted three types of players: casual, active, and serious, with casual players scoring the lowest on all of the assessed dimensions.

Tsaur and Huang (2020) proposed their own three-dimensional model from a study of joggers. The three dimensions included casual tendency (e.g., "Jogging is just one leisure activity among leisure activities that I frequently participate in"), hedonism-focused motivation (e.g., "Participating in jogging is mainly for entertainment"), and ease of withdrawal (e.g., "I can easily go without jogging"). In a later study they surveyed birdwatchers and made an analogous categorization, observed that those who watched without specialized equipment scored higher on the casual dimension than those with specialized equipment. What's more, in line with Stebbins' work, hedonism-focused motivation emerged as the strongest predictor of casual leisure.

Before we finish this section, let's consider whether those who engage in serious leisure gain more from their leisure activities than those engaging in the same activities in a more casual manner (Stebbins, 1997). Testing this idea, Chen and Liao (2019) tested a satiation model wherein enjoyment of casual leisure gradually decreases over time. As a test of this, the researchers played Taiwanese undergraduates an unfamiliar pop song 13, 28, or 36 times, asking them to complete measures before and after the experience. Supporting the model, and perhaps to no one's great surprise, enjoyment dropped with repeated exposure to the song, although participants experienced a small increase in enjoyment by the end as they found novel ways to distract themselves from the song itself. While the study has been used to argue for the fleeting nature of hedonic enjoyment in casual leisure, it does suffer from questions about its ecological validity.[2]

Enjoyment and Media

Researchers have long noted that people consume media (e.g., film, television) for recreational purposes. This point underpinned the work of Rubin (1983), who constructed a measure of nine different uses and gratifications driving media viewers. Among these different uses and gratifications were relaxation, habit, arousal, and, most presently relevant, entertainment (e.g., "Because it's enjoyable"). Those who scored high on entertainment were also more frequent TV viewers, suggesting, to no one's great surprise, that enjoyment contributes to media viewing behavior. The measure has been used numerous times since then, with findings generally supporting the original results.

In accordance with Rubin's findings, Oliver and Bartsch (2010) also recognize that people consume media entertainment because it's fun, although they note that more serious viewers are more prone to moving, thoughtful, and provoking experiences. The researchers constructed a measure assessing the viewer's fun during a film (e.g., "The movie was entertaining") while also assessing other facets of the film, such as whether the film was thought-provoking, left a lasting impression, suspenseful, and had artistic value. We'll talk more about the thought-provoking and deeper appreciation dimensions assessed by some of these variables in later chapters (e.g., Chapter 4, Chapter 6), but for now, let's focus on the results pertaining to fun, the dimension most conceptually similar to recreation. Fun was both the highest-rated dimension and was the dimension most strongly correlated with having a favorable impression of the movie.

In a later study, Hall (2015) gave the same measure to undergraduate baseball fans watching a baseball game. Participants indicated which team won the game, their sense of parasocial friendship and interest in the players involved, their involvement in baseball-related activities (e.g., game attendance), Oliver and Bartsch's (2010) measures of suspense, hedonic enjoyment and appreciation, and emotional responses. Hedonic enjoyment was positively correlated with all of these variables, and was one of the strongest predictors of affective responses to the game.

---

[2] At least insofar as people seldomly (and mercifully) rarely find themselves exposed to the same song 36 times in a row!

Not all studies on this topic looked solely at the link between enjoyment of an activity and affective or behavioral outcomes. Oliver and Raney (2011), for example, differentiated between being entertained by a piece of media and appreciating it. To this end, they constructed a measure of hedonic (e.g., "For me, the best movies are the ones that are entertaining") and eudaimonic (e.g., "I like movies that challenge my way of seeing the world") motivation for watching films. Participants also indicated how much they liked 12 different genres of films. Hedonic motivation was positively related to liking comedies and action films, genres associated with creating interesting or desirable affective states. But hedonic motivation was also negatively related to preference for nonfiction films. A follow-up study found that hedonic motivations correlate with viewers' personality (e.g., optimism, spontaneity, humor). In other words, watching a movie for fun not only predicts consumers' preference for one type of media over another, but can also tell us something about their personality.[3] A later study by Tsay-Vogel and Krakowiak (2016) would similarly show that viewers seeking hedonic pleasures are more willing to suspend moral judgment and subsequently enjoy the experience of viewing morally-questionable characters more than those who don't, suggesting yet another piece of information hedonic information provides us: socio-cognitive processes of viewers during the films.

In a final set of studies, we come full-circle to consider the extent to which hedonic and eudaimonic motivations drive media use among self-described fans of a television show. Taylor (L. D., 2019) asked U.S. participants to rate their identification as a fan of a favorite series (e.g., TV, movies, novels, etc.), their engagement in fan behavior (e.g., consumption, engagement with community), and their eudaimonic and hedonic motivations for media use. Both eudaimonic and hedonic motivation were associated with greater consumption behavior, although highly-identified fans with hedonic motives engaged the most with the fan community. In their own studies of TV fans, Taylor and Gil-Lopez (2020) found that openness to new experiences and cognitive flexibility were significant predictors of eudaimonic motivation, while conscientiousness, neuroticism, and cognitive flexibility were predictors of hedonic motivation.

Taken together, the available research on media consumption makes it clear that entertainment is a significant motivator of media consumption. While hedonic motivation and eudaimonic motivation may both play a role in driving

---

[3] Although Oliver and Raney (2011) treated hedonic and eudaimonic motivation as individual differences between viewers, Bailey and Ivory (2018) would later show that hedonic and eudaimonic states can be elicited through short interventions such as watching a show that reflects one state or another.

fans to watch their favorite shows, hedonic motivation, the pure entertainment value that fans derive from consuming media, can tell us a lot about what fans consume, how much they consume, and the mind and personality of those doing the consuming.

Of course, entertainment doesn't only motivate the consumption of screen media: It's also an important variable in research on sport spectators, being among the strongest predictors of watching sports and fans' positive responses to doing so (Ryu & Heo, 2016). As such, in the final section of this chapter we highlight research assessing the role of entertainment as a motivator of sport spectatorship.

Sport Motivation and Entertainment

In his multidimensional measure of sport fan motivations, Wann (1995) included the dimension of entertainment (e.g., "I enjoy sports because of their entertainment value," "To me, sports spectating is simply a form of recreation"). Wann characterizes sport fans driven by this particular motivation as using sport "as a pastime, not unlike a trip to the movies or an amusement park" (p. 378). Or, as Stebbins might have put it, sport fans may be more accurately categorized as engaging in casual leisure rather than serious leisure.

In line with this idea, Wann, Schrader, and Wilson (1999) found that entertainment was the top-rated motivation of sport fans, and was positively correlated with team identification. This finding is far from unique, as studies since then routinely find that entertainment is among the highest-rated motivations of sport fans (e.g., Daniels & Norman, 2005; Pease & Zhang, 2001; Pugh et al., 2019), predicting both team identification (e.g., Brown-Devlin & Devlin, 2020; Hu & Tang, 2010) and game attendance (Koo & Hardin, 2008).[4] Findings from such studies have shown that:

- Entertainment predicts word of mouth endorsement of attending live events among F1 fans (Kim et al., 2013)
- Entertainment is the highest-rated motivation for baseball, softball, and wrestling fans, and did not differ with respect to sport (James & Ross, 2004)
- U.S. baseball fans are more motivated by entertainment than Japanese fans, although entertainment was the highest rated motivation in both cultures (James et al., 2009)

---

[4] Nor are the findings unique to sport fans: Entertainment is also highly-rated and associated with attendance at performing art events (Swanson et al., 2008). Schroy et al. (2016) likewise found that entertainment motivation was the highest-rated motivation for a variety of different media-based fan groups.

- Australian football fans' loyalty to their teams was predicted by the degree to which entertainment motivated their interest (Kim et al., 2021)

Funk et al. (2004) also included entertainment (e.g., "I attend games because it is an entertaining event for a reasonable price") as a dimension of sport fan motivation in their study, although they labeled their variable "entertainment value," defining it as "the extent to which the affordability of the entertainment contributes to one's attendance at games" (p. 60). In a study of fans of Chinese Professional Baseball League in Taiwan, entertainment value was positively correlated with attitudinal and behavioral loyalty to their favorite team (Wang et al., 2011), a finding replicated in a sample of Turkish football spectators (Yenilmez et al., 2020). A sample of Australian football fans similarly revealed that entertainment value was positively related to team identification (Kim et al., 2021). Thus, although studies worldwide have conceptualized entertainment in slightly different ways—such as the entertainment provided for the price of admission—converging evidence is nevertheless consistent in showing that entertainment strongly predicts fan consumption in sport fans, illustrating the robustness of the association.

In a final set of studies, we consider whether the association between entertainment and fan behavior among sport fans carries over into the digital domain. Seo and Green (2008) constructed a measure of sport fans' motivation to consume online sport-related content. As one might expect by this point, even after controlling for nine other dimensions of motivation, entertainment (e.g., "I use the team's website because it is amusing") was positively correlated with website commitment (e.g., "I am dedicated to being a user of the team's website"). Given that sport fans frequently use social media sites (e.g., twitter, Facebook: Haugh & Watkins, 2016), it is worth knowing, for marketers and fan scholars alike, that entertainment is a unique predictor of the frequency with which fans use such sites (Kang et al., 2015; Li et al., 2019).[5]

Conclusion

It comes as no surprise that recreation and entertainment are important variables in the fan literature, given that fan activities are often thought of as casual leisure activities, and, thus, are activities motivated by the fun fans have engaging in them. A review of the research on casual leisure suggests that

---

[5] Not all studies agree with this conclusion, however: In a study of South Korean students, entertainment motivation was negatively associated with online consumption, intention to purchase merchandise, and intention to attend a game (Sung et al., 2017). Thus, the link between entertainment motivation for visiting sport team websites and frequency of consumption may not be universal, or may need to be qualified by moderator variables.

socializing and enjoyment characterizes these "types" of fans, while media-based research suggests that fans are likely driven by hedonistic desires. Studies looking specifically at sport fans also shows rather definitively that entertainment is among the strongest drivers of both fan-related consumption behavior and identification with, and loyalty to, one's favorite team. The sizable body of fairly consistent research on this topic makes it clear that the entertainment value of one's fan interest must be considered in any model looking to categorize or explain fans.

Chapter 4
Meaning-Making

"What's the meaning of life?" It's perhaps the most vexing question facing humanity, a question motivating spiritual journeys and philosophical discourse alike. The question drives us because we naturally seek to make sense of, and find meaning in, the world around us. Braaten et al. (2019), for example, found that students derive meaning, a sense of growth, and feelings of authenticity from educational settings, all of which is inherently satisfying and which only drives further interest in schooling. In a way, we can't help ourselves from seeking meaning in the things we do.

But what does finding meaning in life have to do with fans? After all, the search for meaning in life is a serious endeavor; can leisure pursuits like listening to music or watching a favorite television show really be expected to provide us with answers to the "big picture" questions?

While we might think of the search for meaning as a vast spiritual or self-reflective undertaking, it may be possible to find significance through seemingly superficial leisure activities (Iwasaki, 2008; Newman et al., 2014). One can develop feelings of significance and purpose by engaging in a leisure activity (Dill-Shackleford & Vinney, 2016) or the activities themselves may be seen as important and meaningful (Oliver & Bartsh, 2010, Oliver et al., 2012). As noted by Vorderer (2011) and Vorderer and Reinecke (2015), leisure activities, while sating hedonic needs, can also be intrinsically valuable as meaningful experiences, something we might call eudaimonic entertainment. Based on such ideas, research on leisure now recognizes both hedonic and eudaimonic motivation for recreation and leisure activities.[1]

In the present chapter we consider this idea that it's possible to derive a sense of meaning from one's fan activities, especially those activities categorized as eudaimonic entertainment. We first review scholarly work investigating the meaning people derive from leisure pursuits like fan activities. We then consider moderators and qualifiers of this link, the mechanisms thought to drive it, and finally some of the ways it can inform our understanding of fan communities and fan consumption.

Types of Meaning

Donald and Havighurst (1959) were arguably the first scholars to systematically study whether people derive a sense of meaning from their leisure

---

[1] This is not unlike the distinction some scholars (e.g., make between "casual" and "serious" leisure described in Chapter 3).

activities. In their work, they defined 12 different benefits that people may gain by engaging in leisure pursuits:

- Connecting with friends
- Contributing to society
- Gaining social standing
- Getting popular
- Financial benefits
- Achievement and accomplishment
- Escaping from work
- Novelty of experience
- Making time pass
- Self-respect
- Pleasure
- Creativity

Two things are worth noting from this list. First, many of these concepts have since made their way into other fan models (e.g., fan motivation, Wann, 1995). Second, of these benefits, only some seem to reflect the idea of gaining a sense of meaning or significance. For example, an activity which fosters a sense of achievement and accomplishment or which allows a person to contribute to society seems to reflect an "inner significance" that we could characterize as meaningful. In contrast, pleasure and financial benefits, while making the activity beneficial, lack in their contribution to inner significance.

Four decades later, Watkins (1999) would similarly examine meaning in leisure activities and note four distinct categories of what leisure is to those who engage in it:

- a means of passing time
- a way to exercise choice
- a way to escape pressure
- a means of achieving fulfillment

It probably hasn't escaped the reader that most of these categories map onto the categories outlined by Donald and Havighurst. The last category in particular most closely approximates what many of us would consider to be a meaningful or significant activity, a category which, as we've seen, scholars have recognized for decades as being part of at least some leisure activities.

Transcendence

A related body of research involves the concept of transcendence. Among other things, transcendence refers to one seeking a sense of purpose that goes beyond themselves. Peterson and Seligman (2004) consider transcendence to be a central virtue across cultures, and it can be thought of both as a trait and as something people develop through engaging in activities that instill awe or hope.

In the context of fans, research suggests that their fan-related activities may contribute to this sense of transcendence, insofar as they create feelings of awe and hope or instill a sense of moral goodness and connection to others. In one study, the authors found that 90.5% of those listening to music, 86.9% watching movies, 80.2% watching TV, 74.7% reading books, and 58.9% listening to podcasts reported being moved, touched, or inspired by the content (Raney et al., 2018). Daily media consumption of such content is tied to perceptions of its meaningfulness and feelings of transcendence (Raney, 2018). Others have similarly found an association between meaningful entertainment experiences and feelings of transcendence in non-media contexts (Rieger et al., 2018; Zhao, 2020).

Moderators
Demographics

While it seems plausible that some fan-related activities will be significant for some people, we wouldn't expect every fan-related activity to be equally significant and meaningful for everyone. Illustrating this point, Sivan et al. (2019) looked at boys' and girls' preferred leisure activities and found, in line with social norms, that boys were more likely to prefer sports than girls. More relevant to the present point, sport preferences were especially meaningful for boys, who obtained a sense of psychological, physical, and social meaning from the activity in a way that girls did not. Such findings suggest that social norms may influence the extent to which people derive meaning and significance from specific fan activities, perhaps influencing the perceived appropriateness of the activity or impacting the way in which they engage in the activity (e.g., superficially instead of passionately).

Other studies have examined whether the link between engaging in fan activities and feelings of meaning generalize to all age groups and cultures. Speaking to the former point, Hofer et al. (2014) observed age differences in the link between affective response and perceived meaning among those viewing films. Specifically, younger adults felt a greater sense of meaning when they watched films regardless of the valence of their affective response to the film. In contrast, older viewers were more likely to only report a greater sense of meaning in response to films that elicited positive affect.

Speaking to the latter point, studies have also assessed meaning and significance derived from leisure activities across cultures. Igartua and Barrios (2013), for example, found that older Spanish fans derive more meaning from their leisure interests than do younger fans, a finding which runs somewhat counter to the findings of the previous study, which was conducted in Switzerland. Other studies directly compare fans from different cultures. In some cases, cross-cultural differences have been observed with respect to deriving meaning from leisure activities (e.g., Odağ et al., 2016), while in other studies, more similarities than differences exist cross-culturally (Iwasaki, 2007).

Taken together, such studies illustrate that the link between fan-related activities and a sense of meaning may be robust and broadly generalize across populations, but the effects are far from uniform across the demographic spectrum.

Motivation

In the introduction to this book we discussed research by Wann (e.g., 1995) showing that fan motivation differs across fans and can predict differences in fan activities. As such, it comes as no surprise that fans differently with different motivations (e.g., eudaimonic or hedonic) may differ in the meaning they derive from their fan-related activities. Tsay-Vogel and Krakowiak (2016), for example, examined hedonic and eudaimonic enjoyment as a moderator of viewer responses to films featuring morally ambiguous characters. Those with more eudaimonic motivations were more likely to experience less moral disengagement (i.e., responding more negatively to the questionably immoral behavior) than those with less eudaimonic motivations. Beyond influencing how people respond to a specific piece of media, fan motivation may also impact media consumption habits more broadly and fans' involvement with fandoms that spring up around particular films or shows (Tsay-Vogel & Sanders, 2017).

Mechanisms

While some scholars have focused their efforts on understanding "when" and "for whom" fan activities contribute to a sense of meaning, others seek to better understand the mechanisms driving these relationships. Dill-Shackleford et al. (2016), for example, studied the extent to which media fans derive a sense of meaning from their fan interest. They found that highly-identified fans experience more meaningfulness than to less-identified fans when watching the show. Critically, this association was driven by the fact that highly-identified fans also had more self-related thoughts while watching the clips which, in turn, were associated with increased perceptions of the media as meaningful. Highly-identified fans also reported less meaning-seeking in their lives, in part because they had already found a sense of meaning, in part, through their interest.

Other studies have suggested that insofar as entertainment media instills a sense of profundity or raises questions about the human condition, it spurs people to reflect on their purpose in life (Taylor, 2021). Others still have pointed to the possibility that narratives can facilitate a sense of empathy which, in turn, leads to feelings of significance and meaning with respect to one's social life (Dill-Shackleford et al., 2016).

Beyond looking at mechanisms leading to a sense of meaning from leisure activities, researchers have also looked at meaning as a mediator itself. Delmar et al. (2018) suggest that media consumption fosters feelings of meaningfulness which, in turn, can impact cognitive-intellectual and social-emotional growth. In a study by Cohen (2016), players of a game that offers knowledge and awareness of genocide and war experienced an increase in feelings of self-efficacy towards these topics because of the meaningfulness of the media to the player (e.g., empathy, identification with the characters). While consuming media for answers to existential questions might not seem like the first reason most of us watch our favorite show, researchers suggest there may be truth to this idea, especially among those who experience awe, inspiration, and empathy from the media they consume (Oliver & Bartsch, 2011).

Applications

Shared Experience and Fandom

Given that fan activities often involve a social component, and given that meaning and significance in life often involves considering people beyond ourselves, it's worth asking whether the meaning some people find in their fan activities impacts, or is impacted by, shared fan experiences.

A study by Wann Hackathorn, and Sherman (2017) sheds light on this possibility. The authors found that participants' identification with the fandom was associated with having found a sense of meaning in their lives. They also found that this relationship was mediated by the extent to which participants felt a sense of belongingness to their fan group. Other studies have similarly shown that feeling like you belonging to a fan group and engaging in fan activities with other fans can make those activities feel more significant and meaningful: A 2019 study by Shabazz found that watching the Super Bowl with your friends and family made viewing the event a meaningful experience.

Materialism

In this final section, we consider the association between materialism—fan purchases and other consumption habits—and a sense of meaning. Intuitively, one might expect these two variables to operate in opposition to one another. After all, content creators who "sell out" are criticized for having forfeited meaning or significance in their art in exchange for monetary gain. People may similarly decry the commodification of deeply meaningful leisure experiences, like someone selling Burning Man merchandise, an event famous for its anti-commercialism. Insofar as materialism represents a cheapened or superficial representation of a meaningful activity, it may constitute a threat to the meaningfulness of that activity.

Gupta (2019) sheds light on this possibility with surprising results: Eudaimonic purchasing predicts greater happiness and satisfaction. Such purchases were seen as fostering rejuvenating, expanding, and consolidating processes that, in turn, made the activities more meaningful to buyers. Other research similarly shows that blanket statements about materialism and its impact on an activity's meaning are overly simplistic. Pandelaere (2016), for example, notes that material purchases done for self-acceptance reasons rather than for the purpose of social status display lead to stronger identification with the interest and the interest having a greater sense of meaning. Such purchases, in turn, lead to more positive outcomes and improved well-being, especially when compared to hedonic purchases, which are more likely to yield negative affect (e.g., regret).

Conclusion

There is a general tendency for people to trivialize leisure activities, especially when those interests are unusual (e.g., Reysen & Shaw, 2016). As such, people often underestimate just how significant, meaningful, and life-changing a person's fan activities can be. As the research reviewed in the present chapter indicates, if we want a complete understanding of fan behavior and the importance of fan activities, we need to consider the significance and meaning behind the fan activities people engage in rather than focusing only on the superficial trappings of the interest itself. In doing so, we'll be able to answer more sophisticated questions about why fans change their thoughts and beliefs in accordance with fan-related content, which fans are the most likely to do so, and when fans are likely to be impacted (positively or adversely) by their interest.

Chapter 5
Direction/Guidance

In Chapter 4 we considered the extent to which fans derive a sense of purpose or meaning from their fan interest. In this chapter we continue this train of thought with a related question: Can fans receive guidance and a sense of direction from their fan interest? We address this question by reviewing two ways fans may have their thoughts, feelings, and behaviors guided by their fan interests: through the norms of their fan communities and from the content itself. We'll then look at fans of the television show *My Little Pony* as a case study, given that many of these fans find guidance and direction from both the show itself and the fandom which developed around it.

Direction and Guidance Through Fandoms and Idols
Fandoms

In the introduction to this book we mentioned social identity theory, which posits that the groups we belong to play a crucial role in the we see and judge ourselves and, by extension, significantly impact how we think, feel, and behave (Tajfel & Turner, 1979; Turner et al., 1987). We'll discuss the theory and its implications in greater depth in Chapter 7, but for now it's sufficient to say that, according to social identity theory, our groups affect the schemas we develop, our stereotypes about others, and are a yardstick against which to compare ourselves (Atwell Seate et al., 2020). They influence our perceptions about what's normal, desirable, and important, and allow us to gauge how we stack up against those criteria. Most important of all, the theory posits that fan groups should be no different from any other group in this respect, allowing us to draw upon research on racial, national, and laboratory-formed groups to better understand fandom dynamics (Atwell Seate et al., 2020; Reysen, Plante, Chadborn et al., 2021).

One way to test whether fan groups guide and direct fans is to look at their impact on the social development of children. Friedman and Rapoport (2020) note that the participatory nature of fandom allows children to observe and internalize norms that, in turn, shape their future behavior. By observing and mimicking the behavior of fans, kids not only learn what constitutes acceptable behavior, but are also likely to seek out and prefer communities who engage in similar behavior. This tendency has been found in studies of youth team sports (Bruner et al., 2017), where team identification helps with the development of interpersonal skills and shapes social behavior and goals, both on and off the field.

The guiding and directing role of fan groups can be found in people of all ages and in fandoms beyond sport. Elliot (2020), for example, looked at the impact being among other music fans in the context of music education. Here, musicians-in-training internalized the norms and behavior demonstrated by older musicians and the professionals to which they aspired to be, including a desire to engage in charity and the perceived value of prosocial behavior. In another study, McInroy (2020) found that participation in online fandom activities provides members of gender and sexual minorities with guidance through the challenges associated with their stigmatized identities. Despite being leisure-focused, these groups nevertheless provide mentorship and model positive behavior, a result also found by Jensen (2017) in the context of groups on social media platforms.

Adult fans can similarly find guidance and direction through their fan groups, as research on sport fans has shown. Henderson (2020) examined two soccer fan communities in Liverpool and Portland. While these groups formed around their members' shared interest in sport, which served as an anchor for the group, they also strongly endorsed norms about the importance of activism and working to improve their community. Henderson notes "They create enclave communities of care, solidarity, and strength for their marginalized members... they leverage the attention cast on elite-level soccer to enter into broader political activism against individuals and institutions that seek to ridicule, disrupt, and crush the vulnerable lives within their communities" (2020, p. ix). In this case, the pro-activism norms of the soccer fan community directed fans' behavior outside the context of soccer, guiding them toward prosocial values and activism.

Fandoms can also guide the behavior of fans in far more mundane ways. Kulczynski (2014) notes, for example, that Madonna fans anticipating her "greatest hits" tour, purchased items from the 80s, including tutu skirts, slouch socks, and large hair bows. Jenkins (1992) similarly notes that fandoms can direct consumption behaviors (e.g., purchasing fan content), while others have even suggested that fan communities (e.g., sport fans) can impact worker productivity and even the stock market (Berument et al., 2005, 2009, 2012).

Celebrities

Beyond the influence of one's fandom, people can also find themselves guided by celebrities and other highly-respected icons and symbols of their fan interest (Berger, 2008). For example, D'Adamo's (2019) work on David Bowie fans reveals that fans are more than just passive followers; by engaging with the celebrity's work, fans feel a sense of connection to the celebrity. For some of David Bowie's fans who view his work through an existential lens, Bowie represents a guiding force and source of direction in their lives. Phillips (2013) similarly found that fans of actor/director Kevin Smith often take to message boards (Boardies) to both reflect on the significance of Smith's work to them and to seek out Smith for approval and direction (e.g., as an aspiring director). These parasocial relationships can be experienced in a manner similar to that of a close friend or relative, with fans being willing to accept guidance and life advice from those they've never personally met or even from fictional characters (e.g., Bernier et al., 2016).

As is often the case with parasocial relationships, the topic is usually discussed in terms of maladaptive outcomes for fans (for more on this see Chapters 26-28). As just one example, Underwood (2017) looked at fans of Zyzz, a bodybuilder who was revealed to be using image and performance-enhancing drugs (IPEDs). Zyzz fans overwhelmingly defended the icon in face of the allegations, ultimately leading to changes in the community's norms and perceptions of IPEDs. Many fans, amateur bodybuilders themselves, began to use IPEDs in response, seeing them as both appropriate and a normal part of bodybuilding. Such fans can thus be said to have had their behavior directed, albeit adversely, by seeing the behavior modeled by a revered icon in their community.

Direction and Guidance Through Narratives and Fan Content

Beyond the influence of other fans or icons within their fan communities, fans can also find their attitudes and behavior guided by the content of their fan interest itself. As media scholars for decades have pointed out, you are what you watch, whether you realize it or not (e.g., Plante, Anderson et al., 2019). Those who find significance and meaning in the media they consume may be especially susceptible to being influenced by its messages; or, to use language introduced in Chapter 4, those with eudaimonic motivation are more prone to self-reflect while consuming media, something called eudaimonic appreciation (Oliver & Bartsch, 2011; Vinney et al., 2019). Such fans are prone to being especially moved and inspired by the content they're viewing (Bartsch et al., 2014; Oliver & Bartsch, 2010; Oliver et al., 2012), reflecting on its relevance to their own experience (Knoblock-Westerwick, 2006). These same fans may find that the content they're consuming provides them with the guidance and direction they need to address problems they're facing, and may even seek their favorite content out for this very reason (Metzger, 2002).

Examples of fans turning to the content of their interests for guidance are fairly easy to come across. Music and television fans often look to songs, stories, and characters as a point of comparison for their own beliefs and behaviors, emulating the behavior they believe (or have been told) will yield desirable outcomes (Click et al., 2013). The effect is especially prominent for highly-identified fans, as seen in work by Plante and colleagues (2018) on bronies, adult fans of the television show *My Little Pony: Friendship is Magic* (we discuss bronies in greater depth in Chapter 29). Highly-identified bronies were more likely to emulate the prosocial behavior espoused in the show's moral lessons when they found themselves in analogous situations (Edwards et al., 2019), a point we elaborate upon in the next section.[1]

Bronies: A Case Study in Guidance and Direction

Bronies are fans of the television show *My Little Pony: Friendship is Magic*, a show which, if its title didn't give it away, contains prosocial messages about friendship, empathy, acceptance, promotion of diversity, and self-expression. Knowing this, and based on what we've learned in the rest of this chapter, we can ask whether bronies' thoughts, feelings, and behaviors are guided by both the brony fandom and by the content of the show itself.

First, research suggests that bronies do, indeed, direct their attitudes and behaviors to be in accordance with the norms of the fandom and the behavior modeled by other fans. More obvious behavioral changes include the creation and transmission of show-related memes and engaging in ritualistic behavior (e.g., giving "hoof-bumps" instead of high-fives). Substantive attitudinal changes also take place as well, such as challenging traditional gender norms and developing a more nuanced and complex understanding of masculinity, especially among highly-identified fans (Edwards et al., 2019; Miller, 2018).

So impactful is the fandom on bronies' thoughts and behavior that bronies often report turning to the show for guidance and direction more than they turn to other, more traditional places. For example, Edwards, Griffin, and Redden (2014) found that bronies consider the show's guiding messages, many of which are an explicit and recurring part of every episode,[2] to be one of the most appealing parts of the show. The fandom itself embraces these moral lessons, normalizing, internalizing, and modeling them in a way that guides many bronies in a manner not unlike how they would be impacted by their relationships with friends and family.

Beyond the impact of fandom interaction, we can also look at how bronies use the show itself as a guiding force. As we've already seen, the prosocial content of *My Little Pony* is associated with greater prosocial behavior (Plante,

---

[1] Of course, not all content-related guidance is prosocial. Williams (2006) found that anime fans often directed their interests toward facets of Japanese culture, even when they lacked the knowledge necessary to do so appropriately (e.g., not knowing how to speak Japanese).

[2] For the first two seasons of the show, every episode would end with the show's main character, Twilight Sparkle, writing a letter to her mentor, Princess Celestia, explaining the episode's morale or lesson.

Chadborn, Groves, & Reysen, 2018), something that many bronies attribute to taking the show's guiding messages to heart. But the show also drives other behaviors. For example, the show's encouragement of creativity and self-expression led many fans to try their hand at drawing and writing themselves (Edwards, Griffin, Chadborn, & Redden, 2014). Chadborn et al. (2017) also note that fans were compelled by the show to purchase and display *My Little Pony* merchandise, something in-line with the show's overarching goal as an advertisement for the *My Little Pony* line of toys (Edwards et al., 2019).

Conclusion

In this chapter we reviewed research showing that fans seek receive guidance and direction from their fan interests and from the communities of fans which form around those interests, even when the interests themselves may seem trivial. As an extension of Chapter 4, which found that fans differ in the extent to which they find meaning and significance in their fan interest, some fans (e.g., highly-identified fans who engage in eudaimonic leisure) are especially likely to change the way they think, feel, and behave in accordance with the values and norms of their fan interests. While we're not suggesting that all fans do (or should) make life-altering decisions based on their fan interests, the attitudes and behaviors modeled by fan content and the surrounding fandom can become internalized and influence fans more than they might think. While certainly not the strongest predictor of fan attitudes and behavior, fan researchers would nevertheless benefit from considering the extent to which fans are guided or directed by their fan interests in models seeking to better understand and differentiate fans.

Chapter 6
Personal Growth

Left to their own devices, humans naturally seek to better themselves. This principle is so foundational to our understanding of human nature that Maslow's (1943) famous hierarchy of needs places self-actualization, the maximizing of a person's talents and capabilities, as the summit for which people strive (after having met more basic needs like food and shelter).

Given the prominence of growth and self-actualization as a motivator of so much of human behavior, it comes as little surprise that people find opportunities for growth and maximization in all of life's domains: their work, family, social groups, and, most presently relevant, their leisure activities. Stebbins (1982) speaks to this idea directly, suggesting that personal growth via self-actualization is a natural outcome of serious or eudaimonic leisure. Empirical evidence also supports this assertion across a variety of fans:

- Interviews with shag dancers reveal that personal growth is a component of their interest (Brown et al., 2008)
- Among gamers, personal growth, including learning to overcome difficult parts of the game, is a significant motivator of their interest (Anderson, 2018)
- Basketball fans indicate that fan participation gives them a sense of personal growth (Chen, 2010)
- Malaysian cosplayers state that building a costume allows them to both learn more about themselves and to grow as a person (Yamato, 2016).

These are just some of the numerous studies suggesting that fans experience a sense of personal growth through their fan activities. While some of this work has been quantitative in nature, much of it is qualitative, with the endeavor of measuring of personal growth itself being characterized by some as spotty and inconsistent (Porter et al., 2010). Taking this grain of salt in stride, the present chapter aims to look at some of the ways researchers have studied personal growth in fans. We shine the spotlight on approaches that focus on eudaimonia, but also survey several other approaches from across the fan literature. We'll see, in-line with research on meaning (Chapter 4) and guidance (Chapter 5), that fan activities can foster a sense of personal growth in fans, even when the activity itself seems, on its surface, to have little to do with self-growth.

Eudaimonia
Eudaimonic Well-Being

One could devote an entire book to summarizing the mountain of research on well-being. In fact, a recent article by Linton et al. (2016) documented nearly 100 different ways researchers have attempted to measure well-being in just the past 30 years. We could hardly do justice to such a complex body of work in just a few paragraphs, and we won't try to here. Instead, we'll briefly note that there's been a general trend in the past few decades to focus on two general clusters of well-being. The first cluster is that of subjective well-being, which includes concepts such as happiness, life satisfaction, and positive affect (Diener, 1984). The second cluster involves psychological well-being which, according to Ryff (1989), includes variables like self-acceptance, positive relationships, autonomy, environmental mastery, purpose in life, and personal growth. Researchers have, at different times, given different names to these two well-being clusters, including two that may be familiar to readers from previous chapters: hedonic well-being (i.e., subjective) and eudaimonic well-being (i.e., psychological; Ryan & Deci, 2001). Regardless of whether one chooses to use these or other labels to describe these two clusters, studies tend to routinely find evidence for them when broad, multidimensional measures of well-being are used (Compton et al., 1996; Keyes et al., 2002).

With this in mind, the present chapter on personal growth will focus primarily on the eudiamonic (or psychological) component of well-being. As we saw in Chapters 4 and 5, eudaimonia tends to be more strongly associated with finding meaning and seeking guidance from one's fan interest, both of which would be expected to contribute to fan growth and self-improvement. We would like to note, however, that in choosing to focus on eudaimonic well-being we are not suggesting that there are no mechanisms through which hedonic well-being may be tied to the personal growth and development of individual fans.

With that caveat out of the way, let's turn to the question of how one goes about assessing both eudiamonic well-being and personal growth? Ryff (1989) suggested assessing the former through a set of six variables, one of which was personal growth. Ryff notes that for optimal psychological functioning, one needs to "develop one's potential, to grow and expand as a person" (p. 1071). Ryff's measure contains items such as "I think it is important to have new experiences that challenge how I think about myself and the world," and "For me, life has been a continuous process of learning, changing, and growing" (Springer & Hauser, 2006). Someone scoring high on this measure is said to be growing toward their potential and developing new useful behaviors and skills (Ryff, 1989), a state most would agree describes someone who is growing.

To illustrate how this scale can be used to answer questions about growth in fans, we turn to one of our own studies in which we assessed fanship, fandom, fan activities, and psychological well-being as measured by Ryff's scale in a sample of undergraduate fans (Reysen, Plante, Roberts, & Gerbasi, 2021). In the first study, participants indicated their favorite fan interest and then rated their degree of fanship, fandom, the number of friends they had who are also fans of the interest, and Ryff's measure of psychological well-being. The personal growth dimension of the well-being scale was positively related to fanship, fandom, and number of friends who were fans. In a second and third study, the researchers again found that personal growth was positively associated with fanship, fandom, attending fan events (e.g., conventions), and consuming fan-relevant media in two different samples of fans. Taken together, the results illustrate the association of both fan activity engagement and interacting with a fan community on perceptions of personal growth.

Eudaimonic Motivation

Ryff's measure is far from the only way we can assess personal growth. For instance, Oliver and Raney (2011) constructed a measure of hedonic and eudaimonic motivations for consuming media. The eudaimonic dimension contains items such as "I like movies that make me more reflective" and "I like movies that challenge my way of seeing the world," neither of which directly measures personal growth, but both of which are measures of a motivational mindset conducive to personal growth. Speaking to this point, the authors found that eudaimonic motivation for media consumption was associated with a need for cognition, intellectualism, and search for meaning in life, while another study found that eudaimonic motivation to consume a favorite fictional story or series was associated with openness to experience (Taylor & Gil-Lopez, 2020). Notably, all of these individual differences lend themselves to both self-reflection and a willingness to better oneself.

The use of eudaimonic motivation in studies has helped to shed light on the importance of personal growth as a driver of fan behavior. For example, eudaimonic motivation was found to significantly predict fandom identification and interaction in a sample of Harry Potter fans (Tsay-Vogel & Sanders, 2017). Eudaimonic motivation has also been associated with intrinsic motivation to watch a TV show (Adachi et al., 2018), preference for certain film genres (Igartua & Barrios, 2013), and enjoying one's preferred video game (Cohen, 2016).

Eudaimonic Entertainment Experience

Eudaimonic entertainment experience represents another approach to the question of leisure activities and their link to personal growth. Wirth et al.

(2012) constructed a measure of eudaimonic entertainment derived in a sample of film-viewers. The measure consists of six dimensions (e.g., purpose in life, relatedness), one of which is entitled competence/personal growth. This dimension is measured with items like "I have a good feeling because the film has made me reflect on myself and my life". When Hofer et al. (2014) used this measure in their own study, they found that the personal growth dimension was positively correlated with feelings of joy after watching a film. Older adults (vs. younger adults) were especially likely to report higher personal growth after viewing a film, suggesting that demographic variables may impact the motivating role of personal growth in fan activities.

Eudaimonic Spectator Questionnaire

In a 2018 study, Delmar et al. surveyed fans of different film and television series to construct a measure known as the eudaimonic spectator questionnaire. The measure assesses two different types of growth, cognitive-intellectual growth (e.g., "I like films and T.V. series that teach me new things") and social-emotional growth (e.g., "I enjoy myself more when we view in a group and we form a community that analyzes and discusses the film or T.V. series"). Given the scales' relatively new status, there is, at the time of publishing this book, no other research applying this measure to the study of media consumption or fan activities. When Delmar et al. defined elements of fan identity (which included pleasure, experience, viewing, collecting, knowledge) in a 2020 paper, these two types of growth were not incorporated, a notable oversight given the potential utility of their measure.

Other Examples of Personal Growth associated with Fans

To this point, we've considered the association between fan growth and both fan activities and identity in the context of eudaimonia-related measures. There are, however, a number of other studies which have assessed personal growth using measures not grounded in the construct of eudaimonia.

Fan Identity and Personal Growth

Vinney et al. (2019) constructed a measure of fan identity that includes three dimensions: enthusiasm, appreciation, and social interaction. Most presently relevant is their "appreciation" subscale, which includes three items. One of the items in this scale ("Has helped me grow as a person") directly assesses fans' perception of personal growth as a result of their fan interest. The scale was found to be positively related to appreciation of the fan interest, but unrelated to other variables of interest (e.g., physical, psychological, or relational well-being.) Given that it's a fairly new measure, there has been, to date, little other research using it thus far.

Sport Team Psychological Commitment

In a sample of U.S. university college students, Keaton (2013) constructed a measure of fans' psychological commitment to the university's football team. The measure contained three dimensions: self-actualization, commitment, and investment. Of particular interest to this chapter is the self-actualization dimension, which contains items directly assessing personal growth (e.g., "Being a spectator of my favorite sport helps me to develop and grow as a person," "Being a spectator of my favorite sport helps me to reach my potential as an individual"). This self-actualization dimension was correlated with fan commitment and investment as well as with an implicit measure of team identification. This latter finding is especially interesting in conjunction with research on eudaimonia and serious leisure which suggests that this sort of deeply-held, non-superficial fan interest is especially likely to lead to a sense of sense of significance (Chapter 4) and seeking direction (Chapter 5) from one's interest; growing as a result of one's fan interest may go hand-in-hand with feeling significance and being guided by the interest in driving fan behavior.

Self-Expansion

In their research on relationships, Lewandowski et al. (2006) proposed a model of self-expansion in which being in a relationship with another person allows someone to enhance themselves by incorporating their partner's knowledge and experience into their own self-concept. Speaking directly to this idea, the measure contains items such as "How much has knowing your partner made you a better person?"

Lee, Bai, and Busser (2019) adapted this measure to assess self-expansion in K-pop fans, in particular the extent to which identifying with the K-pop fan community leads to feelings of self-enhancement. Sure enough, fans who felt this sense of connection to other K-pop fans felt motivated to explore and seek out new experiences via travelling to fan-related tourist sites, arguably an act of self-expansion and personal growth (though seeking out novel experiences). In a similar study Lee, Busser, and Park (2019) also found that this self-expansion in K-pop fans predicted other important fan behavior, including commitment to a celebrity and engaging in more fan activities.

In a study using a different measure of self-expansion (e.g., "How often, when you watch a story, TV show, or movie, do you experience what it would be like to have skills and abilities different from your own?"), Silver and Slater (2019) examined attachment and narrative engagement in TV viewers. Self-expansion was positively associated with anxious and avoidant attachment styles, as well as with a tendency to experience parasocial relationships, transport themselves into narratives, and experience narrative impact. The authors reasoned that people who fail to satisfy intrinsic needs in the real world, including the need for personal growth, may seek to satisfy them through fictional worlds—a finding in accordance with uses and gratifications theory (e.g., Rubin, 1983).

In a final study using yet another measure of self-expansion, Maltby and Day (2017) examined self-expansion in a sample of fans of celebrities. The authors used items such as "When I engage in my activity related to my favorite celebrity I know myself better" to assess growth among fans stemming from activities related to their favorite celebrity. Self-expansion positively predicted participants' attitudes toward celebrities (e.g., feelings of personal connection to celebrities and borderline pathological interests), as well as positive affect, further reinforcing the notion that growth is a significant driver of fan thoughts, feelings, and behavior.

Conclusion

Taken together, the research reviewed in this chapter makes it abundantly clear that personal growth plays an important role in motivating fans from all walks of life. We first found, in the section on eudaimonia, that understanding the growth fans perceive as a result of their fan interests can help us better predict fan-specific behaviors. In such contexts, however, personal growth is rarely assessed by itself, and is instead bundled with other facets of eudaimonia. Nevertheless, growth-related variables are able to predict important variables like consumption behavior, personality traits, affective responses to fan content, and commitment, all of which speak to the importance of devoting time and future research to better understanding the role of personal growth as a driver of fan behavior. This point is only amplified by the other research we reviewed, research where personal growth—again as part of other measures—was similarly associated with variables of practical importance to fan researchers. In short, research from the past three chapters has shown that measuring the extent to which fans take their fan interests very seriously—finding meaning in it, being guided by it, and growing from it—can pay dividends when it comes to helping to meaningfully categorize fans and predict their behaviors.

Chapter 7
Fandom

Given how interesting and varied individual fans can be in the way their interest manifests, it's easy to miss the forest for the trees when studying them. This problem is compounded by the fact that many of the fan-related variables researchers are interested in are individualistic in nature: How much time fans spend on their activity, their personality traits, how strongly they identify with the interest, their motivations, they way they respond emotionally to fan-related stimuli. As such, we frequently consider fan activities as isolated, individualistic phenomena despite the fact that many fan activities, by their very nature, involve other fans (e.g., conventions, forums, sharing fanart and fanfiction).

It's for this reason that researchers have, in recent years, begun paying greater attention to the variable of fandom, the extent to which fans identify with other fans in their fan community. At first glance, one might think that sport researchers have been studying this for decades, given the prominence of team identification measures in the sport fan literature. However, as we note later in this chapter, identification with a sports team (and not with other fans of the team) is more accurately construed as a personal identity (Funk & James, 2004), also known as fanship, a topic to which we'll return in Chapter 15. If you find it difficult to conceptually distinguish between fanship and fandom, don't feel bad: Researchers frequently conflate these two terms (e.g., Rees et al., 2015). As a result, fandom is often overlooked in quantitative studies of fans in favor of fanship, often to the field's detriment.

In the present chapter we attempt to address this oversight and give fandom its due attention as a variable both important and distinct from fanship. We first review social identity and self-categorization, two social psychological theories that constitute the theoretical underpinning for most research assessing fandom identification. Next, we lay out the rationale for considering fandom and fanship (e.g., team identification) as distinct psychological constructs that differently relate to important variables. Finally, we review several measures of fandom identification and demonstrate their utility in studies measuring fandom as a variable distinct from, but related to, fanship.

Social Identity and Self-Categorization Theory

We first mentioned social identity theory in the introduction of this book and briefly did so again in Chapter 5. Here, however, we'll delve more fully into social identity theory and its central tenets along with self-categorization theory, a theory which built upon social identity theory and expanded it.

Social identity theory is founded on the premise that people sometimes view themselves as individuals (e.g., Jenn, a *Doctor Who* fan, compares herself to other *Doctor Who* fans) while, at other times, they view themselves as members of a group (e.g., Jenn compares *Doctor Who* fans to *Star Wars* fans; Tajfel & Turner, 1979). Illustrating both the ease with which people fall into these social identities and the importance of these group identities for behavior, researchers have shown that merely being divided into arbitrary groups in a laboratory (e.g., based on whether you overestimate or underestimate how many dots are on a screen) is enough to elicit discriminatory behavior that favors members of your own group over others (e.g., Tajfel et al., 1971).

Were we to distill social identity theory down to its essence, it would be that people strive to maintain or enhance a positive and distinct sense of social identity. This explains why, in the previously-mentioned studies, participants gave preferential treatment to their own group (i.e., creating a positive group identity) while also distancing themselves from the outgroup (i.e., amplifying the distinctness of one's own group). While they may not be consciously aware that they're doing it, group members are frequently evaluating the status of their group by comparing it with relevant outgroups on important dimensions. Applied to the context of fans, *Doctor Who* fans may find it more meaningful to compare themselves to other science fiction fans (e.g., *Star Wars* fans) than if they were to compare themselves to a largely irrelevant group that doesn't afford meaningful comparisons, like Australian blacksmiths.

Social identity theory also posits that people will engage in strategies to ensure that they belong to high-status, reputable groups. Naturally, the simplest strategy would be to join up with high-status groups. Unfortunately, this isn't always possible or easy. In such cases, researchers have also identified strategies that people use to inflate the positivity of their own group (e.g., challenging the validity of a higher-status group's position, changing the variable on which groups are compared, or selectively distancing or drawing closer to their group when its status is low or high, respectively). With respect to the last strategy, it's possible for group members to vary in their degree of identification with the group—that is, the extent to which they internalize the group as part of their own self-concept. This includes being aware, in the moment, of one's self-categorization as a member of the group, feeling an emotional connection to the group itself, and the evaluation of the group relative to other groups.

Elaborating on the principles of social identity theory, researchers developed self-categorization theory (Turner et al., 1987). Self-categorization theory suggests that there are levels of group inclusiveness: personal (e.g., me vs. another person), intergroup (e.g., America vs. China), and human (e.g., humans vs. insects). Aspects of the person in the group (e.g., readiness to view self as member of a group) and the situation they find themselves in (e.g., being surrounded by similar others) ultimately determine which of these identities will be the most salient. Once an identity is salient, members depersonalize themselves and adopt stereotypical ways of thinking and behaving in line with the norms of the salient group identity. In effect, group members consensually share a set of beliefs about the group's norms and act in accordance with those norms when that identity is salient. To use an example: If someone's Canadian identity is activated (e.g., they're made aware of it) while they're sitting in an airport full of Americans, their attitudes and behaviors may shift to be more in line with the stereotypes associated with Canadians. The effect is greater the more strongly a person identifies with a group.

Together, these two theories represent the social identity perspective, which has been used to explain of a wide range of intragroup and intergroup phenomena, including many facets of fan behavior.

Fanship versus Fandom

The majority of research examining fans' felt connection to the object of their interest has arguably been done through the lens of the social identity perspective (Lock & Heere, 2017). This is due to the popularity of an early measure of team identification (Wann & Branscombe, 1993) created in accordance with the principles of social identity theory. We contend, however, that despite originating from social identity theory, traditional measures of team identification better reflect the construct of fanship than they do the construct of fandom.

To begin, let's clarify our terminology. Fanship represents an individual's psychological connection to a fan interest (e.g., "I am a huge fan of anime"). Fandom, on the other hand, represents an individual's psychological connection to others who share a similar interest (e.g., "I love the anime fan community"). To be sure, there is conceptual overlap between the terms: A person who highly identifies with other anime fans also probably highly identifies as an anime fan themselves. However, the two concepts differ in important ways (e.g., the norms of a team are more ambiguous than the norms of a fandom). As such, while the two variables should be considered strongly correlated with one another, they remain empirically distinct.

As a test of this claim, Reysen and Branscombe (2010) gave measures of fanship and fandom to a sample of fans with a broad range of interests. Factor analysis revealed that the scale items load onto separate factors, suggesting that they are distinct constructs. Despite this fact, most sport fan researchers measure fanship in terms of one's identification as a fan of a specific team while failing to assess their degree of identification with other fans of the team.

The problem is not simply a matter of hair-splitting or pedanticism either. As it turns out, fanship and fandom show different patterns of association with important variables. For example, in a study of sport fans by Yoshida, Heere and Gordon (2015), fandom was a better predictor of game attendance than was team identification (fanship). And in an example from a non-sport fandom, researchers studying a sample of fans of a television show found that fanship (but not fandom) was associated with purchasing official merchandise, displaying group symbols, identification with a character from the show, and disclosing one's fan identity to others (Edwards et al., 2019). On the other hand, fandom (but not fanship) was associated with watching fan-made content, talking to friends about the show, purchasing fan-made products, creating fan content, attending conventions and meetups, and watching reruns of the show. Researchers found a similar pattern in a study of anime fans (Reysen, Plante, Chadborn et al., 2021), where fanship was a stronger predictor of purchasing/collecting official merchandise, frequency of watching anime, and frequency of reading news about anime while fandom was a stronger predictor of fan-related social activities (e.g., attending conventions, talking with non-fans about anime, watching anime with friends). Taken together, such findings suggest that fanship is more strongly associated with fan-related consumption while fandom is more closely tied to social aspects of the fan interest.

With fan research being so heavily dominated by sport fans, and with bulk of this research focusing much more strongly on team identification than on fandom identification, the result has been a greater focus on creating and using measures of fanship than on measures of fandom identification.[1] For this reason, we wish to spotlight the few measures of which do exist that either assess fandom directly or which assess concepts adjacent to fandom.

Measures of Fandom

Sense of Community

McMillan and Chavis (1986) define sense of community as "a feeling that members have of belonging, a feeling that members matter to one another and to the group, and a shared faith that members' needs will be met through their commitment to be together" (p. 9). Incorporating a social identity perspective, Obst, Zinkiewicz, and Smith (2002a, 2002b) examined the construct in a sample of science fiction fans at the Aussiecon 3 fan convention in Melbourne,

---

[1] We should note that there have been efforts (e.g., Bruner et al., 2014) to construct a measure of sport team group identification. However, this measure has been developed to assess players on a sport team rather than fans of a sport team.

Australia. The researchers included items from various measures assessing sense of community and ingroup identification. Factor analyses of the 81 items allowed the researchers to condense and organize the measures into five factors:

- Belonging (e.g., "I feel at home in my science fiction fandom")
- Shared values (e.g., "I have a lot in common with my fellow fans")
- Emotional connection (e.g., "I feel strong ties to my fellow fans")
- Influence (e.g., "I care about what my fellow fans think about my actions")
- Conscious identification (e.g., "I often think about the fact that I am part of my science fiction fandom")

The researchers also included two items assessing overall sense of community (e.g., "In general, I feel that the science fiction fandom has a strong sense of community"). Participants completed the measures with respect to both the science fiction fandom and their local neighborhood.

The results revealed that fans feel a greater sense of community with their fandom than they do with their neighborhood across all five dimensions. In effect, science fiction fans feel more connected to, and more strongly identify with, their fandom than they do to their local neighborhood. The finding wasn't unusual: A 2018 study looking at fans of varying interests (e.g., music, sport, media; Chadborn et al.) found similar results.

In another study, Tsay-Vogel and Sanders (2017) surveyed Harry Potter fans to examine predictors of fandom identification. The researchers included two subscales adapted from the sense of community scale: belonging (e.g., "I feel like I belong in the Harry Potter fanbase," "I feel strongly attached to the Harry Potter fanbase") and interaction with the fanbase (e.g., "The Harry Potter fanbase plays a part in my everyday life," "I contact fellow fans often"). The results showed that number of books read, number of movies seen, and eudaimonic motivation all predicted degree of belonging to the fanbase, while number of movies seen, eudaimonic motivation, and personal growth (negative) predicted contact with the fanbase. The results suggest that consumption behavior and eudaimonic motivation were both significantly associated with feeling a sense of psychological connection to the fandom, a finding somewhat in-line with prior research in that eudaimonic motivation has been linked with fandom, but somewhat at odds with research suggesting that fanship is more strongly associated with fan consumption than fandom (e.g., Reysen, Plante, Chadborn et al., 2021).

Fan Social-Personal Identity Salience

Mindful of the distinction between personal identity (fanship) and social identity (fandom), Shuv-Ami and Alon (2020) conceptualized a continuum between personal identity and fan identity and assessed where sport fans fall between those extremes. They built upon prior work, selecting two items (one for personal identity and one for social identity) to represent each of four different facets of connection to a group: cognitive, evaluative, emotional, and behavioral. For example, the emotional personal identity item ("I have a feeling that I am different from other fans of my team," reverse-scored) reflects feeling like a distinct member of the group while the emotional group item ("I have a sense of belonging to my team's fan base") reflects feeling-based ingroup identification. Factor analysis revealed that personal and social identification were separate factors that loaded onto a single higher-order factor. Other analyses showed that personal (reversed) and social identification both predict fan satisfaction, optimism, and involvement, although they differed with respect to fan loyalty: Only social identity, not personal identity, predicted fan loyalty.

This measure of fandom is fairly unique, both because it strives to assess personal and social identity in a single scale and because it is one of the few measures of group identity to be used with sport fans. The measure is not without its drawbacks, however. For example, the personal identity items were designed to be reversed before analysis. As such, one could argue that the distinction between personal and group identity boils down to differences in how they were coded, which might explain why they both loaded onto a single, higher-order factor. An additional drawback stems from self-categorization theory, which suggests that people are only salient of one identity at any given time. As such, the theory would predict that personal and social identity cannot be simultaneously salient and assessed within a single participant at the same time.

Despite these flaws, this measure's novelty as one of the few measures designed to assess fandom in sport fans makes it a measure worth considering in future studies. For scholars looking to use the measure in their own work, we'd suggest overcoming some of its limitations by reversing the personal identity items and treating both dimensions as a single, combined factor.

Fan Community Identification

Continuing the trend of measures designed to assess fandom identification in sport fans, Yoshida, Gordon et al. (2015) surveyed Japanese soccer and baseball fans. Among a myriad of other variables, they assessed fans' identification with their fan community (e.g., "I really identify with people who follow [insert team]," "I feel a deep connection with others who follow [insert team]"). The measure predicted important fan attitudes and behaviors, including buying and wearing team apparel, word of mouth proselytizing about the team, and frequency of game attendance. In fact, speaking to the last point, the authors conducted a subsequent longitudinal study which found that fandom was a better predictor of game attendance throughout the season than attachment to the team itself (Yoshida, Heere, & Gordon, 2015). More recent studies of Japanese football and baseball fans using a similar measure found that status and distinctiveness—two key social identity variables—mediated the relationship between identification with the sport fan community and felt pride toward facets of the team (e.g., past glory, fight songs: Gordon et al., 2021), providing further evidence for the utility of assessing fans' connections with other sport fans and not just with the fan interest itself.

Tribal Sport Fan Scale

Hedlund (2014) took a similar approach in their study of sport fans, assessing fans' felt connection to a particular college football team ("I consider myself a member of the [insert team] team's fan community," "I am a part of the [insert team] team's fan community," "I am a member of the [insert team] team's fan community"). As in prior research, fandom identification scores were found to predict a variety of fan-related behaviors (e.g., engaging in rituals, intention to attend games, intention to spread positive word of mouth.)

Hedlund would later expand upon the idea of group membership with an 18-item measure assessing the extent to which sport fans feel like a "tribe" (Hedlund et al., 2018) along seven dimensions:

- Sense of community membership (e.g., "I am a member of the [insert team] fan community")
- Geographic sense of community (e.g., "Being a fan of [insert team] helps me to feel connected to [insert city]")
- Social recognition (e.g., "In general, people recognize me as a fan of [insert team]")
- Shared rivalry (e.g., "Fans of [insert team] and I are happy when [insert team] is victorious over their biggest rival")
- Shared knowledge of symbols (e.g., "The logo(s) of [insert team] have important meanings to fans of [insert team] and I")
- Shared knowledge of rituals and traditions (e.g., "Fans of [insert team] and I know the rituals of [insert team]")
- Shared knowledge of people (e.g., "Fans of [insert team] and I know the heroes of [insert team]")

We consider the first dimension—membership—to be a functional measure of fandom, as it closely resembles other measures of ingroup identification. In contrast, the latter dimensions (e.g., knowledge of rituals and people) are best thought of as measures of the outcomes of fandom identification or of other aspects of identification, such as behavioral involvement (see Ashmore et al.,

2004). The scale was later used in a sample of Portuguese soccer fans to distinguish between six clusters of fans (e.g., casual fans, moderate remote fans) that, in and of themselves, predicted attendance and consumption behavior (Hedlund et al., 2019).

Ingroup Identification Measures

Over the years, we have used a variety of ingroup identification measures in our own research. For instance, Reysen, Plante, Roberts, and Gerbasi (2016) adapted a single-item measure of ingroup identification using the inclusion of ingroup in self scale (Tropp & Wright, 2001), a visual measure consisting of a series of overlapping circles representing the self and one's fan group in an increasingly-overlapping fashion. Participants who selected an image with greater overlap are said to identify more strongly with their fan group than those choosing an image with less-overlapping circles. Fandom identification, measured thusly, is positively associated with the perception that one's fandom is distinct relative to other groups.

In other studies we have developed one, two, and three-item Likert-type measures of fandom identification. In Plante, Roberts, Snider et al. (2015) we used a single-item measure ("I strongly identify with others in the [insert group] community") shown in prior research to be valid and reliable (Postmes et al., 2013; Reysen et al., 2013). The measure predicted biologically essential beliefs about one's fan group.

In Plante, Roberts, Reysen, and Gerbasi (2014a), fan identification was assessed using a pair of items ("I am glad to be a member of the [insert group] community," "I see myself as a member of the [insert group] community"). In this study, fandom identification was positively associated with self-esteem and negatively associated with the perception that it would be easy to conceal one's fan membership to non-fans.

The most common variation of our fandom identification measure is a three-item version ("I strongly identify with other [insert group] fans in the [insert group] community," "I am glad to be a member of the [insert group] community," "I see myself as a member of the [insert group] community") used by Schroy et al. (2016). It has been used in studies with numerous different fan groups and has successfully predict a myriad of theoretically and practically important variables including:

- Fan motivation (Schroy et al., 2016)
- Intergroup distinctiveness (Reysen et al., 2017a)
- Felt meaning in life and self-esteem (Ray et al., 2017)
- Perceived function of fandom (Reysen, Plante, & Chadborn, 2017)

- Intention to attend a fan convention (Reysen, Chadborn, & Plante, 2018)
- Immersion into fan-related media (Reysen et al., 2019)

Of the measures related to fandom discussed in this chapter, these means of assessing fandom via ingroup identification are among the most, if not the most used measures of fandom identification employed in the literature, and benefit greatly from being both concise and written in a way that allows them to be used for different fan groups, not just sport fans.[2]

Conclusion

In the present chapter we expanded our concept of fan to include fandom, a social dimension. We reviewed social identity and self-categorization theories, the theoretical backbone of research on fan groups. We then highlighted research distinguishing fandom from the related concept of fanship, noting that a great deal of the research conducted on fan identity to date (especially in the sports fan literature) has overlooked the importance of making this distinction. Next, we explored studies showing not only that fandom identification is especially associated with social beliefs, perceptions, attitudes, and behaviors, but also that fandom is likely a better predictor of variables like game attendance and fan conventions than is fanship. In short, this body of research makes a compelling case for the importance of considering fandom identification alongside fanship in models of fan behavior or when assessing differences between fans or fan groups.

---

[2] As noted at the beginning of this chapter, research on fandom identification is relatively scant. Although we point to a few measures of fandom identification in this chapter, we should note for future researchers that there are a variety of valid and reliable measures of ingroup identification already published for use in other contexts (for a list of such measures see Reysen et al., 2013), including various multidimensional (e.g., Leach et al., 2008), unidimensional (e.g., Doosje et al., 1995), and even single-item measures (e.g., Reysen et al., 2013; Tropp & Wright, 2001).

Chapter 8
Social Interaction

At the beginning of Chapter 6 we introduced Maslow's hierarchy of needs and the presence of self-actualization atop the hierarchy. In this chapter, we'll be looking at one of these more basic needs in that hierarchy, the need for belongingness. Indeed, Maslow (1943) placed the need for belongingness just one step above physiological and safety needs, recognizing that once people have satisfied their need for food, water, and shelter, their need to be part of, and interact with, groups of others is among their next-highest priorities.[1]

So if people satisfy their need for food by eating and their need for security with shelter, how do they satisfy their need for belongingness? According to Baumeister and Leary (1995), people satisfy this innate human need through social interaction and working to integrate ourselves into desirable groups. Brewer (1991) even suggests that satisfying this need for belongingness is one of the main reasons people identify with groups in the first place.

As such, it comes as no surprise that belongingness and the social interaction used to satisfy this desire would underlie so much of fan-related behavior (e.g., fans attending sporting events and conventions, Ahn, 2010; Kim et al., 2019; Thorne & Bruner, 2006; fans creating guides for other fans, Hughes, 2018). In fact, the extent to which fans interact with other fans may well represent one of the biggest differences between those who casually engaging in a fan activity and those who fanatically devote themselves to the task of being part of an elite group of insiders (Smith et al., 2007).

In the present chapter we'll try to better understand why belongingness motivates fan behavior and consider some of ways this may manifest. First, we'll review self-determination theory and optimal distinctiveness theory, two well-established social psychological theories which ground the idea that belongingness needs drive fan behavior. These same theories will also help us to better understand some of the mechanisms thought to drive these associations. Finally, we discuss research specifically assessing belongingness as a predictor of fan-related variables, both in more casual leisure contexts and in a variety of different fan groups.

---

[1] It's also worth noting that, as a tribal species, satisfying even the most basic physiological needs may, itself, be contingent upon belonging to a group. In modern times especially, few of us grow our own food, purify our own water, or build our own homes

Self-Determination Theory: Relatedness

Self-determination theory (Deci & Ryan, 1980, 2000) is, at its core, a theory about intrinsic motivation. The authors argue that for someone to be intrinsically motivated to engage in an activity, that activity should satisfy three psychological needs:

- Competence, being able to learn and demonstrate new skills to continually be growing and developing
- Autonomy, being able to make meaningful decisions about the things that happen
- Relatedness, being able to interact and form substantive relationships with other people

The most relevant of these three needs to the present chapter is the need for relatedness. According to self-determination theory, all else being equal, people will be drawn to activities which facilitate the formation of meaningful relationships. Since fan activities are typically engaged in of one's own volition, self-determination theory posits that fans should be especially motivated to participate in fan activities with a social component. Speaking to his idea, scholars note that sport fans, who could easily stay at home and watch the game from the comfort of their own homes, often choose to go to sports bars to watch games with friends or coworkers (Kim & Mao, 2021). In a study of college student sport fans, for example, those whose fan activities provided a greater sense of relatedness also felt more positive emotions in response to those activities and engaged in more sport-related fan consumption (Kim & James, 2019).

Relatedness has similarly been examined in other contexts, such as watching and playing video games. Qian et al. (2020) surveyed e-sport fans (fans of competitive video games) and found that scores on a measure of relatedness (e.g., "Esports allows me to meet other people online with similar interest to mine") was associated with greater commitment to e-sports and e-sport-related spending. In a similar study, Ryan et al. (2006) found that those who experience a greater sense of relatedness from playing online role-playing games also tend to be more immersed and present in those games, enjoy and play the games more, and expect to play the games more in the future.

Continuing in the vein of media consumption, B. Wang (2019) proposed that relatedness as a motivator of media consumption needs to be considered above and beyond eudaimonic and hedonic enjoyment. Research by Xu and Yan (2011) speaks to this idea: The authors constructed a measure to assess three social dimensions motivating media use:

- Shared interest with immediate friends and family (e.g., "As far as I know, many of my friends/peers watch this show")
- Feeling connected with the broader world through the fandom (e.g., "Knowing that millions of others are also watching this show, I feel myself part of a big family")
- Online communication (e.g., "I'd go to some online forums to read others' comments about this show")

In line with expectations, the authors found that television fans engage in all three forms of socializing, suggesting that social interaction may well be a plausible motivator of media consumption.

Of course, one could argue that not all media fans (e.g., readers of books, viewers of TV shows) co-consume media or discuss the media they consume with their friends or with other fans. Even in such instances, however, there is reason to believe that media consumption activities nevertheless satisfy a person's need for relatedness: the formation of parasocial relationships with media characters. Testing this idea, Adachi et al. (2018) had participants watch television shows and complete measures of both their motivation to watch and their felt connection to the characters. Relatedness with characters (e.g., "I feel attached to the characters in the show") was positively associated with a willingness to recommend the show to others, identification with the show's protagonist, and, most presently relevant, intrinsic viewing motivation

Other studies provide additional evidence that parasocial relationships can satisfy social needs and motivate fan behavior. Studies of sport fans (e.g., Hall, 2015) find that fans' degree of virtual friendship with an athlete (e.g., "I think my favorite player is like an old friend") positively predicts their hedonic enjoyment, appreciation, positive emotional response, and involvement in fan activities. Likewise, when Thomson (2006) examined self-determination in the context of celebrity brands, they found that relatedness (e.g., "[insert celebrity] makes me feel cared about") was positively associated with attachment strength, satisfaction, commitment, and trust of the celebrity's endorsement.[2]

In short: In-line with self-determination theory, many fan activities are intrinsically motivating because they satisfy an innate need for relatedness. Even in fan activities that are themselves solitary, people often form parasocial relationships that can help to drive intrinsic interest in the activity itself (e.g., increased viewership).

---

[2] As a caveat to these findings, the association between relatedness and celebrity attachment tends to decline as individuals age (Ilicic et al., 2016).

Belonging and Distinctiveness

Like self-determination theory, optimal distinctiveness theory can shed light on the social needs driving fan behavior. To describe the theory briefly, Brewer (1991) posits that there are two opposing psychological needs that impact the extent to which people identify with a group: the need for uniqueness/distinctiveness and the need for inclusion/belonging. People prefer to identify with groups that represent an ideal balance between these two needs, although where that balance lies will differ from person to person. Put simply, if a person feels that their personal identity is consumed in the group and that they lack distinctiveness as part of the group, they will be less likely to identify with the group. Conversely, if the result of group membership is to stand out to and be uncomfortably unique, to the point where it prevents them from feeling like they "fit in" in a given context, people may again feel less inclined to want to identify with the group. Ultimately, people will identify the most with groups that allow them to satisfy their need to have a distinct and positive identity while nevertheless feeling a sense of belongingness and shared identity.

Andrijiw and Hyatt (2009) applied the principles of optimal distinctiveness theory to a study of hockey fans, interviewing those who were fans of a nonlocal team. Fans described experiences that were in-line with the theory's predictions, stating that being a fan of a non-local team provides them with a sense of optimal distinctiveness. On the one hand, the fans felt distinct in their local area, supporting a team that others in their region were not supporting. On the other hand, they nevertheless felt a sense of belongingness to their team's fan community through online interactions with other fans. Abrams (2009) found a similar trend among music fans, who tended to prefer music that was neither too popular or unpopular, while other researchers (Reysen, Plante, Roberts, & Gerbasi, 2016; Reysen et al., 2017a) found that fans who feel distinct while nevertheless feeling a sense of belongingness to their fan group reported the highest feelings of connection to their fan group.

Socialization in Casual Leisure

While we've been talking about socialization as a variable that fosters group identification and motivates fan-related behavior, in some contexts socialization itself is the central focus. In their work on casual leisure, Stebbins (1997) suggests that one of the six types of casual leisure is sociable conversation, described as talking with others with no specific purpose other than to socialize. These interactions can happen at any time ranging from waiting for a bus to arrive to planned social events. McDonald et al. (2008) conducted interviews with college students and found that one of the main motivations for visiting bars was to socialize with others.

Socializing with others is a consistent theme throughout the casual leisure literature. For example, in a sample of Hong Kong adolescents about one-third engaged in leisure activities (e.g., club, hobby) specifically to socialize (Sivan et al., 2019). In another example, socializing with others was the most frequently mentioned theme motivating women in the Red Hat Society (Shen & Yarnal, 2010), a group we introduced in Chapter 3. Social motives were also rated higher by attendees at national sporting events than at international ones, suggesting that social interaction is more likely to drive casual (vs. serious) leisure activities (Derom & Taks, 2011). Taken together, these findings illustrate that it is sometimes possible to engage in a leisure activity for the primary purpose of socializing.

Even so, when most people think of fan groups, they're thinking about fans engaging in interest-focused activities, where socializing may be an afterthought, rather than the purpose of the activity. In the next section we turn our attention to such activities and what role, if any, social interaction plays in them.

Social Interaction Motivates Fans

Social interaction plays such an important role in being a sport fan that it's a component of nearly every measure of sport fan motivation.[3] As an illustrative example, Wann (1995) included group affiliation as one of eight motivations driving sport fans (e.g., "One of the main reasons that I watch, read, and/or discuss sports is because most of my friends are sports fans"). While Wann chose the term "group affiliation" in this paper, the construct itself reflects the constructs of group belongingness and social connection to others. In the study, group affiliation was the third-highest-rated reason for being a sport fan, behind only entertainment and eustress. Moreover, group affiliation was among the variables most strongly positively correlated with team identification.

More than two decades later, Wann and James (2019) similarly created a parsimonious measure of sport fan motivation by surveying over 900 sport fans with respect to 34 different motivations. The resulting analyses showed five primary motivations (the "big 5" sport motives) driving sports fans: escape, vicarious achievement, aesthetics, drama, and, of course, social interaction. The emergence of social interaction as a "big 5" motivation, coupled with the fact that social interaction predicts important fan-related outcomes (e.g., commitment to the team, number of games attended, Funk et al., 2009), suggests that social interaction is an essential component of any model of sport fan motivation.

---

[3] And, for that matter, most measures of fan motivation more broadly!

Others using a comparable methodology have found similar results in cross-cultural samples and with respect to other fan interests. Zhang (2017), for example, conducted a multicultural survey of college students in both the U.S. and China regarding their motivations to be a sport fan. Social motivation was found to be an important motivator for both groups: second-highest behind only entertainment for U.S. fans and fourth-highest for Chinese fans. Schroy et al. (2016) similarly assessed various motivations of fandom identification in a variety of samples, including media and fantasy sport fans. Across the different fan groups, a sense of belongingness was one of the strongest predictors of fan identification.

Not every fan scholar has taken the approach of studying multiple motivations to gauge the relative magnitude of social interaction and other motivating factors. Nevertheless, countless studies have looked at belongingness or social interaction and found that this motivational factor predicts:

- Team and fan identification (Chadborn et al., 2017; Gau, 2013; Kulczynski et al., 2016; Trail & James, 2001; Won & Kitamura, 2006)
- Team loyalty and commitment (Trial & James, 2001; Wang et al., 2011; Yenilmez et al., 2020)
- Game and event attendance (Anderson, 2019; Ballouli et al., 2016; Chao, 2010; Cottingham, Carroll et al., 2014; Cottingham, Phillips et al., 2014; Edwards et al., 2019; Funk et al., 2004; Hoye & Lillis, 2008; Kulczynski et al., 2016; Neale & Funk, 2006; Neus, 2020; Schmitt, 2014; Yannopoulos, 2017)
- Enjoyment and valuing of viewing fan-related content (Gau, 2013; Zhang et al., 2004)
- Fan-related purchases (Anderson, 2019; Chadborn et al., 2017; Cottingham, Carroll et al., 2014; Cottingham, Phillips et al., 2014; Edwards et al., 2019; Trail & James, 2001; Yenilmez et al., 2020)
- Media viewing (Anderson, 2019; Chao, 2010; Cottingham, Carroll et al., 2014; Cottingham, Phillips et al., 2014; Trail & James, 2001)
- Importance of the fan activity (Schmitt, 2014)

In a final, telling study, Kim and Kim (2020) surveyed sport fans who used social live-streaming services that allowed fans to interact with one another while watching a sporting event. While social integration was associated with a release of tension, flow, satisfaction, and social well-being, it was unrelated to either team identification or to loneliness. In other words, the study suggests that social integration strategies employed to augment solo viewing experiences may confer some of the benefits of interacting with other fans in-person, but they cannot fully replace face-to-face interaction with other fans, at least when it comes to reducing feelings of loneliness.

Conclusion

In the present chapter we reviewed a sizable body of research strongly supporting the idea that social interaction is an essential driver of both fan identity and fan behavior, both in high-identifying and casual fans. We looked at two social psychological theories, self-determination theory and optimal distinctiveness theory, which suggest that social interaction and belongingness are essential needs that people often satisfy through their fan activities. We've seen, primarily through research on sport fans, but also through research on other fan groups, that social interaction plays a powerful role in fan identification, event attendance, loyalty and commitment, enjoyment, and fan consumption behavior. As such, there can be little doubt that social interaction is an essential driver of fan behavior for many fans, with the extent to which this is the case predicting meaningful and significant differences between fans.

Chapter 9
Novel Experience

One of the appeals of fan interests is their ability to provide us with novel experiences: Media fans can watch larger-than-life fictional characters go on adventures in exotic locations, sport fans enjoy novel match-ups and plays that they, themselves, might be unable to perform, and hobbyists can create objects the likes of which have never been seen before. For people driven to seek out new sensations, feelings, and experiences, it's easy to see the appeal of such novelty.

This novel appeal is the subject of the present chapter. But before we delve into how novelty applies to fan groups, we'll first review research on a cluster of interrelated topics to help us better understand the nuance and complexity of novelty. We start by taking a look at sensation-seeking, arguably the first approach psychologists took to understanding individual differences in the desire for novelty. Next, we discuss arousal-seeking, the pursuit of activities that provide physiological excitement. After that we describe several lines of research focusing on the desire to experience novelty and situational factors that contribute to this desire. Finally, we pull these ideas together with a look at research applying these topics directly to fans and fan behavior.

A Brief History of Sensation-Seeking

The early empirical research using the term sensation-seeking was done by Zuckerman (1979), who conceptualized sensation-seeking as "the seeking of varied novel, complex, and intense sensations and experiences, and the willingness to take physical, social, legal, and financial risks for the sake of such experience" (Zuckerman, 1994, p. 27). Zuckerman and colleagues also referred to the related concept of leisure boredom, an individual difference referring to people who have a fairly low tolerance for stable and unchanging experience and, as a result, are sensation-seeking. As an illustrative example, imagine two people watching the same re-run of a television show over and over again. One of the viewers, high in leisure boredom, is more likely than the other, low in leisure boredom, to grow weary of the re-run and to crave something new, be it a new episode, a new show, or a new activity. This boredom could lead to unorthodox or even deviant leisure activities simply as a means of experiencing something novel (Gordon & Caltabiano, 1996; Iso-Ahola & Crowley, 1991).

While the concepts of sensation-seeking and leisure boredom can be traced back to Zuckerman and their colleagues, they are far from the first to suggest that people seek out experiences that allow them to achieve an optimal level of arousal—that idea can be traced all the way back to Wundt (1893). Nor were they the only ones to conduct studies on this topic. For example, Zubeck (1969), building upon Zuckerman's work, conducted studies showing that those high in sensation-seeking were more likely to become restless in sensory deprivation.

Eventually, the concept of sensation-seeking was conceptualized as a trait by Zuckerman in 1979. Framed in this way, each person has an optimal level of arousal they're seeking to achieve. Some seek to reduce their arousal (e.g., avoiding high-excitement situations) while others, called sensation-seekers, seek out exciting and emotion-evoking experiences (Zuckerman, 1988). Such differences were thought to be grounded in biological differences, such as when people experience a sense of discomfort as they stray from their optimal level of arousal (Zuckerman, 1994).

More than mere speculation, these ideas have been empirically supported over several decades. In some studies researchers induce novelty-seeking and assess the intensity of stimuli participants seek out (Battista, 2011). In others, participants high in sensation-seeking were found to volunteer more for unusual scientific studies, choose more stressful jobs, engage in more risky sexual behavior, and listen to more intense genres of music (Zuckerman, 2008). Differences in sensation-seeking can influence the aesthetic preferences, interests, and media people prefer (Battista, 2011). Early studies (e.g., Zuckerman et al., 1972) found simple differences in aesthetic preferences, with people higher in sensation-seeking preferring more complex shapes than people who were lower in sensation-seeking, who preferred simpler, symmetrical shapes. Later studies would go on to find that sensation-seeking predicts preferences for abstract art (Tobacyk et al., 1981) and art with negative affect (Zaleski, 1984), TV genre (Kremar & Greene, 1999), and violent media consumption (Aluja-Fabregat, 2000). In one particular study of horror film fans, Battista (2011) found that those high in sensation-seeking were more likely to attend horror film screenings. Taken together, such studies illustrate how fans may be drawn to particular fan interests or subcultures on the basis of their sensation-seeking tendencies.

Zuckerman's model of sensation-seeking is not without its critics, however. For example, McDaniel (2003) investigated whether sensation-seeking explains the tendency for men to prefer violent sports more than women. It would seem to follow that sensation-seeking should be primarily found in men, given a 1996 study by Mustonen and colleagues showing that violence was more common among males and those higher in sensation-seeking. McDaniel (2003) found, however, that sensation-seeking does not account for gender differences in violent content preferences and noted that better predictors exist. While it's a far cry from a complete rebuttal of Zuckerman's model, these findings do speak to the idea that sensation-seeking alone can't fully account differences in peoples' aesthetic preferences and fan activities.

Arousal-Seeking

Conceptually related to sensation-seeking is the construct of arousal-seeking, being drawn to experiences or interests that arouse high-excitation, positive emotional states (for a fuller description of this idea see Chapter 11 on eustress). Berger (2008) notes that when people experience a lack physiological arousal, they'll be drawn to arousing situations, either in the real-world or through media. As an example, Berger points out that people who feel distant or disengaged seek out media that offers excitement or positive emotions (Aluja-Fabregat, 2000; Oetting & Donnermeyer, 1998). Regardless of how or why people feel insufficient stimulation (e.g., boredom), they're generally motivated to seek out physiological arousal to compensate.

Other research supports the notion that media consumption is tied to levels of boredom and a need for arousal. Shim and Kim (2018), for example, found that bored media viewers tend to seek out arousing content, binge-watch, and multitask to meet their need for arousal. Studies by Lin and Tsai (2002) and Zuckerman (2014) similarly find that binge-watching is tied to viewers' need to avoid boredom, and is particularly prominent for those high in sensation-seeking.

The association is far from a simple or perfect one, however. For example, Shim and Kim (2018) find that binge-watching fulfills additional needs beyond the need for a particular level of arousal, including enjoyment, control, and social interaction with other fans (for more on these latter two points see self-determination theory in Chapter 8). Put simply, fans binge-watch when other fans suggest doing so, illustrating a social component to the phenomenon. If nothing else, findings like these suggest that arousal-seeking needs to be contextualized among a sea of other important social, cognitive, and personality variables.

Novel Experiences

The desire for novelty has long had a place in the research on leisure travel. As Luo et al. (2020) note, escapism, along with learning, personal enjoyment, stress relief, and the novelty of local culture are just some of the benefits of tourism. For most people, the escapism afforded by seeking out new cultures, people, and experiences different from the ones they're accustomed motivates their desire for travel (Farber & Hall, 2007; Pearce, 1987; Read, 1980). For example, in studies of park visitors, high sensation-seekers were especially likely to partake in a greater number of novel activities and to enjoy the experience (Galloway, 2002; Galloway et al., 2008). Even controlling for age, gender, education, and income levels, high sensation-seekers ultimately spend more money on trips, visit more locations, and engage in more activities during these trips. And while many studies assessing novelty as a motivator of tourism involve more traditional forms of tourism (Hall, 1989; Hall & Zeppel, 1990; Tabata, 1989; Young & Crandall, 1984), recent research has tied this concept to fans and fan-related tourism (Lee & Bai, 2016). For instance, fans often travel to see objects of their fan interest and to be able to share those novel experiences with others (e.g., Jamrozy et al., 1996).[1]

The link between fans and seeking novel experiences has been well-documented, especially sport fans. The emotions associated with being present live at a sporting event can augment the perception of the event's novelty (Madrigal, 2006). Or, to put it another way, while you may have watched hundreds of games on the television, none of them can quite compare to the novelty of experience of seeing the game form the bleachers alongside thousands of other fans. Tsay-Vogel and Sanders (2017) and Kashdan et al. (2004) both note that it's fans' curiosity and intrinsic desire to seek out new content that drives them to find meaning and appreciate novel fan experiences and experiences with their fan communities.

When tied to the concept of screen media, Sherry (2004) notes that sensation-seeking and novelty both contribute to flow experiences—a state of optimal arousal and pure immersion—while watching a television show or film. For those higher in sensation-seeking, this continual desire for novel stimulation leads to increased binge-watching and a willingness to watch shows recommended by others, if only to avoid the possibility of being stuck watching unexciting or repetitive programs (Shim & Kim, 2018; Zuckerman, 2014).

Sensation-Seeking in Fan Groups

In this final section we apply the topics of sensation-seeking, arousal-seeking, and novelty-seeking to the context of fans and fan behavior specifically. As with much of the research on fans, the original research on this subject was conducted on sport fans, such as the relationship between being present at a game and the experience of vicarious winning or losing (Sloan, 1989). The need to seek out such experiences and the arousal they generate is, at least in part, what motivates many sport fans to attend sporting events in-person (Kahle et al., 1996).

While we've reviewed research on novelty-seeking and preference for particular genres of TV or attending a fan-related event, other research considers whether differences in specific fan behaviors may be tied to novelty-seeking and

---

[1] We can think of no better example than fans of the *Lord of the Rings* series, many of whom travel to New Zealand for no other reason than to experience the fantastical village of Hobbiton first-hand. So common are such tourists that states and countries may target promotional tourist campaigns on drawing in these sensation seeking fans.

leisure boredom. For example, Schenk (2009) explains that people prone to leisure boredom who are high in sensation-seeking seek novelty in physical activities, especially those involving a degree of risk-taking. This may explain why some fans seek out sensory-driven behaviors like partying, fan-related pornography, and even conflict and drama: Insofar as people seek to use their leisure activities to attain an optimal level of arousal (Gordon & Caltabiano, 1996), some fans may seek to relieve their boredom through these more intense or novel activities. Work by Humphries (2020) supports this idea, showing that fantasy sport fans who are higher in sensation-seeking are more likely to infuse their interest with gambling, which amplifies the arousal and novelty of their leisure activity. Likewise, sensation- and novelty-seeking are more likely to be associated with excessive celebrity worship among fans (Houran et al., 2005).

Conclusion

Throughout this chapter we've seen how sensory excitement, physiological arousal, and novelty associated with leisure activities—including fan activities—can both pull fans toward particular fan interests and motivate them to engage in specific fan activities. Whether we consider sensation-seeking, arousal-seeking, or seeking out novel experiences, it's clear that individual differences in fans' proclivity toward boredom has a considerable impact on the type of fan they are and the sorts of fan-related activities they engage in.

Chapter 10
Escape

Fan activities frequently involve flights of fantasy and deviations from day-to-day life. Whether it's watching a science-fiction film, playing a fantasy-themed video game, or immersing yourself completely in the drama of a nail-bitingly close sporting event, fan activities can be a refreshing distraction from our jobs, financial concerns, and obligations. But is this escapism enough to explain the allure of fan activities? Can it help us meaningfully compare different fans and predict important outcomes?

In the present chapter we first review some of the different ways scholars have conceptualized escapism before then discussing escapism as a motivator of leisure activities. We then look at research assessing the functional and dysfunctional elements of fans escaping into the media they consume. Finally, we consider escapism in the context of fandom research, noting both how common escapism is as a motivation for fans and how many fan-specific behaviors escapist drives can predict.

Defining Escapism

While there may not be one universally agreed-upon definition of escapism, researchers have nevertheless created useful working definitions of escapism in their own worm. Vorderer and Knolbloch (2000) note that one of the first scholars to discuss escapism was the philosopher Montaigne, who posited that escape from one's normal reality through physical or imaginal travel was a normal and beneficial aspect of mental health. Vorderer and Groben (1992) take this concept one step further, stating that people can actually satisfy important psychological and social needs (e.g., stress relief: Smith, 1988) by escaping the boredom of mundane reality. Across these different approaches is a common thread: People are motivated to partake in escapism if and when doing so satisfies important psychological needs.

Other scholars take a different approach to the study of escapism. Some simply distinguish escapism from related constructs like eustress, noting that eustress is just the means through which people achieve escapism (for more on eustress see Chapter 11; Smith, 1988; Wann, 1995). For others, escapism can be defined on its own, exemplified by Trail et al. (2000), who defined escapism as "a diversion from work and everyday activity" (p. 163). Framed thusly, escapism is something that the average person regularly partakes in. More extreme definitions of escapism also exist, conceptualizing it as a means through which people exposed to trauma or harsh and unjust inequality cope (Gunderman, 2018). Others differentiate between these different types of escapism on the basis of differing underlying mechanisms, noting a difference between "boredom-avoidance" escapism and "thought-blocking" escapism (Valkenburg & Peter, 2006). In the former case, people try to temporarily alleviate a lack of pleasure caused by the status-quo of their day-to-day lives (Lever & Wheeler, 1984). For boredom-avoiders, escape involves trying to keep an idle mind occupied, rather than a more pressing need to avoid unpleasant thoughts or stressful feelings. In contrast, according to the thought-blocking perspective, people throw themselves into activities (e.g., media consumption) to actively avoid or replace these unpleasant experiences with more pleasant ones via more appealing mental or visual imagery and narratives (Berger, 2008; McIlwraith, 1998).

As is often the case in research, there is no need for a winner-take-all approach to escapism. As research by Wann, Allen, and Rochelle (2004) suggests, both stress-blocking and boredom avoidance contribute to self-reported escapism and predict important psychological and behavioral outcomes. Even so, understanding that different types of escapism exist can help us better understand the different activities, functions, and outcomes associated with escapism and when it is more or less likely to be associated with pathology.

Escapism and Leisure

Before escapism was applied to the concept of fans, it was studied as a motivator of leisure and travel. Carden (2006) notes that escape has historically been seen as the number one reason people travel or go on vacation. Uysal and Jurowski (1994) point to escapism as a prime motivator of leisure travel, along with rest, relaxation, and socialization. Manfredo et al. (1996) similarly included the need to avoid environments, social interaction, and activities that people regularly engage in as a motivator of leisure travel. Taken together, there is general agreement that, among other reasons, leisure travel is motivated by escapism, as traveling providing people with a way to pursue interests and experiences that are outside the stress of their daily routine (for more on this see Benckendorff & Pearce, 2012; Sloan, 1989; Trail & James, 2001).

Of course, escapism is neither a permanent nor ideal way to cope with life stresses or dissatisfaction with one's daily routine, at least in the long run (Plante, Gentile et al., 2019). Yet, as a temporary strategy, evidence suggests that escapism through leisure can be effective (Li et al., 2011). As Wann, Grieve et al. (2008, p. 6) note, people who are dissatisfied with aspects of their home, work, or school life frequently use their leisure interests to "temporarily forget their troubles." This is especially helpful in difficult or trying times; as even the negative impacts of war (Wann et al., 1997) or depression (Kim & Oliver, 2013) can be ameliorated at least partly by the escapism afforded by leisure activities (Wann et al., 1997).

While escapism may be little more than kicking the proverbial can down the road, it may be enough to allow people to approach their stressors and problems with a fresh mind and a better mood, making the prospect of coping just a bit more bearable.

Escapism and Media

So far we've discussed the escapism as it applies to leisure activities like traveling, where people leave the places where they work and live to temporarily be somewhere else. But we can also consider escapism in the context of media, with consumers escaping into the fictional world of books, television, movies, or video games, a concept known as narrative transportation (Green & Brock, 2000). In doing so, media consumers may, as with other leisure activities, temporarily draw their attention away from the stresses or mundaneness of day-to-day life (Dy et al., 2020).

While some have discussed escapism in the fairly-grounded context of social media, which is at least somewhat tethered to reality (e.g., Billings et al., 2017), many have focused their attention on media completely detached from the viewer's own experience or, in some cases, completely detached from reality itself. For example, Berger (2008) found that peoples' need for escapism predicts their interest in high-profile, exciting and drama-filled celebrity court trials. Other studies find that binge-watching behavior is motivated by a desire to avoid the pain and discomfort people normally experience in their idle time (Kubey, 1986; W. Wang, 2019). In more media trends, researchers similarly find that the parasocial relationships people form with celebrities (Jenol & Pazil, 2020) while watching live-streams (Blight, 2016) are motivated by a need for escapism (among other needs, like emotional support).

Much of this research paints a fairly bleak portrait of media consumers who seek a "dreamlike world to meet psychological gratifications" that they otherwise lack in the real world (Morgan, 1984). Media, framed thusly, is little more than a temporary and maladaptive coping strategy, one reliant on catharsis (Berger, 2008) or "identifying with a star or hero to the point that one loses oneself in a dream..." (Katz & Foulkes, 1962, p. 384) to manage stress and the discomfort of day-to-day life. The people who engage in escapism through media use are seen as living miserable lives in mundane realities (Zillman & Vorderer, 2000).

More recent research, however, has tried to move beyond this negative perception of media consumers, challenging the assumption that escapism and distraction are the primary motivators of leisure and media consumption. For example, work by Rubin (1981, 1983, 1984) takes a more positive view of media consumption, recognizing that escapism can take on more normal, less dysfunctional forms. Rather than struggling to avoid chronic, crippling anxiety and depression, the average person's escapist tendencies involve coping with little more than the occasional bout of boredom brought about by the humdrum of a mundane or routine life. Those subscribing to this position see escapism through media consumption as something that most people do, a normal and even functional response to a need to occasionally engage in imaginative thought and just one of many ways people satisfy this basic need (Cacioppo & Petty, 1982).

Escapism and Fans

The research we've reviewed thus far has linked escapism with leisure activities and media consumption. As such, it's not much of a stretch to hypothesize that fan activities of all sorts can be driven, at least in part, by fans' desire to occasionally escape daily life. Speaking to this point, Trail et al. (2000) found that escapism is one of two core motivational factors (the other being social interaction) driving fan interests. Others similarly find that escapism is a fairly universal motivator of fan behavior (Chadborn et al., 2017; Fink et al., 2002) and is associated with fan identification (Smith, 1988). With this in mind, let's take a moment to consider some of the ways escapism is associated with fan behavior.

Some of the earliest work on fan motivation focused on sport fans and included, among other motivations, the desire for escapism (McPherson, 1975; Milne & McDonald, 1999; Smith, 1988; Sloan, 1989; Trail & James, 2001; Wann, Schrader, & Wilson, 1999). In this work, scholars found meaningful differences between different types of fans with respect to their escapism motivation. Such differences were noted between viewers of amateur and professional sporting events (Wann, 1995) as well as between viewers of violent and non-violent sports (Sloan, 1989).[1] This association between escapism and sporting event attendance has been explained in part by the fact that sporting events provide thought diversion, recreation, and a change in one's daily routine, all of which are components of escapism (Zhang et al., 2001).

While research on escapism and fans may have started with sport fans, it has since grown to include a myriad of different fan interests. Proudfoot et al. (2019), for example, found that escapism motivates fans' willingness to take fan-themed personality tests (e.g., *Harry Potter* fans completing tests to "sort" them into one

---

[1] In particular, for attendees of professional events, escapism was rated as a stronger motivator than socializing, with the reverse being true for attendees of amateur events (Kim et al., 2008).

of the schoolhouses from the series). For these fans, the tests offer a distraction from daily life, both while taking them and when subsequently sharing and discussing them with other fans (Lee, Lee et al., 2015).

In another example, escapism has been found to be a core motivator of cosplay (Rahman et al., 2012). This likely stems from the fact that the cosplay experience, from designing to crafting to performing, can distract fans from their problems and serve as a break from their daily routine. Madill and Zhou (2021) found this to be the case in their own quasi-ethnographic study of cosplayers.

In a final example, we turn to research on an alumni association whose members support their university's sport team (Schmitt, 2014). In and of itself, being a member of the alumni association was not associated with feelings of escapism. However, members were offered opportunities to engage in club-related activities such as watching a football game. These activities were associated with escapism and enjoyment. Schmitt later noted that club promoters could use this information to promote the organization as an escape from day-to-day stress and routine based.

Having fairly conclusively shown that fan activities can provide fans with a sense of escapism, we can ask whether this phenomenon is expected to operate the same for all fans. The answer, based on empirical evidence, seems to be "somewhat." Kulczynski (2014) found that fans both high and low in fan identification benefit from the escapism provided by fan activities. For example, low-identifying fans attending a concert for a band they only somewhat identify as a fan of nevertheless experience an escape from day-to-day life (e.g., a night away from the kids) just as high-identifying fans do, even if they do spend more time socializing with others or paying more attention to peripheral or tangential features of the experience than to the concert itself.

Even so, some research does suggest that there exists variability in the escapism experienced by fans. Zhang (2017) found that, compared to American sport fans, Chinese sport fans are more likely to be motivated to attend games by boredom avoidance and the desire for escapism. American fans, in contrast, tend to be motivated by social interaction and entertainment. Beyond cross-cultural differences, some individual differences have also been observed. Tinson and colleagues (2017) suggest that parents differ in the extent to which they use their sport fandom as an opportunity to bond with other members of their family as opposed to using it as a means to escape job or family-related stress.

In short, while fan activities of all sorts are often motivated, at least in part, by a desire for escapism, cultural and individual differences may moderate the importance of escapism for fans or the association between escapism and important outcomes.

Conclusion

In this chapter we reviewed a sizable body of research looking at escapism as a motivator of leisure activities. The research has been fairly consistent in showing that most fans benefit from being able to both distract themselves from undesirable stress and to alleviate the humdrum of day-to-day life. Of course, escapism can sometimes be associated with maladaptation, especially when it's a person's sole means of coping or when it's associated with undesirable behavior (e.g., celebrity-stalking). Nevertheless, most fans' engagement in escapism is moderate in frequency and associated with modest short-term benefits for their psychological well-being. Research also suggests that there are important cultural and individual differences in fans' tendency to be motivated by escapism. This variability suggests that it might be possible to use differences in fans' motivation to escape as a means of meaningfully comparing or distinguishing between different fans, a point we will return to in the final chapters of this book.

Chapter 11
Eustress

In general, stress is an undesirable state of affairs. Almost by definition, stress involves discomfort—an undesirable state—grounded in concern about how an unusual or high-stakes situation will play out and one's own ability to cope with that outcome. Most people would jump at the opportunity to avoid having to deal with stress in their lives and, as we've seen in previous chapters (e.g., Chapter 10), people go to considerable effort to escape from stress.

It's against this backdrop that we consider the perplexing topic of eustress, defined by Wann, Schrader, and Wilson (1999) as "a positive form of stress that stimulates and energizes an individual" (p. 115). As an example of eustress, we can imagine a sport fan watching their favorite team playing for the championship. They grip the armrests, sitting on the edge of their seat, their heart racing in the last seconds of the nail-biting game. At a physiological level, this fan is showing all of the hallmarks of stress, but they nevertheless enjoy the experience and actively seek it out. In fact, millions of fans willingly subject themselves to these high-states every week, enjoying the excitement and thrill that they provide.

This is eustress, the enjoyable form of stress that has long motivated many fans to participate in their interest (Madrigal, 1995; Wann, Schrader, & Wilson, 1999). Whether it's because eustress provides fans with a distraction from their day-to-day lives, or simply because the state of exhilaration and the drama associated with eustress is enjoyable to some in and of itself, researchers generally agree that eustress can make certain fan interests exciting and therefore appealing (Funk et al., 2004; Schmitt, 2014).

In this chapter we discuss the role that eustress plays in fans and their interests, paying particular interest to the domain of sports, where eustress has been most frequently studied. We begin with Daniel Wann's seminal work on eustress in sport fans before considering offshoots and applications of this work by other researchers in non-sport domains. We then look more broadly at the concept of eustress beyond a social psychological perspective and the insights this work can offer for future research on this topic.

Sport Motivation and Eustress

You can't discuss the role of eustress in fans without talking about Daniel Wann (1995) and his sport motivation scale. Wann defines eustress in the context of sport fans as "excitement and anxiety that often accompany sport spectating" (Wann, Schrader, & Wilson, 1999, p. 115), and considers eustress as one of many motivators driving sport fans (e.g., escapism, entertainment, aesthetics). Wann, of course, was far from the first to study the concept of eustress (e.g., Elias & Dunning, 1970; Sloan, 1989; Wenner & Gantz, 1989; Zuckerman, 1979). Smith (1988), for example, conceptualized eustress alongside escapism as "the search for excitement represent[ing] one of the most familiar means of escape" (p. 58). Pham (1992) would later tie eustress directly to the fan experience of pleasure via the stress inherent in sports. Nevertheless, while the ideas themselves were not new, Wann was instrumental in popularizing the systematic study of eustress among other fan motivations and the ability of eustress to meaningfully predict other important variables (e.g., Robinson et al., 2005; Wann, 1995, Wann, Schrader, & Wilson, 1999, Trail et al., 2003), including psychological well-being (Wasserberg, 2009), joy (Wann, 2008), and schadenfreude at the loss of an opposing team (Rees et al., 2015).

But it's worth asking why eustress might be an especially poignant motivator of fans, especially if stress itself is generally seen as undesirable? As Wann, Grieve et al. (2008) points out, euphoric stress is born from a need to gain excitement and emotional stimulation, something sport fans do by viewing sports, an idea that harkens back to earlier work by Gantz (1981) and Sloan (1989). Wann, Grieve et al. (2008) notes that sports which offer stronger emotional responses, such as highly-aggressive sports (e.g., boxing, football, etc.), capitalize on the arousing nature of aggression and lead to greater eustress.

Research also suggests that there are individual differences between fans with respect to eustress; some prefer "edge of your seat" excitement, while others prefer aesthetic appeal. Speaking to this idea, James and Ross (2004) examined the motivations of fans of three college-sports: softball, baseball, and wrestling. They found no differences across the three groups with respect to their need for entertainment or social interaction. Where the three groups differed, however, was with respect to eustress: Wrestling fans were the most strongly associated with eustress motivation. This doesn't mean that fans of non-aggressive sports are not motivated by eustress, of course. After all, most sport fans will attest to the fact that they still enjoy the thrill of wondering whether their favorite team or athlete will win. Instead, it suggests that individual differences exist in the extent to which eustress is a motivating factor driving one's fan interest, differences which may explain differences between individuals and between different fandoms.

Beyond Wann

Following in the footsteps of Wann's sport motivation scale, other researchers continued to study eustress in sport fans, including defining it more clearly, conceptually disentangling it from related constructs, finding other ways to operationalize it, and measuring its correlates in fans. As just a few examples:

- Eustress has been linked to a greater likelihood of viewing and attending sporting events (Funk et al., 2009; James & Ross, 2004; Kim et al., 2008)
- Higher eustress scores are associated with greater team and sport fan identification as well as with a greater likelihood of being personally involved in a sport (Fink et al., 2002)
- Eustress is associated with a desire to escape from everyday routine (Samra & Wos, 2014; Schmitt, 2014)
- Eustress is associated with fan well-being (Wasserburg, 2009), including finding meaning in life and a sense of life satisfaction (Grimm et al., 2015; van Zyl & Rothmann, 2014)

As these examples illustrate, researchers have examined eustress in different contexts and applications, all inspired, directly or indirectly, by Wann's examination of eustress through the sport motivation scale (1995). Researchers from other disciplines have also recognized the utility of studying eustress, including those from interdisciplinary fan and leisure studies, marketing, media studies, and communications. They, too, recognize the utility of eustress for populations beyond sport fans.

Non-Sport Eustress

In James and Ross' 2004 study, the authors conceptually replicated prior work by Wann, Schrader, and Wilson (1999) and Wenner and Gantz (1989), the former of which compared eustress in aggressive and non-aggressive sports while the latter found that eustress was present, albeit minimally, in tennis fans. As seen in some of these less aggressive and "quieter" sports, many of these non-aggressive sports (e.g., golf, tennis) typically discourage noise, something that might make it difficult for fans to be involved in, and excited by, the event itself (Benzecry, 2009, 2012). This discouragement of noise and excitement could at least partially explain these findings, as well as why other motivational factors such as being a part of a group or family tend to be stronger motivators than eustress in non-violent sports and why aesthetics and eustress are often negatively associated with one another as motivators of fan interest (James & Ross, 2004; Wann, Grieve et al., 2008).

Research on non-sport fans offers another perspective. In their 2018 work, Trzcinska (2018) discusses K-pop fans, noting that being able to engage with their musical interest (e.g., attending concerts) allows fans a way to satisfy their need for sensory stimulation (among other needs, like self-esteem), which Trzcinska conceptualizes as a form of eustress. Whereas sport fans achieve this stimulation and arousal from the feeling of accomplishment and uncertainty about a game's outcome, music programs and idol competitions allow fans to do much the same thing.

As another non-sport fan example, while perhaps not as exciting as cheering for one's favorite sport team, Proudfoot et al. (2019) notes that fans gain a similar sense of excitement while awaiting the results of fandom-themed personality tests. On one hand, the uncertainty involved in the outcome itself builds anticipation in a manner akin to sport fans waiting for the outcome of a game or, to use an example from literature, fans of a mystery novel reveling in the suspenseful buildup to the climax. On the other hand, the payoff itself also provides fans with a thrill, be it the excitement of getting desirable results from the personality test, having one's favorite team win the championship, or finding out that that one's hunch that the butler did it was correct.

While there has been relatively little additional research on the subject of eustress in non-sport fandoms, the research which has been done speaks to a need for future research to better understand the mechanisms driving eustress as a motivator of fan interest and the differences between eustress in sport fans as compared to non-sport fans.

Eustress and Drama

We finish this chapter by looking back in time, millennia before Wann (1995) and others studied eustress in the context of fan activities and leisure. Aristotle was arguably the first to note that the people often seek out stress via their consumption of drama and tragedy in theater and find cathartic release in the process (Scheff, 1979). Today, the idea of seeking out and reaping benefits from stressful leisure activities resonates just as much with media and sport fans as it does with theater fans in Aristotle's time (Proudfoot et al., 2019). Wann and Pierce (2003) describe the same sense of drama in sport fans, as does Coakley (2003), who argues that fans of violent sports in particular are highly motivated by drama. Such findings suggest that attendance at live events, especially those revolving around aggressive sport or those which incite powerful emotional reactions, are influenced by a combination of eustress and the drama which often accompanies it.

Conclusion

In the present chapter we considered the role of eustress as a motivator of fan interest. Given the thrill associated with uncertainty about future fan-related events (e.g., the outcome of a sporting event), it's easy to see how at least some fans could be drawn to their interest, in whole or in part, by the excitement created by such events. Importantly, the self-chosen nature of these stressors (as opposed to stress created by life circumstances beyond one's control) may contribute to the escapism and novelty they provide, in line with research discussed in Chapters 9 and 10. While the bulk of this research has been done in the context of understanding sport fans, the robustness of the effects and the hint of their applicability to other fan interests (e.g., media fans) is all the more reason for researchers to focus future efforts on better understanding eustress as an important variable for predicting fan behavior and as an individual difference between fans, both within the same fan group and as a mean difference between fandoms.

Chapter 12
Emotion

Given that the word "fan" originates from the word "fanatic," it's no surprise that fans can get emotional, or downright passionate, about the object of their interest. We can find examples of fans experiencing the entire spectrum of human emotion in various fandoms: jealousy about a celebrity's new relationship, exuberance over the triumph of a one's team over a bitter rival, sorrowful mourning over the death of a favorite character from a TV series, anger over a bitter conflict dividing one's fan community, and excitement about an upcoming concert. Fans experience all manner of emotions, some as a direct response to the content of their fan interest, others tied to their identification as a member of a fan community.

In the present chapter we'll delve into the role that emotion plays as both a motivator of fan activities and as a byproduct of participation. We'll first consider some of the underlying reasons why fan activities—despite their leisure and often-trivialized nature—nevertheless yield real and substantial emotions. Next, we distinguish between emotional engagement and emotional connection—emotional responses to the content and to one's identity as a fan respectively—before looking at what research on each of these concepts has to say. Along the way we'll also consider some of the fan groups this work has been applied to and the practical implications of this work for fans and those working with them.

Emotions and Fans

The connection between fan interests and emotions is alluded to in a number of psychological theories. Illustrating this point, Vallerand (1983) draws upon the work of Schachter (1964), Lazarus (1982), Arnold (1960), and Weiner (1981), four influential theories of emotion, to show that they all predict that sport fans should respond emotionally to the object of their interest. With respect to Schacter's work, for example, Vallerand notes that the excitement of watching a game should increase viewers' physiological arousal (see Chapter 11 on eustress) which, in turn, may be misattributed as intense anger or joy, depending on whether one's team wins or loses.

For others, like Gantz (1981), the link between emotion and being a fan lies in the ability of fan activities to satisfy a basic need to experience positive emotional states. Fandoms provide fans with the means to express strong emotions in way that protects them from being perceived as deviants (depending on the interest, of course) while also increasing the likelihood that fans will experience social acceptance from like-minded others. Supporting this position,

Underwood and Olson (2019) found that male bodybuilders in an online forum used their shared interest in bodybuilding to set up a space where they could show emotional vulnerability that might be considered inappropriate for masculine bodybuilders in other contexts.

Other psychological theories can be applied to explain the tie between how and why fans engage emotionally with their fan interest. Maslow (1981), for example, listed emotional connection in his hierarchy of needs. As Zillman (2000) notes, with easier access to subsistence, shelter, and feelings of security, all of which satisfy basic needs, people are have more spare time to direct to emotional needs and activities that allow them to meet those needs. Raney (2006) also points out that people watch sports "because of the emotional rewards they receive from doing so" and experience "positive emotional impacts from their viewing" (p. 340). If this is true, then it should follow that fans are motivated to pursue such fan activities because of the emotional needs they satisfy. Whether it's through emotional responses to the activities themselves or through identification with others who share their fan interest, there are clear theoretical reasons to hypothesize that the emotions evoked by fan activities are a significant draw for fans.

Content vs. Fandom: Two Sources of Emotions

Perhaps the most straightforward way fans' emotions are impacted by their fan interests is by fans engaging with interest-related content. Smith (1988), for example, notes that sport fans experience "strong emotional involvement in the actual outcome - who wins and loses" (p. 55). Echoing this sentiment, Pons and colleagues (2006) state that the emotions fans feel are tied to experiencing the events, shows, games, or products themselves. Rather intuitively, fans' emotional experiences thus often represent a direct response to fan-related content. A 2010 study by Oakes demonstrates this point: The motivation for music fans to attend live performances instead of just listening to a CD stems from, among other things, experiencing stronger emotions in response to the live concert.

Researchers have also found, however, that emotions can be elicited by fans' identification as a fan and their commitment to the fandom itself, and not just by interest-related content. According to Wann and Branscombe (1990), fan identification represents an emotional connection to the interest that goes beyond merely reacting to the content itself. This notion is supported by research on basking in reflected glory, where fans vicariously experience positive emotions like pride from the knowledge that their team has won, despite the fan's lack of individual contribution to the win themselves (Cialdini et al.,

1976). Tellingly, the extent to which this occurs is a product of how strongly the interest is tied positively to the fan's degree of identification with the team.

An even more poignant example of the distinction between emotional connection through identification with the interest rather than through content consumption can be found in the work of Yang (2009). The author examined the Corn fandom, a group of fans who follow the work of Chinese pop star Li Yuchun. The fans made a distinction between fans of the music itself and fans of the singer, noting that the latter invest more "emotion, time, and money in a singer" instead of enjoying and appreciating their songs. The findings demonstrate that even fans make a distinction between emotional engagement with the content and identifying or connecting with the object of fan interest itself.

We finish up our discussion of this distinction by pointing to a body of research showing that emotional responsiveness can be impacted by other important fan variables, like community norms. Benzecry (2009) discusses norms in the opera community, observing that fans frown upon the open expression of emotion in the theater while watching an opera. To be sure, opera fans still experience a sense of emotional connection to opera, and younger, newer fans may even demonstrate this emotional resonance to the chagrin of older fans. As such, community norms can be said to impact when and how emotional engagement can be expressed (Benzecry, 2012), adding yet another level of complexity to the study of emotional responsiveness.

Emotional Engagement: Immediate Responses to Stimuli

A sizable body of research showcases the emotional responses of people to stimuli and experiences associated with their interests—even if this research hasn't always been framed as "fan research." In this section, we'll review some of the different contexts in which this topic has been studied, even when it hasn't been referred to as fan research. We'll also consider some of the variables thought to influence emotional engagement in fans as we peruse this research.

Celebrity Court Cases

One of the most comprehensive deep dives into the topic of emotional engagement in fans stems from a 2008 dissertation by Berger, who examined the appeal of celebrity court cases for fans. While it makes sense that the general appeal of celebrities and the spectacle of trials like that of O.J. Simpson and Michael Jackson would make them highly appealing to viewers, Berger notes that the extent to which people become emotionally engaged in these cases drives their fan-like interest in them. To Berger, the emotional engagement is the primary motivator of fan interest, making the cases entertaining and, ultimately, driving fans' involvement with them.

Parasocial Relationships

Related to the phenomenon of watching celebrity court cases, parasocial relationships involve the formation of intense emotional connections with celebrities and fictional characters, typically in a one-way fashion, where the celebrity or character are unaware of the observer or their intense feelings (Dietz et al., 1991). As one might expect, those who experience parasocial relationships experience disproportionately strong emotional reactions to the object of their affection, often to the point of feeling the same emotional support that they would otherwise feel from a typical relationship (Chia & Poo, 2009). These powerful emotional connections impact the health, well-being, and behavior of those who experience them (e.g., Kim, 2020; Park, Ok, & Chae, 2016), and not always for the better (see Chapters 27 and 28), making it clear that emotional responses to interest-related content can be highly impactful for fans.

Media Consumption

Research on media consumption and narrative transportation has found that people can become so engrossed in a piece of media that, despite its fictional or trivial nature, it can impact their real-world thoughts and behavior (Gerrig, 1993). With respect to emotional responses to fictional narratives (e.g., in literature), transportation can create emotional bonds with the characters in the story and impact consumers' attitudes, beliefs, and behaviors as a result (Green & Brock, 2000).

In a related vein, those interested in understanding the motivations that drive media consumption (e.g., Moyer-Gusé et al., 2011) have suggested that emotional engagement plays an important role (Nabi & Wirth, 2008; Tan, 2008). For example, work by Sherry and colleagues (2006) finds that gamers often play video games to create specific emotional experiences, and that this emotional evocation is one of the primary appeals of video gaming. Other research similarly finds that emotional involvement underpins viewer interest in watching television news (Perse, 1990).

Sport Fans

Cianfrone and colleagues (2011) assessed emotional response as a motivator of sport fans watching sports and playing sport-related video games. They found that fans experienced comparable emotional stimulation whether viewing sports on television or playing sport-themed video games. Delving deeper into these experiences, Cleland et al. (2018) found that football fans become emotionally engaged in the actions of their favorite players and in the ups and downs of the season as they view games and hear stories throughout the season. In fact, the emotions associated with consuming sports often extend beyond specific sporting events themselves and can include both excitement in the days leading up to a much-anticipated game and lingering emotional responses days after the game (Keaton et al., 2014).

Other Motivations Impact Emotional Engagement

In a study by Wann, Brewer, and Royalty (1999), football fans were asked to fill out a questionnaire assessing their emotional state after their team won a home game. Analyses revealed that fans' emotional state after the game was affected by the factors which motivated their interest in football. Specifically, entertainment-motivated fans were the most likely to express positive shifts in mood after the game, while family-motivated fans (e.g., co-viewing as a family activity) experienced less positive emotional responses to the game. In effect, while some of the emotional responses to fan-related experiences are fairly predictable, knowing more about the other motivations driving fans' engagement can help researchers better predict the emotional impact of the game on fans.

Fanship Impacts Emotional Engagement

Another variable impacting fans' emotional response to interest-related activities is their degree of fanship, or felt connection to, and identification with, the object of their interest. For example, Krohn et al. (1998) found that sport fans are likely to attend sporting events to the extent that the events provide them with emotional stimulation. More importantly, however, the emotional stimulation, and by extension fans' willingness to attend events, increases over time. This is presumably because, as fans spend more time involved with a fan interest, they feel a greater sense of connection to that interest (e.g., Kulczynski, 2014). The relationship has been directly tested and found by other researchers comparing fans with respect to their degree of identification (Madrigal, 1995; Wann & Schrader, 1997).

Emotional Connection: Feeling through Shared Identity

While fans can experience emotional responses first-hand from fan-related experiences, its easy to overlook the link between fandom identity and emotional response. This association can perhaps be best understood through a social identity framework (Tajfel & Turner, 1979; Turner et al., 1987 for more on this see Chapter 7). Put simply, a person's emotions are tied, in part, to the groups to which they belong. In the case of fans and their fan communities, their emotional connection to the interest may stem just as much from their identification with other fans as it does from their first-hand response to fan-related activities.

As an illustrative example, Todd (2008) studied participants in a flash mob, noting that they experienced a state of shared emotion. Much of the excitement and positive emotion the participants experienced stemmed not from the act of going to a particular place to being among a bunch of people, but specifically from the fact that they did so with people with whom they identify. This shared sense of community and feeling of collective pride is, itself, a powerful emotional response that is unlikely to be elicited merely by attending the event itself. These shared experiences and the intense positive emotions they create bolster identification with fan communities, elicit powerful emotional responses, and can ultimately bolster fan interest itself.

Sport Fans and Team Connection

In their research, Sutton et al. (1997, p. 15) describe the "personal commitment and emotional involvement" sport fans experience with their favorite teams and the fandoms that arise around them. Milne and McDonald (1999) similarly conceptualize emotional involvement as a component of sport fan identity. This emotional connection to players, teams, and organizations both evokes strong emotions and is fairly resilient to fading over time, in part because it fosters greater involvement in fan activities which, in turn, deepen this felt connection through emotional experiences in a positive feedback loop (e.g., Shank & Beasley, 1998). Shank and Beasley note that both traditional and fantasy sport fans can become deeply emotionally attached to their interests in this manner.

Non-Sport Fans

Similar trends have also been noted in fan communities outside of sport fans. In the context of individual fans, Sandvoss (2005) describes "the regular, emotionally involved consumption of a given popular narrative or text" (p.8), while Booth and Kelly (2013) describe media fans as "audience members who feel an intense emotional connection to a particular media text" (p.57). Importantly, Cronin and Cocker (2019), who consider fans collectively, note that the uniting of fans around a shared interest creates a "shared state of emotional intoxication unlike anything than can be achieved in an individual's life" (p. 282). In other words, while fan experiences themselves often yield strong emotional responses, they are usually amplified when embedded within communities built around a shared interest.

Emotional Connection and Type of Fan

As with emotional engagement, we can ask whether emotional connections between fans are affected by fan-related variables, such as the strength of a fan's identification with the fan community. Sutton, Milne and McDonald (1997) categorized fans into three groups based on their identification as a fan: social fans, focused fans, and vested fans. They found that social fans were low in emotional engagement and primarily sought out entertainment while vested fans experienced intense emotional connections and loyalty to their fan communities,

100

even in the face of loss and poor team performance. Having said that, the authors note that even basic supporters held at least some level of emotional investment in their football club and in the fandom surrounding it, and that differences were more a matter of degree than of kind. Nevertheless, the study suggests that variables such as fanship and fandom may impact the extent to which fans experience emotional responses to interest-related activities.

Applications

We finish this section by briefly considering the practical implications of knowing more about a fan's emotional response to interest-related activities. One practical application is in the domain of marketing, where scholars have long noted that a consumer's emotional connection to a target predicts their interest in purchasing products associated with it.[1] To this end, Thompson et al. (2006) recommend moving away from marketing approaches focused on showing the merits of a product over its competitors to instead focus on emotional branding. The goal, Thompson and colleagues argue, is to foster affective bonds in customers by creating positive emotions. For highly-identified fans, drawing out their emotional responses to their interest can make a product inherently appealing and foster brand loyalty. As an example, associating one's favorite media franchise with a product is often an effective way to create a positive association with the product and its brand. This may be especially effective if the products allow fans to signal their group membership or deepen their affiliation with other fans.

Conclusion

Throughout this chapter we've explored research looking at the role of emotions as a motivator of fan behavior. As this body of work makes clear, fans experience significant emotional responses to both interest-related activities directly (e.g., watching a sporting event, consuming fan-related media) and to their fan communities. We've also seen how this emotional response differs from person to person, for example based on the extent to which fans identify as fans. These emotional responses can predict important fan-related behaviors (e.g., interest in attending events, making fan-related purchases), making them important to take into account when building models that predict fan behavior or to compare fans.

---

[1] This is perhaps no better observed than in recent marketing campaigns seeking to capitalize on feelings of nostalgia, whether for a food product, television show, or video game.

Chapter 13
Materialism

Depending on your interest, being a fan can be a costly proposition. When you consider the cost of going to events (e.g., concerts, conventions, game attendance), purchasing fan-related merchandise (e.g., t-shirts, jerseys, posters, books, memorabilia, physical media), and any equipment required (e.g., art supplies, protective equipment, tools, media-viewing devices), it's not unheard of for fans to spend hundreds or even thousands of dollars on their interests. Given that fan spending can represent multibillion dollar markets (e.g., the Marvel film franchise, professional sports leagues), it comes as no surprise that the material side of fandoms is of considerable interest to scholars and marketers alike.

In the present chapter we'll discuss research on the motivators driving fans to purchase merchandise, attend fan events, and engage in digital spaces where attention is the most coveted currency. We'll also consider the distinction between fanatics, fan tourists, and sport fans with respect to fans' willingness to travel for their interest. Finally, we'll consider collectors and archivists who preserve the fandom and its history through their consumption (and in some cases hoarding) behaviors.

Theorizing on Fan Materialism

Economists, markers, and corporations alike have a vested interest in understanding how and when fans consume, given that fans represent a fairly loyal consumer base (Coffin, 2018). Sport fans frequently find themselves studied in this regard, given the mainstream nature of their interest, their loyalty to their franchises, the multibillion dollar sport fan industry, and a historical tendency for fandom research to focus on sport fans.

The first takeaway message from the research on sport fans as consumers is that sport fans are anything but passive, one-dimensional consumers. Fan communities construct meaning, provide fans with a sense of identity, and guide performative behavior. In fact, Crawford (2004) argues that sport-related consumption is a dynamic relationship between the commodities themselves, the fans who purchase them, and the fan communities which direct behavior and provide a space for commodities to be displayed. Such displays foster a society of spectacle, with fans both observing other fans and being surveyed by the fandom with the hopes of distinguishing fake fans from true fans through interest-related commodities (Moor, 2006). Logos, signs, and merchandise are therefore the means through which fans prove themselves to other fans.

Not everyone shares this optimistic, socio-functional position on fan materialism, however. Some scholars, such as Bishop (2001), argue that the sport fans have become disconnected from the teams they identify with precisely because of marketization. As Debord (1970) notes, sport fans' contact with their favorite team has been displaced by capital and reoriented toward visual consumption (watching) and commodity consumption (official team merchandise). At best, hyper-commodification of sports detracts from the purity of fans' interests while, at worst, it fosters addictive consumption. Even so, there may be cultural variation in this tendency, since maladaptive patterns of consumption are more commonly found among American fans than they are among Korean fans (Lee & Smith, 2007).

Other researchers have developed fan typologies to better predict fan purchasing. Mackellar (2009) divided Elvis fans into four distinct categories: social segment, dabblers, fans, and fanatics. Social segment fans did not identify strongly with others in the Elvis fandom and only attended an Elvis-themed festival for the fun and novelty of the event. This was also the group mostly likely to only spend money on the event itself. Dabblers had a more moderate sense of fan identity, but were also unlikely to spend money on anything except kitschy items. Fans who identified much more strongly with the Elvis fandom were also much more willing to participate in more Elvis-themed events regardless of cost, and were more likely to purchase collectables. Finally, fanatics, the highest-identifying fans, indicated that Elvis was a central part of their identity. They were the most likely to spend money on travel, to spend thousands on authentic items, and were especially likely to transform their houses into shrines dedicated to The King.

In sum, researchers take different approaches to studying fans' purchasing and consumption behavior. Whether framing consumption as an indicator of group display, lamenting the commodification of fandom, or simply predicting which fans will and won't consume, researchers have had a lot to say about when and what fans purchase.

In the sections which follow, we'll focus our attention on specific forms of purchasing and consumption behavior to see whether we can learn anything additional about fans based on their tendency to engage in specific acts of consumption.

Merchandise

Purchasing merchandise, especially top-dollar, officially-licensed merchandise, is a top priority for fans and a subject of great importance to content producers and distributors. As such, researchers – especially those in marketing –have a strong incentive to better understand what motivates fan spending.

Intuitively, the extent to which one identifies as a fan is perhaps the most-studied motivator of fan spending. Speaking to this point, a theory by Lee and colleagues (2011) proposes that sport fans' intention to purchase merchandise is strongly predicted by, among other things (e.g., disposable income: Lee et al., 2013; Hedlund & Naylor, 2020), their identification with a team, attitudes towards the brand, and past experiences with the brand. The model is largely in-line with other lines of research showing that purchasing sponsorship products at a sporting event is predicted by the extent to which fans identify with their favorite sport team and believing that such purchases are normal behavior in the fan community (Madrigal, 2000).

In another study, Boyal and Magnusson (2007) found that collegiate basketball fans were especially susceptible to team marketing, although it depended in part on which of three fan groups they fell into (i.e., alumni, community members, current students). As a general rule, however, highly-identified fans are more likely to feel positively about the sponsors of their fan interest (Gwinner & Swanson, 2003) and to be more willing to purchase team-related merchandise (Kwon et al., 2007). In fact, fan identity has been shown to be the strongest predictor of purchasing sports-related merchandise among collegiate sport fans (Shapiro et al., 2013), a trend which, as we'll see throughout this chapter, is not limited to sport fans.

Events

Like purchasing fan-related products, those who identify the most with their fan interest have the strongest desire to be seen as members of the fan community and, as such, are the most motivated to attend fan-related events (Ballouli et al., 2016; Iso-Ahola, 1980; Kim, Trail, & Magnusen, 2013; Murrell & Dietz, 1992; Parry et al., 2014; Pentecost, 2009; Reysen, Chadborn, & Plante, 2018; Trail et al., 2017). Speaking to this point, researchers studying rugby fans similarly find that fans' personal attachment to the sport predicts future game attendance (Hill & Green, 2000). Likewise, in a study of Latino sport fans, wanting to be affiliated with a team and a desire to socially demonstrate one's connection to the team was found to predict future game attendance (Harrolle et al., 2010).

Such studies are consistent with other findings regarding fan consumption, including the theory of planned behavior (see Chapter 2). Recall that, according to the theory, a person's intention to engage in a behavior is driven by their prior engagement in the behavior, positive attitudes toward the behavior, and perceptions of the group's norms regarding the behavior. These same factors predict whether fans attend interest-related events, be they hockey fans (e.g., Cunningham & Kwon, 2003) or media fans (Reysen, Chadborn, & Plante, 2018).

Of course, fan identification with the interest or its surrounding fandom is far from the only predictor of event attendance. Among sport fans, for example, we can look at aspects of the team itself: One study found that football fans were more willing to attend games if their team had a record of winning and was fairly evenly matched in skill with the opposing team (Iso-Ahola, 1980). Other studies have looked at the event itself. Koo and company (2008) found that behavioral intentions to attend future women's basketball games were predicted by the anticipated outcome of the game, the quality of the staff and workers at the game, and the cleanliness, atmosphere, and organization of the venue where the game was being held. Likewise, Wann, Bayens, and Driver (2004) found that fans are especially likely to attend an event when they believe that tickets are scarce.

Having said all of this, the frequency with which fans attend events may not actually be a great indicator of how much money they're willing to spend on their interest. Researchers studying fans of the Pennsylvania State University football team found that the fans spent less money per game as the number of games they attended increased (Godbey & Graefe, 1991). This makes a great deal of sense: If attending games is a part of a fan's regular routine, rather than being a novel event, fans may be less likely to see it as special and worth spending a lot on the way one might on a vacation or one-time event.

The evidence in this section suggests that fan identification is an important predictor of whether fans will attend an interest-related event, even if identification is not the only relevant predictor. As with almost any behavior, a complex interplay of cognitive, situational, and affective factors ultimately determines event attendance, although it is possible to predict a fair amount of variance in attendance habits based on fan identification alone.

Fan Tourism

Researchers have become increasingly interested in studying fan-related tourism in recent years. According to this fan-as-tourist paradigm, fans often travel to fulfill psychological needs related to their fan identity (Krupa & Nawrocka, 2020; Lundberg & Lexhagen, 2014; Reichenberger & Smith, 2020). One model adopting this paradigm proposes that fan-based tourism involves the co-creation of communities at distinct locations; in other words, fans travel to interact with other fans, past, present, and future, in fan-relevant spaces (Reichenberger & Smith, 2020).

Other research taxonomizes fans into categories based on their motivation for travel and tourism. Krupa and Nawrocka (2020), for example, make a distinction between fanatics, sport fans, and fan tourists. Fanatics, highly-identified fans (Mackellar, 2006), spend a lot on both authentic commodities and on fan-related travel experiences. They tend to be emotionally involved and committed to their fandom, sometimes to a fault (Krupa & Nawrocka, 2020). Fanatics also tend to travel farther and spend more money on accommodations (Mackellar, 2009), although they are also the most difficult to please as customers.

Sport fans can be distinguished from fanatics based on the fact that, for sport fans, traveling and tourism is a central part of their fan interest (Krupa & Nawrocka, 2020). In a study of marathon and horse-racing fans, social motivations were the primary drivers of traveling to sporting events (Malchrowicz-Mosko & Chlebosz, 2019). In other studies, nostalgia has also been found to play an important role (Cho et al., 2019). Sport fans also take practical considerations into account: In a sample of fans from Brazil and Hong Kong looking to travel internationally, both the safety of the location and the level of excitement were primary concerns (Uvinha et al., 2018).

The final taxonomic group, fan tourists, differs from fanatics in that they tend to show less fervor and emotional volatility and differs from sport fans by feeling less need to travel to prove their fan identity (Krupa & Nawrocka, 2020). Even so, fan tourists exhibit motivations similar to both fanatics and sport fans, using travel to satisfy social needs, although they satisfy these needs and interact with their respective fandoms in different ways. Fans of novels (bibliophiles) tend to go on literary travels outside established touring events, preferring instead journeys to destinations featured in their favorite novels or to locations known for particular authors (MacLeod et al., 2018; Surratt, 2021). On the other hand, music festival fans tend to visit large, highly organized events that create an illusion of intimacy, such as the King Biscuit Blues Festival in Helena, Arkansas (Fry, 2014). In their research on music fan tourism, Bolderman and Reijnders (2017) conclude that music festivals provide fans with a space to develop their identity alongside like-minded others.

Engaging with Interest-Related Media

While we tend to think of consumption behavior in terms of material purchases, fans expend resources other than money to engage in their fan interest. In the digital era, where attention is a commodity which can be bought and sold (Coffin, 2018), marketers and corporate interests are just as interested in fans' time and attention as they are in their bank accounts.

Fans spend a great deal of this time and attention on fan-related media, a point we discussed in Chapter 2. And, like with other spending habits, the more strongly fans identify as fans, the more they are willing to "spend" their time and attention consuming interest-related television, radio, and websites (Parry et al., 2014). In a 2000 thesis, De Carlo found that sport fans, relative to other television-centered fandoms, were more intentional and deliberate with their viewership, but also more emotionally invested in what they choose to watch. Highly-identified sport fans also engage in more information-seeking behaviors (e.g., researching a game prior to viewing) and pursue more follow-up content post-viewing (Gantz et al., 2006). In other words, a lot of fan-related viewing a means of information gathering in addition to being a source of entertainment (Hong & Raney, 2007).

Collecting

In this final section we look beyond purchasing the occasional interest-related commodity to instead consider collecting behavior, where fans accumulate and organize fan-relevant items, often in a systematic manner. The phenomenon itself is hardly new: Sherlock Holmes fans often wrote to Sir Arthur Conan Doyle with requisitions for autographs from Holmes to add to their collections (Brombley, 2017).

According to Mackellar (2009), collecting is similar to other forms of fan materialism, in that the extent to which fans collect is predicted by how strongly they identify as a fan. Among fanatical Elvis fans, authentic item collecting often takes priority over simply collecting trinkets and novelties, something a more typical fan would be interested in.

Staiger (2005) takes a different approach, categorizing collectors directly based on the type of collecting behavior they exhibit: systematic, fetish, and souvenir. Systematic collectors accumulate and organize items to better understand to transmit knowledge about their fan interest. Television fans who collect VCR tapes would be an example of a systematic collector, someone who archives lost, condemned, or ethereal artifacts (Bjarkman, 2004). This form of collecting is also similar to vinyl record collectors, who similarly view themselves as archivists of their interest (Anderton, 2016). In contrast, fetish collecting, akin to hoarding, involves collecting as a means of self-gratification (Staiger, 2005). Shoe collectors, for example, may curate and exhibit their collections on YouTube with the ultimate goal of accumulating an even larger collection of shoes (Scaraboto et al., 2017). Finally, souvenir collecting involves curating a collection of autobiographical items representing the story one's own unique experience in the fandom (Staiger, 2005). Such items include badges from fan conventions, tickets to sporting events, and autographed merchandise from music festivals. In this case, the items collected provide a sense of meaning, linearity, and narrative for the fan's fandom experience.

Conclusion

The present chapter explored the motivations underpinning fan materialism and interest-related spending. The most apparent trend emerging from this body of work is that identifying with one's fan interest predicts fan spending, be it on merchandise, fan-related events, or fan tourism. Other factors also play a role in fan spending, including the event or commodity in question, the fan community, and one's social needs (Krupa & Nawrocka, 2020; Lundberg & Lexhagen, 2014; Reichenberger & Smith, 2020). This may stem from the fact that such spending may fulfill different purposes for different fans (e.g., Staiger, 2005). Given this variability, as well as the ability for consumption-related variables to predict important fan outcomes, fan materialism is an important variable to consider when comparing fans or when attempting to predict fan behavior.

Chapter 14
Loyalty

When we think of loyalty, we might imagine a soldier vowing to lay down their life for their country, a lover resisting the temptation of infidelity, or a congressperson who stays true to their ideals when tempted with lobbyist money. But what does it mean for a fan to be loyal? What misstep or temptation constitutes disloyalty to one's fan interest?

In the present chapter we describe fan loyalty as relatively exclusive engagement in a single fan interest, be it a single team, sport, brand, celebrity, show, or hobby (Tokuyama & Greenwell, 2011). Or, as put by Scanlan et al. (1993), it's a prolonged, continuous "intensity of desire." In other words, loyal fans are highly-focused on, and devote their time and effort to, pursuing a single fan interest to the exclusion of others.

In this chapter we investigate whether the concept of fan loyalty is useful for fan scholars. We begin by considering different approaches to studying fan loyalty before discussing variables associated with it. In doing so, we show that the distinction between "loyal" and "fair-weather" is far from superficial and may prove useful for meaningfully categorizing different fans and predicting differences in their behavior.

An Interdisciplinary Approach to Fan Loyalty

In a trend we've seen repeatedly throughout this book, the earliest research on fan loyalty was done on sport fans. Specifically, researchers looked at fans' loyalty toward their favorite sports and toward their favorite teams. For a quintessential example of the latter, look no further than the long-suffering fans of the Chicago Cubs baseball team. Until recently, Cubs fans embraced the title of "lovable losers" after a 108-year streak without winning the World Series. Despite this century-long dry spell, Cubs fans remained passionately devoted to a team that it seemed unlikely would ever win the World Series again, a testament to just how loyal sport fans can feel toward their teams and the fact that loyalty is about more than just sticking with a team when they're having a good season.[1]

Funk et al. (2000) examined how this sort of team loyalty develops. They argue that social identity and self-categorization processes (see Chapter 7) play a considerable role, fostering a sense of commitment to the team. Returning to our example, being a Cubs fan is a group identity, one that both satisfies social

---

[1] We discuss the Chicago Cubs again in Chapter 21, including the recent shattering of one of the longest dry spells in sport history and its implications for Cubs fans.

needs for fans (e.g., belongingness, distinctiveness) and which sustains itself through ingroup biases and outgroup derogation (e.g., "We're the most loyal fans there are!," "We don't bandwagon like the fair-weather fans of other teams!"). While it might have been difficult to "suffer alone" as a Cubs fan, the task becomes much simpler when you're with other suffering fans, satisfying your need for social interaction along the way.

One place to look for research on fan loyalty is in the literature on marketing and consumer behavior, where the bulk of this research has been done (Theodorakis et al., 2013). Loyalty is key from a marketing perspective, given its association with consumer engagement (e.g., buying merchandise and attending related events), positive attitudes toward the interest, word-of-mouth marketing, recruitment of new consumers, resisting the allure of competitors, and ensuring consistent consumption despite bumps in the road (Dick & Basu, 1994; Iwasaki & Havitz, 2004; Maxton, 2019; Stevens & Rosenberger, 2012). Put simply, creating loyal consumers is the goal of any business, whether we're talking about loyalty to a brand, a team, a network, a show, or a celebrity. Knowing how to create this loyalty and the profits it can yield drives much of the research on this topic.

In recent years, however, there has been a steadily-growing body of psychological research aimed at understanding the mechanisms driving loyalty. To use a recent example, Kim, Morgan, and Assaker (2020) examined the mechanisms underlying loyalty in sport fans and found that increased involvement is the key to turning fan motivation into loyalty. Social and cognitive processes like these are gradually becoming the focus of research instead of the behavioral outcomes of loyalty.

Of course, to get a complete picture of the complex and multi-faceted phenomenon of fan loyalty, one would ideally focus on both the marketing research (with its focus on creating loyalty and its behavioral outcomes) and the psychological research (with its focus on mechanisms driving these effects; Jacoby & Chestnut; 1978; Oliver, 1999). In pursuit of this nuanced approach, researchers have, at different times, construed loyalty itself in terms of its attitudinal, psychological, and behavioral components (Chen, et al., 2009; Dick & Basu, 1994; Jacoby & Chestnut, 1978; Oliver, 1999; Olsen, 2007; Rosenberg et al., 2019; Stevens & Rosenberger, 2012). We consider what research on these different types of loyalty has found in the next section.

A Model of Different Types of Loyalty

Early scholars recognized three approaches to studying loyalty: attitudinal loyalty, behavioral loyalty, and an approach that combines the two (Jacoby & Chestnut, 1978). Attitudinal loyalty describes how a person's investment in their interest builds positive feelings toward that interest. These positive feelings create a sense of commitment which, in turn, leads to behavioral loyalty, including purchases, engagement, and participation in interest-related activities. Some researchers prefer to study how attitudinal loyalty creates behavioral loyalty, while others prefer to focus their attention either on the antecedents of loyalty or its outcomes.

Others still, such as Oliver (1999), elaborate on the complexity of this approach with a multi-stage model. The first stage, called the conative stage, involves thinking about one's interest and choosing to identify with it. Next comes the affective stage, wherein positive perceptions of the interest become positive attitudes toward the interest (the attitudinal loyalty stage). For example, if a person experiences a good feeling while watching a film they may form positive attitudes toward the film franchise. The affective stage gives way to action loyalty (or behavioral loyalty) where the fan now participates in activities, purchases products, or otherwise engages with others in the context of their interest. Oliver's stages integrate much of the existing literature on attitudinal and behavioral loyalty, explaining loyalty and fan-related behavior as an interplay of psychological factors.

Having distinguished between attitudinal and behavioral loyalty, we can ask whether, and how, these two closely-related concepts are associated with one another. Iwasaki and Havitz (1998) were among the first to investigate how involvement in one's interest mediates the shift from attitudinal loyalty to behavioral loyalty. As Tachis and Tzetzis (2015) note in their work on sport spectators, being involved in one's sport influences their perceived commitment which, in turn, creates a sense of attitudinal loyalty and contributes to feelings of behavioral loyalty.

In a recent study, Yun et al. (2020) found that brand image moderates soccer fans' attitudinal loyalty while team brand image moderates behavioral loyalty and mediates attitudinal loyalty. The complex interplay of these variables, their antecedents, and outcomes demonstrates the trickiness of disentangling them empirically. Despite their conceptual overlap, they are not one and the same, and need to be recognized as such (e.g., Kang, 2015).

Predicting Loyalty

Among the variables expected to predict fan loyalty, identification with the target is one of the most frequently-studied. As one example, Stevens and Rosenberger (2012) studied Australian rugby fans' loyalty toward their favorite team. The authors found that fans' sense of team identity, along with their involvement in fan-related activities, contributes to feelings of loyalty. Sidani went one step further in their 2019 thesis, finding that fan identification drives loyalty most strongly when fans first become interested in the team, before they've become further attached to their interest, which helps to facilitate the process of becoming loyal.

Outside the domain of sport, Wu et al. (2012) found that self-reported identification and feelings of trust in other fans contribute to feelings of loyalty. In a an experiment on loyalty in music fans, Obiegbu et al. (2019) found that intense brand engagement, socialization, and identification all contributed to fans' feelings of loyalty. More importantly, however, they observed that fans take an active role in fostering a sense of loyalty, choosing to seek out other highly-engaged and passionate fans and congregating with them in online and offline communities.

Others studying the antecedents of loyalty have focused not on identification with the target interest, but rather on the impact of broad social influences on loyalty (e.g., countries where sport is a national pastime). For example, Desai (2017) commented on the impact of the country's national interest in a sport as a moderator of the effect of a team's loss on loyalty toward the team. They note that in many studies there is a tendency for loyalty to buffer some of the effects of a team's loss on reduced attachment to the team. In Desai's research in South Africa, however, they found no such effect, noting that a team's loss of a game was associated with decreasing team loyalty regardless of loyalty. In contrast, a 2019 study by Rosenberg and colleagues of Brazilian football fans found that socialization and feelings of vicarious achievement contribute to fans' sense of loyalty to their team. Taken together, these studies suggesting that social norms (e.g., a country's affinity for a sport) may play an important role in the extent to which people experience feelings of loyalty toward an interest and in the association between loyalty and subsequent behavior.

Researchers have also considered whether demographic variables can predict fan loyalty. A study by Toder-Alon and Brunel (2018) finds that loyalty increases with age: Younger fans have a more focused set of interests, but with age these interests build and are bolstered by a sense of commitment that may yield more predictable consumption behavior. Likewise, Keaton (2013) observed that those who become fans at a younger age tend to become more loyal fans, learning loyalty through observation and indoctrination with time.

The variables described in this section are far from the only factors thought to drive fan loyalty. Dwyer (2011) found that involvement in sport and fantasy sport activities improves attitudinal loyalty, while Bodet and Bernache-Assollant (2011) found that transaction-specific satisfaction predicts loyalty above and beyond identity and game attendance in a sample of French hockey fans. In short, there are multiple paths to fan loyalty, and no one variable single-handedly predicts which fans will develop into committed, loyal fans and which fans will abandon their interests when the going gets tough or when another interest comes along. That said, sufficient evidence exists to point to social identity and engagement-related variables as being fairly consistent predictors of fan loyalty.

Brand Loyalty

As previously mentioned, much of the research on loyalty originates from studies testing whether brand loyalty predicts consumer behavior. Brand loyalty, in this context, is defined as "a deeply held commitment to rebuy or patronize a preferred product or service consistently in the future… despite situational influences and marketing efforts having the potential to cause switching behavior" (Oliver, 1999, p. 34). Consumer loyalty is fairly analogous to fan loyalty (e.g., loyal fans sticking with a team despite difficult seasons and repeatedly choosing to spend time and money engaging in team-related behaviors). In fact, studies of marketing and consumer purchasing habits similarly find that attitudinal and behavioral loyalty predicts repeat purchasing and other consumer behaviors, in line with research on fan loyalty (Bauer et al., 2008; Kaynak et al., 2008).

Min (2019) made the comparison between fan and brand loyalty more directly in their own work on sport tourism which, as Yoon and Uysal (2005) point out, is akin to a "product that can be resold (revisited)." Tsiotsou (2017) similarly blurred the link between fan loyalty and brand loyalty in their work on sport team brand management and loyalty. The authors note that involvement (along with other variables like self-expression and trust) all impacted fans' loyalty and willingness to switch teams during bad seasons.

As the study by Tsiotsou (2017) suggests, brand loyalty is also similar to fan loyalty in the sense that trust is important to building loyalty in both (Wu et al., 2012). Reichheld and Schefter (2000) note that people must first develop a sense of trust in a product or organization before a sense of loyalty can develop. This trust fosters a sense of identification with the target which, when coupled with commitment, increases the likelihood of engagement with the target and loyalty toward it (Min, 2019; Tsiotsou, 2017), a finding which could be taken straight out of the pages of a fan research journal.

Conclusion

The research in this chapter represents a brief review of the much larger literature assessing the role of loyalty in fans. We've discussed distinctions between different types of loyalty (e.g., attitudinal, behavioral), different mechanisms through which fan loyalty can develop, and some the outcomes of fan loyalty, but there remain a vast range of additional questions in this literature.

For example, in their 2021 study of football fans, Ay and Kaygan make a distinction between the consumption of official content and fan-made content, raising questions about whether it's worth distinguishing between loyalty to one's fan community, to a team, and to a franchise. Additionally, questions remain about the nature of the association between attitudinal and behavioral loyalty and whether there are meaningful differences between brand loyalty and fan loyalty with respect to these variables.

Putting aside these questions for now, we can at very least note that the available research shows us that fan loyalty can vary considerably between fans and that this difference is important when it comes to predicting how fans think, feel, and behave toward their fan interest.

Chapter 15
Fanship

The term fanship describes the degree of psychological connection a person feels with a specific fan interest. It's conceptually different from, albeit related to, fandom identification, the degree of connection someone feels with other fans (see Chapter 7). It also happens to be one of the most-studied fan dimensions and the variable closest to the broad question: "Just how much of a fan is that person?"

Given that a majority of fan studies focus on sport fans, it comes as little surprise that most studies that measure fanship do so by measuring the extent to which fans identify with a particular sport team. In fact, this tendency is so common that many fan researchers view team identification as one of the most important variables for predicting fan behavior. Speaking to this importance, a meta-analysis found that team identification is among the strongest predictors of sporting event attendance (Kim et al., 2019).

Since fanship is such an important variable for fan researchers, it only makes sense to devote a chapter to better understanding fanship and the vast body of research on the subject. We begin by reviewing some of the measures designed to assess fanship in the domain of sport fans—that is, measures of team identification. We then review research outside the context of sports fans, taking a look at fanship measures that don't ask about someone's identification with a particular team.[1] Thought the chapter, we'll also be showcasing fanship's impressive predictive power across a wide range of attitudes, beliefs, feelings, and behaviors.

Fanship in Sport Fans
Sport Spectator Identification Scale

The first, and arguably most-used measure of team identification was developed by Daniel Wann and Nyla Branscombe and called the sport spectator identification scale (SSIS; Wann & Branscombe, 1993; e.g., "How important is being a fan of K.U. basketball to you?" from *not important* to *very important*). The utility of the measure is hard to overstate given its application to predicting countless facets of fan identity and fan behavior. For example, a cursory glance

---

[1] This chapter is not an exhaustive review of all of the different measures of fanship. While this is the case throughout this book, it is especially the case in the present chapter, as there have been so many different measures of fanship over the years, many of which have only seen sporadic use (e.g., Gantz & Wenner, 1995; Kim, 2003; McGuire, 2002; Pease & Zhang, 2001).

just at work done by Wann and colleagues has found connections between team identification and...

- Collective self-esteem (Wann, 1994)
- Psychological well-being (Wann, 2006a)
- Belief in trustworthiness of others (Wann & Polk, 2007)
- Belief that one can influence a game's outcome and emotional responses to wins and losses (Wann, Dolan et al., 1994)
- Knowledge of the sport (Wann et al., 1997)
- Willingness to anonymously injure an opposing team's coach or player (Wann, Peterson et al., 1999)
- Willingness to anonymously cheat to help one's favorite team (Wann et al., 2001)
- Consumption behavior, including willingness to spend money on a ticket, willingness to wait in line for a ticket, and time consuming media related to the team (Wann & Pierce, 2003)
- Positive emotions and a lack of depression, negative emotions, and alienation from others (Branscombe & Wann, 1991)

Given the utility of team identification as a concept, other researchers adapted Wann's measure for use in their own work. The results similarly show that fanship predicts a wide range of fan-related variables in sport fans from all walks of life, including:

- Basking in reflected glory, positive emotions, and satisfaction with game attendance in U.S. women's college basketball fans (Madrigal, 1995)
- Perceived quality of the team's brand in samples of U.S. students, alumni, and community members who were all fans of college basketball (Boyle & Magnusson, 2007)
- School satisfaction, academic and social integration, and sense of community among U.S. undergraduate college students (Clopton, 2005)
- Knowledge of the sport, number of games attended, and spending on team-related merchandise (Greenwood, 2001)
- Job commitment, satisfaction, involvement, and motivation among people who work on the business side (e.g., accounting, sales, facilities) of professional sports (e.g., baseball, basketball: Swanson & Kent, 2015)
- Perception of the team's corporate social responsibility, merchandise purchases, and positive word-of-mouth in Canadian major junior hockey fans (Morrison et al., 2020)

• Intention to attend future games (but only if the team performed well, among low-identified fans) in a sample of Japanese football fans (Matsuoka et al., 2003)

• Motivation to consume, intent to purchase team-related merchandise, satisfaction, and team loyalty in a sample of Brazilian soccer fans (Silveira et al., 2019)

In short, the SSIS is one of, if not the most, frequently-used measures of team identification and, by extension, fanship, in the fan literature. It's been used by researchers to studies fans of different sports from different parts of the world and has proven useful in predicting all manner of fan-related variables. It is, however, not the only measure of fanship that exists.

Team Identification Index

Trail and James (2001; see also James et al., 2002) constructed their own short, three-item measure of team identification called the team identification index (TII). It overlaps considerably with Wann's SSIS, asking fans to indicate how important the team to themselves, how much others recognize the participant as a fan of the team, and the extent to which the participant self-categorizes as a fan of the team.

As with the SSIS, the TII predicts important fan-related variables. For example, in a measure of U.S. baseball fans, the TII predicted different fan-related motivations (Trail & James, 2001). In a later study of U S men's college basketball fans, Trail, Fink, and Anderson (2003) used three slightly different items to assess team identification ("I consider myself to be a "real" fan of the basketball team," "I would experience a loss if I had to stop being a fan of the team," and "Being a fan of basketball team is very important to me") and found that, measured this way as well, team identification predicts fan motivation and an expectation that the team will do well in an upcoming game.

The TII gained traction in the literature, being picked up by researchers studying fans in other contexts. For instance, Gray and Wert-Gray (2012) surveyed a variety of U.S. sport fans and found that team identification strongly predicts fan consumption and positive word-of-mouth—in some cases even more so than satisfaction with the team's performance. In a study of Texas minor league baseball fans, Lee, In, and Seo (2015) found that team identification predicts a sense of belonging and interest in attending future games. The measure has also found use internationally, with Wu and colleagues (2012) showing that scores in Taiwanese baseball fans predict trust in their team and its players as well as intentions to attend future games.

As a final demonstration of the utility of the TII, Trail et al. (2017) conducted a longitudinal study on a sample of U.S. college students. The authors found that team identification was preceded future game attendance, representing one of the rare few studies (in a field dominated by cross-sectional research) to be able to hint at causal direction due to its longitudinal design.

Team Identification

Gladden and Funk. Gladden and Funk (2001, 2002) constructed their own four-item (e.g., "It is important that my friends see me as a fan of my favorite team") measure of team identification. In a 2001 paper the authors found that the measure was positively correlated with escapism, nostalgia, and pride in one's community. The measure was later used in a study examining the association between team identification and meaning attached to licensed products in US undergraduate sport fans (Apostolopoulou & Papadimitriou, 2018). The authors found that team identification was positively associated with buying merchandise, having positive experiences, associating with other fans, and a tendency to see one's team as representatives of the participant's geographic region.

Gwinner and Swanson. Gwinner and Swanson (2003) developed a slightly different six-item measure of team identification. Their measure was adapted from a measure of organizational identification (Mael & Ashforth, 1992) to be used in a study of fan support for their team's corporate sponsors. Team identification correlated positively with recognition of, favorable attitudes toward, and patronage of the team's company sponsors. Similar results were found in a sample of Australian rugby players, where team identification was associated with greater bias toward one's own team and its sponsors (Mahar & Weeks, 2013). Likewise parents of kids that attending an NBA basketball camp showed an increase in identification with the team sponsoring the camp (Walsh et al., 2017).

Gwinner and Swanson's measure has also proven useful in predicting fan attitudes and behaviors that have nothing to do with corporate sponsorship (or with sports themselves, in some cases):

- Team identification predicts greater commitment to one's team and a greater willingness to consume products related to the team (Fairley et al., 2014)
- Team identification predicts greater affective empathy toward their favorite team in a sample of Turkish soccer fans (Argan et al., 2018)
- Koenig-Lewis et al. (2018) found that British Premier League soccer fans who strongly identified with their teams also interacted positively with other fans and engaged in more positive word-of-mouth sharing of the team with others

- Team identification predicts positive affect, greater work engagement, and better work performance in Greek football fans (Gkorezis et al., 2016).

Kwon and Armstrong. Continuing the trend of researchers who constructed their own measures of team identification, Kwon and Armstrong (2004) constructed a measure specifically for use with college students that consisted of three dimensions: team identification (e.g., "When someone criticizes the [sports teams name], it feels like a personal insult"), school identification (e.g., "The [insert university] successes are my successes"), and commitment ("I do feel emotionally attached to the [insert team]"). In their first study of U.S. university students they found that each dimension positively predicted buying team-related merchandise, a finding later replicated with respect to the impulse-buying of team merchandise (Kwon & Armstrong, 2006).

Kwon and Trail (2005) also tested the validity of a single-item measure of team identification ("Overall, I am a fan of the team") in a sample of U.S. college students. The measure was positively correlated with the longer measure of team identification and did a fairly good job predicting behavioral outcomes such as purchasing and wearing merchandise and watching games.

Dimmock et al. When creating their own measure of team identification, Dimmock and colleagues (2005) built upon existing measures from social identity theory (see Chapter 7 for more on this). The result was a 15-item, three-dimensional measure of team identification comprised a cognitive-affective identification dimension (e.g., "I think of my favorite team as part of who I am"), a personal evaluation dimension (e.g., "I have a lot of respect for my favorite team") and an other-evaluation dimension (e.g., "Others respect my favorite team"). The original study found that greater overall team identification predicts greater ingroup favoritism, while a subsequent study of Greek and Australian students found that all three factors predict positive word-of-mouth and intention to attend future games (Theodorakis et al., 2010).

*TEAM*ID*

Heere and James (2007) created their own measure of team identification, called the TEAM*ID scale, which contains six dimensions:
- Private evaluation (e.g., "I am proud to think of myself as a fan of my college football team")
- Public evaluation (e.g., "Overall, my college football team is viewed positively")
- Interconnection of self (e.g., "The college football team's successes are my successes")

- Sense of interdependence (e.g., "My destiny is tied to the destiny of the college football team")
- Behavioral involvement (e.g., "I am active in organizations that include mostly fans of my college football team")
- Cognitive awareness (e.g., "I know the ins and outs of my college football team")

In their original study, each dimension was positively correlated with psychological commitment to the team. In other studies, team identity was also positively related to purchasing team merchandise, media consumption, and game attendance (Heere et al., 2011; Katz et al., 2018). The measure has also proven to be fairly stable over time in longitudinal research, both over a one year period (Lock et al., 2014) and over a three year period (Katz & Heere, 2016).

Points of Attachment

In this final section of fanship in sport fans we consider a slightly different measure, one that doesn't focus exclusively on team identification. In their points of attachment scale, Trail, Robinson et al. (2003) assess the degree of connection that college sport fans feel with various aspects of their favorite sport, not just with their favorite team. The measure itself contains seven subscales measuring fan identification with:

- The team (e.g., "I consider myself to be a "real" fan of the [insert team] team")
- The players (e.g., "I consider myself a fan of certain players rather than a fan of the team")
- The coach (e.g., "I am a fan of the [insert team] because they are coached by Coach [insert coach]")
- The community (e.g., "I am a fan of [insert team] because it enhances the community image")
- The sport (e.g., "[insert sport] is my favorite sport")
- The university (e.g., "I identify with the university rather than with any specific university team")
- The level of sport (e.g., "I consider myself a fan of collegiate [insert sport], an not just one specific team")

In a 2003 study, Trail and colleagues used the scale to test the association between sport fan identification and fan motivation in American college football fans. The first thing they noticed was that the seven dimensions of identification fell into two higher order constructs. The first assessed fan identification with the organization: team, coach, community, university, and players. The second construct represented fan identification with the sport itself, consisting of identification with the sport and with the level of the sport.

Results from the study showed that different motivations predicted different facets of sport fan motivation. For example, being motivated by a desire for vicarious achievement predicted organizational identification, but not sport identification. In contrast, spectator-related motivations (skill, aesthetic, drama, knowledge) predicted sport identification, but not organizational identification. To use an illustrative example, feeling good when the team is winning is linked to identifying with the team and the university, while those who appreciate the beauty and skill of the game identify more with the sport and the level of the sport in general. Robinson and Trail (2005) found similar results in both college basketball and American football fans.

Researchers have (e.g., Kwon et al., 2005) questioned whether all seven dimensions of the scale are necessary. In their own study, Kwon et al. (2005) administered the scale without the community identification subscale and found that team identification most strongly predicted basking in reflected glory, satisfaction with game experience, intention to purchase merchandise, and the number of games fans attended. In fact, other dimensions of identification added predicted little additional variance above and beyond what was predicted by team identification, suggesting that there is little point to assessing identification with anything other than the team.

Taken together, the research in this section both highlights the importance of team identification to the concept of fanship and illustrates the utility of fanship for predicting fan attitudes and behaviors. Of course, the research discussed thus far has only focused on sport fans; we'd be remiss if we didn't address more recent research on fanship and its application in the context of non-sport fans.

Fanship in Non-Sport Fans

When it comes to measures of fanship in non-sport fans, we turn first to the measure developed by Reysen and Branscombe (2010), one of the first measures developed explicitly for use in non-sport fan contexts. The measure consists of 11 items (e.g., "I strongly identify with my interest," "My interest is part of me") assessing the extent to which fans identify with their interest. Importantly, the measure is worded in a way that is independent of content from any specific interest, meaning it can be flexibly used for in any sample of fans.

In the original study by Reysen and Branscombe (2010), the authors found that their measure of fanship was empirically distinct from a measure of fan group identification (i.e., fandom). Moreover, fanship was significantly positively associated with fan behaviors (e.g., frequency of participation), distancing oneself from non-fans, perceived group entitativity, and collective happiness.

Chadborn et al. (2017) used the measure in a study about fanship, fan motivation, and display of group symbols in a sample of fans with various interests. Fanship was positively associated with several fan motivations (i.e., meaning in life, escape from daily hassles, and making social connections), as well as with frequency of buying fan-related merchandise and displaying said merchandise to others.

Schroy et al. (2016) used a shortened, three-item version of the measure ("I am emotionally connected to being a [fan of interest]," "I strongly identify with being a [fan of interest]," "Being a [fan of interest] is part of me"), in three different samples of fans. As with Chadborn et al. (2017), fans' degree of fanship was associated with one's motivation to be a fan, although the authors found that the association differed between fan groups (i.e., belongingness was positively associated with fanship for some of the fan groups, but not for all of them).

Shaw et al. (2016) also used the three-item measure to examine predictors of fan entitlement—the belief that a person is owed unearned special treatment—in intrafandom interactions with content creators across various fan groups. Fanship significantly predicted fan entitlement, at least in two of the fan groups (anime and fantasy sport fans).

In other studies, fanship has been found to predict:
- Self-esteem, meaning in life, distinctiveness, and having social needs (Ray et al., 2017)
- Psychological well-being in a sample of anime fans (Reysen et al., 2017b)
- Word-of-mouth proselytizing about one's fan interest in a sample of general fans (Plante, Chadborn, & Reysen, 2018)
- Concert attendance, motivation to attend concerts, and spending at concerts (Kulczynski, 2014)
- Happiness, self-esteem, social connectedness, and consumption behavior in a large sample of K-Pop fans (Laffan, 2020)

Together, studies like these illustrate the importance of fanship as a predictor of fan-related variables (e.g., consumption, behavior, attitudes, well-being, social interaction). The work also illustrates that this association is not limited to sport fans, despite sport fans comprising the bulk of participants in research on this topic.

Other Fanship Measures

As a brief aside, this final section draws readers' attention to a series of measures that, while perhaps not directly assessing fanship, or doing so only as part of a broader measure, are nevertheless close enough to fanship conceptually that they bear mentioning in a chapter on fanship.

One such measure was developed by Pentecost and Andrews (2010), who examined Australian fashion fans' purchasing behavior. The measures assesses thoughts regarding fashion (e.g., "I carefully follow what is happening in the fashion world") and the extent to which fans identify as fans of fashion (e.g., "I am an avid fashion fan"). The latter dimension was positively associated with greater spending on clothes, in line with earlier research linking fanship to consumption behavior. Lee and Jung (2018) would later adapt the measure for use in a sample of Korean participants, asking about their favorite brands (e.g., Samsung, Apple). Greater brand-related identification was, as one might predict based on Chapter 14, associated with greater brand loyalty.

Biscaia and colleagues (2018) took a slightly different approach in their own study of Portuguese sport fans, one that we might call a stakeholder perspective. They proposed a four-dimensional scale assessing feelings of power (e.g., "I can exert power within the club"), urgency (e.g., "I exhibit urgency in my relationships with the club"), external legitimacy (e.g., "My claims are viewed by the club as legitimate") and internal legitimacy (e.g., "I consider myself to be a real fan of my team"), the last dimension of which is reminiscent of other fanship measures. Structural equation modeling found that while power predicts intention to attend games and purchase merchandise, the magnitude of this association is about half of that observed for internal legitimacy, the dimension most closely reflecting fanship. In other words, the fanship-related variable is the strongest predictor of consumption-based fan behavior in the study. Other studies find similar effects, relating fanship-adjacent variables to online consumption behavior like viewing a team's website (Seo & Green, 2008) and using team-related social media sites (Haugh & Watkins, 2016).

Conclusion

In the present chapter we reviewed the research on fanship by exploring a multitude of different measures of fanship and their use in predicting important fan-related variables. While much of this research has focused on sport fans, so much so that the most frequently-used measure of fanship was developed specifically for use with sport fans (Wann & Branscombe, 1993), more recent work has broadened the field's focus and found analogous results in the context of non-sport fans.

Regardless of the fan group under study, fanship is consistently one of the strongest predictors of fan-related attitudes, beliefs, and behaviors, especially when it comes to consumption behaviors like game attendance and fan purchases. Given this importance, fanship is one of the most important variables to consider for those studying fans, whether they intend to predict fan behavior or to measure differences between fans on almost any other psychological or fan-related dimension.

Chapter 16
Uniqueness

As anyone who was once a teenager can attest, humans strive to be distinct from one another and to feel unique, even if the desired degree of uniqueness differs from person to person (Snyder & Fromkin, 1980). In general, people dislike being seen as overly similar to others. In response to such comparisons, we often change our attitudes or our behavior to make ourselves more unique. In fact, entire industries are built around selling people ways to express their creativity, to be unconventional, and ultimately to avoid being too much like those around them (Tian et al., 2001).

In the present chapter will consider this idea that people are driven toward an optimal level of uniqueness through the fan groups they belong to. We begin by briefly reviewing research linking fan identity to uniqueness more generally before delving into specific examples of fans seeking uniqueness in sport, music, and low-status, stigmatized fan groups. Throughout it all, we'll be considering different ways to assess one's need for uniqueness and some of the implications of this work for important fan behaviors like fandom identification and fan-related consumption.

Social Identity Theory, Uniqueness, and Fan Groups

Studies have shown that people in groups are generally motivated to distinguish themselves (preferably in a positive manner) from members of other groups, especially when direct comparisons are being made (Mlicki & Ellemers, 1996). We can see evidence of this behavior in the context of inter-brand rivalries (e.g., drivers of BMW versus Mercedes-Benz vehicles), where consumers of both brands feel distinct from one another (and aligned with others who share their taste in products, Berendt et al., 2018). Findings like these also mirror research on sport fans: NFL fans purchase team apparel to distinguish themselves from out-group members—in this case, fans of other teams (Sierra et al., 2012).[1] It seems plausible that a need for uniqueness could be driving fan identification and these specific fan behaviors, both of which allow fans to positively differentiate themselves from others.

---

[1] The need to distinguish oneself from a negatively-viewed outgroup is especially strong among sport fans relative to other fan groups. For comparison, the need for distinction and outgroup derogation is stronger in sport fans than it is for fans of either the Marvel and DC comic book franchises, a fairly famous brand rivalry (Havard, Grieve et al., 2020).

If this were the case, then it should follow that threatening fans' sense of uniqueness should increase pro-fandom attitudes and behavior while also making them more likely to derogate and differentiate themselves from members of other fandoms (Branscombe et al., 1999). Studies suggest that this is precisely what happens. Studies of sport fans reveal that they are highly sensitive to uniqueness threats, like the possibility that their team's stadium may change its name to that of a corporation, citing concerns about the possible loss of their team's distinctiveness (Reysen et al., 2012). In studies of media fans, uniqueness threats (e.g., an artist or another fan creating a character similar to one of yours) are often met with hostility (Reysen et al., 2020a) or selectively adopting essentialist beliefs about one's fan group to more clearly distinguish it from other fan groups (Plante, Roberts, Snider et al., 2015).

In short, the available evidence suggests that fans are motivated, in part, by a need to feel unique and by their fan interest's ability to satiate that need. Of course, uniqueness isn't the only need being satiated, nor is this idea incompatible with the notion that fan groups also provide fans with a sense of belongingness (Abrams, 1994; Brewer, 1991; Hoverd et al., 2012; Leonardelli et al., 2010). Fandoms provide fans with the opportunity to be optimally distinct through flexible boundaries and structured subgroups (Hornsey & Hogg, 1999; Leonardelli et al., 2010), which draws fans further into fan interests and the communities that arise around them.[2] This, in turn, may impact other behavior important to fan researchers, including consumption (Papyrina, 2012; Shore et al., 2011) and relationships (Slotter et al., 2014).

Having established the importance of uniqueness as a motivator of fan behavior, at least through the lens of social identity theory, we next turn our attention to the manifestation of this principle in three different groups of fans.

Sport Fans

Most fan-related phenomena are studied in the context of sport fans first. Optimal distinctiveness theory, however, may be the exception to this rule (Dimmock & Gucciardi, 2008). In fact, compared to other fan groups, there has been relatively little research focusing exclusively on the topic of optimal distinctiveness in sport fans.

This isn't to say that there hasn't been at least some research more broadly focusing on the subject of uniqueness in sport fans. Richardson and Turley (2006), for example, found that football fans perceive themselves as distinct (in

---

[2] One interesting moderator of this effect may be nostalgia. Studies suggest that the need for distinctiveness decreases and group conformity increases in the presence of feelings of nostalgia (Fan et al., 2020). As such, for fandoms grounded in feelings of nostalgia, distinctiveness or uniqueness may be less of a motivator.

128

a superior way) from other fans. Goldman and colleagues (2016) similarly find that fans of a team often look for ways to distinguish themselves not just from fans of other teams, but also from other members of the same team. Goldman's (2014) work comes even closer to the dualism of optimal distinctiveness theory, showing that South African rugby fans experience both a need to be distinct from other fans (e.g., other teams) and a need to be similar to other fans (e.g., of the same team). And in their work on hockey fans cheering for a non-local team, Andrijiw and Hyatt (2009) find that the fans experience uniqueness by being different from other fans in their area while still belonging to the community of fans who share their favorite team.

More recently, Shuv-Ami and Alon (2020) developed a scale to directly assess optimal distinctiveness in fans by comparing fans' personal identities to their social identities. The measure, developed and validated in samples of Israeli basketball fans, uses questions like "I have my own way of being a fan of my team" and "I identify with the nationalistic / ideological fans of my team" to assess the ways fans negotiate the competing needs of being unique and belonging to their fan community. The measure has proven useful in predicting fan attitudes, including optimism about the team and satisfaction with the team and the surrounding fandom.

Music Fans

Brewer (1991) argues that teens and young adults pursuing optimal distinctiveness seek out groups which, on the one hand, provide a sense of homogeneity within the group while, on the other hand, are perceived as highly unique or unusual to outgroup members (such as their parents). Many music subcultures fall into this category. Studies show, for example, that music fans often conform to norms and stereotypes about the genre when it comes to behavior and style (North & Hargreaves, 1999), relationships (Selfhout et al., 2009), and political orientations (North & Hargreaves, 2007). More importantly, the music fans who identify most strongly with, and invest the most in (e.g., time and money), their musical interest tend to prefer moderately distinct genres of music, neither too mainstream nor too obscure, including heavy metal, alternative/indie, Motown, easy listening, soul, house, acid, rock 'n' roll, and funk (Abrams, 2009).

Artists and brand managers are keenly aware of this optimal distinctiveness "sweet spot." As such, they use impression management (Snyder & Swann, 1976) to create a sense of authenticity and typicality that allows fans to both feel included in the fan community while also standing out from fans of other musicians (Borgstedt, 2008). In a study of adolescent music fans in Germany, the typicality of an artist's music and images predicted feelings of optimal distinctiveness in fans (Cohrdes & Kopiez, 2015). As managers have known for a long time, artists and musicians should aim to foster a stable and devoted fanbase by balancing the need to be distinct from other musicians and the need to be seen as normal and typicality enough so as to not be alienating to potential fans.

Low Status Fans

Like with other fan groups, members of low-status, stigmatized fandoms similarly have a dual need to be distinct and to fit in. In fact, the low-status, stigmatized nature of some fan groups may strike the perfect balance between these needs, creating a sense of distinctness from popular culture while fostering a strong sense of community through the shared experience of stigma. This dynamic has been observed in the brony community, where adult fans of the television show *My Little Pony* frequently find themselves on the receiving end of stigma from mainstream media, but nevertheless report a strong sense of kinship and community with other bronies. As a result, the need for belongingness and the need for distinctiveness underpinned identification as a brony for many in the fandom (Edwards et al., 2019). Similarly, anime fans surveyed both online and at fan conventions report higher group identification when they feel both a high sense of belonging and distinctiveness (Reysen et al., 2017a), a finding which has been found in other media-based fandoms (Reysen, Plante, Roberts, & Gerbasi, 2016).

Conclusion

In the present chapter we explored theories of uniqueness and optimal distinctiveness (Brewer, 1991; Snyder & Fromkin, 1980) and their application to fan groups. We've seen that people have a need to be perceived as distinct from others (Snyder & Fromkin, 1980) and respond aversively to threats to that distinctiveness. People temper this need with a contradictory desire to fit in with others (Brewer, 1991). While there has been comparatively little work assessing optimal distinctiveness directly, the work which has been done helps researchers better understand fan attitudes, behavior, and identification (Andrijiw & Hyatt, 2009; Dimmock & Gucciardi, 2008) across a variety of fan groups, from sport fans to music fans to stigmatized fans of non-mainstream media. More research is needed to improve our understanding of uniqueness as a motivator of fans and its potential utility when it comes to making important distinctions both across and within fan groups.

Chapter 17
Creativity

Before we begin this chapter, we'd like you to consider all of the different ways you can use a brick. Stop reading for one minute and think about the different things you could use a brick for, regardless of how uncommon or impractical they may be.

Now, take a moment to consider the following three words: "Sandwich," "Foot," and "Golf." Think of a word or concept that connects them—what they all have in common?

The two tasks you just did are two commonly used measures of creativity, known respectively as the Alternate Uses Task and the Remote Associates Test. You might have noticed that the two tasks felt quite different from one another. The first prompted you to generate a multitude of answers, and is measure of (among other things), generativity, a facet of creativity. The second task, on the other hand, wasn't about generating a multitude of answers, and instead required you to consider a multitude of possibilities to arrive at the one that fits the criteria provided ("Club").

The two tasks represent two of the many different ways researchers have tried to measure creativity. In fact, the study of creativity is a story of scholars trying to nail down what, precisely, creativity is and what we can learn about creative people, activities that involve creativity, and catalysts for creativity.

Regardless of how you define creativity, however, we can probably agree that many fan-related activities involve an element of creativity—creating novel content inspired by a favorite show, imagining inventive plays to outsmart the opposing team, or devising the perfect way to cosplay a non-human-shaped character. As such, we can speculate on the role of creativity and its association with fan behavior. We dive into this very topic in the present chapter after briefly reviewing some of the scholarly work on creativity.

Defining Creativity

Psychological research on creativity can be traced back to at least the mid-19th century (Runco & Jaeger, 2012). After more than a century of work and countless studies approaching creativity from different perspectives, no one researcher has come up with a universally agreed-upon definition of creativity. Despite this lack of consensus there was research needing to be done, and so scholars generally got by with one variation or another on the loose consensus that creativity, whatever it is, involves the ability to generate ideas that are original, useful, and non-obvious.

A couple of examples from the scholarship on creativity illustrate just how vast the subject is and the number of different disciplines that have weighed in on it. Sternberg (2006), for example, conceptualizes creativity as an investment, using the allegory of economics to suggest that creative people "buy low and sell high" when it comes to ideas (p. 87), meaning they recognize the potential in older, lesser-known ideas and transform them into innovative new concepts, practices, commodities, or discourses.

As another illustrative example, Unsworth (2001) developed a taxonomy of creative behavior centered around two dimensions: the type of problem and the motivation driving the person involved. Problem type indicates the extent to which the problem is open-ended or closed-ended in its form, labeled "discovered" and "individual," respectively. With respect to the person involved, one must consider the extent to which they are motivated for psychological (internal) reasons or for social (external) reasons. The two axes form four quadrants which demarcate four types of creativity: proactive creativity (open-ended, internal), contributory creativity (closed-ended, internal), expected creativity (open-ended, external), and responsive creativity (closed-ended, external). Proactive creativity involves seeking opportunities to be creative while contributory creativity involves providing a solution or innovation to an established problem. Expected creativity involves being in a position where one is expected to find problems and develop creative solutions for them and, finally, responsive creativity refers to creative behaviors that are a response to a clearly outlined situation where the person involved has little creative choice available to them.

A full review of the literature on creativity is beyond the focus of this chapter, of course. For now, it is sufficient for our purposes to show that creativity has been construed in a multitude of ways and that there is no one "right" way to measure or study creativity. Likewise, studies illustrate the wide range of topics to which creativity has been applied, ranging from studying how best to foster creativity, predicting individual differences in creativity, and the links between creativity and other outcomes such as leadership or intelligence. Most presently relevant to this chapter's purpose, however, is the body of research linking creativity to fans and fandom, both in general and with respect to specific fan behaviors.

Creativity in Fandom

Creativity has come to play an increasingly central role in fan culture as media consumption habits shift from a paradigm of passive viewing toward a more participatory culture where fans themselves become content producers (Jenkins, 1992, 2018). With the advent of the internet, fans are becoming increasingly able to find and distribute their own fan-made content, with modern media-based fans spending almost as much time engaging with fan-created content as they do with canonical content (Edwards et al., 2019). But the phenomenon of viewer-as-producer dates back to before the internet, back to the fans of the original *Star Trek*, who some have suggested created the first fanfiction (or, at very least, popularized it) as a means of further exploring the show's characters and their relationships, (e.g., romantic relationships between Captain Kirk and Mr. Spock, Bacon-Smith, 1992; Jenkins, 1992).

But productive fandom is much more than just writing fanfiction. As another example, fans often craft replicas of devices, costumes, or settings in the media they love. This is perfectly demonstrated in fans of the band Daft Punk who regularly create their own versions of the band members' iconic helmets as a way to transform a symbolic representation of the band into a material artifact (Hills, 2014). In other fandoms, creators construct detailed models and figures of everything from robots and mecha to *Doctor Who*'s iconic TARDIS, operating within an economic space that provides creative commodities to fans outside of official, corporate-driven economies (Godwin, 2016).

Conceptualized thusly, it seems like creative expression may motivate people to join or participate in fandom-related activities—and this is almost certainly a draw for at least some fans. It could also be argued, however, that simply belonging to a fandom may foster creativity in fans. In a study testing this idea, researchers found that when people were put into a group with a highly-creative person (in this case, a star performer), they became more creative themselves (Kenworthy et al., 2020). Jenkins (2018) even suggests that fandom is a place where creativity itself is a currency among fans. Given the abundance of fan-generated art and producer communities online (e.g., Youtube, Archive of Our Own, Fanfiction.net, tumblr, furaffinity, twitter, DeviantArt: Winter et al., 2021), as well as the public display of interest-related artistic content (e.g., cosplayers, art commissions: Garon, 2017), this would certainly seem to be the case. Harrington (2018) even argues that such creative expression follows fans into older adulthood and may preserve psychological well-being far better than a daily Sudoku puzzle ever could.

Keeping this in mind, let's turn our attention to two well-documented examples of creativity in fan communities: fanfiction writers and cosplayers.

Creativity in Fan Fiction and Writing Communities

Fanfiction refers to the creation of alternative texts that either spin off from, extend, or change the canon of a piece of media content (Jenkins, 1992, 2018). One of the first observations of significant fanfiction production among fans originates from women in the *Star Trek* fandom who created works which, among other things, explored hypothetical relationships between protagonists that were not depicted in the television show itself. Today, one would be hard-pressed to find a media fandom that doesn't have at least a fledgling fanfiction community, if not its own repository for fanfiction (sometimes alongside fan-produced artwork).

Fiske (1992) conceptualized fanfiction as existing within a shadow cultural economy, one where fans create, exchange, sell, and share artifacts and commodities outside of official corporate economies (e.g., a television network's official merchandise store). Of course, the success and spread of such works varies considerably, ranging from fanfiction writers who only share their stories with other writers or in small, independent publications (e.g., zines) to works such as *Fifty Shades of Grey* by E. L. James, one of the best-selling books of the past decade that originated as a fanfiction spinoff of the *Twilight* series of novels by Stephani Meyers (Reunders et al., 2017). While not every piece of fanfiction becomes popular enough to influence mainstream culture, the practice of fanfiction is sufficiently prevalent in fan culture that pedagogical researchers have begun to use the practice of writing fanfiction to engage primarily school students in writing education and literacy development (DeLuca, 2018; McConnel, 2019).

Of particular note from both the early *Star Trek* fanfiction and, perhaps to an even greater extent exemplified by the *Fifty Shades of Grey* franchise, sex and relationship tension are often a core aspect of the fanfiction genre (Bacon-Smith, 1992; Jenkins, 1992; Reunders et al., 2017). Fans of *Star Trek* would often explore homoerotic overtones in the relationship between Captain Kirk and Mr. Spock while, decades later, fans of the *Harry Potter* franchise created a number of queer works around the character of Albus Dumbledore, especially after the series' author, J. K. Rowling, disclosed that the character had always been envisioned as gay (Tosenberger, 2008). Jenkins (1992) argued that sexualized fanfiction often stems from a lack of sex (or a particular kind of sexual relationship, such as gay relationships) within a media canon, with fans finding personal meaning and exploring personally-relevant sexual and romantic themes through the creation of fanfiction to overcome their absence in the canon. While these themes often include queer identities and relationships, fan-fiction can also involve more niche or specific subjects, such as "mpreg," which explores the dynamic of men getting pregnant (Reunders et al., 2017), pony-themed erotica among fans of *My Little Pony*[1] (Bailey & Harvey, 2019; Edwards et al., 2019), and of course, BDSM in *Fifty Shades of Grey*.[2]

The frequent presence of sexual content in fanfiction has led many to perceive fanfiction and those who produce and consume it as deviant. We'd be remiss if we didn't counter this perception by pointing out some of the positive aspects of these works. As Jenkins (1992) points out, sexualized fanfiction serves a purpose within the broader context of cultural lack, offering a way for individual fans to explore facets of their identity and create spaces to foster creativity and acceptance outside of the dominant corporate and cultural hegemony. Sereda (2019) similarly argues that her experience of sexual fanfiction was emotionally therapeutic, offering a way to experience life situations culturally unavailable to her as a lesbian. Dreisinger (2018) discussed the role of *Twilight* fanfiction for people with disabilities, highlighting the work *Forgive Me for Loving You* by an author with the handle "LisbethsGirlfriend," as well as others which focus on disability in the context of *Twilight*. And, in the context of *My Little Pony* fanfiction, researchers suggest that fanfiction allows readers to explore themes of nonconformity with respect to mainstream conceptions of masculinity, compulsory heterosexuality, and intellectual disability (Bailey & Harvey, 2019; Ellis, 2015; Pramaggiore, 2015).

Taken together, the research on fanfiction suggests not only that fanfiction is prevalent across a multitude of media-based fandoms, but that this act of creativity allows fans to make interest-related content more meaningful and relevant to them. But fanfiction is not the only creative act engaged in by fans, as we'll see in the next section.

Creativity in Cosplayers

Fiske (1992) argued that fan communities create economies of cultural capital wherein those with more capital hold a higher degree of status among fans. One of the primary ways fans achieve this higher status is to demonstrate their creativity as an indicator of their devotion to the fan interest, one intended to be observed and appreciated by other fans. In doing so, many cosplayers hold

---

[1] Fanfiction in the *My Little Pony* fandom is rife with examples of niche or specific content that is otherwise not found in the children's television show. Crome (2014), for example, notes that Christian fans of *My Little Pony* have used fanfiction to negotiate their religious identities and fan interests, exemplified in Brain Jacko's "Putting My Idol on the Altar."

[2] It bears mentioning here that, despite displaying the superficial trappings of BDSM throughout the story, the relationship portrayed in *Fifty Shades of Grey* has been heavily criticized by those in the BDSM community for its portrayal of consent (and troubling lack thereof).

considerable cultural capital within their fan community, being looked up to for the creativity, technical skill, and social confidence needed to create, wear, and perform as one's favorite character among other scrutinizing fans (Winge, 2006). As Lome (2016) points out, cosplaying is an act of creativity, both a wearable form of visual art and as a piece of theatrical performance. And, in line with what you'd expect from those who achieve status through their creative pursuits within a fandom, cosplaying is associated with a greater sense of community with one's fandom (Reysen et al., 2018a).

Emphasizing the fact that cosplay is, at its core, a creative pursuit, Kane (2017) notes that cosplayers are motivated by the challenge of engaging in creative processes like designing, constructing, displaying, and performing their art for other fans. Lamerichs (2015) further points out that cosplayers are also driven by the opportunity to develop new, creativity-based skills, often unseen by the public, especially since nearly all cosplayers create their own costumes (Lotecki, 2012). In fact, the skills needed for cosplaying often go far beyond just sewing an outfit. As Vardell and colleagues (2020) point out, cosplayers develop sophisticated information literacy skills to help them find crucial information about cosplay concepts and ideas.

Similar to fanfiction, cosplay provides fans with a creative role-playing space within which they can express themselves through their favorite characters while simultaneously taking on features of the characters (Lotecki, 2012). Themes of gender-bending and queer identity are common among those who cosplay, allowing cosplayers to explore these elements of themselves in a manner that's likely to be received positively by other fans.

Of course, positive reception is not always guaranteed. One study of cosplayers found that cosplayers are sometimes stigmatized for their gender, race, or weight (Lome, 2016). As Hines (2020) points out, there is often a lack of people of color in media, which leads to a lack of representation in cosplaying culture that can ultimately stifle or discourage the full range of a creator's creative expression. N. Taylor (2019) also recognized the problem, arguing that the normalization of cosplay within Afrodiasportic communities is one important way of providing people of color with a way to experience alternative ways of being and reclaim self-visualization in public spaces.

Conclusion

In the present chapter we briefly introduced different conceptions of what it means to be creative before delving into research showing that, regardless of how one construes creativity, one can hardly deny that creativity abounds in fan culture. Far from being passive consumers of media, many fans engage in acts of creativity that range from amateur drawings of one's favorite character to writing and sharing fanfiction with other fans to the creation of elaborate cosplays performed in front of other fans. While the present chapter has primarily focused on fanfiction and cosplay as two representative creative fan pursuits, each fandom possesses its own idiosyncratic culture of creativity and innovation (Reysen & Branscombe, 2010).

Fandoms provide fans with a space within which to innovate, explore facets of themselves, and to build upon the creative products of like-minded others. In this shadow cultural economy (Fiske, 1992) where creativity is a valued commodity (Jenkins, 1992), fans benefit from their creative endeavors, whether through social acceptance and status from other fans or well-being at being able to explore and express an otherwise stigmatized part of themselves. For this reason, future research on fans and fan culture would do well to explore the role of creative pursuits in fan spaces, both looking at individual differences in fans' tendency to do so and at fandom-level differences in the opportunities they afford fans to engage in creativity and share the fruits of their work with other fans.

Chapter 18
Aesthetics

Aesthetics describes the viewing of something as an art form, appreciating it for its sensory appeal and artistic value. One who finds beauty in the way a chime sounds as the wind blows through it or in the delicate blend of flavors and aromas in a cup of coffee can be said to be appreciating the aesthetics of these experiences. Aesthetics contributes significantly to the affective appeal of an experience, and so it follows that activities we enjoy and seek out may, to some degree, be activities that we consider to be aesthetically appealing. Fan research would seem to agree with this assertion, whether in the context of media fans appreciating the sights and sounds of their favorite show or, as Smith (1988) suggests, finding sport fans who appreciate the "beauty and creativity" of an athletic performance (p. 58) where others might not.

In the present chapter we make the case that aesthetic appeal should be considered as variable important to our understanding of fans and fan behavior. We begin by speaking broadly about the link between aesthetics and fan interests before delving into two very different examples of aesthetics in fandom: fandoms based around content that's artistic by design (e.g., music and poetry) and fandoms based around content where aesthetic appeal is not the primary purpose of the activity (e.g., sport).

Aesthetics and Fan Interest

There is considerable contention in the field of aesthetic psychology about the definition, components, and precise nature of aesthetics, aesthetic experiences, and the emotions they both yield (Leder & Nadal, 2014; Menninghaus et al., 2019; Skov & Nadal, 2020). Some scholars contend that aesthetic experiences necessitate the creation of positive emotions and experiences (Menninghaus et al., 2019), while others argue that aesthetic emotions emerge under challenging or difficult circumstances (Hagtvedt & Vohs, 2017). Illustrating just how abstract such conceptualizations can be, Chatterjee (2017) argues that aesthetic experience has less to do with a particular emotion and more to do with the convergence of past, present, and future in a single moment.

Regardless of how you operationalize aesthetics, you can probably agree that aesthetic experiences are those which elicit powerful emotions and can have a significant impact on us. We see this principle demonstrated in a study by Djikic and company (2012) in which participants were randomly selected to read either an essay or a short story. Those who evaluated the work as artistic (e.g., having aesthetic components, regardless of genre) were more likely to feel that an aspect of themselves had changed as a result.

In a related line of work from media psychology, researchers have shown that meaningful or appreciative (aesthetic) experiences differ from entertainment-centered experiences in important ways. Oliver and Bartsch (2010), for example, report on a series of studies showing that aesthetic-focused movies that cause the audience to experience moving or thought-provoking experiences lead to feelings of appreciation, whereas movies centered merely on entertainment lead to feelings of fun instead. Oliver and Raney (2011) would later report that some movie viewers pursue what they label "eudaimonic" motivations, or a desire to consume media as a means of truth-seeking, existential exploration, and meaning making. Movie genres dedicated to human virtue, drama, or biography/documentary are the most likely to elicit these types of emotions in viewers, although even light-hearted comedies or action movies can have aesthetic appeal (Oliver & Bartsch, 2011).

When he laid out the motivations that drive sport fans, Wann (1995), included aesthetic appreciation of the sport itself as a motivator. Considering some of the other motivators (e.g., eustress, escapism, entertainment, group affiliation), one might not expect aesthetic appeal to rank especially high. As it turns out, this couldn't be further from the truth: Aesthetic appreciation was among the highest-rated motivators for sport fans, second only to entertainment. Moreover, aesthetic appeal has since been shown to predict important fan-related variables including one's identification with their fan community (fandom), felt loyalty to their favorite team, intention to purchase team-related merchandise, and a tendency to consume sport-related media (Trail & James, 2001). Similar trends have been observed in other fandoms, with aesthetics motivating anime and video game cosplayers (Loteki, 2012; Reysen et al., 2018a), fans of *My Little Pony* (Edwards et al., 2019), and members of other media-related fandoms (Schroy et al., 2016). In each of these groups, artistic appreciation for interest-related content was a significant driver of fans' interests.

Music and Poetry

Music fans, both in general and of a particular genre or artist, often experience feelings of awe, an aesthetic experience also common among those viewing visual art (Silvia et al., 2015). In fact, in a study looking at reactions to visual scenes and musical pieces with respect to their capacity to elicit aesthetic experiences, the authors found that those higher in openness to experience were more likely to experience awe while listening to music than they were to viewing visual scenes.[1] Speaking more to the role of individual differences in aesthetic experiences, empathy is associated with aesthetic appreciation in unfamiliar, sad music (Eerola et al., 2016). Three responses, in particular, were associated the with sad music: Relaxing sadness, associated with peaceful and positive experiences, moving sadness, characterized as existential and salient sadness, and nervous sadness, associated with anxiety or fear.[2]

In a manner analogous to music fans, fans of poetry similarly appreciate the aesthetics of their interest, as outlined by Knoop and colleagues (2016). In their work, the authors found that assessments of poetry and music are the most similar when it comes to measures of aesthetic response to different interests. One reason why poetry and aesthetic appreciation may go hand in hand stems from the fact that poetry's form is, itself, often considered to be aesthetic, especially when a poem uses systematic recurrence or repetition throughout. Menninghaus and company (2017) use an example from Shakespeare: "All days are nights to see till I see thee." This fairly small line contains a multitude of aesthetically intriguing features, including iambic meter, all of the words consisting of one syllable, repetition of words ("see"), words with similar endings, alliteration, and even a paradox. When poems use these features, emotional responses and aesthetic evaluations are heightened (Menninghaus et al., 2017). More importantly, Kraxenberger and Menninghaus (2017) note that a person's appreciation for poetry as a medium also weighs heavily on how they rate the aesthetic quality of a poem, with highly-identified poetry fans experiencing greater aesthetic appreciation for a piece of poetry than non-fans do.

Sport

While music and poetry are aesthetically appealing by design, it might be challenging to argue that sporting events, rooted first and foremost in the spirit of competition, are, themselves, artistic and aesthetic experiences. Even so, in a meta-analysis of 119 studies, aesthetics emerged as the strongest motivator for

---

[1] In case you were wondering, the song in question was "Hoppipolla" by Sigur Rós.
[2] According to Fleischer (2015), these experiences, while potentially intense, may be unstable or transitory due to the mass production and readily-available state of music streaming online, which can create a "musical superabundance" (p. 256) that desensitizes listeners from appreciating the aesthetic experience of an individual piece of music.

fans to attend a sporting event (Kim et al., 2019).[3] We can see the resilience and generalizability of this relationship through a few representative studies:

- In Kwon and Trail's (2001) work, aesthetics was the second-strongest motivator of sport viewership
- In a study of Indian sport fans, aesthetics was ranked third overall as a motivator of fan experience, and was especially impactful on Indian women, who watched sports for their creative expression (Yousaf et al., 2015)
- Among Israeli football (soccer) fans, aesthetic appeal was significantly positively associated with team identification (Cohen, 2017)
- American baseball fans not only identify more with their team than Japanese fans do, but they also prioritize aesthetics more as well; in contrast, Japanese fans were much more motivated by family and social motivations (James et al., 2009)
- Even in a rough-and-tumble sport like roller derby, fans are especially drawn to the aesthetic experience—more so even than baseball fans are to baseball (Pugh et al., 2019)
- High-identifying fans of equestrian sport were more motivated by the aesthetics of the sport than were low-identifying fans; among high-identifying fans, aesthetics was second only to entertainment as a motivating factor (Daniels & Norman, 2005)

When it comes to fans' motivation to watch specific sports, Wann and Wilson (1999) originally believed that fans motivated by aesthetics would prefer non-aggressive sports, in part because other facets of aggressive sports (e.g., excitement and eustress) might be more salient and because aggression itself might not be especially appealing aesthetically. On the contrary, however, aggressive sport fans are motivated by aesthetics just like fans of other sports are. To explain this, Brett (2017) argues that there are particular aesthetics that mixed martial arts (MMA) fans appreciate. To better understand this, Brett proposed two thresholds in the response to violence: repugnance and transcendence. Fans fall into repugnance when violence is too excessive or one-sided, or when the violence observed is against the rules. In such situations, violence shifts fans from being entertained by the spectacle to concern for the victims of the violence. However, when violence becomes transcendent, fans describe the matches as sublime experiences, marveling at the skill, technique, and ability of the fighters. Indeed, in the work of Seungmo and their colleagues

---

[3] According to Wang and colleagues (2013), however, the relationship is not a simple one, and may be moderated by other factors, such as the well-being of the person watching the sport.

(2008), who analyzed the motivations of MMA fans attending events, aesthetics was the third-highest motive, behind only drama and interest in the sport itself.

Sport researchers have also considered whether the appeal of aesthetics to sport fans also holds for fans of e-sports. Studies seem to suggest that this is the case: At least one study has found that the motivations driving e-sport event attendance are similar to those of traditional sport fans, including a similar tendency for aesthetics to predict event attendance (Pizzo et al., 2018). One difference among e-sport fans, however, is the fact that online viewers are more motivated by aesthetics than in-person viewers are (Sjöblom et al., 2020).

Video game fans—that is, fans of non-competitive, solo game experiences—are likewise motivated by aesthetics. For example, Oliver and company (2015) found that engaging with the stories and relating to the game leads to greater aesthetic appreciation for it beyond merely enjoying the game. Games with artistic environments for players to interact with further tap into this aesthetic motivation and can yield better learning and retention of in-game tasks (Lohse et al., 2016). In studies of virtual reality games players enjoy the games more when they allow players to customize their appearance, and thus the aesthetic experience, of their in-game avatar (Cuthbert et al., 2019). In fact, one need not customize their own avatar to achieve this effect: Toh (2016) went one step further, showing that customizable features of the game (e.g., customizing the appearance of one's weapon) can be enough to satisfy aesthetically-motivated players.

Conclusion

As we've seen throughout this chapter, aesthetic appreciation of one's fan interest motivates fans, not only for "traditionally" aesthetic interests (e.g., poetry, music), but also for interests rarely considered in terms of their aesthetic appeal (e.g., video games and sports). Aesthetic motivation, in turn, predicts fan interest (e.g., fanship) and fan behavior (e.g., attending a game). For this reason, models of fan behavior should consider the aesthetic appeal of the activity for fans to more accurately predict fan-related variables.

Chapter 19
Knowledge

By definition, fans are people who are enthusiastic about their interests. As such, it would seem to follow that they would seek out and accumulate knowledge and expertise relevant to that interest (Reysen & Branscombe, 2010). While some of this knowledge acquisition undoubtedly occurs through engagement with the content and with other fans, some fans are motivated by this process of knowledge acquisition itself, which may drive them to seek out more interest-related content (Trail, Robinson et al., 2003). This may, in fact, be the appeal of fan-based websites, which provide fans with the knowledge and information they're looking for (Hur et al., 2007).

In short, fan activities often involve, and are frequently motivated by a desire for, some degree of learning or knowledge acquisition, fostered and supported by fan communities through archiving and knowledge-sharing behavior. In the present chapter we explore these ideas in the context of sport and video game fans. We then discuss fandoms as communities of practice that enable the learning and development of experts. Finally, we look at the role of knowledge seeking among fans in the development of information literacy skills.

Fandom Expertise

Expertise is defined as developing skills within a specific domain and maintaining those skills through deliberate practice for an extended period of time (e.g., Ericsson, 2014; Ericsson et al., 1993). Traditionally, expertise research has focused on how people become highly-skilled in highly-specific domains, including athletes (Swan et al., 2015), musicians (Ericsson et al., 1993), SCRABBLE players (Tuffiash et al., 2007), and taxi drivers (Maguire et al., 2000). More recently, however, researchers are beginning to recognize the expertise that fans develop with respect to their interests. Given their enthusiasm (Reysen & Branscombe, 2010), fans can spend hundreds or even thousands of hours engaging with, researching, and exploring their fan interest, an essential element in the development of expertise, albeit in a relatively underappreciated domain.

Below we review the limited research on fan-related expertise by considering two of the groups in which it has been most studied: sport fans and video game fans.

Sport Fan Expertise

One of the most surprising findings in the research on sport fan expertise is the fact that sport fans who score high in sports-related knowledge demonstrate many of the same cognitive effects as other, more traditional experts. For example, in two studies of baseball fans, those scoring high in baseball-related knowledge experienced reduced ability to disambiguate words associated with baseball terminology relative to a low-knowledge control group (Wiley et al., 2018). Or, to put it another way, high-knowledge baseball fans found it harder to disambiguate a word like "bats" than low-knowledge controls, who found the task rather simple. In another study by Ricks and Wiley (2010), baseball fans high in baseball-related knowledge were presented with plausible player/position phrases: "The reliever is at the mound;" The manager is at the mound;" "The catcher is at the mound" (p. 2177). These phrases were then paired with implausible player/position phrases, such as: "The pinch runner is at second base;" "The reliever is at first base;" "The pitcher is at the bullpen" (p. 2177). The results found that high-knowledge fans were much more susceptible to the "fan effect," making more errors and taking longer to recall the implausible sentences than low-knowledge fans. In other words, their expertise was causing them to make predictable patterns of errors, a pattern similarly observed in volleyball fans (Tomasino et al., 2012). Together, these studies demonstrate that the acquisition of domain-specific expertise operates the same in expert fans as it does for experts in other domains as exhibited by fans' developing the same patterns of cognitive errors.

In the same way that non-sport experts can benefit from their expertise (e.g., becoming a highly-paid professional), sport fans can also use their fan-related expertise to their benefit. Fans can make use of their vast sport-related knowledge when betting on the outcomes of games, although they are far from immune to biases and as such, may not perform much better than chance (Cantinotti et al., 2004; Mercier et al., 2018; Na et al., 2019). A study of soccer suggests that expertise may provides fans with the illusion of control in their bets, rather than actually leading to better-than-chance performance (Khazaal et al., 2012), although this isn't always the case: When betting on horse races, fans with high domain expertise do perform better than chance, at least in the short run (Landouceur et al., 1998).

Video Game Expertise

Expertise researchers have also begun to consider expertise among video game fans. Game-related expertise has been found to coincide with a variety of other cognitive benefits including executive control (Li et al., 2020), spatial location memory recall (Bonny et al., 2016), reaction time and processing speed (Kowal et al., 2018), and fluid intelligence (Kokkinakis et al., 2017), at least when these variables are assessed in the context of playing video games (Kowal et al., 2018). As Röhlcke and colleagues (2018) note, time spent playing a video game predicts improved performance in a manner consistent with Ericsson's (1993) conceptualization of expertise as deliberate practice over time.

Other research has focused less on those who play video games and more on those who watch e-sports. Studies find, for example, that e-sport fans are often motivated by the acquisition of relevant knowledge (Carter et al., 2017), just as sport fans are similarly motivated, in part, by a desire to learn more about their favorite game (Pizzo et al., 2018). This same desire for knowledge is present in both online e-sport viewers and in live attendees (Sjöblom et al., 2019).

To this point we've noted that fans, regardless of their fan interest, can and do acquire specific knowledge and can become experts, in-line with what has been observed in more traditional studies of expertise. In the next sections we'll consider where this knowledge acquisition comes from and how fan communities themselves are structured in ways that facilitate knowledge acquisition.

Communities of Practice and Archiving

The concept of communities of practice is grounded in social learning theory and was developed by Wenger (1988) for use in the context of business and governmental institutions. The theory posits that learning occurs through social participation and has the side-effect of altering our sense of social identity in the process. Wenger (1988) outlined three factors at play in communities of practice: a shared sense of purpose, opportunities for engagement, and a relevant skill set. Steenkamp (2018) would later draw upon Wegner's work and apply it to the context of fandoms, arguing that fandoms operate as communities of practice through its members organizing, sharing domain-specific knowledge, and creating meaning. While evaluating online fan communities, Steenkamp speculated that when fandoms operate as communities of practice they grow and can sustain themselves. One such practice is through the act of archiving. In an exploration of Disney fans who archive relevant information for their fandom, Clément (2019) observed that archiving, interpreting, and disseminating fan-related knowledge is an important inter-group task undertaken by fans at all levels of fandom involvement. Clément also notes that this work is valued by the community, with some fans using their knowledge as a means to distinguish themselves as being higher in status than more "ordinary fans."

In his own work on fandom, Hills (2015) refers to this tendency for fans to engage in archivist work as archontic fandom. Hills notes, for example, that fans of *Doctor Who* developed the TARDIS Data Core, an archive of knowledge about the *Doctor Who* series which fans can contribute to and use as a reference. As the *Doctor Who* franchise continues to reinvent itself and become increasingly complex, the archive becomes increasingly important to fans, who rely upon it to keep abreast of changes in the series over time. In a similar fashion, fans of *The Elder Scrolls* franchise developed The Imperial Library to house and organize the vast amount of in-game text (Jansen, 2018).

Fans' motivation to engage in archiving behavior may stem from the unstructured nature of their interest's canon. As described by Jansen (2018), organizing and supplementing existing canon both provides fans with a sense of structure and cohesion for their fan interest while also providing status and prestige to those who do this work. While both Hills (2015) and Jansen (2018) discuss archontic fandom within Web 2.0 spaces, this behavior is far from a new phenomenon: Fans from the 1980s and 1990s, for example, would record television shows on their VCRs, doing so for similarly archivistic reasons (Bjarkman, 2004). The prevalence and persistence of this sort of behavior speaks volumes to the importance of organization, archiving, and, more generally, of fan-related knowledge to fans.

Information Literacy

Information literacy has become an increasingly essential set of skills for traversing the modern digital environment. This is especially true in an economy where knowledge is a currency unto itself, where consumers and producers are expected to "recognize when information is needed and have the capacity to locate, evaluate, and use [information] effectively" (Bundy, 2004, p. 3). Digital fandom, as both a community of practice and as a place where expertise can be developed, is no different in requiring information literacy among its members. As an illustrative example, information literacy is an essential skill for anime cosplayers who need to conceptualize, design, and perform their cosplay, relying heavily on techniques and hard-earned knowledge from others in the fandom (Lotecki, 2012). Speaking to the importance of information literacy in serious leisure, Demasson (2016) describes four functions of information literacy among fans: acquiring new information, helping share knowledge with the fandom, increasing self-awareness, and entertainment. Conceptualized thusly, information literacy is both a personally fulfilling process and is embedded within the structure of the fandom itself.

Speaking to the role of information literacy in a specific fandom, McMullen (2018) studied it in the context of music fans. Specifically, they looked at four categories of relevant behaviors:

- Giving information, which involves framing, sharing, and publishing information for others to find and use
- Seeking information, which involves searching and scanning information for utility

- Gathering information, which involves organizing and surveying collected information
- Communicating, which involves exchanging information with others and framing it within the social/context

Popular music fans were found to engage in all four behaviors online as a means of better understanding their interest, feeling closer to it, and sharing that information with other fans, fostering social connections.

Information literacy has also been shown to be important to video game fans, primarily those who play multiplayer games. A study of *Minecraft* players found that game-specific literacy developed as players provided one another with social and technical support (Arismendi, 2020). Additionally, after a 24-week period, *Minecraft* players showed an increase in media literacy skills more broadly (Morgan, 2015). Two studies of *World of Warcraft* players similarly found that information literacy skills were critical for effectively engaging with the game and with the game's fan community (Martin et al., 2012; Martin & Steinkuehler, 2010).

Conclusion

In the present chapter we summarized several bodies of scholarly work which all suggest that knowledge acquisition and the development of expertise is important to fans. Because fans are active and enthusiastic in their pursuit of their interests (Reysen & Branscombe, 2010), and because knowledge acquisition plays an important role in improving both individual engagement and social interaction with other fans (Hur et al., 2007; Trail, Robinson et al., 2003), fan communities have developed sophisticated systems of knowledge exchange. Through these systems of exchange, which incorporate communities of practice (e.g., archiving: Hills, 2015; Steenkamp, 2018) and emphasize information literacy skills (McMullen, 2018), fans learn knowledge and acquire the skills needed to become more informed fans. As a result, sport fans and video game fans alike can become experts and show the same cognitive markers of expertise that researchers find in more traditional experts (Röhlcke et al., 2018; Tomasino et al., 2012).

Taken together, the research makes it clear that fans not only acquire interest-related knowledge over time, but are motivated to pursue their interests because they provide them with the opportunities to learn, grow, and contribute to a collective body of knowledge. Despite being commonly overlooked as a motivator of fan behavior, it is important for researchers to consider fans' drive for knowledge acquisition in studies aiming to better understand fan attitudes, motivations, and behavior.

Chapter 20
Self-Esteem

Numerous social psychological theories are based on the premise that people are motivated to create and maintain positive self-evaluations through their own actions and through the groups to which they belong (Hoyle et al., 1999; Sedikides & Gregg, 2003; Vignoles et al., 2006). As an example, this idea underpins terror management theory, which posits that self-esteem buffers people against the existential fear of death (Burke et al., 2010; Pyszczyski et al., 2015). It's also a crucial part of social identity theory, where Tajfel and Turner (1979) argue that people seek to belong to groups that ultimately reflect well on and bolster their self-esteem.

Given the importance of self-esteem as a fundamental motivator of human behavior, the present chapter considers the association between self-esteem and both fanship and fandom. First, we briefly review ties between psychological theories involving self-esteem and the concept of fanship in general. We then delve into specific associations between self-esteem and fanship, including the association between self-disclosure of one's fan identity and self-esteem and self-esteem in the context of celebrity worship. Throughout it all, we'll see the crucial role that self-esteem plays in fanship and fan behavior, a finding very much in line with what we would predict based on existing social psychological research (e.g., Tajfel & Turner, 1979).

Self-Esteem and Fan Identification

As you'll recall from Chapter 7, researchers utilizing Tajfel and Turner's (1979) work on social identity theory distinguish between individual self-esteem and collective self-esteem. When it comes to individual self-esteem, people seek to create and maintain positive evaluations from others belonging to valued groups. When it comes to collective self-esteem, people contrast the groups they belong to against other groups to gauge their value, doing so strategically so as to maximize their own sense of value. These concepts, as well as social identity theory in general, were devised to apply broadly to all social groups, meaning the same principles that apply to religious, political, or national groups should also apply to fan groups.

For example, we can see evidence of the importance of individual self-esteem to fan behavior if we imagine a sport fan's favorite team wining a championship. The fan probably feels a sense of vicarious pride from their team's accomplishment, despite not being a member of the team themselves (for more on this see Chapter 21). We can also see evidence of collective self-esteem in the tendency of sport fans to, all else equal, draw closer to winning teams and distance themselves from losing teams (Bizman & Yinon, 2002). By being a member of the more desirable group, fans can make downward social comparisons to other, less-desirable groups, bolstering their own sense of worth (Reysen & Shaw, 2016). Fans have also been shown to engage in ingroup favoritism, giving preferential treatment to fans of their own interest over fans of other interests (Edwards et al., 2019), a finding which would also be predicted by social identity theory.

Taken together, there is ample reason to believe that fans gain self-esteem benefits from their identification with a fan group. In fact, evidence suggests that fans structure their fan identities around the self-esteem enhancing aspects of their fandoms (Vignoles et al., 2006). For this reason, we would expect self-esteem to play a motivating role in driving fanship and fandom, as well as to motivate participation in fan-related activities.

Self-Esteem as Fan Motivation

In his research on the factors motivating sport fanship, Wann (1995) identified eight possible motivators, one of which was self-esteem. If, indeed, self-esteem motivates fanship, it should be possible to find positive associations between fans' self-esteem scores and their identification with their sport or with a particular team. Speaking to this point:

- Self-esteem is associated with fan identification and fan-related behavior in varsity sport fans (Wann, Schrader, & Wilson,1999; Wann, Brame et al., 2008)
- In a study of Turkish sport fans, Sari et al. (2011) found that commitment to one's team predicts greater self-esteem
- Greek soccer fans were motivated by self-esteem regardless of whether the team was a local one or a distant one (Lianopoulos et al., 2020)
- Hu and Tang (2010) found that self-esteem motivation positively predicts fan identification in a sample of Taiwanese baseball fans.
- Higher self-esteem motivation predicts less switching of favorite teams and greater team loyalty in a sample of Taiwanese sport fans (Yun-Tsan, 2017)
- Self-esteem motivation is associated with engaging in fan-related activities in a sample of e-sport fans (Cushen et al., 2019)

While research linking self-esteem motivation to fanship and fan behavior has primarily been done in the context of sport fans, similar results have been found in other fan groups (e.g., Edwards et al., 2019; Proudfoot et al., 2019; Ray et al., 2017; Schroy et al., 2016). Alongside other motivations, such as entertainment-seeking, desiring eustress, and wanting to belong to a group, satisfying one's need for self-esteem is among one of the strongest drivers of fan engagement for fans, sport or otherwise.

Disclosure and Self-Esteem

While we discuss the significance of disclosing one's fan identity at length in Chapter 25, we'll briefly discuss it here because of its relevance to self-esteem in fans. To understand this relevance, we turn to the rejection-identification model by Branscombe and colleagues (1999). In this model, the researchers lay out the paradox of identifying with a stigmatized and its implication for self-esteem. On the one hand, social identity theory posits that people gain much of their self-esteem through the groups to which they belong. On the other hand, when a group is highly-stigmatized, it represents a threat or liability to one's self-esteem.

As such, one might expect fans of stigmatized interests to avoid this problem by abandoning their fandoms and identifying instead with a different, higher status, group. This may not be easy, possible, or desirable to do in some cases. We know, for example, that racial minorities have little choice over whether they belonging to a stigmatized group. Likewise, while a member of a stigmatized religious group could change their affiliation, they might prefer not to do so if it would result in distancing from one's friends and family or lead to an existential crisis. And while we don't wish to equate fan identities with racial or religious identities, it is possible that, in at least some contexts, fans may analogously find it difficult (if not to the same extent) to disidentify with their interests for a multitude of reasons.

In such cases, the rejection-identification model predicts that instead of trying to abandon or switch one's group affiliation, group members may "double down" on the group, identifying more strongly with it. Despite the stigma they experience, they may nevertheless find resilience through the social support of their similarly-suffering cohort and may even reframe the stigma as a source of self-esteem. For example, a person who grew up in a low-income neighborhood may flip the stigma of being impoverished into a positive by espousing the virtues of anti-materialism.

With this in mind, let us consider members of stigmatized fan groups. On the one hand, they could deny or conceal their fan identification to avoid the stigma associated with belonging to a fringe or non-mainstream fan group (Plante et al., 2014a; Reysen & Shaw, 2016). This strategy is adopted by at least some fans, who limit the people they discuss their fan identification with (e.g., Edwards et al., 2019) out of fear of harassment, rejection, or bullying. According to the minority stress model (Meyer, 2003), however, concealment can worsen self-esteem and lead to worse psychological health in the long run compared to people who are able to be open about their stigmatized identity (DeJordy, 2008; Frable et al., 1990; Lane & Wegner, 1995; Miranda & Storms, 1989; Pachankis, 2007; Quinn & Chaudoir, 2009; Smart & Wegner, 1999).

For this reason, instead of concealing their stigmatized fan identity, some fans embrace it, increasing both their fanship and their self-disclosure, an act which brings them closer to their fellow fans and, by extension, provides them with greater social support. This has been observed in members of stigmatized media fans (Reysen & Shaw, 2016) who report greater feelings of self-esteem and acceptance (Mock et al., 2013), belongingness (Tague et al., 2020), and well-being (Reysen et al., 2018b, 2018c) to the extent that they disclose their stigmatized fan identity to others.

To summarize, while fan identity is often associated with the self-esteem benefits that come with group membership more generally, the relationship is far from a simple one. When one's fan identity is stigmatized, it can be just as much a liability for one's self-esteem as it is an asset. To get a complete picture of the association between fan identification and self-esteem, one must consider factors like stigma, identity concealment, and the benefits and drawbacks of fan group membership, which may differ across fandoms and from fan to fan within a given fandom.

Celebrity Worship

In this final section we consider the somewhat contentious body of research linking self-esteem to celebrity worship, a topic we discuss in greater depth later in this book (e.g., Chapters 26-28). On the one hand, evidence suggests that those who engage in intense celebrity worship also tend to have higher self-esteem (Ashe et al., 2005; North et al., 2007). This makes a certain amount of sense if the worship involves a parasocial component, where fans feel a sense of attachment or connection with the celebrity. To put it simply, a person has to feel pretty good about themselves to imagine that a celebrity would be drawn to them over any of their countless other adoring fans. Indeed, research shows that celebrity worship is associated with fans' rating of their own attractiveness (Swami et al., 2011), suggesting that high self-esteem fans may "shoot for the stars" and imagine themselves with their favorite celebrities.

On the other hand, evidence suggests just the opposite, that self-esteem is negatively associated with celebrity worship (Cheng, 1997; Chia & Poo, 2009; Reeves et al., 2012). One can imagine, for example, that insofar as a parasocial relationship with a celebrity represents a means of compensating for feelings of loneliness or a lack of face-to-face interaction with others, it may be associated with lower self-esteem.

The matter is confused further still by studies which find no association whatsoever between celebrity worship and self-esteem (Engle & Kasser, 2005; Liu, 2013; Maltby & Day, 2011). One possible interpretation of these findings is that the two phenomena really are unrelated, and that studies to the contrary represent the exception rather than the rule—variability in the estimation of a null effect. Another possible interpretation is that there are important and, as of yet untested, moderators impacting whether the association between self-esteem and celebrity worship. Failing to take such moderators into account could lead to an "averaging out" of positive and negative effects, giving the appearance of there being no association.

For now, there is insufficient evidence to suggest that any of these answers is more correct than the others, and more research is clearly needed on the subject. For now, however, we can say that the question of celebrity worship—a form of fanship—and its association with self-esteem is being considered by fan scholars and that its answers may prove important, both to understanding those who worship celebrities as well as to understanding fans more generally (e.g., the distinction between healthy and pathological fan behavior, a point we return to in Chapter 27).

Conclusion

The field of social psychology views self-esteem as a crucial human need, something apparent by its presence in numerous highly-influential social psychological theories (e.g., social identity theory, terror management theory). Given this importance, we considered the role that self-esteem may play in fan-related phenomena, including fanship and fan-specific behaviors. We also reviewed the complexity of these associations with respect to stigmatized identity concealment and celebrity worship, emphasizing that more research is needed on the role of self-esteem in fandoms, but hinting at the potential importance of self-esteem for models aiming to better understand fans and fan behavior.

Chapter 21
Desirability

In the previous chapter we discussed how fans may be motivated to pursue their fan interests, in part, because those fan interests provide them with a sense of self-esteem. In the present chapter we expand upon this idea by discussing the related concept of desirability, or public collective self-esteem—belonging to a group that is viewed favorably by others. We begin by defining collective self-esteem and once again drawing upon social identity theory to understand the implications of collective self-esteem for the well-being of fans. We then consider how members of stigmatized fan groups—fan groups low in desirability—engage in impression management strategies to counteract the negative effects of stigma.

Collective Self-Esteem

To understand the concept of collective self-esteem, we once again turn to Tajfel and Turner (1979) and social identity theory, which posits that people are motivated to belong to desirable groups in service of their self-esteem. This collective self-esteem, or the aspects of one's sense of worth that come from their group membership, was categorized into four distinct facets by Luhtanen and Crocker (1992):

- Membership esteem, which describes the extent to which a person actually considers themselves to be a member of the group
- Private esteem, which refers to how positively someone feels about being a member of a particular group
- Public esteem, which refers to how positively the group is viewed by the public, regardless of how a person personally feels
- Identity, which indicates how influential the group is on a member's own self-concept

While the original context for this work was not fan groups, fan researchers would adapt parts of the model for use in the context of sport fans. For example, Heere and James (2007) developed the TEAM*ID measure, a multidimensional construct which assessed fans' identification with their favorite sport team. One of its dimensions is referred to as public evaluation, or how positively fans believe their group is evaluated by outgroup members—a concept akin to what Luhtanen and Crocker would call public esteem. The measure has been used by other researchers, such as in samples of Australian soccer fans (Lock et al., 2014; McDonald et al., 2016) which found that fans' awareness of their team was associated with increased public evaluation and that some categories of fans (e.g., "community-focused fans") were driven to their interest precisely because of the positive public perception of the team.

Converging evidence for the importance of public esteem for fans comes from research linking fan identification to psychological well-being. According to the team identification-social psychological health model (TISPH), identifying with a local sport team directly increases self-esteem and psychological well-being (Wann, Dimmock et al., 2003; Wann, 2006a, 2006b; Wann et al., 2009; Wann & Weaver, 2009). Most presently relevant, the model predicts that fans of distant teams—who presumably are not looked upon fondly by fans of the local team—do not receive the same well-being benefits that local fans do. Support for this assertion has been found in both American and non-American fans (Wann, Dimmock et al., 2003; Wann, Dunham et al., 2004), as well as both in university classrooms, dormitories, and attending university sporting events (Wann, Durham et al., 2004; Wann, Walker et al., 2005).[1] Other studies of sport fans find that attending fan-related events bolsters the benefits of team identification (Wann, Brame et al., 2008; Wann, Martin et al., 2008) by, among other things, creating a sense of public esteem, a finding which has also been observed in non-sport fans (e.g., Reysen et al., 2017b).

Avoiding Stigma through Impression Management

As we note elsewhere in this book (e.g., Chapter 25), fan groups are not perfectly interchangeable in the eyes of the public: Some fan communities are considered normal or desirable, while others are considered deviant or degenerate (Reysen & Shaw, 2016). Fans of mainstream interests such as football, video games, The Beatles, or Harry Potter benefit from the prototypicality of these interests—they're the sorts of interests that come to mind when people imagine a fan. In contrast, fans of more fringe or less-popular interests like the Insane Clown Posse, *My Little Pony*, or Barbie dolls suffer from the non-prototypicality of their interests and are perceived as abnormal. These fans of unusual interests may struggle with issues of public esteem, especially if faced with unflattering portrayals of their interest in the media or hostility toward their interest from the general public.

In these low-desirability fan groups, members may engage in impression management strategies to reduce the stigma directed toward their fandom and improve its public perception (Schlenker, 1980). Leary and Kowalski (1990) posit that this impression management is a two-component process that involves both impression motivation and impression construction. Impression motivation

---

[1] There is some evidence to the contrary, however, with at least one study suggesting that fans of distant teams do, in fact, receive the same well-being benefits as local fans (Lianopoulos et al., 2019).

refers to monitoring public impressions and trying to close the gap between the desired impression and the current public image. Impression construction refers to the impression that one is trying to create. Viewed through this theoretical lens, fans of stigmatized interests are motivated to engage in behaviors aimed at creating a more desirable, mainstream-appealing image of their fandom to reduce the discrepancy between how fans see their fandom (i.e., positively) and how society at large views their fandom (i.e., negatively).

There is some preliminary evidence to suggest that fans of stigmatized communities do exactly that. For example, Reysen, Plante, Chadborn and colleagues (2021) found that members of stigmatized media-based fandoms perceive themselves as stigmatized and often selectively disclose their identities to others to avoid negative evaluation. These stigmatized perceptions are not illusory, as other studies have shown that outgroup members do, indeed, tend to see these fans as detached from real life and socially awkward (Reysen, Plante, Roberts, Gerbasi, Mohebpour, & Gamboa, 2016). Fans are thus motivated to behave in ways that counter these stereotypes. They may, for example, emphasize the charity and social justice work their fandom does to demonstrate warmth and social awareness. As an example of this in the anime fandom, fans promote norms of empathy, social justice, and prosocial behavior (Reysen, Katzarska-Miller et al., 2020), all of which may help to rehabilitate the image of anime fans. Similar acts of charitable giving, concern for others, empathy, and helping have been observed in other stigmatized fan communities (Chadborn et al., 2016; Edwards et al., 2019; Plante, Chadborn, Groves, & Reysen, 2018).

Taken together, the paucity of research applying an impression management framework to fan cultures suggests that fans may engage in prosocial behavior, in part, as an impression management strategy to improve the public evaluation of their fandom. To be fair, it's also likely that fans engage in charitable giving and prosocial behavior as a virtue in and of itself. But it probably helps that these behaviors also improve the desirability of the group which, in turn, improves the fandom's ability to satiate fans' need for collective self-esteem.

BIRGing, CORFing, BIRFing, CORSing, and GORFing

According to Tajfel and Turner (1979), an important part of collective self-esteem is the need for a group to maintain a high level of status; if not, ingroup members will struggle to feel positively about their membership in the group (Ellemers et al., 1999). Using sport fans as an illustrative example, one easy way to gain status and feel positively about a team in to be in the enviable position of winning frequently or even being league champions. But, as research shows, a team's performance directly influences fans' willingness to associate with the team, even among highly-identified fans (Bizman & Yinon, 2002), meaning that teams which have a poor season may put fans in a difficult situation, representing a threat to their self-esteem. To better understand how fans derive the most benefits from teams' successes and preserve their identity's desirability in the face of failures, researchers have found evidence of five different identity management strategies called BIRGing, CORFing, BIRFing, CORSing, and GORFing.

Basking in reflected glory (BIRGing) was first described by Cialdini and his colleagues in 1976. The authors found that college football fans would wear their school's colors more after their team won a game than after they lost, a finding that was replicated decades later (Jensen et al., 2016), demonstrating its robustness. In the case of BIRGing, fans capitalize on the desirability of their team after a victory and experience increased collective self-esteem as a result.

When one's team loses, fans may engage in a second strategy to preserve self-esteem called cutting-off-reflected-failure (CORFing; Snyder et al., 1986). In CORFing, fans do the exact opposite of BIRGing: they distance themselves from the team, leaving their team colors at home and choosing to compartmentalize and limit that facet of their identity, since it represents a liability to their self-esteem. As one would expect, highly-identified, lifelong fans are more likely to BIRG than CORF, while less-identified fans (e.g., bandwagon fans) are more likely to CORF than to BIRG (Wann & Branscombe, 1990), although at least one study has challenged this association (Trail et al., 2012).

Beyond BIRGing and CORFing strategies to protect public esteem, Campbell and company (2004) introduced two additional, somewhat counterintuitive strategies, called basking in spite of reflected failure (BIRF) and cutting off reflected success (CORS). BIRFing is described as a demonstration of extreme loyalty in fans who, despite their team's losses, maintain positive feelings toward their team. Studies show that highly-identified fans are the most likely to BIRF (Aiken & Campbell, 2005), as seen in a study of Chicago Cubs fans. Recall from Chapter 14 that the Chicago Cubs are a baseball team which, until recently, were renowned for their prolonged inability to win the world series. The study found that the most highly-identified Cubs fans were the ones who engaged in the most BIRFing, demonstrating their die-hard loyalty to the team (Jensen et al., 2018). In doing so, Cubs fans earned the nickname of "lovable losers," a demonstration of admiration from outgroup members that allowed fans to preserve their self-esteem by steadfastly embodying the virtue of loyalty, a desirable trait.

In a strategy related to BIRFing, fans may also participate in CORSing to preserve an underdog identity or as a form of nostalgia for a team that consistently loses (Campbell et al., 2004). Speaking to this idea, Aiken and Campbell (2005) found a positive association between CORSing behavior and age, with older fans of a team being more likely to deny a team's wins because of nostalgia and tradition. In the wake of the Cubs' recent world series win after more than a century, it's likely that some long-time Cubs fans will find themselves CORSing to preserve their identity as the lovably loyal losers.

In a final identity management strategy, fans may engage in glory out of reflected failure (GORF), a phenomenon wherein fans experience a boost in self-esteem after seeing their despised rivals lose to another team (Havard, 2014; Havard et al., 2019). GORFing can be considered a form of downward social comparison or schadenfreude, where fans delight in, and feel better about themselves after, the downfall of a rival, even if their own team was not responsible for the defeat (Havard et al., 2018). GORFing also occurs outside of sport fans spaces, such as when highly-identified fans of Disney theme parks celebrated the failure of a park owned by Universal Studios, a rival of Disney (Havard, Wann et al., 2020).

The existence of these different identity management strategies makes it clear that fan groups are an important enough part of fans' self-esteem, otherwise there would be no need for fans to engage in these strategies in the first place. In addition to situational influences on fans' use of these strategies, researchers have also suggested that individual differences (e.g., personality traits) and demographic variables (e.g., age) may influence fans' willingness to engage in some of these strategies (e.g., Brown-Devlin et al., 2018). These findings demonstrate just how complex the association between fans, group identification, and self-esteem, collective or otherwise, really is.

Conclusion

In the present chapter we explored the desirability of one's fan community, the effort fans put into preserving this desirability, and the impact of this desirability on fan well-being. We saw how collective self-esteem plays an important role in maintaining the psychological well-being of ingroup members (Wann, Dimmock et al., 2003; Wann, 2006a, 2006b; Wann, Keenan et al., 2009; Wann & Weaver, 2009) and that fans can maintain their collective self-esteem by selectively interpreting their favorite team's wins and losses. We also saw that members of stigmatized fan communities are motivated to manage outsiders' perception of their fandom as a means of counteracting stigma (Leary & Kowalski, 1990; Schlenker, 1980). Considered within the broader framework of social identity theory, this chapter concludes, as did the previous chapter, that fans are highly motivated to maintain a positive self-image through their fan groups, and may engage in an interesting variety of behaviors and mental gymnastics to do so. For this reason, group desirability is a variable worth keeping in mind for researchers looking to study fan behaviors and distinctions between fan groups, in particular differences between desirable, mainstream fan groups and stigmatized, fringe fan groups.

Chapter 22
Economic Motivation

Money makes the world go round. It's a sentiment that reverberates through song lyrics and in the lay philosophies of the rich and the poor alike. At its core, the statement posits that human behavior—societies and individuals alike—is driven by monetary incentive. But does this notion, which seems self-evident when it comes to our professional lives, also hold true for our leisure and recreation activities? Are the things we do for fun really motivated by profit?

Early theorists postulated that economic motivations for fandom engagement stem from a combination of American pro-capitalist sentiments and from being socialized to prioritize economics and partake in risky behavior (e.g., gambling), especially among men (Chorbajian, 1978; Smith & Abt, 1984). Years later, researchers empirically studying the motivations of sport fans suggest that our hobbies and a drive for profit can occasionally co-exist (Wann, 1995).

The bulk of the research on the economic motivations of fans has focused specifically on gambling behavior in sport fans (Braverman et al., 2011; Hobson, 2015; Mahan et al., 2012; Mercier et al., 2018; Mowen et al., 2009). Other work has focused not on economic motivations specifically, but rather on the relative importance of economic motivation compared to other motivations in different fan groups (Schroy et al., 2016). With this in mind, this chapter focuses on economic motivations as a driver of fan behavior, focusing particularly on sport fans and gambling behavior, but also considering a fruitful direction for future research: Other, non-gambling ways that profit economically from their fan interests.

Gambling

According to Smith and Abt (1984), adult men have a propensity for gambling that can be traced to growing up in an American society that prioritizes capital accumulation and to engaging in childhood play which encourages risk-taking and gambling. In their work, the authors use the example of marbles, a childhood game in which children wager their own marbles to potentially acquire those of their opponent.[1] As children develop, Smith and Abt argue, their preferences shift to more complex games that retain similar gambling mechanics (i.e., poker, craps, slot machines).

Fan activities are only a stone's throw away from these ideas: The same logic driving children from playing marbles to casino games can also explain, in part,

---

[1] Other examples from the authors' own youth include Pogs, Crazy Bones, and collectable card games.

how kids find themselves growing up into fans whose interests are incentivized by the potential economic benefits those interests afford. We can see this, for example, in the global sport gambling industry, which has an estimated value of $80 to $380 billion (Hobson, 2015). Most would agree that gambling is part of the sport fan community, whether one personally engages in gambling or not.

As a counterpoint, some might argue that those who gamble on sports are not "real fans," and that their profiting off their interest distances them from it or undermines their interest in the sport, the team, or the fan community. Research suggests otherwise, however: Sport fans who gamble on the outcomes of games tend to be more involved with, and identify more strongly with, their favorite team as compared to those who don't gamble (Mowen et al., 2009). And while this team identification might not be related to the amount of money fans are willing to gamble, it is related to fans' tendency to participate in the act of gambling in the first place (Mahan et al., 2012).[2] As for whether sport fan identification predicts problematic or extreme gambling behavior, while it's true that young, single men are among the most likely demographic to both have gambling problems and to be sport fans (Hing et al., 2016), research also suggests that sport fans who gamble tend to be less impulsive in their gambling habits than those with a gambling disorder (Braverman et al., 2011; Mowen et al., 2009).

In recent years, researchers studying sport fans have noted numerous parallels between sport fans and fans of e-sports, leading to questions about whether e-sport fans similarly gamble on the results of competitive video game leagues. As with fans of more traditional sports, younger men are the most likely to bet on outcomes of e-sports tournaments (Abarbanel et al., 2020). Also similar to sport fans, a desire for additional excitement (see Chapter 11 on eustress) is among the primarily drivers of e-sport related gambling (Denoo et al., 2021), with wagers adding an extra sense of weight to the games. Future research will likely further examine these parallels though, in all likelihood, e-sports is just a new outlet for the same interests and behavior.

Fantasy Sports: A Modern Way to Bet on Sports

As a more modern alternative to betting on the outcomes of specific sporting events, many sport fans go one step further, participating in fantasy sport leagues. In fantasy sports, fans build a hypothetical team roster from the league's current pool of athletes (Martin et al., 2020; Tacon & Vainker, 2017). Over the course of a season, players' fantasy teams "compete" against one

---

[2] Also worth noting, an interest in astrology predicts sport gambling behaviors, which may relate to the ingroup superstitions and rituals that sport fans engage in with respect to their favorite team (Mowen et al., 2009).

another via aggregated statistical data derived from the players' actual statistics during that season. Team scores are compiled and, at the end of the season (or however long the agreed-upon length of the fantasy season is) the fantasy team with the most points wins (Martin et al., 2020.) This basic fantasy sport league structure has been applied to a number of different team-based sports (e.g., soccer, volleyball, polo), but the most popular fantasy sport by far is American football.

Fantasy sports is far from being a niche hobby. According to a survey conducted by the Fantasy Sports and Gaming Association (2021), an equal number of sport fans (19%) participate in both sports-related betting and in fantasy sports,[3] with other research suggesting that these categories are distinct, but highly-overlapping (Mahan et al., 2012).[4] In fact, an estimated 45.9 million Americans and Canadians participate in fantasy sports (Fantasy Sports & Gaming Association, 2021). With the average fan investing $653 in fantasy sports in their lifetime, the fantasy sport industry may be worth as much as $26 billion. Much of this investment takes the form of entrance fees paid to the fantasy sport league for each team submitted, which is then redistributed to the winners at the end of the season. And, as one might imagine, these payoffs represent much of the impetus for participation.

Fantasy sports are also financially lucrative for those besides the fans who participate in them. It's not uncommon, for example, for fantasy teams and fantasy leagues themselves to have corporate sponsors. As such, fantasy sports are often considered a form of consumer behavior, one where fans' economic and social motivations are funneled into profits for the owners of fantasy sports leagues and for those lucky few who win (Flanigan, 2014; Tacon & Vainker, 2017).

Like gambling on individual sporting events, those who participate in fantasy sport leagues, drawn in by the allure of economic incentives, might be assumed to be "lesser" fans than those whose interests are motivated by love of the game itself. However, studies of fantasy sport fans are comparable to those of sports bettors, with those who engage in fantasy sports identifying more strongly with the sport as well as with the professional leagues (e.g., the National Football

---

[3] Practical considerations, such as legality, may lead to an underestimation of actual interest in fantasy sports. For example, in the same 2021 study by the Fantasy Sports and Gaming Association, 79% of fantasy sport fans indicated that they would be more likely to participate in sport-related betting if their state were to legalize it.

[4] In a study further elaborating on this point, Houghton and colleagues (2019) found that more materialistic fans are more likely to engage in sport betting while less-materialistic fans tend to prefer fantasy sports.

League) than those who don't engage in fantasy sports, with the caveat that they may not identify as strongly with a real team, choosing, instead, to focus on their own fantasy team (Lee et al., 2013). Flanigan's 2014 study goes one step further, finding that fantasy players are not only more loyal to their favorite team, but are also more likely to consume team- and sport-related products. Supporting this position, the Fantasy Sports and Gaming Association (2021) reports that fantasy sport fans are more likely than other fans to visit a sports bar and consume athletics-related products (e.g., shoes).

In short, the available evidence suggests not only that a many sport fans partake in fantasy sports, but that most of these fans are among the most highly-identified fans. Converging evidence for this conclusion comes from demographic data which shows that, similar to sport gambling, those who participate in fantasy sports are primarily young, middle class men (Roy & Goss, 2007; Ruihley & Billings, 2012) high in football-related knowledge (Lee, Kwak et al., 2011). Of course, this doesn't mean that women don't participate in fantasy sport leagues: The same studies suggest that women make up about 20% of fantasy sport fans. A qualitative investigation by Blain (2014) suggests that some of the reasons for this smaller proportion of women include gender-related gatekeeping, not having enough time, and not having friends to participate with.

This research should also not be taken as a suggestion that fantasy sport fans are driven solely by economic incentive. For example, several of the studies above also found that fantasy sport fans are also motivated by other, non-economic interests (e.g., self-esteem, team identification). Even so, it's hard to deny the centrality of economic incentives as a motivation for sport-related betting and engaging in fantasy sports.

Artistic Commissions and Fan Labor

We've spent most of this chapter discussing the economic benefits of fan-related gambling. And while gambling is the most-studied way to profit from one's fan interest, it's far from the only way one can do so. Theoretical work agrees with this notion, arguing that fandoms allow for the transfer of cultural capital, unlike the purely economic capital one earns from work (Duchesne, 2005; Fiske, 1992; Geraghty, 2014; Jenkins, 1992). As an illustrative example of what an exchange of cultural capital might look like, Fiske (1992) describes fan communities operating as a shadow cultural economy where discussions, writings, art, and collecting are exchanged between fans in a series of symbiotic relationships that exclude corporations (e.g., TV networks). As Godwin (2016) notes, however, there is also economic capital to be gained from fandom behavior, such as makers who create and sell customized one-sixth scale action figures.

But if these economic opportunities exist in non-sport fan spaces, and if fans can be motivated by such opportunities, why are they not more frequently discussed and studied in the academic literature? Noppe (2011) identifies three reasons. First, there is an aversion to describing fandoms as linked to commodity culture for fear of trivializing or reducing fan interests as mere materialism and encouraging corporations to meddle.[5] Second, fanart often exists in a precarious legal space, caught somewhere between fair use laws and copyright infringement. Lastly, many wish to idealize fan communities as gift economies despite obvious economic thresholds for participation in some fan spaces (e.g., the costs of attending fan conventions).

Regardless of what theoretical work says on the matter, one can find examples of financial incentive and economic motivation in specific fandoms. In media-based fandoms, for example, there is a vital and flourishing community of artists-as-vendors. These artists operate, according to Dodson (2020), according to neoliberal principles such as prioritizing individualism (e.g., commissioning art of original characters), commodifying ideas through purchasing representations of one's characters, and a deregulated art market wherein artists participate in a microcosm of the free market. Or, as Godwin (2016) might put it, original characters and their representations are cultural capital, but economic motivations are what drive artists to take on commissioned work and sell other commodities for the fandom at large to consume— with many making their living this way.

To date, there has been a relative dearth of research on the microeconomies of specific fandoms and on the relation between cultural capital and economic capital—especially in non-sport fandom. But the existence of markets and small, independent content creators who make their living off the fandoms while simultaneously being part of them speaks volumes to the need for more research. Researchers, fans, and content creators alike would benefit from further investigation of how these economies function and their role in the economic motivation driving at least some fans to their interest.

Conclusion

The present chapter investigated the role of economic incentives as a motivator of engagement in fan-related activities. As Wann (1995) notes, much of the research on economic motivation has been in the domain of sport fans, focusing on the role of sport-related gambling and, more recently, fantasy sports. Far from being at odds with one another, gambling and fantasy sports are

---

[5] Of course, this seems to ignore the fact that fans themselves are often defined, at least in part, by their consumption of fan-related commodities (e.g., media).

associated with fanship, rather than detracting from fans' interest. Of course, economic motivation is far from the strongest motivator of fan interests, although this may vary from fandom to fandom (e.g., media fans vs. sport fans) and from fan to fan (e.g., artists and content creators vs. passive consumers). The lack of work on non-sport fandoms needs to be addressed in future research to better understand both the role that economic motivation plays in predicting important fan-related variables and to help researchers better appreciate the broad range of activities that may satisfy fans' economic motivation.

Chapter 23
Accomplishment

Achievement refers to the sense of accomplishment and competence someone feels in response to something they've done. People feel a sense of achievement after completing a difficult or laudable task, usually accompanied by a wave of positive emotions (e.g., contentment, happiness, exhilaration). These positive emotions, coupled with a boost in self-esteem and the possibility of gaining social status, make the promise of achievement a powerful driver of human behavior. Given that achievement motivates human behavior ranging from athletic achievements to their careers to great works of art, we can ask whether it can motivate fans and interest-related behavior.

The topic has been studied primarily in sport fans. In this context, Fink et al. (2002) define vicarious achievement as "the need for social prestige, self-esteem and sense of empowerment that an individual can receive from their association with a successful team" (p. 198). In other words, sport fans can derive a sense of achievement vicariously, through the achievements of others related to their fan interest. The link between one's fan interest and achievement need not be vicarious, either. It's possible, for example, that non-sport fans may feel a sense of achievement through the production of a valued piece of fan art, through cosplay, or through their contribution to resources valued by other fans (e.g., wikis, forums).

In the present chapter we consider the possibility that a sense of accomplishment may drive such fan behaviors by reviewing research and theory relevant to achievement in fans. We begin with a brief review of fan labor, where fans engage in acts of productivity that, in and of themselves, may yield a sense of achievement. Next, we discuss examples of serious leisure (e.g., gardeners) who, in a similar vein, gain a sense of achievement through their own accomplishments. Shifting gears to sport fans, we then revisit basking in reflected glory (BIRGing) and self-determination theory and consider their application to understanding achievement as a motivator of sport fans. Finally, we look at research directly assessing vicarious achievement as a motivator of sport fans.

Fan Labor

Fan labor refers to any work (typically unpaid) that one carries out in association with their fan interest. Examples of fan labor include the creation of fan art, fan videos (e.g., music videos), fan fiction, or online podcasts about one's fan interest (Savit, 2020). Fan labor can also involve volunteering at fan-related events such as conventions (Peaslee et al., 2014) or moderating fan forums and chat rooms online. Disney fans engage in acts of fan labor when they collect and organize the history of Disneyland and act as custodians of this knowledge (Clément, 2019), as do media fans who construct meticulously-organized online repositories of knowledge about their favorite show (e.g., fan wikis). To put it simply, there's no shortage of fan labor to be found in fandoms.

Given that fans usually have full-time jobs or are full-time students, it's a wonder that they opt to give away their labor for free in their spare time. Studies suggest that at least part of the reason why is because of the sense of achievement fans derive from producing something, especially if the product is valued by other fans. For example, anime fans often report feeling a sense of achievement after all the work they put into constructing a cosplay (Wang, 2010). Fans who write and share online video game walkthroughs note feeling a sense of pleasure from the achievement of what is, in most cases, a fairly lengthy process (Hughes, 2018). In a similar vein, those who create mods for video games report a sense of achievement, especially when their mod is recognized and revered by the gaming community (Moody, 2014; Poor, 2014). In effect, the labor fans expend creating something for, or contributing to improving, the fan community leads to positive feelings of achievement, feelings which can, in turn, make engaging in such behaviors self-reinforcing.

Serious Leisure

Back in Chapter 3 we learned that Stebbins (1982) coined the term "serious leisure," using it to describe the growing phenomenon of people taking their leisure activities, well, seriously (e.g., working to make money to support their leisure). In opposition to more casual leisure, Stebbins characterizes serious leisure as involving perseverance, making leisure activities into a career, requiring the application of effort and knowledge, strongly identifying with the fan community, and, most presently relevant, as being rewarding by providing fans with a feeling of accomplishment.

Gibson and colleagues (2002) drew upon the idea of serious leisure in a study of University of Florida football fans. There, they observed many of the hallmarks of serious leisure described by Stebbins, including fans' sense of achievement and happiness when their favorite team won. This same sense of accomplishment has been noted in interviews with others who do serious leisure, including recreational gardeners (Cheng & Pegg, 2016) and surfers (Sotomayor & Barbieri, 2016).

As Stebbins notes, another sign of serious leisure is that those who engage in it often take on an identity related to the interest. Put this way, serious leisure may be another way to describe highly-identified fans, which would ground this phenomenon squarely in the domain of social psychology (alongside concepts like BIRGing and self-determination theory).

Self-Determination Theory

So far we've talked about the need for achievement, but we've yet to show any evidence that achievement does, in fact, motivate human behavior. To understand how, we turn to self-determination theory (Deci & Ryan, 1980, 2000), which posits that humans have three important needs (competence, relatedness, and autonomy) that are essential for growth, well-being, and flourishing. Importantly, people are intrinsically motivated to take part in behaviors insofar as those behaviors satisfy these needs. For the present chapter, we'll focus primarily on the need for competence and the idea that, all else equal, people are more attracted to activities if those activities afford them the opportunity to gain and demonstrate a sense of competence.

As an illustrative example, imagine that someone works on a task and receives negative feedback on their performance. It's not hard to imagine that, if this were you, you might feel less intrinsically motivated to continue working on the task, especially when you imagine how motivated you would feel if you received positive feedback about your performance. Framed thusly, feeling a sense of achievement bolsters one's motivation to continue doing the thing that led to the sense of achievement. In the context of sport fans, if spectating when one's favorite team wins a game provides fans with a sense of vicarious achievement, this activity should satisfy their need for competence and therefore be sought out in the future. Vignoles et al. (2006) go one step further, suggesting that self-efficacy—or a sense of competence—is one of the main reasons why people belong to groups, fan groups or otherwise.

Tying self-determination theory more directly to fans, Ryan et al. (2006) studied video game fans and found that players' sense of competence was related to game enjoyment, well-being, and immersion. In other words, gamers' positive feelings about the game stemmed from the sense of competence and achievement that they provide. Qian et al. (2020) tied the idea even more directly to fans, surveying 1,100 e-sport fans and found that fans' degree of felt competence predicted both greater commitment to e-sports and more word-of-mouth transmission of e-sports to others. In short, the available evidence available suggests that the extent to which fan interests provide fans with a sense of achievement should impact fans' motivation to participate in fan-related behavior and to identify with the interest itself.

Basking in Reflected Glory

Elsewhere in this book (e.g., Chapter 12, Chapter 21) we've mentioned the concept of basking in reflected glory. Given its importance to the study of fan motivation, it's worth taking a brief detour to more fully describe the research, its findings, and its relevance to the topic of achievement in fans.

In their now-classic series of studies, Cialdini et al. (1976) examined undergraduate fans' connection to their varsity football team. In Study 1, every Monday, from the third to the last week of the college football season, the researchers counted the proportion of students in classes who were wearing clothing emblazoned with the symbol of their university. The researchers also noted whether the university's football team had won or lost a game that weekend. The results were clear across the seven universities in which the study was conducted: Students were more likely to wear a symbol of their university after a recent win than after a recent loss.

In a follow-up study, the researchers called students and asked them to do a short quiz. Students were randomly assigned to a positive or negative feedback condition, where they were told that they had either performed well on the quiz or not, respectively. The researchers then asked the students about the outcome of a recent game where the university's football team had either won or lost. The dependent variable was whether students would use the word "we" in their response to describe the team's performance (e.g., "we won," as opposed to "they won"). Students who received positive feedback on about their quiz performance, and thus presumably felt pretty good about themselves, showed no difference in their usage of the word "we" to describe their team after a win or a loss. The same could not be said for the students who were told they performed badly on the quiz. These students, who had just experienced a blow to their self-esteem, were more likely to reply with "we" to describe their team's win than they were when describing their team's loss, which they usually described by saying "they lost." Notably, this occurred despite the fact that none of the students were, themselves, players on the team: They were basking in reflected glory (BIRGing or, in the case of losses, cutting off reflected failure, CORFing).

Cialdini et al.'s research yielded decades of follow-up studies. For example, Snyder et al. (1986) asked U.S. college students to work in groups on a problem-solving task. After the task, the groups were told that they had either performed well, performed poorly, or were given no information at all about their performance (control condition). Participants were then given an opportunity to wear a team badge. In line with Cialdini's findings, if participants were told that they had performed well, they were more likely to wear the badge (BIRGing). The reverse was also true: if the team performed poorly, participants were less likely to wear the badge (CORFing).

Other creative examples abound in this literature. Fan, Billings et al. (2020), for example, analyzed tweets (coding for words like "we" and "us" vs. "they" "them") coming from fans after their team or the opposing team scored a goal. They found that BIRGing occurred more when fans' teams were winning (vs. losing). In a somewhat darker, but nevertheless fascinating study, Campbell et al. (2021) coded the obituaries of people who lived where a professional sport team had a winning and then losing season (or visa versa) to see whether the team had been mentioned. The results showed that the local team was mentioned more often in obituaries when they were having a winning (vs. a losing) season.

While BIRGing and CORFing have thus far been discussed in the context of sport fans, the effects are not limited only to sport fans. Miller (2009) found that after the 2008 U.S. presidential election, signs endorsing Barack Obama, the winner of that election, were displayed for longer than signs for his opponent, John McCain. Moreover, ratings of both candidates before and after the election showed an increase in Barack Obama's favorability (BIRGing) and a decrease in favorability of John McCain (CORFing), a trend that has continued in subsequent U.S. presidential elections.

BIRGing and CORFing, as we've discussed, are tied to one's sense of self-esteem (e.g., Lianopoulos et al., 2020). But it's also worth noting that these phenomena also reflect peoples' drive to feel a sense of achievement. As we've seen, fans seek to connect themselves with something or someone who has achieved something. For those who highly identify with the achiever, the achievement is experienced as their own, satisfying their need for achievement. While this is obvious in sport fans, the same may be true in non-sport fans, when the fan's movie, book, TV show, or band is viewed positively and becomes popular in mainstream media, fans may feel that they, themselves, can share in that accomplishment, perhaps even contributing to it in some small way. In line with the research from self-determination theory, this ability to derive a sense of achievement vicariously through one's fan interest may explain at least some of the motivation underlying at least some fans' interests.

Vicarious Achievement Motivation

While achievement was not included in Wann's (1995) frequently-used multidimensional measure of fan motivation, it has appeared in subsequent measures and models (Kahle et al., 1996; Milne & McDonald, 1999). Below, we highlight research using two different measures of fan motivation that explicitly include achievement as a motivator of sport fans to see whether research on sport fans has, in line with research on self-determination theory in video game fans, similarly reports an association between feelings of achievement and fan-related variables.

Trail and James

In Trail and James' (2001) sport fan motivation scale, one of the nine dimensions they assessed measured fans' feelings of achievement (e.g., "I feel like I have won when the team wins"). In a sample of U.S. baseball fans, specifically those who were season ticket holders, the authors found that achievement was positively correlated with team identification, loyalty, and consumption behavior. Subsequent research on basketball fans similarly found that, among the different motivations assessed, vicarious achievement was the strongest predictor of team identification (Fink et al., 2002).

Numerous other studies using fans of different sports from different regions have consistently shown the importance of vicarious achievement as a motivator of fan behavior. To list just some examples which have used variations of Trail and James' measure:

- In a study of U.S. college football fans, vicarious achievement was singled out among other motivations (e.g., aesthetics, knowledge) for its association with spectating behavior (Trail, Robinson et al., 2003)
- In a study of U.S. college basketball fans, achievement loaded more strongly onto a higher-order factor than did other motivations (Trail, Fink, & Anderson, 2003)[1]
- Achievement motivation predicted game attendance and watching games on television or online in U.S. college basketball fans (Chao, 2010), e-sport fans (Anderson, 2019; Sjöblom et al., 2019; Xiao, 2020), and in other fans (Kang et al., 2014; Kim et al., 2019)
- Achievement motivation is positively associated with watching and following sport- and e-sport-related media (Krier, 2017; Sjöblom et al., 2019; Xiao, 2020)
- Achievement motivation predicts greater intent to purchase merchandise in baseball fans (Park, Suh, & Pedersen, 2016) and in e-sport fans (Anderson, 2019)
- A study of undergraduate baseball fans found that vicarious achievement led to team identification which, in turn, was associated with BIRGing, suggesting that achievement-motivated fans choose to identify with winning teams and then express this association to others (Kwon et al., 2008)

---

[1] As a caveat, we should note that in terms of mean ratings, achievement is typically one of the lower-rated motivations—though this doesn't necessarily detract from its predictive utility or association with other important fan-related variables (Robinson & Trail, 2005; Robinson et al., 2004).

- A longitudinal study found that vicarious achievement predicts greater subjective well-being in fans (Kim & James, 2019)

Studies such as these reveal the robustness of fan achievement as a motivator of fan-related attitudes and behavior. However, it is possible, if unlikely, that these results may be an idiosyncrasy of Trail and James' scale. As such, we consider additional research using an second measure of fan achievement.

Funk et al.

In a 2003 study, Funk et al. used their own measure to assess motivation in fans of U.S. women's basketball. The results found, in line with the research above, that vicarious achievement predicts fans' level of support for their team. In subsequent studies using similar measures, vicarious achievement was also found to be correlated with team loyalty in the Chinese Professional Baseball League in Taiwan (Wang et al., 2011), team identification in baseball fans from South Korea and Japan (Won & Kitamura, 2006), intention to purchase merchandise in a sample of Turkish soccer fans (Yenilmez et al., 2020), and game attendance in Australian football fans (Neale & Funk, 2006). From football fans to Formula 1 fans (Ballouli et al., 2016), regardless of how vicarious achievement is assessed, the results are consistent: Fans who derive a sense of accomplishment from the sports they watch are driven to engage more strongly with those sports.

Conclusion

In the present chapter we reviewed research on fans and their felt sense of achievement. Fans, regardless of what their specific interest might be, often experience a sense of achievement from their interest, either from their own fan- or leisure-related labor or vicariously, through the achievements of their teams, as is the case with BIRGing sport fans. A wealth of research has looked at vicarious achievement as a motivator of fan-related attitudes, identity, and behaviors in sport fans and shows that, regardless of the specific sport, country, or measure used, achievement seems to motivate fan engagement. As such, there can be little doubt that achievement is a variable worth considering in any model looking to understand fan motivation, trying to predict fan behavior, or trying to distinguish between different types of fans.

Chapter 24
Exclusivity

Often, when we picture a fan, we imagine someone with a singular interest: A football fan decked out in their team's apparel, a fan of a particular musician cheering loudly at a concert, or a fan of a particular TV show cosplaying as their favorite character at a fan convention. And why shouldn't we? After all, fans are defined by their passionate interest in a particular topic, so it makes sense to conceptualize fans engaging in that singular interest.

However, nothing in the definition of fan necessitates that they are limited to just one interest. Or, to put it another way, there's no reason why the football, music, and TV show fan we just imagined couldn't be the same person. As the poet Walt Whitman famously noted, humans are complex and contain multitudes; this is just as true of our interests as it is for any other facet of human experience.

This being the case, it's rather surprising that there exists relatively little research looking at the variable of fan focus—that is, the tendency for some fans to focus their attention on a single interest while others divide their focus across numerous interests. Instead, the vast majority of fan research focuses on single fan interests in isolation, with relatively little consideration given for the other interests a fan may have (Delia, 2015). By doing so, researchers are missing out on the opportunity to compare those who do and do not focus their interest on a single fandom on other important fan variables. They also miss out on the opportunity to more broadly study the potential benefits (and drawbacks) of having multiple fan identities.

In the present chapter we explore what limited research exists on the subject of fan focus, considering different perspectives on the focused fan. We also, where possible, compare and contrast this work against research that does look at multiple fan groups or which considers fans with a multitude of different interests.

Assessing Singular Fan Identities

Most fan studies, in particular those from a social psychological perspective, have focused their attention on one fandom at a time. From older studies on railroad enthusiasts to fans of *Star Trek* and *Star Wars*, there is no shortage of studies which look at the behavior of members of a single fandom and use those observations to make universal claims about fans in general.

Of course, it was only a matter of time before researchers would begin to recognize the limitations of this approach, such as the fact that fans often belong to multiple fandoms, making it difficult to study fandoms in isolation tricky.

Some researchers responded by broadening their research focus to directly examine this phenomenon, looking at the psychology of having multiple fan identities in a way that builds upon social identity research (e.g., Heere & James, 2007; Trail, Fink et al., 2003).

In the wake of this growing awareness, however, some scholars noticed that there was a lingering, unanswered question: What about fans who really are fans of only a single interest? Unfortunately, there has not been an organized, concerted effort to systematically tackle this questions, although individual researchers have been slowly chipping away at facets of it. The works of Tapp and Clowes (2002) and Tapp (2004) represent perhaps the most comprehensive attempts to do so.

In Tapp and Clowes (2002), the researchers focused on creating a typology of fans and the researchers who study them. This was primarily done from a marketing and consumer perspective. For example, the authors note that sport fans identify more strongly with their favorite sport than the average consumer does with their favorite brands or commodities. Identification with a particular team turned out to be useful information for marketers, as those loyal to a single team were more likely to attend home and away games than were fans of multiple different teams (for more on this, see Chapter 14.) Focused fans were also more likely to say that their team winning was more important to them than the entertainment value of the game, although they still found games entertaining even when their team lost.

Tapp (2004) expanded upon Tapp and Cloves (2002). In this study, a number of highly committed, highly-focused fans revealed that their fan interests were highly important and significant in their lives. One such participant mentioned that if a fire were to break out in their house, they would run in to save their programs and tapes from attended games, pausing, as an afterthought, to add that they would also save their wife and kids. Focused fans tended to be older and more settled, with fewer other commitments and a history of engagement with the fan interest. Focused fans were also found to have the biggest overlap between their group identity and their self-identity, leading to bigger gains when their team was doing well, but also bigger blows to their self-esteem when their team was doing poorly.[1]

Focused Fans

In Tapp and Clowes' work we find differences between focused fans of a single interest (or fans with multiple interests but who have singled out one

---

[1] Focused fans were also compared to collectors, who not only committed to a team and attended events, but also acquired merchandise, demonstrating both behavioral and attitudinal loyalty to the team.

interest as central) and fans who more evenly distribute their focus across several interests. Completely focused fans are likely to be rare relative to fans with a more diverse set of interests, given that an important tenet of social identity theory is that people have multiple group identities (e.g., vocations and avocations, gender, political affiliation, religion, etc.) and that those who focus on a single facet of their identity tend to experience detrimental effects when their identities are challenged.

In more recent years, researchers have begun examining these rarer, highly-focused fans while studying individual fan communities. For example, Sotomayor and Barbieri (2016) examined different types of surfers by talking to shop owners. While many of these types did not appear to be defined by an exclusive focus on surfing, one group, described as beach bums, was notable in having dedicated their lives exclusively to surfing and to little else.

A study by Häkkänen-Nyholm (2020) went one step further, examining Bruce Springsteen fans that were either exclusive or highly-focused fans. Examining the 600 fans from the US, Canada, Europe, South America, and South Africa, the average length of their fan interest in Springsteen was 30 years, with an average attendance of 27 concerts. More than half of participants listened to his music daily and more than half reported that Springsteen's work comprised the majority of the music they listened to. These descriptions sound like indicators of highly-focused fans. The researchers found that these highly-focused fans, despite engaging in a form of celebrity worship toward Springsteen, did so in a largely non-pathological fashion (e.g., a Springsteen fanclub), and found that their intense interest grew milder with age.

Research on fan focus has also shown that fan interest exclusivity varies predictably with age and with identity development. Younger fans in particular tend to become more focused on singular fan interests. As an illustrative example, teenage and young adult fans of *My Little Pony* tended to strongly adhere to their identity as a fan of the show, seeing it as a defining feature of themselves, often to the exclusion of other interests—at least at first (Edwards et al., 2019). Over time, however, some of these fans branched out and explored other, related fan communities, or they would simply become less focused on their fan interest as other commitments like school, work, and family became priorities for them, representing a shift toward a more complex and multifaceted sense of identity.[2] As for those who entered the fandom when they were older,

---

[2] For some converging evidence, Lee, McMahan et al. (2015) found that gender roles and the expectations that come with them (e.g., providing for children) reduce the amount of focus people can devote exclusively to their fan interests and hobbies—in this case, birdwatching.

they were more likely to treat *My Little Pony* as just one of their many other interests.

In the case of Häkkänen-Nyholm's Springsteen fans, it's worth noting that many were older, but nevertheless focused fans, some having identified as fans for decades. Age, in this sense, may push fans toward a fork in the road: With time, fans may learn to branch out and develop other interests. For those who don't, they may become increasingly passionate and focused on their interest.

Focus and Serious Leisure

Serious leisure, as we mentioned in Chapter 3, refers to, among other things, fans who are highly-committed in their engagement with a particular interest (Stebbins, 1982). It differs from casual leisure, which tends to refer to popular or mainstream fan interests that are easily-accessible and which tend to involve less commitment. Using the example of Taekwondo students, Lee et al. (2005) note that students who persevere, discover meaning and knowledge from the sport, and become highly familiar with its intricacies can be said to be engaging in serious leisure. Compared to those who engage with an interest more casually, serious leisure practitioners are especially committed (and focused) to their interest.

Commitment is an important component of serious leisure as it describes the level of physical and psychological effort fans are willing to devote to its pursuit (Lee & Ewart, 2019). For non-committed fans, who lack skills, knowledge, and experience to engage in an activity in a fulfilling manner, they may not be able to maintain their interest or integrate into a fandom of more committed fans. Lee and Ewart used mountain climbing as an example, noting that climbers must put in the time learning safe climbing techniques before they can participate in outdoor climbing trips. Heuser (2005) used the example of lawn bowlers who, with time, focus, and commitment, become organizers, judges, coaches, and eventually convention panelists and organizers. Perseverance also helps fans maintain their focus in an interest in the face of adversity (e.g., Lee, Gould et al., 2017), such as serious sport fans whose interest in their favorite team is resistant to losing streaks in a way that isn't true for bandwagon fans (Shipway & Jones, 2008). In short, research repeatedly shows that commitment, perseverance, and focus are all essential components of serious leisure (Heo et al., 2012; Lee, 2013; Lee, Bentley et al., 2017; Stebbins, 2007).

Serious leisure has also been compared to the concept of a leisure career (Stebbins, 2007). As fans focus their time and effort on their interest they progress and reach milestones (e.g., becoming a convention organizer) much like someone with a professional career (Kane & Zink, 2004). Also like a career, with time, an increase in commitment leads to a strengthening of personal and social identities linked with that activity (Heo et al., 2012; Lyu & Oh, 2015). With time, those who seriously pursue their leisure activities begin to surround themselves with like-minded others as the activity becomes a more prominent and defining feature of who they are. And, by extension, they find themselves with less and less time for other, non-career-related activities (e.g., other fan interests).

Having said all of this, there is no one way to examine exclusiveness of, or focus on, a leisure activity. It's possible, for example, to assess the scope of the interest itself, the level of skill needed to engage in it, or the structure and organization of the community surrounding the interest and the way it categorizes and describes its most fervent members. In other research by Unruh (1980), the authors discuss the idea of ranking fans with respect to their level of identification, involvement, and focus in the activity. In other research still (e.g., Tapp, 2004; Tapp & Clowes, 2002) the researchers looked for differences in the levels of commitment between focused fans (e.g., those treating the activity as serious leisure) and more casual fans. None of these approaches is the "right" approach, but represent a range of options available to researchers looing to study this topic.

Exclusive Engagement

In previous sections we described theorizing and research on fan focus, including those who spend a considerable amount of their time on a single interest and who may identity strongly with that interest. This work, however, has not focused specifically on exclusive fans—those who have only a single fan interest to the exclusion of any others.

An important tenct of social identity theory is that people juggle multiple group identities across situations to maintain a distinct and positive sense of self (Tajfel & Turner, 1979; Turner et al., 1987). Because of the utility of switching between identities, it makes sense why, theoretically speaking, one would expect to find relatively few examples of fans with only a single, exclusive interest-based group identity. The closest the fan literature gets to studying this possibility is the work of Hillman et al. (2014) who examined exclusive fan communities on Tumblr. Hillman et al. observed that many fans use the blogging platform to create their own hyper-specific blogs where they create art and interact with other fans members with respect to a single fan interest. While it's debatable whether these fans should be considered exclusive fans, Hillman et al.'s work does shed light on the important role that websites play in fostering highly-specific, single-interest communities.

Other researchers may have gotten closer to studying the elusive exclusive fan. For example, those studying fans of specific sports have looked at the process of internalizing one's fan identity and the varying extent to which fans do this (Delia, 2015). In doing so, they note that the highest-identifying fans, those who have most internalized their interest, may do so to a level that borders on exclusivity. Kolbe and James (2003) lay out three distinct levels of internalization, starting with an initial interest and proceeding to exclusive focus, "the formation of a distinct and exclusive preference for a sport team" (Funk & James, 2004, p. 10). Delia (2015) points out that at among exclusively-focused fans, their favorite sport team can be used to satisfy a number of psychological needs to the point where their personal identity overlaps substantially with the team, with their interest becoming highly representative of who they are.

Conclusion

Fan focus and exclusivity are important variables that can predict the motivations, behaviors, and even well-being of fans. Much of the existing research, in line with social identity theory, suggests that exclusive focus on a single fan interest may be to the fan's detriment. For instance, research suggests that fans who are more willing to join other fan interests tend to experience less loneliness and less depression (Wann & Ensor, 2001), while other work suggests that belonging to multiple fan groups can buffer fans against the detrimental effects that come from experiencing a falling out with any one fan interest (Reysen, Plante, & Chadborn, 2021).

Even so, there has been relatively little empirical research examining truly exclusive fans, and only slightly more research examining the dimension of fan focus. The research which does exist seems to suggest that fan focus and exclusivity exists along a continuum and may be related to demographic variables such as age. This relationship may be a complex one, however, as younger fans may be more exclusive in their focus as a byproduct of a still-developing identity while older fans may be more exclusive as a product of spending decades engaging in their preferred activity. Research on serious leisure offers possible inroads to the topic of fan exclusivity, suggesting a theoretical framework within which to conceptualize focused fans (e.g., as those fans who engage in serious leisure or career fans).

For now, however, the subject of fan focus and exclusivity remains a subject ripe with potential, one that will almost certainly yield insights into fan behavior for researchers who pursue this line of inquiry.

Chapter 25
Self-Disclosure

As we've discussed in previous chapters (e.g., Chapter 7, Fandom), a person's fan group is often an integral part of who they are—a social identity. People strategically manage their social identities such as these to maintain a positive and distinct sense of self (Tajfel & Turner, 1979; Turner et al., 1987). Among the various identity management strategies available to them is the decision to withhold self-disclosure: Should they let others know they are a part of a group, or conceal that part of themselves from others (a topic we introduced in Chapter 21.) On the one hand, disclosing a desirable or valued social identity reflects well on someone and earns them the prestige and status that comes with membership in a desirable group. On the other hand, disclosing a stigmatized or undesirable identity can bring scorn and ill-repute, something which could people to keep that part of themselves hidden. Members of any group—fan or otherwise—often find themselves faced with such decisions.

Ample evidence suggests that at least some fans have little problem with being open (or even boisterous) about their fandom membership, both to other members of their fan group as well as to non-fans (Reysen, Plante, Chadborn et al., 2021). As an example, beyond merely spectating sporting events, sport fans often adorn themselves and their belongings (e.g., lockers, cars, homes) with logos and symbols of their favorite teams, doing so to signal their group membership, especially at times when their team is doing well and reflects positively on them (Bishop, 2001; Chadborn et al., 2017; Cialdini et al., 1976; Crawford, 2004; Moor, 2006).

But research also suggests just the opposite to be true: Some fans deliberately conceal their fan identity from others, particularly from those who know them the least well, in an effort to protect themselves against stigma. Members of stigmatized fan groups may do this despite the fact that it represents a potential threat to their long-term psychological and physical well-being (Mock et al., 2013; Reysen, Plante, Chadborn et al., 2021).

With these two possibilities in mind, the present chapter explores the desire of some fans to self-disclose their fan identity and the extent to which this happens in small, stigmatized subcultures as well as in non-stigmatized, mainstream fan communities. We also consider the topics of deviant leisure, the consequences of stigma on the well-being of those belonging to these deviant groups, and why concealment over self-disclosure may seem like a viable strategy for fans facing considerable stigma.

Self-Disclosing Behaviors

A central component of identity management is the decision about whether to express one's belonging to a specific group and the ways one can demonstrate this to others (Banister et al., 2005; Grossberg, 1992). In the case of non-fan groups, people may display symbols of their identity (e.g., flags, clothing, symbols) or simply declare their group membership to others. In many ways, fans are no different: They collect, archive, and display artifacts of their fan groups to demonstrate their connection to their fan communities (Banister & Hogg, 2004; Borer, 2009; Chan et al., 2012; Derbaix et al., 2002; Geraghty, 2014; Levine et al., 2005). Fans can also proselytize their interest to others, sometimes in the hope of recruiting new members to the group, other times simply as a means of asserting their distinctiveness from others (Edwards et al., 2019). As an illustrative example, bronies—self-identified adult members of the *My Little Pony* fandom commonly wear clothing related to the show. In doing so, they not only signal their identity to other bronies, but they may also raise questions from non-fans about the show, which can lead to conversations about it and suggestions that the curious inquirer watch the show for themselves.

Regardless of how, precisely, fans choose to disclose—be it through wearing of merchandise, talking to their work colleagues about their interest, or simply being "caught" participating in a fan-related activity (e.g., watching a show on break)—it's worth asking whether the tendency for a fan to disclose their fan identity tells us something meaningful about the fan themselves. Speaking to this question, studies show that fans who openly display their group membership identify more strongly as fans and feel more committed to the group than those who conceal or avoid actively displaying their group membership (Jones, 2014, 2015). In fact, displaying one's fan interest may even be a viable strategy for newer fans to find and make friends who share a similar interest (Chadborn et al., 2017). Research has also shown that more openly displaying one's fan interest increases fans' sense of belonging to the fan group (Wann & Branscombe, 1990) and can both demonstrate and reinforce the norms of the fan community (Holt, 1995; Vigil, 1988).

In short, fans of all sorts—from mainstream sport fans to subcultures built around fringe media—engage in behaviors intended to display their fan identity to others. The reasons for this are multitudinous, ranging from a personal desire to befriend new fans to the systemic reinforcement of group norms. But despite the many reasons to display one's fan interest, as well as the myriad of ways to do so, fans vary considerably in the extent to which they choose to do so. In the next section, we consider whether the nature of their fan community may play a role in this decision.

Not All Fandoms are Created Equal

Fan culture is popular and even encouraged in some domains (e.g., marketers, mainstream media) and, as a result, most people would probably consider themselves to be a fan of something. Even so, not all fandoms are viewed in a positive light, although the stigma surrounding fan cultures is far from randomly distributed. Studies suggest that the further a particular fan interest strays from what is considered prototypical (the most representative member of a category), the more likely it is that members of that fan community experience stigma (Reysen & Shaw, 2016). For example, sport fans and fans of mainstream musicians are typically what people imagine when they think of a fan. As a result, people seldom bat an eye or direct stigma toward fans of football, NASCAR, basketball, Michael Jackson, The Beatles, and Pink Floyd. However, fan communities perceived as being atypical experience stigma and prejudice toward them. This has been found to be the case for the comparatively non-mainstream fans of the Grateful Dead, the Insane Clown Posse, and *My Little Pony* (Reysen & Shaw, 2016). In other studies, science fiction fans (as compared to sport fans) are often perceived as less socially and physically attractive (Cohen et al., 2017; Seate et al., 2020). And while the content of *Star Trek* or comic books is not, itself, especially negative or worthy of condemnation, its non-mainstream nature can often lead to unflattering perceptions of these fans[1] (Cusack et al., 2003; Lopes, 2006), which may, understandably, disincentivize them from wanting to self-disclose their fan identity to others. But what about people who are fans of content that, in and of itself, is considered deviant or reprehensible by mainstream culture?

Deviant Leisure

As we've seen, simply being a fan of a non-prototypical fan interest can be enough to get someone stigmatized by mainstream culture. This being the case, things can only get worse for fans of deviant leisure, activities or interests centered around topics that society has deemed taboo or morally questionable in and of themselves (Stebbins et al., 2006). Researchers of deviant leisure conceptualize it as activities caught somewhere between "cool-individualism," and the transgression of hyper-regulated neoliberal spaces, where people are typically viewed, first and foremost, as consumers (Raymen, 2016; Rayman & Smith, 2019). Criminologists view deviant leisure enthusiasts as participating in a system of normalized harm, which can include anything from explicitly illegal

---

[1] This is certainly not helped by unflattering media portrayals of characters with non-mainstream fan interests. As characters in television shows like *The Simpsons* and *The Big Bang Theory*, science fiction and comic book fans are often painted as obsessive, socially awkward, and in a generally unflattering light.

activities, such as auto theft, child trafficking, or violence (Berdychevsky, 2018; Drozda, 2006) to far more legally-grey spaces like parkour enthusiasts who flaunt property laws in regulated cityscapes (Raymen, 2016).[2]

Traditionally, scholars of deviant leisure have tended to focus their attention away from those who explicitly break the law to instead focus on fan groups whose transgressions involve the violation of cultural mores. As an example, vampires define themselves as possessing an energy deficit, one which must be supplemented by donors of either psychic energy or blood (Williams, 2008, 2009). They organize themselves into covens or clans and practice occultism, something which runs counter to the predominantly Protestant American culture in which they reside. In another example, the BDSM (Bondage/Discipline, Domination/Submission, Sado-masochism) community is perfectly legal, but falls under the umbrella of deviant leisure due to their (consensual) intertwining of aggression and sexuality, something which discomforts mainstream culture and its fairly conservative, religious-based norms about sex (Berdychevsky, 2018; Williams, 2009).

Regardless of how, precisely, one defines deviant leisure, the point remains: Some interests are, in and of themselves, considered deviant and, therefore, its fans are often stigmatized simply for being fans of it. In the same vein as fans of non-taboo, but nevertheless non-mainstream fan interests, deviant leisure enthusiasts may find themselves in situations where they would prefer not to disclose their interests to others—be it their friends and family, their colleagues at work, strangers on the street, or authority figures.

Stigma and Well-Being

Humans are, at our core, social creatures who thrive when we belong to groups of like-minded others. One of the primary reasons people identify with groups is because of the sense of self-esteem they experience through group membership, both in terms of favorable ingroup attributions and in terms of downward social comparisons to members of less-desirable outgroups.

But when the group one belongs to is deemed taboo or is stigmatized, it becomes difficult to maintain the benefits of group membership while simultaneously trying to shield one's self-esteem from the threat of stigma-by-association (Tajfel & Turner, 1979). The concern is a valid one: Being part of a stigmatized group can lead to, among other things, poor psychological well-being, substance abuse, and reduced relationship quality (Balsam & Szymanski, 2005; Doyle & Molix, 2014; Schmitt et al., 2014; Stock et al., 2017). As such,

---

[2] As Raymen and Smith (2019) point out, deviant leisure need not require legal transgression, pointing to the legal, but nevertheless ecologically-destructive practice of maintaining ski resorts in the Swiss Alps to cater to well-off skiing enthusiasts.

there is a certain logic to trying to avoid the detrimental effects of stigma by pursuing identity concealment strategies which would allow group members to retain the benefits of group membership (e.g., social support) while avoiding stigma they experience from those outside the group.

Despite the intuitive appeal of concealment as a strategy, however, research suggests that prolonged concealment can be harmful (Meyer, 2003). Insofar as concealment requires people to be in a constant state of hypervigilance, monitoring their own behavior and the behavior of others for signs of inadvertent disclosure, concealment leads to a constant state of anxiety, something which, itself, has been associated with a range of physiological and psychological problems. To name just a subset of the problems which can arise, the decision to keep a stigmatized part of one's identity from others has been associated with excessive self-monitoring, rumination, intrusive thoughts, anxiety, chronic stress, and psychological dissonance (DeJordy, 2008; Frable et al., 1990; Lane & Wegner, 1995; Miranda & Storms, 1989; Pachankis, 2007; Quinn & Chaudoir, 2009; Smart & Wegner, 1999). Despite these consequences, however, people may nevertheless choose to conceal their identity, even in cases where they see their group as being a highly permeable one, where the ability to join and leave is fairly simple (Plante et al., 2013). This may well be the case for most fandoms, where people may join and leave of their own volition.

As mentioned, however, while one can choose to conceal their stigmatized identity to avoid problems in specific situations, there are benefits to both belonging to a group and, more specifically, to openly disclosing one's belonging to the group, however stigmatized it may be. According to the rejection-identification model (Branscombe et al., 1999), a model we first introduced in Chapter 20, people who experience stigma due to the groups they belong to may respond by increasing their group identification and engaging in self-disclosure to mitigate the negative effects of stigma. For example, a gay man who expects to experience stigma in the workplace may identify more strongly with the LGBTQ+ community as a source of social support which, in turn, provides them with the social support and confidence they need to self-disclose in the workplace and alleviate the anxiety associated with concealing their gay identity. Evidence for this has been found in the context of racial minorities, people with disabilities, and sexual minorities (Branscombe et al., 1999; Giamo et al., 2012; Scroggs & Vennum, 2021; Tabbah et al., 2016).

There is also some preliminary evidence suggesting that the rejection-identification model operates in fan communities as well. Among members of highly-stigmatized media fans, those who identify more strongly with their fan group also tend to disclose more and, by extension, feel a greater sense of self-acceptance (Mock et al., 2013) and belongingness (Tague et al., 2020). Self-disclosure in the anime fandom has also been found to be especially prominent among cosplayers, who report higher levels of psychological well-being than other anime fans (Reysen et al., 2018b). While research is far from finished on this subject, it does illustrate the importance of identity disclosure for members of stigmatized fan groups and some of the possible mechanisms at play driving (or preventing) this disclosure from happening (e.g., feelings of group belongingness).

Conclusion

In this chapter we've explored the desire for fans to self-disclose their fan identities, both as a function of the magnitude of their interest (Reysen & Branscombe, 2010) and as a way for members of stigmatized fan communities to alleviate the negative effects of stigma (Mock et al., 2013; Reysen et al., 2018b; Tague et al., 2020). We've seen how fan groups use symbols as a means of demarcating ingroup boundaries, often through the consumerist mode of purchasing commodities for the purpose of adorning themselves and signaling their identification to others, both fans and non-fans alike (Bishop, 2001; Crawford, 2004; Moor, 2006).

We've also seen that while some fans, typically those with mainstream interests (e.g., sports, music) are free to project or self-disclose their identity without consequence, others experience adverse consequences of doing so. This is often the case in members of less-mainstream, but non-deviant fan interests (e.g., anime fans, *Star Trek* fans), but also for fans of interests that fall full under the label of deviant leisure (e.g., parkour, BDSM, vampires), who may experience, at best, social ostracism (e.g., BDSM, vampires) and, at worse, legal consequences.

Finally, we discussed how, despite identity concealment seeming like an ideal way to avoid the adverse consequences of group membership, this strategy carries with it its own detrimental effects, including many of the problems associated with chronic anxiety. Instead, research suggests that being able to self-disclose and openly identify with one's fan community, even in the wake of accompanying stigma, is generally a net positive for fans, providing them with a sense of belonging and self-esteem.

In sum, a fan's decision to conceal or self-disclose their fan identity says a lot about their particular fan interest, their identification with the interest and with the fan group, and their psychological and physiological well-being. For this reason, it's important for researchers studying fans to seriously consider focusing some of their attention on this topic to better understand important distinctions between fans and the impact of fan activities and belonging to fan communities on fans themselves.

Chapter 26
Physical Attraction

When we think about fans, we imagine people who passionately pursue an interest for its own sake: Football fans who spectate for the love of the game, gamers who play because they enjoy the thrill that accompanies beating a difficult stage, and media fans who spend long hours writing fanfiction or cosplaying. When conceptualized thusly, it almost seems insulting to suggest that someone's interest might be "skin-deep," or little more than "mere attraction" to a character, celebrity, or athlete. The unspoken implication behind this assertion is that physical attraction is a shallow or superficial way to engage with one's interest. For this very reason, scholars have been pressured to stop including measures of physical attraction in their fan studies (Fink et al., 2002; Woo et al., 2009).

And yet, examples abound suggesting that such attraction plays a non-trivial role in many fans' interests. For example, about 30% of anime fans report having waifu or husbando—that is, they consider (sometimes jokingly, sometimes not) an anime character to be their wife or husband (Reysen, Plante, Chadborn et al., 2021). Such attraction can stem from physical attraction to an actor or character, exemplified by a veritable sea of fan-made erotic and pornographic images and fanfiction (e.g., Edwards et al., 2019; Reysen, Plante, Chadborn et al., 2021; Santos, 2020). Even fans of music, a non-visual medium, have been shown to be motivated, at least in part, by physical attraction to a band member (Kulczynski et al., 2016).

To better understand the role of attraction in fans, the present chapter delves into research on physical attraction and the formation of parasocial relationships with media characters and celebrities—a topic with a surprising amount of scholarship devoted to it (Liebers & Schramm, 2019). We begin with a look at research on attraction as a motivator of sport fans. Next, we consider comparable research on attraction to celebrities and other public figures, including idols, before delving into the extensive literature on parasocial relationships. Finally, we look directly at the extent to which sexual attraction motivates media fans and drives their fan interest.

Athlete Attractiveness

Before exploring whether physical attraction indeed drives fans' interest in sport, it's worth taking a quick detour to look at the research on what makes for an attractive athlete in the first place. Despite the subjectivity inherent in questions of attraction, there have been attempts to systematically study attractiveness in athletes. One approach, for example, is founded on the assumption that players who get the most attention from fans are also the most attractive. Dietl et al. (2018) tested this idea by examining the physical attractiveness of tennis players (operationalized as facial symmetry)[1] and television viewership for that player's games. The study found that when it came to female (but not male) athletes, greater attractiveness was, indeed, related to higher viewership. Analogous results were found by Mutz and Meier (2016), who gathered data on the frequency in which male and female soccer players were Googled. Specifically, they considered the amount of time players were on the field, the number of goals scored, and research assistants' ratings of the players' attractiveness. The data showed that while performance predicted being more popular with respect to Google traffic, attractiveness also mattered—both for male and female players. In short, the available evidence seems to suggest that fans prefer athletes who are both skilled and attractive, at least when it comes to their spectating and online search behavior.

Advertisers are keenly aware of this fact. Researchers find, for example, that female athletes appear partially-clothed in about 81% of advertisements (Grau et al., 2007). Male fans respond positively to these sexualized ads, even if doing so undermines the perceived competence of the athlete in question (Greenwell et al., 2017). In other words, in at least some cases, pure appreciation for competition and the drive to be the best can sometimes take a backseat to the physical appearance of the athlete in question.

Motivated by Physical Attraction

It's one thing to observe that sport fans are sometimes attracted to their favorite athletes, but another thing entirely to suggest that this attraction drives their interest. To address this question, we turn to a study of sport fans by Trail and James (2001) in which they included a measure of physical attraction (e.g., "An individual player's "sex appeal" is a big reason why I watch") alongside eight other possible motivations. Physical attraction was significantly correlated with several of the other motivations, including achievement, aesthetics, escape, and the players' physical skill. After controlling for the other motivations, however, physical attraction was not significantly related to the number of games fans attended, their identification with, or loyalty to, the team, or their sport-related media consumption—although it did predict merchandise purchasing.[2]

---

[1] This idea is grounded in principles of evolutionary psychology which suggest, and find evidence that, all else equal, people are more attracted to symmetrical faces as an indicator of good physical health.

[2] As mentioned in this introduction of this chapter, results like these, which only hint at the possibility that physical attraction may play a small role in some fan behaviors, have

Other studies have similarly tested whether physical attraction and sex appeal played a role in motivating fan behavior:

- Madrigal (2006) found that male (vs. female) sports were rated higher on physical attractiveness which, in turn, was correlated with a greater likelihood for fans to watch, although male and female fans scored similarly in their physical attraction to athletes (Aygün & Demir, 2020)
- Physical attraction is associated with intention to attend a baseball game (Park et al., 2016) and a live e-sports event (Sjöblom et al., 2019)
- A meta-analysis of sport fan studies found that perceived physical attractiveness is associated with event attendance (Kim et al., 2019)
- Physical attraction scores were related to the extent of a person's gambling behavior in a sample of sport gamblers in Spain (Lopez-Gonzalez, 2020)
- Cottingham, Carroll et al. (2014) found that while physical attraction was the lowest rated motivation for fans, it was positively related to enjoying violence in sport and escapism

But not all studies agree with the conclusion that physical attraction is associated with greater fan motivation:

- Physical attraction was positively, but non-significantly correlated with frequency of travel to support one's favorite Australian rugby team (Hoye & Lillis, 2008)
- Macey et al. (2020) did not find a significant relationship between physical attraction and watching e-sports
- Physical attractiveness was negatively associated with posting about e-sports on social media (Anderson, 2019)
- Physical attraction negatively predicted purchasing merchandise and intention to attend future events (Cottingham, Phillips et al., 2014)

Taken together, the literature on physical attraction and its role as a motivator of fan-related behavior in sport fans is mixed. We might suggest that physical attraction is one of the weaker motivators of sport fan behaviors, far from the most significant or impactful, but it's certainly not negligible. This is all

---

led to considerable pushback. In a study published the following year (Fink et al., 2002, pp. 199-200) "the physical attraction subscale was deleted at the athletic department's request." Further, "physical attraction was removed due to the request of the athletic department where the survey was conducted because they did not want to acknowledge that people might be motivated to attend games because of the attractiveness of the athletes" (Woo et al., 2009, p. 44). The physical attraction subscale does not make an appearance again in Trail's work after 2001, although other researchers have included the physical attraction dimension in their own research.

speaking in the context of sport fans, however, who represent only a fraction of the fan population. We next consider whether physical attraction may play a bigger role in the attitudes and behaviors of non-sport fans.

Attraction to Celebrities and Public Figures

While not necessarily studied as a "fan interest" per se, there exists a considerable body of research on celebrity worship which can help shed light on the motivations of other, non-sport fans. As an illustrative example, Stever (1991) interviewed people who like celebrities and found four common themes: the celebrity is a hero or role model, mystique surrounding the celebrity, appreciation for the celebrity's talent, and, most presently relevant, sex appeal. In a later study, Stever (2008) administered a measure of these different dimensions to fans about to attend a Josh Groban concert. They found that fans perceived Josh Groban as a role model, entertainer, and a sex symbol. Others have similarly suggested that sexual attraction (e.g., "I have fantasies of an intimate nature about my favorite celebrity") may be linked to the fan experience (e.g., Sheridan et al., 2006). For example, music fans' physical attraction to a band member predicts not only their degree of fanship, but also the number of concerts attended, the amount of money the fans were willing to pay, and their willingness to travel to see a concert (Kulczynski, 2014).

Idol Worship

Related to the concept of attraction to celebrities is idol worship, particularly in Southeast Asian countries where researchers have been studying the phenomenon for decades (Yue & Cheung, 2019). A recurring theme in this body of work is the attraction and illusionary feeling of romance that fans often feel toward idols. For example, Cheung and Yue (2000) surveyed students in Hong Kong and Nanjing about their favorite pop stars and found that the students especially valued attractive stars who met the criteria for illusory romance, although this romanticism was more important for pop stars than for role models (Yue & Cheung, 2000).

Researchers continued along this line of work to construct an idol worship questionnaire that assesses the motivations underlying liking a celebrity, although the specifics of the questionnaire have changed over time (e.g., Cheung & Yue, 2011; Liu, 2013; Yue et al., 2010; Yue & Cheung, 2000, 2019) At various times, the scale has included the dimensions of attachment, identification, romanticization, idealization, intimatization, consumption, and commodification. At present, we'll focus specifically on the romantization dimension (e.g., "I wish that I would become the lover to my idol," "I consider my idol as my dream romantic partner").

Cheung and Yue surveyed students in Hong Kong and other Chinese cities about idols in a series of studies (Cheung & Yue, 2011, 2019). Of the different motivational dimensions measured, romanticization was rated the lowest of the motivators; even so, they were nevertheless positively associated with being a member of an idol fan club. In another study of students in Hong Kong, Liu (2013) found that romantic fantasy was the highest-rated dimension of idol worship and, like in the 2011 Cheung and Yue study, it was related to being in a fan club. Taken together, these results suggest, in line with research on celebrity worship, that idol worship also involves an element of physical attraction, even if physical attraction is far from the strongest motivator.

Parasocial Relationships

To this point, we've primarily discussed feelings of physical or sexual attraction toward celebrities. But what about circumstances when attraction becomes more than a crush or vivid daydream, when it gives way to feelings of attachment, closeness, and intimacy toward people who are unaware of, or cannot, reciprocate those same feelings? It's here that we delve into the realm of parasocial relationships, a topic we've already briefly touched on in Chapter 12.

In a 2009 study, Spinda and colleagues surveyed NASCAR fans, asking them about the extent to which they experienced symptoms of parasocial relationships with their favorite drivers, which included a mixture of relationship (e.g., "The driver makes me feel comfortable, as if I am with friends") and romantic attraction (i.e., "I find my favorite driver to be attractive"). The results showed that female (vs. male) fans were more likely to feel greater parasocial attachment, something which, itself, is positively associated with other motivations for watching (e.g., self-esteem, social interaction), intention to watch, an affinity for NASCAR, favorable attitudes toward corporate sponsors, and identification with NASCAR as a sport. In short, not only were female fans more likely to experience parasocial relationships, but these experiences predicted fan-related behavior.

In an entirely different context, Song and Fox (2016) surveyed female Chinese players of dating video games. They asked players about their game-playing habits, identification with their avatar, parasocial relationships (e.g., "I felt I was in a relationship with him when I was playing the game"), and romantic beliefs (e.g., "I believe that to be truly in love is to be in love forever"). The authors found that greater playing of romantic video games predicted greater identification with the main character which, in turn, predicted parasocial relationships and, ultimately, romantic beliefs. Like the NASCAR study above, these results illustrate the association between fan interests and parasocial relationships, including the possibility that fans' parasocial relationships have implications for their beliefs outside the context of the fan interest.

Parasocial Romance

In a related line of research, Tukachinsky (2010) developed a measure to assess different types of parasocial relationships including physical love (e.g., "I find X very attractive physically"), emotional love (e.g., "For me, X could be the perfect romantic partner"), and friendship. Physical love—a measure of physical attraction—emerged as the highest mean among all of the dimensions when it came to rating one's favorite media character. Illustrating the generalizability of this tendency across media formats, Liebers and Schramm (2017) similarly assessed parasocial romance toward a favorite book character. They found that physical and emotional attraction played an important role in predicting parasocial relationships, one that mediated the association between perceived similarity to the character and experiencing a parasocial relationship. From such studies it seems that, across media formats, fans' feelings of romantic parasocial attraction to media characters (including fictional ones) predicts important fan-related behaviors, including attachment and identification with the characters and fans' preference for specific media characters.

In their own study of parasocial romance and its potential long-term impact, Erickson and Dal Cin (2018) asked a sample of U.S. college women if they had a crush on a celebrity when they were younger (ages 12-14), along with questions about parasocial relationships and as romantic parasocial attachment. This new measure contained three dimensions: affective (e.g., "My relationship with [this person] made me feel happy"), cognitive (e.g., "I wanted to know as much as I could about [this person]"), and fantasy (e.g., "I often daydreamed about [this person]," Erickson et al., 2018). Parasocial romantic experiences as a teenager predicted heterosexual romantic scripts, experiences of passionate love, and relationship-contingent self-esteem. While modest in magnitude, parasocial romances do impact peoples' current understanding of, and experiences with, relationships. Fantasizing about media figures and the romantic parasocial relationships these fantasies yield (e.g., Liebers & Straub, 2020) can, in line with research on parasocial relationships more broadly, impact fans outside the context of their fan interest.[3]

---

[3] In fact, other research (e.g., Adam, 2019; Schnarre & Adam, 2018) has shown that parasocial romances and related fantasies are seen by some partners as a form of relationship infidelity. This suggests yet another way that parasocial relationships, despite being "not real," nevertheless have real-world consequences for those who experience them.

Sexual Attraction as a Motivator of Media Fans

In this final section we move beyond parasocial relationships and celebrity worship to consider the role that sexual attraction (not just physical or emotional attraction) plays in the motivation of media fans. Given the prominence of explicit fan-created content (e.g., fanart, fanfiction) in fandoms like *My Little Pony*, *Harry Potter*, *Star Trek*, and *Supernatural*, as well as the general tendency for sex to motivate a great deal of human behavior, we can ask whether sexual attraction to fan-related content is a draw for fans.

Assessing this possibility, Schroy et al. (2016) examined the motivations of three different fan groups and the relation of those motivations to fans' fanship and fandom scores. Among the multitude of motivations was sexual attraction, which averaged at about the midpoint of the scale for some groups and below it for others. More importantly, sexual attraction did positively predict fanship scores for some of the fan groups, but not for others. The same could not be said for fandom scores, however, which were unrelated to sexual motivation across the fan groups. These results suggest that, at least for some fan groups, sexual attraction to aspects of the interest may facilitate a deeper connection to the topic itself, but seem to have minimal impact on fans' engagement with other fans.[4]

One possible explanation for differences in the link between sexual motivation and fanship across fandoms may stem from the availability or centrality of sexual content to the interest itself. For example, while there is undoubtedly erotic content available to curious sport fans, it may be less prevalent, less openly talked about, and harder to find, than, say, hentai (explicitly sexual) content in the anime fandom. Even so, in preliminary studies assessing the role of sexual attraction in media fandoms with significant pornographic content, only a small minority of fans spontaneously mentioned that pornography was an important initial draw to their interest in open-ended questions (Reysen et al., 2017c).

Conclusion

Fans' physical, emotional, and sexual attraction to celebrities and characters tied to their fan interest is a taboo topic, both to academics studying the subject and among fans themselves. Speaking to the former point, Trail's department did not appreciate his findings that college students may be attending games because of the attractiveness of the athletes. Speaking to the latter point, some fandoms have seen movements to deny or outright purge sexual facets of the

---

[4] Given that pornography use and masturbation are largely private subjects that people may be reluctant to discuss with one another, it makes sense that sexual attraction to fan-related content has little impact on how fans connect and engage with other fans.

interest, either as an idealistic stance against the perceived "cheapening" or "trivializing" of the interest or, more pragmatically, as a means of defending against stigma and criticism from non-fans.

Despite the taboo which exists around the subject, however, it's impossible to deny the existence of sexuality and the role that attraction plays to fans of almost any interest. In fact, this idea is so ingrained in internet culture that it was enshrined in the "rules of the internet" as "rule 34," which posits that if something exists, there is also pornography of it. Empirical research would seem to support the notion, at least partially, that attraction and sexual interest can motivate fans to consume fan-related content and feel a sense of attachment to their fan interest—be it a celebrity, a fictional character, or the interest itself (e.g., a show). And, as we've seen, this physical attraction is far from inconsequential: It predicts everything from spectatorship to live event attendance to fans' own beliefs and attitudes about relationships.

While the available evidence is far from suggesting that physical attraction is among the most important drivers of fan behavior, there is ample evidence to suggest that it is a variable worth at least considering, both because of its association with other important fan-related variables and because it is a variable which differs so considerably from fandom to fandom and even between fans within a given fandom.

Chapter 27
Pathology

The pathological fan is one of the oldest stereotypes placed upon people passionate about a hobby or interest in the 20th Century (Jenson, 1992). In the post-industrial, rapidly-modernizing West, fans were seen as fanatics seeking validation through parasocial relationships and losing all sense of perspective and reason when it came to their interest. Jenson (1992) argued that such criticisms of fandom, both from society at large and from academia, are a displacement of the central critique of modernism, that modern society has fragmented social bonds and created isolated, atomized individuals at the mercy of media influence. Fans, conceived of thusly, are reduced to loners with an obsessive interest that isolates them from their decaying communities, as "frenzied, crowd member[s], suffering from the disease of contagion" (p. 13).

While much of the 20th Century was spent decrying fans as the folk devil of modernity (Cohen, 1972), the 21st Century seems to be turning over a new leaf: Fans and fandoms have become far more normalized and accepted by mainstream society and scholars alike. Whether it's because multibillion dollar industries have sprung up around popular fan interests or because of the sheer number of people openly embracing their fan identity, there has been a general shift in the conceptualization of fans away from obsessive loners and zealous mobs. Even so, despite mounting evidence that fan communities provide social support and contribute to fans' psychological health (Ray et al., 2017, Schroy et al., 2016; Tague et al., 2020; Wann, 1995), the pernicious specter of dated fan stereotypes lurks in the shadows.

In the present chapter we aim to shed light on these stereotypes. First, we discuss research on the notion of fans as obsessive loners, returning to the topic of celebrity worship. We then shift our attention to scholarly work on fans as frenzied mobs, using the example of violence and rioting in sport fans, one of the best-studied fan-related phenomena. In both cases, we discuss whether there is a kernel of truth to the conceptualization of fans as pathological and its potential implications.

The Obsessive Loner

While fans may be characterized by their passionate interest in something (e.g., Reysen & Branscombe, 2010), the manner in which this passion manifests varies dramatically from person to person. In most cases, interests manifest as moderate consumption of the interest, reasonable displays of group identity, engagement in fan-related activities, and purchasing fan-related material. In some cases, however, the manner or extent to which the interest manifests can be problematic, bordering on pathological. Numerous researchers have weighed in on the how, when, and why of this possibility.

For example, Vallerand and company (2003) note this distinction in their work on harmonious and obsessive passion. They define harmonious passion as the internalization of one's interest into their identity through flexible, controlled, and enjoyable interest-related experiences. In contrast, obsessive passion is just the opposite, marked by uncontrollable, rigid, and compulsory attachment to one's interest. Conceptualized thusly, the potential benefits or drawbacks of an interest are a product of the type of passion the fan experiences toward their interest.

Another model aiming to explain the process of pathological fanship is the absorption-addiction model. Outlined by McCutcheon and colleagues (2002), the model posits, using the example of celebrity worship, that a combination of mental health problems and isolation from others contributes to pathological fanship. While fandoms centering around a particular celebrity are relatively harmless and comparable to other fan communities, pathological variants of this fandom have been increasing over time (McCutcheon et al., 2002; McCutcheon & Aruguete, 2021), possibly due to increasing rates of depression, anxiety, conformity pressure, and social isolation during the same period (Geiger & Davis, 2019; Goodwin et al., 2020; Holt-Lunstad, 2017).[1]

In their model, McCutcheon and colleagues (2002) conceptualize interest in a celebrity as falling into three tiers. At the entertainment-social level, people seek out information about the celebrity, enjoy the celebrity's content, and discuss the celebrity with friends. At the next level, the intense-personal level, people will start developing parasocial feelings toward the celebrity and compulsively think about them. Finally, at the borderline-pathological level, celebrity worship becomes obsessive, with people overidentifying with their interest and archiving information about their fixation.

Far from being a trivial distinction, the extent of a person's celebrity worship has been linked to an array of mental health concerns. Some, for example, have linked celebrity worship to an unstable sense of self, or social atomization (Brooks, 2021; Reeves et al., 2012). Others, such as Maltby and colleagues (2001), have found a correlation between borderline-pathological celebrity worship and symptoms of anxiety and depression. Celebrity worship has also been linked to obsessive thoughts (Brooks, 2021), fantasy proneness and dissociation (Maltby et al., 2006), self-harm and substance abuse (Zsila et al.,

---

[1] In the wake of recent global financial crises, a pandemic, and social upheaval, the notion of fans as obsessive loners may be due for a revival (McCutcheon & Arguuete, 2021).

2020), eating disorders (Aruguete et al., 2014), and problematic gambling (Lian et al., 2019). It's also been associated with a number of social and interpersonal problems (McCutcheon, Gillen et al., 2016), including a propensity toward neuroticism, narcissism, and a lack of humility (Ashe et al., 2005; Greenwood et al., 2018; Huynh & McCutcheon, 2021; Maltby et al., 2011), and has even been linked to a willingness to not convict a fictitious celebrity accused of murder (Wong et al., 2010). In short, celebrity worship, as an example of excessive and obsessive fan behavior, can have detrimental consequences both for the idolator, but also for those around them. It would therefore seem that there is some cause for concern, at least when it comes to the more extreme manifestations of fan interest.

But, as we've pointed out in previous chapters (e.g., Chapter 7 on fandom), fan interests are rarely a solitary experience. As such, might we expect even more dire consequences when obsessed or excessive fans congregate?

The Frenzied Crowd

Research on social contagion and group dynamics suggests fairly grim prospects for excessively enthusiastic fans who find themselves in a group of similarly-passionate zealots (Jenson, 1992). According to Ward (2002), sport fan-related violence occurs often enough that it can be studied, predicted, and ultimately broken down into three stages based on the severity of the behavior involved. In the first phase, often in response to frustration (e.g., over their team losing), fans engage in verbal assaults or throwing items in the arena at other fans, officials, or players. As tensions escalate into the second phase, physical violence breaks out between individual fans or with security, and a number of small brawls may break out in the stands. "Pitch invitations" (p. 459) may also take place, where a group of fans will rush the opposing fan group to literally trample the opposition. Finally, as aggression levels peak, violence begins to spread to outside the stadium and into the surrounding neighborhoods. As Ward (2002) notes, this pattern of fan aggression has be found around the world, although it's been documented most frequently at soccer games in Europe, South America, and Africa.[2]

While some researchers have documented the trajectory and magnitude of fan-related violence as a problem, others have attempted to explain why it

---

[2] Ward (2002) also speculates that Americans may not fight as much at games due to voyeuristic violence: American sports are more visually violent than, say, soccer, and so American fans may experience violence cathartically without instigating it themselves. Having said that, aggression research would wholly disagree with this supposition, suggesting instead that viewing violent sports only increases levels of aggression, rather than decreasing them cathartically (e.g., Arms et al., 1979).

occurs. Some researchers note, for example, that while environmental factors such as heat, alcohol, and behavioral modeling contribute to fan violence, the biggest predictor of violence at sporting events is the extent to which individual fans identity with the team (Wann, 2005). Researchers suggest that sport fans are not especially aggressive in and of themselves (Wann, 1993, 1994; Wann, Fahl et al., 1999; Wann et al., 2002), but rather are moved to aggression due to group identity processes coupled with the context of the sporting event itself. Recall that people, including fans, attach themselves to groups to maintain a positive self concept (Tajfel & Turner, 1979). When those groups are challenged directly (e.g., one's favorite team loses), people are often motivated to defend their groups, especially when other outlets or strategies are unavailable (e.g., cutting off reflected failure, Snyder et al., 1986).

Speaking directly to this idea, a series of studies found that highly-identified sport fans were more likely to exhibit higher levels of verbal aggression than less-identified fans (Wann, Carlson et al., 1999). Further speaking to the importance of context, studies have also shown that the violence of the event itself plays an important moderating role: attendees at more aggressive sporting events (such as hockey games) engage more frequently in aggressive verbal behavior than those attending less aggressive events (like basketball games, Wann et al., 2000). A study of college students at the University of Kentucky even found that those who highly identified with the school's basketball team were more likely to engage in unscrupulous behavior if it meant helping out their team (Wann et al., 2001). Studies like these illustrate how fan identification and context can drive otherwise mild-mannered, well-behaved fans to immoral or aggressive behavior.

Skeptical readers may find themselves doubting whether evidence of verbal aggression or a willingness to behave unscrupulously can truly inform questions about more serious aggression like brawling or rioting. Fortunately (or perhaps unfortunately), research has similarly documented the same processes at work in more extreme examples of violence. For instance, Zani and Kirchler (1991) studied Italian soccer fans and found that group norms permitting or even encouraging violence do, in turn, instigate violence in fans. Analogous findings have been noted in highly-identified American fans who are more likely to consider committing a violent act against the opposing team or players after their team experienced a loss (Wann, Culver et al., 2005). As perhaps the most tarnished of silver linings, however, Wann, Peterson and company (1999) did find that while highly identified sport fans were more likely to injure the star player of an opposing team, they drew the line when it came to their willingness to commit murder.

As we mentioned, team identification is only one part of the broader picture of fan violence. In a relatively new development of research, Ben Larkin suggests that collective narcissism in sport fans (2017) may moderate the link between team identity and violence at sporting events (Larkin & Fink, 2019). Moreover, Wakefield and Wann (2006) introduced the concept of the "dysfunctional fan," one characterized by confrontational behavior, complaining, alcohol consumption, and favoring away games, while still others have linked fan violence to being a bully as a child and beliefs about the appropriateness of using verbal aggression (Courtney & Wann, 2010; Donahue & Wann, 2009). In short, consistent with Wann's theory of sport fandom, while fan identification plays a crucial role in predicting violence and other extreme fan behavior, it's important to also consider important individual differences (i.e., fan dysfunction) if one wants to predict which highly-identified fans are the most likely to misbehave during fan events (Wann, Waddill et al., 2017).

Conclusion

In the present chapter we explored two pathological archetypes of fandom: the obsessed loner and the frenzied crowd (Jenson, 1992). The obsessed loner is exemplified by the celebrity idolator, whose obsession with their fan interest leads them to personal and social dysfunction ranging from anxiety and depression to interpersonal conflict and narcissism. Unfortunately, while there are healthy expressions of celebrity centered fandom, it seems that celebrity worship, including the more pathological kind, has only increased over the past couple of decades as people feel increasingly more lonely, depressed, and anxious.

The other pathological archetype, the frenzied crowd, was discussed in the context of sport fans and violence at sporting events. Through this work, we observed that a combination of team identification and individual differences can interact to explain how fairly mundane sport fans may be driven to violence in exceptional circumstances, a finding very much in-line with the central principles of social psychology.

Jenson (1992) argues that the unflattering archetypes of fans are a silent critique of modernity. Ward (2002), on the other hand, suggests that the concern with violent sport fans may be a cultural boogeyman. While both seem to suggest that concerns about extreme or pathological fan behavior constitute a moral panic or hand-wringing over nothing more than people with hobbies, one can hardly ignore the research suggesting that fandom does have a pathological side, even if it is the notable exception rather than the rule. It is important and worthwhile to consider the propensity for fans to engage in pathological behavior when trying to paint a complete picture of fans and fan behavior, if only to better understand how and when rare cases of pathological fan behavior are likely to take place.

Chapter 28
Special Bond

The bond between fans and content creators (e.g., performers, celebrities) has been described by some scholars as akin to religious devotion (Ferencz, 2013). Of course, unlike religion, most fans would not be willing to die for their favorite celebrity in the way that zealous followers of a religion might (Reysen, 2006). That said, however, the magnitude and nature of the felt bond between followers and the objects of their affection may be driven by similar psychological processes. If so, the special bond that fans have with their interest may have attitudinal and behavioral implications not unlike the effects of religion. Examples abound illustrating this possibility, from business owners naming their business after a band they felt a personal connection to (Gunderman & Harty, 2016) to sport and other fans who are strongly influenced by the norms they've internalized from the teams and fan groups they identify with (Heere & James, 2007; Otmazgin, 2016; Plante et al., 2014b).

With this in mind, in this, the final chapter of our literature review, we consider the special bond fans have with fan-related objects. Perusing the fan literature reveals that the nature of this bond is fairly ambiguous, residing somewhere in the overlap between fanship (Chapter 15), fandom (Chapter 7), and parasocial connections (Chapters 26 and 27). In the present chapter we'll circle back once more to the topic of parasocial connection and celebrity worship, focusing particularly on research that tries to characterize the nature of this felt bond and its implications for those who experience it.

Parasocial Connection

Tukachinsky and Stever (2019) recently developed a model to explain the stages fans go through when developing a relationship or bond with their particular fan interest. The model draws upon research on parasocial relationships (perceived relationship with a character or celebrity) and parasocial interactions (interacting with characters, such as yelling at them through a television screen) and assumes that parasocial relationships are experienced psychologically in a manner analogous to real-world relationships (Eyal & Rubin, 2003).

Specifically, the model posits four stages in bond formation, starting with the most superficial connection and becoming deeper and more significant with time. In the first stage of relationship development—initiation—people are initially exposed to the interest (e.g., a character or celebrity). They scrutinize the character with a sense of uncertainty, relying heavily on existing schemas as they form their first impression. In the second stage—experimentation—

interested viewers are motivated to learn more about the character or celebrity, gauging the degree of fit between the character and themselves. By seeking more information, they reduce their uncertainty about the character and form a clearer opinion of how they feel about the character. It's during this period that the person goes from a mere observer to potentially liking the character or celebrity.

During the third stage of parasocial development—intensification—fans who like the character or celebrity begin to solidify a sense of relationship with them. The fan views the character as a friend and feels a sense of commitment to the relationship. They begin seeking out relevant media (e.g., interviews, social media) to satisfy their own needs, such as improving their mood after a bad day. Imagined parasocial interactions also begin to increase in frequency as fans think more about the character in their day-to-day lives. During this stage, fans are unlikely to counter-argue anything the character or celebrity says and, instead, find themselves increasingly persuaded by them. A sense of trust and intimacy has been forged with them.

In the fourth and final stage—integration/bonding—fans experience a sense of fusion or oneness with the character or celebrity. While a truly reciprocal relationship is virtually impossible (e.g., marriage), fans at this stage have nevertheless incorporated the character into their own self-concept, defining themselves, in part, by the character. In addition to engaging in behaviors typical of highly-identified fans (e.g., collecting, attending conventions, reading/writing fanfiction, interacting with fellow fans), fans in this "special bond" stage may also develop more pathological behaviors (e.g., surgery to look like their favorite celebrity), although instances of such extreme behaviors are relatively rare.

This model is perhaps the best representation of research focusing directly on fans experiencing a special bond toward their fan interest. While promising, at the time of writing there has yet to be a significant body of research applying the model to specific fan groups or even validating measures of model-relevant variables.

Celebrity Worship

In a line of research related to, but more specific than the work described above, McCutcheon et al. (2002) constructed the celebrity worship scale which, as its name suggests, assesses the extent to which people feel a sense of connection with a celebrity—to the point of worship or excess at the upper end of the scale.

To develop the scale, the researchers began by using Wann's (1995) model of fan motivation to assess entertainment, group affiliation, self-esteem, and escape motivation in a group of celebrity fans. The researchers also included a measure of pathological over-identification, a novel dimension. Analyses found evidence for two factors, one representing a tendency toward fantasy (e.g., "I love to talk with others who admire my favorite celebrity") and the other assessing potentially pathological tendencies (e.g., "I am obsessed by details of my favourite celebrity's life").[1]

Maltby et al. (2002) would later revise the measure, renaming it the celebrity attitude scale. The revised measure had a three-factor structure: entertainment/social (e.g., "My friends and I like to discuss what my favorite celebrity because it means a good time"), intense/personal feelings (e.g., "I consider my favorite celebrity to be my soulmate"), and mild pathological attitudes (e.g., "I often feel compelled to learn the personal habits of my favorite celebrity"). For the purpose of the present chapter, we're most interested in the intense-personal subscale, as this factor closely resembles the concept of experiencing a special bond with one's fan interest. The measure has been shown to have good test-retest reliability (Griffith et al., 2013) and, in their own work, Maltby et al. (2002) found that the intense-personal subscale predicts theoretically-relevant variables, such as lower extrinsic religious motivation.

In the rest of this chapter we review some of the ways the celebrity attitude scale, and especially the intense-personal subscale, has been applied to various domains of research as an illustration of how theoretically important it is for fan researchers to assess fans' felt bond to their interest and its characters / celebrities.

Body Image

Several studies have suggested that the intense-personal dimension of the celebrity attitude scale is related to negative body image, particularly for women. For example, Swami et al. (2009) surveyed undergraduate women in the UK about celebrity worship and acceptance of cosmetic surgery. Scores on the intense-personal dimension were positively associated with stronger beliefs about the benefits of getting cosmetic surgery, greater social motivation to get cosmetic surgery, and a greater willingness to consider getting cosmetic surgery. In similar studies, intense-personal scores also predicted a preoccupation with one's own body image (Maltby & Day, 2011), body dissatisfaction (Swami et al., 2011), and attention to body shape in adolescent girls (Maltby et al., 2005). While these findings don't directly relate to fan-related attitudes or behavior, they do illustrate one of the more subtle and often-overlooked ways a person's

---

[1] Despite analyses suggesting that the scale had a two-factor structure, the two factors were strongly correlated with one another, hinting at the possibility that the scale might be assessing the same single dimension in two slightly different ways.

fan interest—and the bonds they form with fan-related content—can impact the way they see the world around them and their understanding of themselves.

Materialism

Other research has applied the intense-personal dimension of the celebrity attitude scale to understanding fans' materialistic attitudes and behaviors. In one such study, Aruguete et al. (2020) found that the intense-personal dimension was associated with being present-focused (e.g., "I only act to satisfy immediate concerns, figuring the future will take care of itself"), valuing material goods (e.g., "I like to own things that impress people"), and feeling a sense of relative deprivation (e.g., "I feel resentful when I see how prosperous other people like me seem to be"). Other studies have shown similar associations in U.S. college students (Reeves et al., 2012) and in southeast Asian samples (Chia & Poo, 2009). Studies have also found that this intense-personal dimension predicts the belief that materialism contributes to happiness (e.g., "I'd be happier if I could afford to buy more things:" Green et al., 2014). In short, one's felt bond to their fan interest may predict or explain some of the consuming behavior (e.g., collecting, attending live events) observed in highly-identified fans.

Shedding light on this possibility, a study of Bruce Springsteen fans found that an intense-personal bond with the singer was positively associated with watching Springsteen on YouTube, listening to his music, and consuming information related to his music online (Häkkänen-Nyholm, 2020). Likewise, shoppers at a mall in India were surveyed regarding the extent to which they worshipped a celebrity who endorsed a particular product (Singh & Banerjee, 2019). Feeling a strong personal bond with the celebrity was associated with more positive attitudes toward advertisements featuring the celebrity and greater intention to purchase the product.

Well-Being

A sizable body of research has also focused on assessing the well-being of fans in relation to the bond they feel to their interest, stemming, in no small part, from questions about the potential pathology of fans (see Chapter 27 for more on this). With this in mind, some have asked whether feeling an intense-personal connection with a celebrity or other object of one's fan interest is an indicator of well-being, good or bad.

Numerous studies from the UK characterize the link between special bond and well-being to be a fairly maladaptive one. Specifically, intense-personal bonds have been associated with:

- Somatic symptoms, anxiety, and depressive symptoms (Maltby et al., 2001)

- Negative coping, negative affect, depression, and anxiety (Maltby, Day, McCutcheon, Gillett et al., 2004; Maltby & Day, 2017)
- Obsessive-compulsive disorder and dissociation (Maltby et al., 2006)
- A lack of cognitive and flexibility and social complexity (Maltby, Day, McCutheon, Martin, & Cayanus, 2004)
- Neuroticism (Maltby et al., 2003; Maltby et al., 2011)
- Narcissism (Ashe et al., 2005)
- Reduced self-concept clarity, self-esteem, and life satisfaction (Reeves et al., 2012)
- Drug addiction (Shabahang et al., 2020)
- Drug use, self-injury, and suicide attempts (Zsila et al., 2020)
- Problematic internet use and maladaptive daydreaming (Vally et al., 2021)

In short, evidence is mounting that intense-personal bonds with one's interest, if not directly driving pathology, may, at very least, be an indicator of other problems.

Not all research on the subject agrees with this conclusion, however. Ashe and McCutcheon (2001), for example, did not find evidence that shyness or loneliness were related to celebrity worship. Likewise, McCutcheon et al. (2003) found no evidence that intense-personal bonds were significantly related measures of cognitive deficits, a finding that was replicated in a subsequent study (McCutcheon et al., 2012). And while intense-personal scores were negatively related to self-esteem for women in a Hong Kong sample, the same result was not obtained for men in the sample (Liu, 2013). As such, there remain open questions about precisely when, and for whom, a strong bond with one's interest may signal maladaptation in fans, although research does seem to suggest that such bonds are more likely to indicate problems than functionality, as least in the way they're presently assessed.

Relationships

Given the well-documented link between intense-personal bonds with the object of one's fan interest and well-being, as well as the intuitive lay theory that people form parasocial bonds as a means of compensating for loneliness or relationship problems, it's surprising that comparatively little research has examined the nature of one's relationships and their association with intense-personal bonds with celebrities. What little research does exist, however, seems to suggest that the association is a fairly negative one.

In one study, for example, intense-personal dimension scores were positively associated with dependence in one's romantic relationships, including possessiveness, jealousy, and insecurity about whether or not one's connection to their partner will dissolve (McCutcheon, 2002). Linn (2013) found analogous findings in their own study, linking an intense-personal bond with a celebrity to attachment anxiety in women who seek contact with male celebrities. Finally, Giles and Maltby (2004) surveyed British adolescents (between 11 and 16 years of age) regarding their attachment style when it came to their peers and their parents and found that intense-personal bonds to a celebrity predicted less secure attachment. The researchers went on to suggest that pseudo-friendships with celebrities may help fans to make up for a lack of close attachment with their peers or their families. While the body of research on this topic may not be as burgeoning as the work on well-being, it nevertheless points to a similar trend, that a special bond with the object of one's fan interest may be a sign of maladaptation.

Conclusion

While the notion of having a special bond with the object of one's fan interest has been ambiguously operationalized in past research, varying, at times, between assessing fanship, fandom, and parasocial relationships, fan researchers often conceptualize it as a closely felt, personal bond between some fans and their interests. The two closest lines of research on this topic include work on parasocial relationships and the intense-personal dimension of the celebrity attitudes scale (with one item on the scale explicitly asking about a "special bond"). With respect to parasocial relationships, highly-identified fans are the ones most likely to have forged a special bond, one in which their own sense of self has come to include the object of their interest. With respect to the intense-personal dimension of the celebrity attitudes scale, a significant body of research reveals that this bond predicts an unfavorable self-perception, materialism, reduced well-being, and relationship issues. And while the research we've reviewed may seem only tangentially related to fan behaviors, other work has more directly shown that this close bond can predict obsessive or obnoxious fan behaviors (McCutcheon, Arguete, McCarley, & Jenkins, 2016), in line with findings linking this special bond with maladaptation.

In closing, the present chapter has shown that it's important to consider the special bond that some fans have with their interests when attempting to understand fan motivations, distinctions between fans, and fan attitudes, beliefs, and behaviors. While such special bond may not be all that common among fans, they may prove highly informative about those who do experience them.

Chapter 29
Development of the CAPE Model of Fan Interest

The book thus far has been a testament to the mountain of work scholars have devoted to understanding the psychology of fans. We've looked at 28 of the most apparent or distinct variables from the literature, variables studied by hundreds of researchers in the context of dozens of different fan groups Through it all, we've seen enough trends and commonalities to conclude that the psychological processes underlying fan activities (e.g., motivation, social dynamics, identity) are not mere idiosyncrasies of any particular fan group; despite variation between specific fandoms and within any given fandom, the same fundamental processes seem to be at play in sport fans, media fans, and hobbyists.

Even so, there has been little work attempting to consolidate and integrate this vast literature on fan psychology. Instead, as is often the case in interdisciplinary academia, scholars publish in the journals of their own field using the terminology and models of their discipline and are generally incentivized to innovate rather than review and integrate what already exists. Mindful of this, what follows is our humble attempt to overcome these limitations with a sort of "unified model of fans," one with three specific goals:

> 1. To non-redundantly assess all relevant dimensions of fan identity in a manner that considers and accounts for conceptual overlap between dimensions
> 2. To reliably and concisely assess these dimensions in a fandom-general fashion—that is, using items that can be flexibly applied to fans of all interests
> 3. To predict outcomes both theoretically important to researchers and practically important to fans and those working with fans

In service of these goals, we've run a series of seven studies on five different fan groups over the past five years with a combined sample of $N = 7,772$. In the present chapter we outline the nature of these samples and the conditions under which the data were gathered. We then describe the creation of an initial pool of questions and the dimension reduction and confirmatory factor analyses that allowed us to arrive at our four-factor CAPE model, assessed with an 18-item scale. In Chapter 30, we establish the predictive validity of each of the CAPE model's four factors based on evidence from our set of seven studies. Finally, in Chapter 31 we test the CAPE model's ability to predict outcome variables of interest to researchers and those who work both with and within fandoms.

The Studies

Between 2016 and 2019 we conducted a series of seven studies on fan groups we were familiar with based on our own prior research. In this section we briefly describe the nature of these samples and the protocols under which data were collected. To make this chapter manageable in length (not to mention bearable to read), we'll spare the reader an exhaustive list of every measure assessed in every study and, instead, direct curious readers who want to know the specifics of the measures used in each study to Appendix A.

General Undergraduate Fans

As is common in psychological research, our first two samples consisted of undergraduates recruited at a large university in the United States Midwest in 2016 and 2017. The first sample included $N = 372$ undergraduates who were self-identified fans of something (e.g., media, sports, music, hobbies). The participants completed the half-hour survey online in exchange for course credit. The survey's focus was on 112-items assessing 28 different facets of fans drawn from prior research (see Appendix B for the entire list of items) alongside a few outcome variables of practical and theoretical interest (e.g., fan behaviors such as spending money, individual differences such as trait transportation, and well-being). The data from this study would be factor-analyzed and used to reduce the original 112-item scale to a more manageable, non-redundant measure.

The second study served as a conceptual replication of the first. We recruited a new sample of $N = 462$ undergrads fans who did not take part in the first study. Participants completed the same 112-item version of the scale assessing facets of fan interest alongside some additional theoretically and practically-relevant items (e.g., perceived stigma, production / consumption behavior, demographic variables).

These first two studies form the empirical foundation upon which the CAPE model and scale were derived. Importantly, they also represent a conglomerate of different types of fans: Across the two studies, 40.1% of participants identified as sport fans, 27.6% as media fans, 24.5% as music fans, and 7.8% as hobbyists. The use of a heterogeneous sample of different fans is an essential part of these two samples, as they inform the second stated goal of our research, to develop a psychological model of fans that can be flexibly used across fan interests. In other words, the model which resulted from these studies cannot be said to be an idiosyncrasy of any one fan group, since it was derived from a sample of different types of fans.

The result of this pair of studies was an 18-item scale assessing the four dimensions of the CAPE model. Having thus developed the scale, we next sought to assess its utility for samples of specific fandoms. We therefore tested the scale in four different fan groups, each of which served as a test the scale's reliability, predictive validity, and ability to predict outcome variables of interest in samples with their own unique quirks and eccentricities.

Furries: A Stigmatized, Non-Prototypical Fandom

While no universally agreed-upon definition exists with respect to what, precisely, a furry is, more than a decade of research has led us to broadly define them as people with a fan-like interest in media (e.g., animation, stories, music, games) that prominently features characters who are anthropomorphized animals or humans with animal-like traits (Plante, Roberts, Reysen, & Gerbasi, 2015). As with other fans, furries' interests manifest in various ways including the development of furry-themed avatars or representations of the self (i.e., "fursonas"), costuming (i.e., "fursuits"), creating, viewing, or commissioning artwork or writing, roleplaying, and interacting with other furries in online forums or in-person at meet-ups and conventions.

Much of our prior research on furries has focused on the heavily-stigmatized nature of the furry fandom, owing, in no small part, to popular media portrayals of furries as sexual deviants or as maladjusted and dysfunctional (Plante, Roberts, Reysen, & Gerbasi, 2017). Indeed, research by Reysen and Shaw (2016) illustrates that furries are among the most heavily-stigmatized fan groups studied, with many furries reporting significant bullying and stigma from those around them and in professional contexts (Roberts et al., 2015). Despite this considerable stigma, however, furries nevertheless rely on the furry fandom for social support (Mock et al., 2013). As a result, furries tend to identify fairly strongly with their fan group when compared to members of other fan groups (Schroy et al., 2016).

To obtain a large and representative sample of furries, in 2017 we recruited N = 1,870 self-identified furries from 62 different countries by recruiting through furry-themed forums, podcasts, social media outlets, and through word-of-mouth signal boosting from the organizers of large furry conventions. Participants completed the survey, which was part of a broader study of the furry fandom, in exchange for entry into a gift card draw. In addition to the final 18-item version of the CAPE scale, the survey also included questions about spending habits, fan identity disclosure, self-expression, personality traits, well-being, and fandom-related behavior (e.g., gatekeeping, helping other fans).

Star Wars Fans: A Mainstream Fandom

In 2018, in a manner similar to our methodology for studying furries, we conducted an online survey of N = 1,925 self-identified fans of the *Star Wars* franchise. Since the first film's original release in 1977, *Star Wars* has grown into one of the largest and most internationally-recognized media franchises in history. In stark contrast to the fringe and highly-stigmatized furry fandom, the final film in the "sequel trilogy" of films grossed more than $1 billion in the American box office alone (IMDbPro, 2020), with various films in the franchise being prominently hyped up, discussed, and reviewed in mainstream media outlets—including the airing of a trailer for one of the films during the 2018 Super Bowl.

As with furries, *Star Wars* fans were recruited through a variety of websites, forums, and social media pages frequented by *Star Wars* fans in exchange for entry into a gift card draw. The study, which was also part of a larger study of *Star Wars* fans, had participants complete the 18-item CAPE scale as well as questions pertaining to their fantasy engagement, elitist beliefs and behavior, subgroups within the *Star Wars* fandom, specific fan behaviors, and participant well-being.

Anime Fans: An International Fandom

Anime is a bit of a catch-all term referring to various sorts of animation (e.g., acetate cells, digital animation, Claymation, stop-motion puppetry) that share one thing in common: they all originate from Japan (Clements, 2018). In contrast to western styles of animation, anime distinguishes itself through its elevation of the medium—including complex and often dark storylines in ways that take animation more "seriously" than the more light-hearted western cartoons of the time, many of which were predominantly targeted toward children. As a genre, anime is complex and multi-faceted, including themes and categories as diverse as science-fiction, warrior and samurai, robots, slice-of-life high school stories, religion, and pornography (Drazen, 2014).

The anime fandom is especially interesting to researchers for several reasons. For one thing, it is international in scope, being produced and present in at least 138 different countries (Clements, 2018). This makes the anime fandom ideal for assessing similarities in fans across cultures while holding the content of the interest itself fairly constant. For another thing, the anime fandom straddles the line between mainstream acceptance and marginalization. On the one hand, more than 60% of all animated television worldwide is considered anime, with the children's show *Pokémon* representing the single-most viewed cartoon series in the world, viewed as it is in 68 different countries (Napier, 2005). On the other hand, despite its global popularity as a genre, anime fans (especially adult fans) frequently find themselves on the receiving end of stigma (Reysen, Plante, Chadborn et al., 2021). For instance, one study found that undergraduate students associated anime fans with being obsessed, introverted, pale-skinned, and nerdy, consuming anime for the purpose of escapism (Reysen, Plante, Roberts, Gerbasi, Mohebpour, & Gamboa, 2016; see also Reysen, Plante,

Roberts, Gerbasi, & Shaw, 2016). Likewise, anime fans frequently find themselves dealing with misconceptions about anime fans as both excessive (e.g., otaku) and perverted (e.g., hentai, Reysen, Plante, Chadborn et al., 2021).

In 2018 we conducted a large-scale study of anime fans that, unlike the previous studies up to this point, recruited participants from both a regional fan convention and from online sources (e.g., popular anime forums and fan websites). The result was a sample of $N = 2,232$ anime fans who completed both the 18-item CAPE scale and a number of questions assessing demographics, subgroup membership, spending habits, fan behaviors (e.g., elitism, gatekeeping, help-giving), and well-being.

Bronies: A Fandom in Decline?

The final two samples were drawn from a fan group known collectively as "bronies", a group we've mentioned on several occasions throughout this book. The term "brony" is a portmanteau of the words "bro" and "pony," and refers to a (typically adult man) fan of the television show *My Little Pony: Friendship is Magic* (Edwards et al., 2019). Unlike the other fan groups mentioned above, which have existed for decades, the brony fandom largely originated in 2010 with the start of the fourth generation of the *My Little Pony* franchise.[45] In the beginning, many of the adult men viewing the show did so ironically, goaded into it as a joke by internet forums. Before long, however, fans were drawn to the show's quality animation, dynamic characters, back and forth in-jokes with the show's writers and animators, and an extensive culture of fan-made content.

Like furries and anime fans, bronies are frequently stigmatized, owing, in no small part, to their perceived violation of gender and age norms by virtue of being adult men watching a show targeted toward young girls (Edwards et al., 2019). Like furries, bronies frequently report feeling a sense of camaraderie and belongingness to the brony fandom (e.g., through slogans like "join the herd"). In fact, a sizable minority of bronies (approximately 20%) themselves identify as furries, having either discovered the brony fandom through their interest in furry or discovered furry through their interest in the brony fandom.

Nevertheless, bronies, as a group, differ from furries in several notable ways. Perhaps most importantly, the furry fandom is largely decentralized and not based around any one media franchise or content creator. In contrast, the brony fandom (like *Star Wars* fans) is centered around a single media franchise. As a result, when the show ended its nine-season run in 2019, coinciding with the

---

[45] This is not to say that there were not fans of *My Little Pony* before 2010, of course. However, the term "brony" and the popularity of the show with adult male fans began with the fourth generation of the show in 2010, not with the show's earlier generations in the 80s, 90s, and 2000s.

final year of the fandom's largest convention, Bronycon, the future of the fandom was thrown into doubt. And while a new generation of *My Little Pony* looms on the horizon, it remains to be seen whether the fandom itself will weather the winds of change or will scatter and be assimilated into other, related fandoms.

Interested in these questions and in the relevance of the CAPE model for predicting attitudes and behaviors in a fandom facing an existential crisis, we conducted two studies of the brony fandom. The first study took place at the world's largest brony convention in 2018 ($N = 221$) while the second took place both in-person at a brony convention and online in 2019 ($N = 690$). In addition to the 18-item CAPE scale, the study included questions similar to those of the above-described studies. The studies also assessed questions about the perceived future of bronies' fan interest and the brony fandom itself, including participants' trajectory into (and possibly out of) the fandom, their thoughts about the end of the show, and their expectations about the future of the brony fandom.

Model Construction

Recall that the first stated goal of this project is to develop a measure that non-redundantly assesses all relevant dimensions of fan identity while accounting for any conceptual overlap. To this end, we first scoured the available literature for every fan-related measure that we could. After doing so, we went through each item in every scale one at a time, adding it to the pool of possible items as long as it was not extremely similar to an existing item in the pool. The result was an initial pool of 239 survey questions.

From there, we organized conceptually-similar items into groups, resulting in 28 dimensions or subscales, each of which has been covered by a chapter in this book. At that point, however, the items were not evenly distributed across the 28 dimensions: Some dimensions had as few as three items, while others had as many as 18 items. For the purpose of making each subscale as comparable as possible, we picked the four items that we felt most represented each dimension in a face valid manner. In the case of subscales with fewer than four items, we created supplemental items to try and capture the essence of the dimension without being too similar to the existing items. The resulting 112-item measure, including the source of every question, can be found in Appendix B (the final 18-item scale is presented in Appendix C).

In the interest of deriving a scale that would be relevant to as many different fandoms as possible, we gave the 112 items to two independent samples of undergraduates who identified as a fan of something. Importantly, we avoided selecting for any specific types of fans. In the first sample we conducted a principal component analysis aimed at empirically deriving the factor structure of our 112-item measure. In our second sample we tested the replicability of the resulting factor structure using a confirmatory factor analysis.

Dimension Reduction

Having collected data about the 112 fan-related items from our first undergraduate sample, we ran a principal component analysis, entering the average scores for each of the 28 subscales as individual items to make the analysis manageable in scale. We chose a principal component analysis to reduce the number of unnecessary items from the measure where possible. We applied an oblimin rotation based on our findings from the literature review that many of the 28 dimensions would correlate with one another, meaning that rotations which assumed orthogonality of the dimensions (e.g., a varimax rotation) were wholly inappropriate. Finally, we established a minimum factor loading cutoff point of $|.40|$ to consider an item as loading onto a factor.

From there, we carried out an iterative process of running the analysis, observing the resulting pattern matrix, eliminating dimensions with a single subscale loaded onto them, cutting subscales which significantly cross-loaded onto multiple dimensions, and getting rid of subscales which did not load significantly onto any of the dimensions. After several iterations, the result was a four-dimension solution which explained 76.16% of the observed variance. The four dimensions, of commitment, asset, present, and expression form the backbone of the CAPE model and are described below.

Commitment

By far, commitment explains the most variance of the four CAPE dimensions at 52.00%. The commitment dimension is comprised of six of the subscale average scores: loyalty, knowledge, magnitude, participation, fandom, and materialism, with loyalty representing the most strongly-loaded subscale. Collectively, these subscales share a common theme in relating to the extent of a fan's committed to their fan interest, be it in terms of trivia known, engagement in fan-related activities, amount of merchandise owned, interaction with other fans, or devotion to the interest itself. In colloquial terms, we can think of the commitment dimension as a fan's one's answer to the question "Just how big of a fan are you?"

Asset

The dimension which we have labeled "Asset" accounts for 10.14% of explained variance in our model and assesses the extent to which fans benefit tangibly or intangibly from this specific fan interest. This is reflected in the four subscales that comprise the asset dimension: economic benefits, self-esteem gained from the fan interest, a sense of accomplishment derived from the interest, and the exclusiveness with which one focuses on this particular interest.

While the last subscale may, at first glance, seem unrelated to the first three, we note that many of the benefits fans derive may be specific to one particular interest (e.g., being a vendor at a particular type of fan convention, or deriving a sense of accomplishment from being well-known in one fandom—despite being largely unknown to other fandoms). In lay discourse, this dimension reflects the question "Do you get anything out of being a fan of this?"

Presence

This is the "weakest" of the four dimensions, accounting for just 6.17% of the variance in our model. Its name refers to the idea that, for some fans, their interest is just something to occupy their attention in the here-and-now. This is encapsulated in the three aspects that make up the presence dimension: it provides them with a sense of escapism, it's a source of sensory novelty, and it offers an experience of eustress. This dimension can also be thought of as a form of "hedonic satisfaction" or what Stebbins (1982, 1997) might have called "casual leisure;" It reflects the extent to which a fan interest scratches that itch for excitement or just provides fans with something novel to break up the monotony of their day-to-day life.

Expression

The expression dimension accounts for a unique 7.85% of the variance in our model. It can be thought of as the significance one ascribes to their fan interest above and beyond its superficial or face content—what the interest means for them, in a way that may differ considerably from other fans. This is apparent from the dimension's subscales, which include aesthetic beauty, finding meaning in the fan interest, growing as a result of the fan interest, the fan interest's ability to allow one to feel unique, and in the ability of the interest to foster and permit creative expression. Conversations about fan-content interactions, critical and personally significant readings and retellings of fan narratives, and the ability to see a fan interest as more than the sum of its parts are all reflected in this dimension, which is also reminiscent of what Stebbins (1982) might have called "serious leisure."

The Second Study

Model Replication

In our first study of undergraduate students we found evidence for a four-dimensional model of fans comprised of 18 out of 28 of our original dimensions. Despite the sample being based on a sizable sample of fans with diverse interests, however, there is no way to know from a single study whether the four-dimensional CAPE model's structure is resilient or merely an idiosyncrasy of the sample. To test this, we conducted a second study in a new, larger sample of undergraduates. The methodology was much the same, recruiting participants who were fans of different interests and assessing the nature of that fan interest using the same 112 items representing the same 28 empirically- and theoretically-derived factors from the existing literature.

The results were subjected to a principal axis factor analysis this time, namely because the intent of this second study was not to reduce the number of items in the questionnaire but, rather, to be a confirmatory factor analysis which assesses the resiliency of the CAPE model's four-factor structure as derived in the first study. The same iterative process was used using the same elimination criteria, resulting in the same four-dimensional structure observed in the first study. About the only notable differences between the two datasets were that in the second study, the model accounted for a smaller overall percentage of variance (67.15% versus 76.16% in the first study) and that the expression dimension explained relatively more variance (8.00%) than the asset dimension (4.98%) in the second study, reversing the trend observed in the first study. Commitment remained the greatest predictor of variance (50.67%) and presence remained the weakest predictor of variance (3.51%), replicating the results of the first study.

Scale Creation

While these two undergraduate studies suggest that the four-dimensional organization of the CAPE model's 18 subscales is fairly resilient, it's worth noting that the structure is based on data from a total of 72 items (see Appendix B). This is a bit unwieldy for use in studies aiming to assess a multitude of other factors. As such, we deemed it necessary to create an abbreviated version of the scale, one that largely replicates the model's four-dimensional structure and captures the essence of the subscales, but does so more concisely.

To accomplish this, we conducted a reliability analysis on each of the 18 constituent subscales in the first and second studies, calculating the item-total correlations for each item. For each of the 18 subscales we chose the item with the highest item-total correlation, arguing that these items most strongly represent the subscale's underlying concept. The result was an 18-item version of the CAPE scale (see Appendix C) with a single indicator representing each of the 18 different subscales.

We next factor analyzed the 18-item scales from both undergraduate samples and found evidence for the same underlying four-dimensional structure. As one might expect, given that the analysis was based on 18 individual items rather than on 18 averages representing composites of each subscale, the structure of the four dimensions was a bit more variable. For example, in the first undergraduate sample, the "meaning" subscale cross-loaded onto both the

"Commitment" and "Asset" dimensions. In the second sample, the "growth" subscale's factor loading on the "Asset" dimension was slightly below 0.40.

These few small and inconsistent discrepancies aside, however, the overall factor structure and the pattern of relationships between the dimensions and their constituent subscales was preserved. For this reason, the 18-item CAPE scale was used in all subsequent studies and, for consistency's sake, is the scale used in all subsequent analyses in Chapters 30 and 31.

Illustrating the reliability of the dimensions, Table 29.1 below lays out the reliability of the four dimensions across seven different studies. Importantly, three of the four dimensions consistently reach acceptable levels of reliability (Commitment, Asset, and Expression). Presence, previously found to be the dimension predicting the least variance, is consistently the least reliable of the dimensions—although it is worth noting that this should, if anything, make it increasingly difficult to find relationships between the present dimension and outcome variables of interest. As we'll see in later chapters, significant relations can be found between presence and other variables despite this relatively low reliability.

Table 29.1

Cronbach Alpha Values for Each of the CAPE Dimensions Across 7 Different Samples of Fans

Study	Commitment	Asset	Presence	Expression
GEN1 (Undergrad)	.862	.767	.645	.866
GEN2 (Undergrad)	.839	.787	.627	.854
Furry	.843	.709	.554	.810
Star Wars	.884	.752	.670	.810
Anime	.829	.739	.540	.767
Brony 2018	.817	.720	.439	.790
Brony 2019	.833	.707	.612	.797

Conclusion: Fans in a Four-Dimensional Space

In the following chapters we will be assessing the validity of the four-dimensional fan scale and its ability to predict both theoretically and practically important outcome variables.

But before we do that, let's pause for a moment to contextualize the CAPE model and its implications for fan research. Specifically, we should ask ourselves what, precisely, it means to say that there are four primary dimensions upon which to assess fans?

Let's start with what the model does *not* say. The CAPE model does not imply that there is no value to assessing subscales beyond the 18 that made it into the final model. Few would argue, for example, that concepts such as "recreation," "desirability," and "sexual attraction" are not worth studying in the context of fan groups. Instead, there may be reasons why specific subscales did not make it into the final model. For instance, scores on the "recreation" subscale averaged almost 6.00 out of a possible 7, with a standard deviation that was only about half of that for the "growth" subscale. This suggests that some of the subscales may suffer from range restriction issues that limit their utility when it comes to meaningfully distinguishing between different fans; if almost every fan finds their interest enjoyable, the variable can tell us very little about significant differences between fans. The same can be said, in the opposite direction, for "sexual attraction," which had an average score of about 2.64 out of 7, suggesting that, at least for most fans, this is not an especially relevant variable. It's absolutely possible that for specific fan interests—notably those with more sexual content or in which sexuality is normalized—it's possible to observe more than floor effects. But insofar as the present goal is to develop a model to assess variables relevant to most fan groups, it would seem that subscales assessing "sexual attraction" or "recreation" may be too idiosyncratic or too lacking in variance to be of use.

But what about subscales such as "desirability," which scored around the midpoint of the scale and which showed a level of variability comparable to the other subscales? In such cases, it may be that the variable itself is too distinct or tangential to other variables to be of theoretical interest. For example, if the social desirability of a fan interest is completely orthogonal to the other subscales assessed (e.g., one's knowledge of the fan interest, the aesthetic appeal of the interest, interest in material trappings of the interest), then it would have been dropped from the factor analysis as a single-item factor. This doesn't mean that social desirability of a fandom is not a facet of fan interest worth considering: A sizable body of research has focused on this very topic (e.g., Reysen, Plante, Roberts, Gerbasi, Mohebpour, & Gamboa, 2016), and has illustrated the impact of belonging to stigmatized fan groups on outcomes such as well-being (e.g., Mock et al., 2013). Instead, it simply means that such variables should considered outside of, or in addition to, the CAPE model.

The CAPE model also does not imply that fans of all interests will score in a comparable fashion on all of the dimensions, or that there will, for certain, be meaningful fandom-level differences on the dimensions. The model says nothing about the relative importance of various motivations as drivers of fan interest or about whether a fan interests are necessarily beneficial for fans' well-being. In and of itself, the CAPE model does not assess fans' specific attitudes or the norms of a particular fandom.

Instead, the CAPE model is a multidimensional space within which to begin meaningfully comparing different fans. Typically, when people compare two different fans, the most salient comparisons are those based superficially on the content of the fan interest itself: Comparing a *Doctor Who* fan to a *Battlestar Galactica* fan based on differences between the shows itself. While such content-based comparisons are certainly useful in some contexts (e.g., anthropological, media studies), there is little reason to believe that the underlying psychology of a *Doctor Who* fan and a *Battlestar Galactica* fan differ substantially—no more than any two people differ significantly in their personality on the basis of whether their favorite color is blue or green or whether they prefer vanilla over chocolate.

For perspective, it's useful to consider the CAPE model alongside other multidimensional models of individual differences, the most famous of which may well be the Big Five model of personality. Using the Big Five dimensions, two different people can be meaningfully compared within a five-dimensional space, quantifying the extent of their differences in ways that, paired alongside other research, allow psychologists to make predictions about their attitudes, beliefs, and behaviors. The CAPE model allows psychologists to analogously compare two fans from two entirely different interests (e.g., a model train enthusiast and a fan of Italian horror films) using a common vernacular and a common conceptual space that allows researchers to both quantify differences between the fans and to predict differences in their thoughts, feelings, and behaviors.

In the following chapters, we assess the extent to which the CAPE dimensions do exactly that, starting first with fairly easily predicted relations to help validate the dimensions themselves before moving into some of the more surprising, interesting, or practically useful outcomes.

Chapter 30
Validation of the CAPE Scale

In the preceding chapter we described the creation of the CAPE model—a four-dimensional model derived from existing research which allows fans of different interests to be meaningfully compared. We also described the development of a concise, 18-item scale to reliably assess these four dimensions across a variety of samples to predict theoretically and practically relevant outcomes. But before we can assess the utility of the CAPE scale, we must first validate it. After all, a reliable scale with a replicable structure is unlikely to do us much good if we can't don't know what, precisely, it is measuring.

To this end, the present chapter aims to test the predictive validity of the CAPE model's four dimensions. Specifically, we'll consider data from the seven studies described in the previous chapter to further explore each of the CAPE model's four dimensions with respect to whether our characterization of each one holds conceptual water. To some, this may seem like a redundant exercise. For example, since we derived and labeled the commitment dimension from, among other things, fan responses to the magnitude item "I am one of the biggest fans of this interest," should we not, by definition, assume that the dimension will predict scores on a measure of fanship, a conceptually similar variable which asks questions like "I strongly identify with [fan interest]"?

Not necessarily. When we derive a model's dimensions, we are, in essence, extracting common variance from the indicators of that dimension. In the case of the commitment dimension, magnitude is only one of its six subscales—and not even the indicator with the strongest item-scale correlation. It's therefore entirely possible (albeit unlikely) that the magnitude subscale covaries with the other subscales in the commitment dimension for reasons beyond the subscales' shared association with the concept of strongly identifying as a fan (e.g., shared method variance between the specific items).

For this reason, we are conducting a check of the predictive validity of the CAPE scale, assessing the extent to which each dimension is positively associated with variables that, conceptually, it ought to be associated with. In doing so, we can be more confident that the dimensions are, in fact, tapping into the conceptual variables which we are claiming they are. In the rest of this chapter we will go through the model, one dimension at a time, and assess its ability to predict, relative to the model's other dimensions, conceptually critical variables.[1]

Commitment

Recall from the previous chapter that the CAPE dimension we've labeled commitment is a composite of six conceptually-related subscales:

- The extent to which fans feel a sense of loyalty to a particular fan interest
- Fans' self-reported knowledge about a particular fan interest
- The magnitude of fans' identity as a fan of a particular interest
- The extent to which fans participate in interest-related activities
- Fans' identification with other fans of the same interest
- The extent to which fans own merchandise associated with their fan interest

By assessing the predictive validity of the commitment dimension we're asking how uniquely or relatively strongly it predicts measures of involvement or devotion to one's fan interest relative to the other three CAPE dimensions.

Years as a Fan

Perhaps one of the most face-valid behavioral measures of one's commitment to their fan interest—and specifically to the idea of being loyal to one's fan interest—is to simply measure how many years they've been engaging in their fan interest.[2] We asked this question to four of our seven samples: furries, anime fans, and two different samples of bronies.

In furries, commitment was the CAPE dimension most strongly associated with years of furry identification ($b = 1.696$, $SE = .198$, $p < .001$),[3] although presence was also significantly (albeit negatively) associated with years as a furry ($b = -.704$, $SE = .182$, $p < .001$). In contrast, neither asset nor expression were significantly associated years of identifying as a furry ($ps > .110$).

These findings were not unique to the furry sample, however. A similar pattern of results was also found in anime fans, with commitment being the CAPE dimension most strongly associated with years spent identifying as an

---

[1] Unless otherwise stated, this is done through multiple regression analyses, allowing each of the four CAPE dimensions to simultaneously predict the variable in question. This represents a more stringent, conservative test of the association than a simple zero-order correlation because it assesses the ability of a CAPE dimension to uniquely predict an outcome while controlling for the other three dimensions.

[2] For information about the specific measures used throughout this chapter see Appendix A.

[3] We have chosen to present unstandardized regression coefficients throughout this book to maximize the intuitiveness of the results in the context of the original scale.

anime fan ($b = 1.232$, $SE = .156$, $p < .001$) and presence being significantly negatively associated with years as a fan ($b = -.752$, $SE = .143$, $p < .001$). Unlike furries, however, expression was also positively associated with years as a fan ($b = .427$, $SE = .177$, $p = .016$) and asset was negatively associated with years as a fan ($b = -.520$, $SE = .180$, $p = .004$), albeit both more weakly so than either commitment or presence, respectively.

The only exception to this trend could be found in our 2018 study of bronies, where presence was the only variable significantly associated with years as a brony ($b = -.403$, $SE = .170$, $p = .019$; all other $ps > .173$). Lest we conclude that the link between commitment and years as a fan ends with bronies, however, the 2019 sample of bronies found evidence for the previous trend, with commitment in that sample being the only CAPE dimension to predict years as a brony ($b = .311$, $SE = .152$, $p = .041$; all other $ps > .818$).

Expected Engagement Post-Show

One component of the commitment dimension speaks to loyalty, which would seem to include a willingness to *continue* being a fan of a show if its original content were to suddenly come to the end. This was far from a hypothetical scenario for the bronies we studied in 2018, who were facing the imminent end of the show *My Little Pony: Friendship is Magic*. When asked whether they expected to continue engaging in fan activities after the end of the show, commitment was the only one of the CAPE variables significantly associated with anticipated participation ($b = .253$, $SE = .043$, $p < .001$). The other three dimensions, in contrast, did not significantly predict scores on this measure (all other $ps > .057$).

Fan Elitism

Another component of the commitment dimension is the subscale of fan-relevant knowledge, assessing the extent to which fans accumulate an almost encyclopedic knowledge about their interest as a result of the time they've invested in it. Related to this concept is fan elitism, wherein some fans—typically those who have been fans for longer or who are more invested in an interest—consider themselves to be more knowledgeable about the interest than others (Plante et al., 2020).

In a sample of *Star Wars* fans we found that, of the CAPE dimensions, commitment was the most strongly tied to feelings of fan elitism ($b = .269$, $SE = .018$, $p < .001$), although the asset dimension was also positively associated with elitism ($b = .126$, $SE = .023$, $p < .001$) and the presence dimension was negatively associated with elitism ($b = -.067$, $SE = .018$, $p < .001$). Expression, in contrast, was not significantly associated with feelings of elitism among fans ($b = .034$, $SE = .023$, $p = .141$).

The same pattern of results was found in anime fans, with commitment again being more strongly associated with elitism ($b = .237$, $SE = .022$, $p < .001$) than either the asset ($b = .109$, $SE = .025$, $p < .001$) or presence dimension ($b = -.118$, $SE = .020$, $p < .001$). Once again, expression was not significantly associated with elitism ($b = -.023$, $SE = .025$, $p = .343$).

The same could not be said for our 2018 sample of bronies, however, in which none of the CAPE dimensions were associated with feelings of elitism ($ps > .304$). One possible explanation may be the somewhat relatively lower internal reliability found for the elitism scale ($\alpha = .688$) compared to that in the *Star Wars* ($\alpha = .747$) and anime samples ($\alpha = .783$), although this is unlikely to fully account for the discrepancy between the samples. If nothing else, we can say that the link between the commitment dimension and elitism is perhaps more tenuous than the link between commitment and years as a fan or anticipated future engagement with the interest.

Fanship: Fan Identity

An important component of the commitment dimension is the extent or magnitude to which fans consider themselves to be fans, a concept captured by the variable of fanship (Reysen & Branscombe, 2010). Given the importance of fanship to any study of fans, it was assessed in nearly all of our samples (the exception being our undergraduate samples.)

Across the five samples, commitment was consistently found to be the CAPE dimension most strongly associated with fanship scores. This was the case with furries, where commitment ($b = .520$, $SE = .031$, $p < .001$) and expression ($b = .394$, $SE = .032$, $p < .001$) were the only two dimensions significantly associated with fanship (all other $ps > .059$). It was also the case with *Star Wars* fans, where commitment ($b = .651$, $SE = .024$, $p < .001$), significance ($b = .191$, $SE = .030$, $p < .001$), and presence ($b = .084$, $SE = .024$, $p < .001$) were all significantly associated with fanship, but the asset dimension was not ($b = -.021$, $SE = .031$, $p = .489$). In anime fans, where all four dimensions were significantly tied to fanship scores, commitment was again the most strongly associated with fanship ($b = .556$, $SE = .026$, $p < .001$), beating out asset ($b= .067$, $SE = .030$, $p = .028$); expression ($b = .351$, $SE = .030$, $p < .001$), and presence ($b = .191$, $SE = .024$, $p < .001$). The same could also be said in both brony samples: In the 2018 sample, commitment was more strongly associated with fanship ($b = .612$, $SE = .073$, $p < .001$) than expression, which was also positively associated with fanship ($b = .214$, $SE= .083$, $p < .001$) while neither asset nor presence were ($ps > .314$), with an almost identical trend, including comparable magnitudes, observed in the 2019 brony sample (commitment: $b = .642$, $SE = .046$, $p < .001$;

expression: $b = .308$, $SE = .051$, $p < .001$; asset and presence were non-significant, $ps > .071$).

Taken together, these findings provide robust evidence that the concept of fanship, as one would predict, is most strongly tied to the CAPE dimension of commitment. In contrast, fanship was only sporadically or inconsistently found to be associated with the other CAPE dimensions.

Engaging in Fan-Related Activities

Beyond merely identifying as a fan, factor analyses also revealed that commitment is associated with the extent to which fans actively participate in fan-related activities. We can look at these fan activities both in general and with respect to specific activities.

Fan-Related Activities in General

Across four samples, commitment was the CAPE dimension most strongly associated with a composite measure of engagement in different fan activities. In a sample of *Star Wars* fans, for example, although all CAPE dimensions were positively associated with general engagement in fan activities, commitment was more strongly associated ($b = .298$, $SE = .204$, $p < .001$) than the dimensions of asset ($b = .069$, $SE = .032$, $p = .029$); expression ($b = .100$, $SE = .031$, $p = .001$), and presence ($b = .197$, $SE = .024$, $p < .001$).

Other samples followed the same pattern of results, with commitment being the dimension most strongly associated with fan activities, although only some of the other CAPE dimensions were significantly associated from sample to sample. In anime fans, commitment ($b = .546$, $SE = .024$, $p < .001$) was more strongly associated with fan activity engagement than presence ($b = .058$, $SE = .022$, $p = .009$), while expression was negatively associated ($b = -.059$, $SE = .028$, $p = .033$) and the asset dimension was non-significantly associated ($b = -.024$, $SE = .028$, $p = .385$). In the 2019 brony sample, commitment was again the most strongly associated with activity engagement ($b = .361$, $SE = .035$, $p < .001$) relative to asset ($b = .098$, $SE = .037$, $p = .008$) and expression ($b = .083$, $SE = .039$, $p = .031$), while presence was not ($b = -.033$, $SE = .031$, $p = .282$). Finally, in perhaps the strongest evidence linking commitment to engaging in fan activities, commitment was the only CAPE dimension significantly associated with activity engagement ($b = .264$, $SE = .035$, $p < .001$; all other $ps > .055$).

Specific Fan Activity: Convention Attendance

Beyond a general look at fan engagement, we can also find some evidence for an association between commitment and specific fan activities—such as the frequency with which fans attend fan conventions. This was the case with furries, for whom commitment ($b = 2.406$, $SE = .415$, $p < .001$) was the dimension most strongly associated with the number of conventions fans had attended relative to the asset dimension (b = .820, SE = .404, p = .042), and expression, which was negatively associated with convention attendance (b = -.987, SE = .434, p = .023). Presence was, in contrast, not significantly associated with convention attendance for furries (b = -.226, SE = .380, p = .552).

As one might expect for a variable as noisy and multiply-determined as convention attendance, the evidence for this association was far from perfect. For example, in our sample of anime fans, commitment was, as with furries, found to be strongly positively associated with the number of cons fans had attended (b = .764, SE = .232, p = .001) and was more strongly associated, in magnitude, than either presence (b = -.651, SE = .213, p = .002) or expression (b = .299, SE = .263, p = .257). Commitment was not, however, the dimension most strongly associated with convention attendance in anime fans: In this case, asset (b = .923, SE = .268, p = .001) was more strongly associated with convention attendance. Despite fluctuations in the relative strength of commitment as a predictor across these two samples, it was nevertheless a fairly consistently strong predictor of a specific fan activity, in line with its tendency to be the strongest CAPE predictor of fan activities more generally.

Nature of Fan Activity Participation

In addition to asking fans about the specific activities they engage in, we asked them about the way in which they engaged in those activities. For instance, we asked our undergraduate participants whether the nature of their participation was active and productive as opposed to being more passive and consumptive. The results revealed that commitment was significantly more strongly associated with an active participation style (b = .569, SE = .066, p < .001) than the asset dimension was (b = .239, SE = .066, p < .001), although both were significant. In contrast, neither expression nor presence were associated with the extent to which a fan's interest-related activities were active in nature (all ps > .093).

Fandom: Identifying with Other Fans

Another important subscale of the Commitment dimension involves the extent to which fans identify not only as fans of the interest itself, but also the extent to which they interact and identify with other fans.

To this end, we asked participants in one of our undergraduate samples to indicate the extent to which their fan activities involved a social component (e.g., shared consumption). Tellingly, commitment (b = .552, SE = .081, p < .001) was the only one of the CAPE dimensions significantly associated with the measure of shared activity participation (all other ps > .087).

Going beyond merely interacting with other fans in the course of one's usual fan activities, we were also able to assess the extent to which fans identify with the broader fan community, also known as fandom (see Chapter 7). Across five samples of specific fan groups, we find consistent evidence that, as predicted, the commitment dimension is a better predictor of fandom than the other CAPE dimensions.

For example, in our sample of furries, while expression ($b = .256$, $SE = .032$, $p < .001$) and presence ($b = .108$, $SE = .028$, $p < .001$) were significantly associated with fandom scores, commitment scores were the most strongly associated with fandom ($b = .471$, $SE = .031$, $p < .001$; Asset: $b = .032$, $SE = .028$, $p = .927$). A similar pattern emerged with *Star Wars* fans, where commitment ($b = .480$, $SE = .025$, $p < .001$) was more strongly predictive of fandom than the only other significant predictor, presence ($b = .210$, $SE = .025$, $p < .001$; other $ps > .224$). The same was true for anime fans: Despite all four CAPE variables predicting fandom scores, commitment was the strongest predictor ($b = .437$, $SE = .027$, $p < .001$; asset: $b = .122$, $SE = .032$, $p < .001$; expression $b = .171$, $SE = .031$, $p < .001$; presence: $b = .287$, $SE = .025$, $p < .001$). Finally, we observed the same pattern of results in the two brony samples, with commitment emerging as the strongest predictor of fandom scores in 2018 (commitment: $b = .391$, $SE = .085$, $p < .001$; asset: $b = .180$, $SE = .088$, $p = .042$; all other $ps > .061$) and in 2019 (commitment: $b = .507$, $SE = .043$, $p < .001$; expression: $b = .208$, $SE = .048$, $p < .001$; presence: $b = .123$, $SE = .038$, $p = .001$; asset: $b = .010$, $SE = .046$, $p = .828$).

Together, these findings indicate that the social component of one's fan interest is most strongly encompassed by the CAPE dimension of commitment, despite the tendency for the social facets of one's fan interest to overlap to a lesser degree with other dimensions (e.g., asset).

Materialism and Fan-Related Spending

The final commitment subscale indicates the extent to which fans spend money on or collect memorabilia and merchandise of their interest. The link between these concepts is a fairly intuitive one: The more devoted a person is to an interest, the more they may feel compelled to represent that interest through the accumulation of stuff pertaining to it.[4] It would therefore make sense that measures of fan-related spending behavior should be tied most strongly to the CAPE dimension of commitment.

---

[4] Or, for a cognitive dissonance interpretation that turns cause-and-effect on its head: Fans who spend more on fan-related merchandise may justify their purchases post-hoc by convincing themselves that they must be devoted and committed to the fan interest and that the activity itself is more important to them.

Value of Interest-Related Merchandise Collection

In our 2019 study of bronies, we asked fans to estimate, in $USD, the approximate value of their total collection of *My Little Pony* merchandise (which may include, but is not limited to plushies, figurines, artwork, cosplay materials, and clothing—to name just a few: Edwards et al., 2019). Commitment emerged as the only CAPE dimension which significantly predicted the value of fans' merchandise collection ($b = 836.973$, $SE = 244.590$, $p = .001$; all other $ps > .382$). In particular, fans with more expensive collections tended to have higher commitment scores than fans with less expensive collections.

Willingness to Spend $250 on Fan Interest

Providing converging evidence for the above relation, we asked participants in one of our undergraduate samples and in our furry sample to indicate their willingness to spend $250 on a single purchase related to their fan interest. Undergraduate fans' commitment scores were the strongest of the CAPE dimensions to predict scores on this measure ($b = .665$, $SE = .083$, $p < .001$) relative to asset ($b = .399$, $SE = .086$, $p < .001$), presence ($b = -.153$, $SE = .075$, $p = .042$), and expression scores ($b = -.025$, $SE = .074$, $p = .732$). The same trend was observed in furries, where commitment scores ($b = .546$, $SE = .051$, $p < .001$) were more strongly associated with willingness to spend than expression, which was also significant ($b = .112$, $SE = .054$, $p = .037$) and either asset or presence, neither of which were significant ($ps > .100$).

Annual Spending on Specific Fan-Related Merchandise

As a final set of measures of fan materialism, we asked furries and anime fans to indicate how much money they had spent in the past 12 months on various fan-related merchandise: physical artwork, digital artwork, erotic artwork, and on platforms designed to support independent content creators.

With respect to physical artwork, none of the CAPE variables predicted annual spending among furries (all $ps > .496$). In contrast, among anime fans, commitment was significantly associated with spending more on physical artwork ($b = .426$, $SE = .032$, $p < .001$), albeit to a comparable extent as expression ($b = .440$, $SE = .036$, $p < .001$); asset ($b = .160$, $SE = .037$, $p < .001$) and presence ($b = .238$, $SE = .029$, $p < .001$) were also significantly associated with spending on physical artwork.

When it comes to digital artwork, the results were more consistent and in-line with predictions. For furries, commitment was the only CAPE dimension associated with spending on digital art ($b = 106.486$, $SE = 45.495$, $p = .019$); all other $ps > .118$). For anime fans, while commitment was not the sole significant predictor, it did emerge as the strongest predictor ($b = .557$, $SE = .031$, $p < .001$)

relative to expression (b = .364, SE = .036, p < .001), presence (b = .158, SE = .029, p < .001), and asset (b = -.034, SE = .036, p = .351).

A similar trend emerged with respect to erotic artwork: For furries, commitment was again the only CAPE dimension significantly associated with spending on erotic artwork (b = 35.549, SE = 13.234, p = .007; all other ps > .217). Among anime fans, commitment (b = .331, SE = .031, p < .001); and presence (b = .308, SE = .028, p < .001) were the two strongest predictors, although asset (b = .120, SE = .036, p = .001) and expression (b = .200, SE = .035, p < .001) were also significantly associated with spending on erotic content. We will return to this association between commitment and sexual fan content specifically in the next chapter.

Finally, when it comes to supporting independent content creators through funding platforms such as Patreon, we find again that commitment is the dimension most consistently associated with spending. For furries, commitment was the only significant predictor of spending on such platforms (b = 19.192, SE = 7.735, p = .008; all other ps > .470). For anime fans, commitment was significantly associated (b = .106, SE = .041; p = .010), although it was not more significantly associated than the other dimensions of asset (b = .142, SE = .048, p = .003) or presence (b = .134, SE = .038, p < .001); in comparison, expression was not significantly associated (b = -.091, SE = .047, p = .052).

Taken together, these findings make a compelling case for the fact that the side of fan culture most associated with its material trappings is best captured by the CAPE dimension of commitment. While the occasional exception to this trend was observed, it's clear that commitment is associated with materialism in line our predictions based on the overall structure of the CAPE model, its dimensions, and their constituent subscales.

Asset

The next CAPE dimension, entitled "asset," refers to a composite of four subscales loosely connected to the idea that one's particular fan interest is something they benefit from in a tangible or intangible way:

- The extent to which fans benefit economically from their interest
- Fans' tendency to derive a sense of self-esteem from their involvement with their interest
- The tendency for fans to feel a sense of accomplishment resulting from their fan-related activities
- The extent to which fans' interests are limited exclusively to one specific fandom, as opposed to a multitude of different fandoms

As with the commitment dimension, we can assess the extent to which the asset dimension uniquely or distinctly predicts the extent to which one's fan interest is an asset to them relative to other interests they may have.

Content Production

One of the most direct ways a person's fan interest can be an asset to them is if they produce fan-related content that they subsequently profit or receive positive attention from. To this end, we asked undergraduates fans to indicate the extent to which they do or do not produce content related to their fan interest.

With respect to extent to which participants produce fan-related content, asset was the CAPE dimension most strongly associated with it ($b = .322$, $SE = .073$, $p < .001$), although expression was also a significant predictor ($b = .269$, $SE = .069$, $p < .001$; all other $ps > .203$). A related question about the extent to which participants do *not* produce fan-related content proved consistent in its findings: Asset was again most strongly predictive dimension for this outcome ($b = -.402$, $SE = .098$, $p < .001$), while presence was the only other significant predictor ($b = .330$, $SE = .092$, $p < .001$; all other $ps > .212$).

These findings provide initial, albeit tangential, support for the idea that the asset dimension of the CAPE model is associated with the extent to which fans benefit from their fan interest. While we have not, to date, specifically assessed the extent to which participants sell or otherwise profit from the content they create, it seems to follow that those who create fan-made content should be more likely than those who don't to materially benefit from the selling of such content. Future research on this topic would benefit from targeting content creators (e.g., artists, writers) who sell their products to fans, assessing this subscale in a more direct fashion and allowing for a comparison of those who score high and low on the asset dimension with respect to such measures.

Receiving Help

While the previous section construed financially benefitting from a fan interest as a product of selling fan-made content, this is far from the only way fans can derive material value from their fan interest. Another possibility stems from receiving financial help from other members of the fandom—be it in the form of donations, financial assistance, a place to live rent-free, or being able to split travel or hotel costs at a convention.

To assess this idea, we asked several different samples to indicate the extent to which they had received different forms of help (including several types of financial help) from other fans. In the first sample of undergraduate fans asset was the dimension most strongly associated with receiving help ($b = .373$, $SE = .064$, $p < .001$), although expression was also positively associated ($b = .186$, $SE = .054$, $p = .001$; all other $ps > .363$).

Subsequent studies carried out the same procedure in specific fan groups with comparable results. In a sample of furries, for example, the asset dimension (b = .109, SE = .028, p < .001) was significantly associated with receiving help, along with commitment (b = .128, SE = .028, p < .001) and presence (b = .071, SE = .026, p = .006; but not expression: b = .031, SE = .029, p = .297). In a sample of anime fans, the asset dimension (b = .121, SE = .022, p < .001), alongside expression (b = .101, SE = .021, p < .001) and presence (b = .043, SE = .017, p = .013), was associated with receiving help from other fans in a way that wasn't the case with commitment (b = .029, SE = .019, p = .125). The only sample in which receiving help was unrelated to the asset dimension was the 2018 brony study, in which only expression was modestly associated with receiving help (b = .189, SE = .085, p = .026; all other ps > .151).

While these findings don't point to asset as being unique among the CAPE dimensions with respect to being associated with receiving help (i.e., expression), they do suggest at least some relation between the asset dimension and the notion of benefiting in some way from one's fan interest—a finding that is only strengthened by converging evidence from the previous findings about content production.

Self-Esteem from Fandom

To date, we've yet to run a study directly assessing the extent to which fans' self-esteem is directly affected by being part of a fandom, interacting with other fans, or by engaging in fandom-related activities. We have, however, assessed the self-esteem of fans in several of our studies, allowing us to assess the extent to which trait self-esteem is associated with the asset dimension of the CAPE model—on the assumption that those benefiting more from the fandom will show greater self-esteem than those who do not.

Preliminary evidence for this idea can be found in both our *Star Wars* and anime samples. Among *Star Wars* fans, the asset dimension is significantly positively associated with self-esteem (b = .157, SE = .051, p = .002), as is the commitment dimension (b = .211, SE = .039, p < .001). In contrast, the presence dimension is negatively associated with self-esteem (b = -.263, SE = .039, p < .001) and the expression dimension is not associated at all with self-esteem (b = -.016, SE = .050, p = .745). Asset is also similarly positively associated with self-esteem in the anime sample (b = .100, SE = .049, p = .040) along with commitment (b = .152, SE = .042, p < .001), while presence is negatively associated with self-esteem in anime fans (b = -.204, SE = .039, p < .001) and expression is unrelated (b = .028, SE = .048, p = .557).

However, evidence from two samples of bronies calls into question the robustness of these findings. In a 2018 sample, commitment was the only CAPE dimension found to be significantly associated with self-esteem ($b = .334$, $SE = .142$, $p = .019$; all other $ps > .800$). In a subsequent 2019 study, commitment was again found to be positively associated with self-esteem ($b = .165$, $SE = .061$, $p = .007$) while presence was negatively associated with self-esteem ($b = -.255$, $SE = .055$, $p < .001$). In contrast, neither asset nor expression were significantly associated with self-esteem ($ps > .485$).

Taken together, the data provide only modest evidence at best for a link between asset and trait self-esteem. However, it should be noted that one need not predict a relationship between trait self-esteem and the asset dimension for it to nevertheless be true that asset is tied to one's use of the fandom for self-esteem bolstering purposes. After all, research suggests that people often rely on their social groups for self-esteem (e.g., Tajfel & Turner, 1979). As such, there may not be any reason to suspect trait-level differences in fans' level of self-esteem relative to non-fans (or relative to those who rely on the fandom for self-esteem versus those who do not). Instead, it will be useful for research on this subject to more directly assess the association between the asset dimension and a behavioral measure of self-esteem protection using the fandom—perhaps experimentally, using a self-esteem threat and subsequent assessment of fans' reliance on fan identification in response to the threat.

Fan-Related Status

Another important benefit subsumed under the asset dimension involves the sense of accomplishment or achievement one associates with one's fan involvement. This may stem from the sheer volume of content consumed, from knowing more than typical fans do, or being more recognized and revered among fans. Regardless of where the sense of achievement comes from, it is common for people to feel a sense of growth and accomplishment in the things they do—including their leisure activities (e.g., self-determination theory, Deci, 1980; Deci & Ryan, 2000). To this end, feeling a sense of accomplishment—including comparing ourselves to other fans and feeling better than them (e.g., downward social comparison, Wills, 1981)—should be beneficial to fans, making the fandom an important asset for them as such.

To test this, we asked participants in three different samples of fans (furries, anime fans, and bronies) to complete a measure of intrafandom status—the extent to which they felt like they would be held in especially high regard by other members of their fandom.

In our sample of furries, the CAPE dimension of asset ($b = .298$, $SE = .033$, $p < .001$), along with the dimension of commitment ($b = .289$, $SE = .034$, $p < .001$) were positively associated with felt intrafandom status. In contrast, presence was negatively associated with felt status (b = -.142, SE = .031, p < .001) and expression was unrelated (b = -.044, SE = .035, p = .211).

Our sample of anime fans similarly found a positive association between asset and intrafandom status (b = .206, SE = .028, p < .001), although commitment was more strongly associated with status (b = .446, SE = .024, p < .001). Like with furries, presence was again negatively associated with status (b = -.094, SE = .022, p < .001) and expression was again not significantly associated with it (b = -.036, SE = .027, p = .185).

Finally, and perhaps most importantly, in our 2018 sample of bronies, asset was the *only* CAPE dimension significantly associated with intrafandom status (b = .200, SE = .098, p = .043; all other ps > .086). These findings further suggest that asset may be the CAPE dimension most consistently associated with status.

Exclusiveness of Fan Interest

A final important component of the asset dimension centers on the idea that if a fan interest is especially beneficial to a fan, it is likely to be fairly unique in that regard. Put in colloquial terms, a Jack-of-all-trades is a master of none, meaning that a person who splits their attention and effort among a wide range of fan interests is unlikely to be able to invest the time and effort into any one fandom needed to benefit from it (whether in terms of achieving status through knowledge or fame, forging deep and meaningful relationships, or establishing a presence in the fan market).

Speaking to this idea, we asked undergraduate participants to indicate the exclusiveness of their particular fan interest. The results revealed that asset was, by far, the CAPE dimension most strongly associated with exclusiveness of fan interest (b = .523, SE = .054, p < .001), with commitment being the only other dimension positively associated with exclusivity of interest (b = .111, SE = .052, p = .032; all other ps > .283).

In a distinct, but related vein, we asked members of specific fandoms (i.e., furries, bronies) to indicate whether they had other fan interests and, if so, to indicate the extent of their interest in those other fandoms. The data were largely in line with our undergraduate results. For furries, the asset dimension was associated with having less interest in other fandoms (b = -.134, SE = .037, p < .001), with presence being the only other dimension significantly (if positively) associated with other interests (b = .079, SE = .036, p = .028; all other ps > .297). And while none of the CAPE dimensions were significantly associated with the extent of other fan interests in the 2018 sample of bronies (all ps > .202), in the 2019 sample asset was the only dimension significantly associated with having less interest in other fandoms (b = -.212, SE = .092, p = .022; all other ps > .108).

Taken together, the findings for the asset dimension, while not quite as strong and consistent at those for the commitment dimension, nevertheless provide preliminary evidence for the dimension's predictive validity. In particular, it would appear that the asset dimension largely predicts fan attitudes and behaviors in-line with what we would expect from fans for whom their fan interest was beneficial to them, making their specific fan interest an invaluable asset to them.

Presence

The third CAPE dimension is labeled "presence," and it pertains to a set of three subscales assessing the extent to which fans engage in their fan activity in service of superficial, moment-to-moment hedonism:

- As a means of escaping the dreary monotony of day-to-day life
- To facilitate novel sensory experiences
- To experience thrill or excitement associated with uncertainty (i.e., eustress)

To date, the presence dimension is the least-validated of our four dimensions, lacking, as it does, a strong test of the latter two subscales. Nevertheless, at least with respect to its first subscale—the one which most strongly loads onto the presence dimension, numerous measures exist as an opportunity for validation testing.

Fantasy Engagement

The fantasy engagement scale was developed to assess the extent to which a person's engagement in fantasy activities is largely beneficial (positive) or dysfunctional (negative: Plante, Reysen, Groves et al., 2017). One component of this scale is an assessment the frequency with which people engage in fantasy activities. Insofar as this represents a general tendency for people to allow themselves to drift from reality to focus instead on fantasy worlds, we can use frequency of fantasy engagement as a proxy measure for a person's desire for escapism.

With this in mind, we assessed frequency of fantasy engagement in our undergraduate samples. Presence was found to be uniquely associated among the CAPE dimensions with frequency of fantasy engagement (b = .140, SE = .070, p = .045; all other ps > .521) in one of our samples. And while it was not as strongly associated with frequency of fantasy engagement as commitment (b = .320, SE = .029, p < .001) in the second sample, presence (b = .193, SE = .029, p < .001) did, along with asset (b = .167, SE = .038, p < .001) and expression (b = .208, SE = .038, p < .001), significantly predict frequency of fantasy engagement. As such, of the four CAPE dimensions, presence was the one most consistently associated with frequency of fantasy engagement.

Immersion into Fictional Worlds

In the same vein as frequency of engaging in fantasy activity, we have also asked fans about their general tendency to be immersed or "transported" into fictional settings as another measure of their desire for escapism (e.g., Green & Brock, 2000). In one of our samples of undergraduates, presence was the CAPE dimension most strongly tied to a trait measure of transportability ($b = .173$, $SE = .037$, $p < .001$), relative to expression ($b = .149$, $SE = .036$, $p < .001$), asset ($b = -.236$, $SE = .041$, $p < .001$), and commitment ($b = -.034$, $SE = .040$, $p = .403$).

In later studies, we assessed immersion into fan-related media specifically, rather than a general tendency to become transported into fictional stories in general. In a sample of furries, presence ($b = .106$, $SE = .027$, $p < .001$) was a significant predictor of immersion, though it was not as strong a predictor as commitment ($b = .265$, $SE = .030$, $p < .001$) or expression ($b = .275$, $SE = .031$, $p < .001$), and was about as strong a predictor as asset ($b = -.077$, $SE = .029$, $p = .008$). In a sample of anime fans, however, presence did emerge as the strongest predictor of immersion into fan-related media ($b = .241$, $SE = .022$, $p < .001$), stronger than either commitment ($b = .137$, $SE = .024$, $p < .001$), expression ($b = .164$, $SE = .027$, $p < .001$), or asset ($b = -.017$, $SE = .028$, $p = .537$). Running contrary to this trend, however, in a 2018 sample of bronies, neither presence nor asset were significantly associated with immersion (both ps $> .059$), while commitment ($b = .238$, $SE = .072$, $p = .001$) and expression ($b = .241$, $SE = .081$, $p = .003$) were. In short, evidence linking presence to immersion into fictional worlds is somewhat sporadic, a finding somewhat inconsistent with the previous finding linking presence more generally to escaping into fantasy.

Expression

The final CAPE dimension, labeled "expression," involves five subscales organized around the central concept of finding self-expression, beauty, or meaning in fan content in a way that transcends the surface level of the content itself:

- The extent to which fans appreciate the beauty of interest-relevant content
- Finding significance or meaning in interest-relevant content
- Feeling a sense of growth or personal development inspired by, or as a direct results of, their fan interest
- Feeling a sense of personal distinctiveness or uniqueness based on their identification as a fan of an interest

- Feeling more creative as a result of engaging in interest-related activities

As with the other dimensions, validating the expression dimension and its measure will consist of assessing its association with measures related to these concepts beyond what is predicted by the other CAPE dimensions.

Being a Content Creator

While it is conceptually difficult to quantify and compare the extent to which two people find aesthetic appreciation in the content of their respective fan interests, we may be able to assess beauty and aesthetics in another way: By assessing the extent to which fans engage in acts of artistic creation, either through drawings or through writing. In service of this goal, we assessed the extent to which those who do and do not identify as artists and as writers in different fan groups compare to one another with respect to their scores on each of the CAPE dimensions. Unlike the previous analyses in this chapter, the present analyses will involve a series of *t*-tests.

Artist vs. Non-Artist

In a sample of furries, artists scored significantly higher than non-artists on three out of four of the CAPE dimensions (commitment, asset, and expression); there was no difference in presence scores between furry artists and non-artists (see Table 30.1). For *Star Wars* fans, artists scored significantly higher than non-artists on measures of expression and presence, but did not differ on measures of commitment or asset (see Table 30.2). For anime fans, artists scored higher on measures of expression and asset, but not on measures of commitment or presence (see Table 30.3). Finally, for bronies, artists scored significantly higher than non-artists on all measures except presence (see Table 30.4).

Taken together, across four samples, expression was the only dimension on which artists scored consistently higher than non-artists.

Table 30.1

CAPE Variables in Furry Artists and Non-Artists

Dimension	Group	Mean	SD	t(df)	p-Value
Commitment	Artist	4.43	1.30	$t(1651)$ = 2.946	.003
	Non-Artist	4.25	1.26		
Asset	Artist	3.50	1.30	$t(1648)$ = 6.667	< .001
	Non-Artist	3.08	1.30		
Presence	Artist	4.60	1.18	$t(1650)$ = .510	.610
	Non-Artist	4.57	1.19		
Expression	Artist	4.86	1.31	$t(1651)$ = 4.512	< .001
	Non-Artist	4.58	1.36		

Table 30.2

CAPE Variables in Star Wars Artists and Non-Artists

Dimension	Group	Mean	SD	t(df)	p-Value
Commitment	Artist	4.17	1.46	$t(1923)$ = .887	.375
	Non-Artist	4.10	1.47		
Asset	Artist	2.34	1.24	$t(649.210)$ = 1.172	.242
	Non-Artist	2.26	1.14		
Presence	Artist	4.29	1.40	$t(1923)$ = 1.962	.050
	Non-Artist	4.14	1.41		
Expression	Artist	3.94	1.32	$t(1923)$ = 5.012	< .001
	Non-Artist	3.56	1.38		

Table 30.3

CAPE Variables in Anime Artists and Non-Artists

Dimension	Group	Mean	SD	t(df)	p-Value
Commitment	Artist	4.01	1.38	t(2230) = 1.865	.062
	Non-Artist	3.88	1.28		
Asset	Artist	2.62	1.72	t(595.709) = 3.827	< .001
	Non-Artist	2.37	1.25		
Expression	Artist	4.63	1.32	t(614.537) = 1.166	.244
	Non-Artist	4.55	1.23		
Presence	Artist	4.28	1.35	t(610.620) = 7.777	< .001
	Non-Artist	3.72	1.25		

Table 30.4

CAPE Variables in Brony (2019) Artists and Non-Artists

Dimension	Group	Mean	SD	t(df)	p-Value
Commitment	Artist	4.39	1.26	t(688) = 2.650	.008
	Non-Artist	4.10	1.33		
Asset	Artist	3.10	1.24	t(688) = 3.070	.002
	Non-Artist	2.79	1.17		
Presence	Artist	4.42	1.27	t(688) = .698	.486
	Non-Artist	4.34	1.30		
Expression	Artist	4.67	1.37	t(688) = 3.611	< .001
	Non-Artist	4.26	1.35		

Writer vs. Non-Writer

In the same manner as with artists, we compared writers to non-writers across the same four samples of fans. In the furry sample, writers only scored significantly higher than non-writers on the expression dimension; scores on the other dimensions did not differ (see Table 30.5). For *Star Wars* fans and for anime fans, writers scored higher than non-writers on all four dimensions (see Tables 30.6 and 30.7). Finally, writers and non-writers did not differ significantly on any of the measures for bronies (all *p*s > .088).

As with the data on artists, the data on writers shows that the expression dimension is the CAPE dimension most consistently associated with the tendency to identify as a creator of fan-related content—an act of creation that involves, among other thing, an appreciation for aesthetic principles. While far from a perfect validation of this subscale, it provides preliminary evidence for the aesthetics subscale of the expression dimension.

Table 30.5

CAPE Variables in Furry Writers and Non-Writers

Dimension	Group	Mean	SD	t(df)	p-Value
Commitment	Writer	4.36	1.23	$t(949.787) = .339$	.735
	Non-Writer	4.30	1.29		
Asset	Writer	3.31	1.25	$t(1648) = 1.330$	.184
	Non-Writer	3.22	1.28		
Presence	Writer	4.59	1.14	$t(1650) = .285$	.776
	Non-Writer	4.57	1.21		
Expression	Writer	4.79	1.29	$t(1651) = 1.994$	.046
	Non-Writer	4.65	1.37		

Table 30.6

CAPE Variables in Star Wars *Writers and Non-Writers*

Dimension	Group	Mean	SD	t(df)	p-Value
Commitment	Writer	4.25	1.49	$t(1923) =$ 2.617	.009
	Non-Writer	4.06	1.46		
Asset	Writer	2.43	1.18	$t(1923) =$ 3.879	< .001
	Non-Writer	2.21	1.15		
Presence	Writer	4.39	1.34	$t(1195.192)$ $= 4.642$	< .001
	Non-Writer	4.08	1.43		
Expression	Writer	4.02	1.33	$t(1923) =$ 8.007	< .001
	Non-Writer	3.48	1.36		

Table 30.7

CAPE Variables in Anime Writers and Non-Writers

Dimension	Group	Mean	SD	t(df)	p-Value
Commitment	Writer	4.05	1.34	$t(2230) =$ 2.714	.007
	Non-Writer	3.86	1.29		
Asset	Writer	2.60	1.23	$t(652.225)$ $= 3.602$	< .001
	Non-Writer	2.37	1.14		
Presence	Writer	4.76	1.27	$t(2230) =$ 3.729	< .001
	Non-Writer	4.52	1.24		
Expression	Writer	4.14	1.30	$t(2230) =$ 5.872	< .001
	Non-Writer	3.74	1.27		

Found Meaning in Life

We assessed the extent to which a sample of undergraduate fans indicated that they had found a sense of meaning in their life as a test of the idea that, for some fans, their fan interest may allow them to find a sense of significance, direction, or purpose. In line with this hypothesis, expression was the only one of the CAPE variables significantly associated with having found meaning in one's life ($b = .117$, $SE = .054$, $p = .033$; all other $ps > .213$). While this does not mean that all fans find meaning through their fan interest, it does suggest that for those fans characterized by higher scores on the expression dimension, it may be the case that at least some of the meaning they found in their life may have stemmed from their fan interests.

Fursonas as Ideal Selves

While we did not directly assess measures of growth or uniqueness in our studies, we did ask our sample of furries several questions pertaining to their fursonas, defined as a furry-themed avatar or representation adapted by the vast majority of furries (Reysen et al., 2020b). Most presently relevant are three characteristics of fursonas. First, furries tend to identify fairly strongly with their fursonas. Second, furries tend to create fursonas that allow them to distinguish themselves from other furries (with respect to species, color, name, etc.). Finally, furries tend to describe fursonas that represent idealized versions of themselves. Taken together, insofar as furries identify with fursonas that, almost by definition, allow furries to distinguish themselves uniquely among other furries, furries' identification with their fursona constitute a proxy measure for their feelings of distinctiveness or uniqueness. Moreover, insofar as those same fursonas represent idealized versions of themselves, this may represent an opportunity for furries to use their fan interest in service of personal growth, to become more like their idealized selves. With this in mind, we assessed the extent to which the CAPE dimensions, and expression specifically, predict both one's identification with their fursona and their belief that their fursona represents their idealized self.

Speaking to the former point, expression was the dimension most strongly tied to furries' identification with their fursona ($b = .350$, $SE = .039$, $p < .001$) relative to commitment ($b = .217$, $SE = .038$, $p < .001$), presence ($b = .071$, $SE = .035$, $p = .039$), and asset ($b = .029$, $SE = .036$, $p = .429$). Speaking to the latter point in particular, expression was again the dimension most strongly associated with seeing their fursona as an idealized self ($b = .293$, $SE = .047$, $p < .001$) relative to commitment ($b = .116$, $SE = .045$, $p = .010$) and to asset and presence, neither of which were significant ($ps > .176$).

Positive Fantasy Engagement

As a final form of predictive validity, we assessed the extent to which the creativity subscale of the expression dimension was associated with a proxy measure of creativity, the positive fantasy subscale of the fantasy engagement scale. The scale contains, among other things, an item assessing the extent to which participants' engagement in the fantasy activity is a source of creative inspiration or muse for the participant (Plante, Reysen et al., 2017). As such, we can use the positive fantasy engagement subscale as a proxy measure for one's use of their fan interest in service of creativity.

In an undergraduate sample we found, as predicted, that positive fantasy engagement was most strongly associated with the expression dimension (b = .348, SE = .069, $p < .001$), was only modestly associated with presence (b = .168, SE = .173, $p = .018$), and was not significantly associated with either commitment or asset ($ps > .297$). A similar pattern of results was found in a sample of *Star Wars* fans, for whom expression was, again, the dimension most strongly associated with positive fantasy engagement (b = .645, SE = .029, $p < .001$) relative to Asset (b = -.094, SE = .029, $p = .001$), commitment (b = .069, SE = .022, $p = .002$), and presence (b = .146, SE = .022, $p < .001$).

Taken together, the results in this section provide preliminary evidence for the validity of the expression dimension of the CAPE model. While there is significant need for future studies which more strictly and directly test the extent to which the CAPE dimensions uniquely predict subscales of the expression dimension, there is sufficient evidence at present to suggest there is at least merit to the expression dimension as a valid psychological construct, one distinct from the other CAPE dimensions.

Conclusion: Validity of the CAPE Scale

Throughout this chapter we have tested the predictive validity of the CAPE model and its four constituent dimensions by using the CAPE scale in seven studies of different fan groups and assessing the unique and distinct predictive abilities of the dimensions with respect to variables that represent conceptually relevant variables.

While far from a perfect validation, the results of the present chapter suggest that the CAPE dimensions do a fairly good job predicting relevant conceptual variables. In a few cases the dimensions did not uniquely (or even most significantly, relative to the other dimensions) predict relevant conceptual variables. However, in most cases, even when the dimension was not unique or the strongest predictor of a relevant conceptual variable, it did, at very least, predict unique variance.

Future research is needed to fine tune and more precisely validate the CAPE model and its associated scale. For the time being, however, we suggest that the scale has been sufficiently validated to warrant testing its ability to predict more conceptually distant, interesting, and ultimately practical outcomes of fan attitudes, feelings, traits, and behaviors—the focus on the next chapter.

Chapter 31
Utility of the CAPE Scale

To this point we've established the four-dimensional model of our empirically-derived CAPE model. We've also preliminarily validated the CAPE scale—a measure of these four dimensions—across seven different samples representing a myriad of different fan groups. It now remains for us to test the scale's utility and applicability to a wide range of fan-related topics, including its ability to predict specific fan thoughts, feelings, and behaviors, its relation to relevant psychological variables, and its ability to discriminate between fans of one demographic category over another.

Fan Attitudes / Behavior

It goes without saying that fan scholarship is an interdisciplinary field that includes, but isn't limited to, marketing, media studies, social psychology, anthropology, and sociology. Common among these fields is a scholarly interest in better understanding the way fans behave and the attitudes driving those behaviors. To this end, we consider the utility of the CAPE scale in predicting these variables of interest.

Type of Fan Interest

A question that commonly arises among fan scholars is whether or not there are quantifiable differences between fans of different interests, be it differences between fans of different sports, differences between fans of different music or television genres, or differences between media fans and hobbyists more broadly. The CAPE model may be able to shed light on such questions, as we demonstrate in our findings from two studies using the CAPE scale. In the two undergraduate samples participants identified either as sport fans, media fans, music fans, or as hobbyists. They also completed the CAPE scale. Armed with this data, we are able to compare how each type of fan scores, on average, on each of the CAPE dimensions, allowing us to test whether there were significant differences between different types of fans. Moreover, if differences are observed, the CAPE model allows us to meaningfully quantify and describe the nature of these differences. Participants' aggregated scores were shown in Table 31.1.

Table 31.1

Means and Standard Deviations of CAPE Scores in Two Undergraduate Samples of Sport Fans, Media Fans, Music Fans, and Hobbyists

Dimension	Sport Fans	Media Fans	Music Fans	Hobbyists
Commitment	5.17 (1.18)[a]	4.04 (1.43)[b]	4.55 (1.34)[b]	5.17 (1.26)[a]
	4.98 (1.32)[a]	4.24 (1.31)[b]	4.43 (1.44)[b]	5.19 (1.37)[a]
Asset	3.31 (1.34)[a]	2.38 (1.22)[b]	3.10 (1.35)[a]	3.95 (0.92)[a]
	3.07 (1.42)[a]	2.58 (1.32)[b]	2.82 (1.37)[a]	4.11 (1.41)[c]
Presence	4.73 (1.40)[a]	4.80 (1.38)[a]	4.48 (1.47)[a]	4.69 (1.41)[a]
	4.50 (1.40)[a]	4.90 (1.23)[a]	4.42 (1.50)[a]	4.67 (1.17)[a]
Expression	3.51 (1.53)[a]	3.52 (1.66)[a]	4.69 (1.41)[b]	4.81 (1.37)[b]
	3.38 (1.46)[a]	3.37 (1.51)[a]	4.45 (1.49)[b]	4.72 (1.32)[b]

Note. The top number in each row refers to the first undergraduate study, while the bottom number refers to the second undergraduate study. Values sharing a superscript in each row did not significantly differ from one another.

When it comes to the commitment dimension, sport fans and hobbyists score significantly higher than either music fans or media fans in both the first ($F(3,363) = 16.756$, $p < .001$, partial $\eta^2 = .122$) and second study ($F(3,425) = 10.093$, $p < .001$, partial $\eta^2 = .067$). A comparable trend was observed with respect to scores on the asset dimension, with sport fans, music fans, and hobbyists all scoring significantly higher than media fans in the first study ($F(3,362) = 16.503$; $p < .001$, partial $\eta^2 = .120$) and in the second study— although hobbyists also scored significantly higher than the other types of fans ($F(3,424) = 11.714$, $p < .001$, partial $\eta^2 = .077$).

Trends change a bit when it comes to expression scores: On this dimension, music fans, along with hobbyists, scored higher than either sport fans or media fans in the first study ($F(3,363) = 17.252$, $p < .001$, partial $\eta^2 = .125$) and in the second study ($F(3,424) = 18.439$, $p < .001$, partial $\eta^2 = .115$).

Finally, the four types of fans did not significantly differ with respect to scores on the presence dimension in the first study ($F(3,361) = 1.120$, $p = .341$, partial $\eta^2 = .009$) and differed only very modestly in the second study ($F(3,425) = 2.686$, $p = .046$, partial $\eta^2 = .109$).

Taken together, these findings hint that the possibility that fans of different interests may differ in ways that can be quantified. For instance, media fans tend to score the lowest with respect to commitment, asset, and expression while hobbyists, by contrast, tend to score the highest on these same dimensions. This may indicate a tendency for media fans to have a relatively low bar for entry (e.g., simply turning on a show and watching a few episodes) relative to hobbyists, for whom there may be a more sizable investment for entry (e.g., learning a skill or obtaining the requisite equipment).

The data also suggest that sport fans tend to score higher than music fans on measures of commitment, while the trend reverses with respect to the expression dimension. One possibility is that sport fans are better characterized by knowledge, devotion, or time spent on a particular team while, for music fans, their interest may be better characterized by its significance, meaning, and inspirational qualities for the listener.

It's also rather telling that the four groups did not strongly differ with respect to their scores on the presence dimension, the dimension thought to be most strongly tied to escapism and pathological engagement styles (see later in this chapter for more on this). This suggests, in a manner analogous to prior research (e.g., Plante, Reysen et al., 2017), that the possible dysfunctionality of a fan interest may have little to do the content of the interest itself.

Willingness to Travel for Fan Interest

In one undergraduate sample of fans we asked participants to indicate their willingness to travel for their fan interest—something we might expect to predict based on fans' CAPE commitment score—in two different ways. First, we asked them to indicate, in miles, the furthest they had ever traveled for their fan interest (e.g., to attend a event). The results revealed that, as predicted, of the four CAPE dimensions, commitment ($b = 71.79$, $SE = 103.711$, $p = .003$) was, along with asset ($b = 63.971$, $SE = 23.643$, $p = .009$) significantly positively associated with distance traveled. In contrast, expression and presence scores were not ($ps > .711$). A comparable pattern of results was obtained with a second indicator, asking participants to indicate, on a Likert-type scale, their willingness to fly to another city for their fan interest. Again, commitment ($b = .563$, $SE = .084$, $p < .001$), along with asset ($b = .304$, $SE = .087$, $p = .001$), were positively associated while expression was not ($b = .068$, $SE = .075$, $p = .361$). This time, however, presence was slightly negatively associated with traveling for one's fan interest ($b = -.174$, $SE = .076$, $p = .022$).

Fan-Related Dreams

Assuming that fans spend a non-trivial amount of their time thinking about and engaging in their fan interests, and given research showing that the content of a person's waking thoughts can impact the content of their dreams (Cartwright et al., 1984), we assessed whether the CAPE dimensions might predict the frequency with which fan content makes its way into fan's dreams.

In a sample of *Star Wars* fans, commitment (b = .150, SE = .032, p < .001), asset (b = .313, SE = .042, p < .001), and expression (b = .122, SE = .041, p = .003) were all significant positive predictors of frequency of dreaming about fan content. In contrast, presence was not (b = .048, SE = .032, p = .134). And, demonstrating that this association is not limited just to *Star Wars* fans, the exact same pattern of results was observed in a sample of anime fans (commitment: b = .195, SE = .046, p < .001; asset: b = .252, SE = .053, p < .001; expression: b = .276, SE = .052, p < .001), with presence again emerging as the only dimension not associated with interest-themed dream content (b = -.041, SE = .042, p = .325).

While it remains for future research to explain precisely why commitment, asset, and expression all predict greater dream content while presence does not, one possibility has to do with the amount of time fans spend time thinking about their interest during their waking hours. It makes sense that highly committed fans would spend more time both actively engaging in, and thus thinking about, their fan interest. These same fans may also spend a great deal of time learning more about their interest (e.g., researching facts or trivia). Likewise, fans who benefit (e.g., financially or in terms of social support) from their interest may think of their interest frequently in response to specific setbacks or threats (e.g., working at an upcoming convention to pay bills). Finally, fans characterized by the expression dimension may spend a great deal of time elaborating upon, finding significance in, and brainstorming new content based on their interest.

In contrast, insofar as the presence dimension is characterized by transient or fleeting engagement in a fan activities for hedonic reasons, they might think about them less and, as such, presence might not be as strongly associated with dream content, although it remains for future research to test this possibility more directly.

Parasocial Relationships

We asked a sample of undergraduate fans to complete a measure assessing the extent to which they tend to develop parasocial relationships with fictional characters or with celebrities (Liebers & Schramm, 2017, 2019) related to their own fan interests. The data revealed that commitment (b = .201, SE = .051, p < .001), asset (b = .197, SE = .052, p < .001) and, to a lesser extent, expression (b = .114, SE = .045, p = .012), were both positively associated with parasocial relationships, while presence was not (b = .064, SE = .046, p = .164).

As was the case with dreaming, this finding may reflect a tendency for fans characterized by high commitment, asset, and expression scores to spend a considerable amount of time thinking about their fan interest beyond the moments when they actively engage in them. In contrast, those for whom fan activities represent a temporary distraction or a moment of escapism (presence), there may be less emotional investment and felt connection to the interest itself, reducing the likelihood of a parasocial relationship forming.

Cosplay

We asked a sample of anime fans whether or not they considered themselves to be a cosplayer. We next compared the extent to which cosplaying and non-cosplaying anime fans differed with respect to the CAPE dimensions (see Table 31.2). The results revealed that cosplayers scored significantly higher than non-cosplayers on all four of the dimensions. This finding is fairly significant because, among laypersons, cosplay is often thought as an indicator of whether someone is a hardcore fan or a more casual fan.[1] In contrast, the present findings suggest that the distinction between cosplaying and non-cosplaying anime fans may be multifaceted and nuanced, extending far beyond the magnitude of their fanship or the frequency with which they watch a show to include the elements of expression or the hedonic enjoyment characterizing the presence dimension.

Table 31.2

CAPE Variables in Anime Cosplayers and Non-Cosplayers

Dimension	Group	Mean	SD	$t(df)$	p-Value
Commitment	Cosplay	4.25	1.31	$t(2230) = 7.340$	$< .001$
	No Cosplay	3.81	1.28		
Asset	Cosplay	2.94	1.30	$t(2230) = 9.765$	$< .001$
	No Cosplay	2.31	1.10		
Presence	Cosplay	4.87	1.23	$t(2230) = 5.191$	$< .001$
	No Cosplay	4.50	1.25		
Expression	Cosplay	4.44	1.35	$t(2230) = 10.315$	$< .001$
	No Cosplay	3.7	1.24		

---

[1] This is far from unique to anime fans. Among furries, for example, is it commonly believed among newer members of the fandom that those who wear elaborate and expensive fursuits represent devoted or committed "lifestylers," while those who lack a fursuit are frequently seen as "casual."

Figure Collecting

In an analogous fashion, we compared whether anime fans who identify as collectors of anime-themed figurines differ from non-collectors respect to their scores on the CAPE dimensions (see Table 31.3). As with cosplay, figurine collectors scored significantly higher than non-collectors on all four of the dimensions. The commitment dimension was also notably strongly associated with figure collecting relative to the other dimensions, a finding in-line with findings from the previous chapter showing a link between commitment and the value of one's interest-related merchandise collection.

Table 31.3

CAPE Variables in Anime Figurine Collectors and Non-Collectors

Dimension	Group	Mean	SD	t(df)	p-Value
Commitment	Collect	4.66	1.21	$t(2230) =$ 15.260	$< .001$
	No Collect	3.69	1.24		
Asset	Collect	2.79	1.22	$t(731.168)$ $= 7.783$	$< .001$
	No Collect	2.31	1.22		
Presence	Collect	4.84	1.23	$t(2230) =$ 5.471	$< .001$
	No Collect	4.49	1.25		
Expression	Collect	4.26	1.30	$t(2230) =$ 8.531	$< .001$
	No Collect	3.70	1.26		

Hentai Fans

Hentai refers to sexually explicit anime-themed content and is a rather divisive subject among anime fans (Reysen, Plante, Chadborn et al., 2021). To assess whether the CAPE dimensions shed light on possible differences between fans who do and do not consume hentai content, we asked anime fans whether or not they were also fans of hentai and compared their scores on the CAPE dimensions (see Table 31.4). Asset and presence were both fairly modestly associated with being a hentai fan, while commitment was more strongly associated with being a hentai fan. In contrast, expression was not associated with being a hentai fan.

Table 31.4

CAPE Variables in Hentai Fans and Non-Hentai Anime Fans

Dimension	Group	Mean	SD	t(df)	p-Value
Commitment	Hentai Fan	4.09	1.29	t(2230) = 5.033	< .001
	No Hentai	3.80	1.29		
Asset	Hentai Fan	2.49	1.17	t(2230) = 2.238	.025
	No Hentai	2.38	1.16		
Presence	Hentai Fan	4.69	1.26	t(2230) = 3.427	.001
	No Hentai	4.50	1.24		
Expression	Hentai Fan	3.88	1.26	t(2230) = 1.466	.148
	No Hentai	3.80	1.30		

These findings are a bit surprising, at least with respect to commitment. When it comes to presence, one might expect it to be associated with hentai consumption, given that presence is largely associated with hedonic enjoyment. With respect to commitment, however, it is sometimes assumed that fans who are interested in fan-themed pornography are somehow "lesser fans" or that theirs is a more superficial interest than those who don't consume fan-themed pornography. If anything though, the present findings suggest that those who spend the most time engaging with their fan interest are also the most likely to be fans of explicit content. Speaking to this idea, we also asked anime fans to indicate the frequency with which they consumed hentai content. Commitment was the only CAPE dimension significantly positively associated with frequency of hentai consumption ($b = .255$, $SE = .047$, $p < .001$; all other $ps > .189$).

Fan Shipping

As we've mentioned elsewhere in this book, erotic fanfiction has existed for almost as long as modern fandoms have existed (Jenkins, 1992). Shipping is a big part of erotic fanfiction, its name a play on the word "relationship." Put simply, shipping involves fans creating—either in written fanfiction, fan art, or simply in discussions and hypotheticals—romantic relationships between (usually established) characters (Reysen, Plante, Chadborn et al., 2021). Given the conceptual proximity of shipping to pornography and hentai use (as shipping often, but not always, involves sexual relationships between characters), we might hypothesize that the same CAPE dimensions which predict hentai consumption would also predict shipping. This couldn't be further from the truth, however. In a sample of *Star Wars* fans it was found that expression ($b = .214$, $SE = .060$, $p < .001$) and presence ($b = .489$, $SE = .047$, $p < .001$) were both positively associated with shipping behavior while commitment, defying expectations, was negatively associated with shipping ($b = -.253$, $SE = .046$, $p < .001$; asset: $b = .064$, $SE = .061$, $p = .293$).

It remains to be seen whether this apparent contradiction in results is the product of differences in the content or norms of the anime and *Star Wars* fandoms (e.g., the acceptability of pornographic content) or whether we observe the same distinction between viewing hentai content and the act of shipping among fans within the same fandom. One potential key difference between the two may be the association of expression with shipping but not with hentai. This speaks to the idea that shipping is a far more deeply-held, personal, and self-expressive activity than is the consumption of hentai, despite both often involving erotic content. Regardless of the specific mechanisms involved, the results speak to the importance of considering the nature of the fans involved—rather than only looking at the content itself—to get a complete picture of the motivations driving fan behaviors like erotic content consumption.

Fan Proselytizing

For many fans, one of their initial points of exposure to their interest is through word-of-mouth transmission from a friend, family member, or colleague (Edwards et al., 2019). As such, it would be helpful to know the factors that predict which fans are the most likely to proselytize or spread the word about their fan interest—something researchers have already began to study (Plante, Chadborn, & Reysen, 2018). To this end, we asked undergraduate fans of various interests to indicate the extent to which they proselytize their fan interests to others. The results showed that the CAPE dimension of commitment

($b = .611$, $SE = .052$, $p < .001$) was very strongly associated with this tendency, along with, albeit to far lesser extent, the asset dimension ($b = .290$, $SE = .054$, $p < .001$). In contrast, neither expression nor presence were associated with proselytizing ($ps > .478$).

Intuitively, it makes sense why commitment would be strongly tied to proselytizing: Given that fandom is a defining component of commitment, and insofar as proselytizing, among other things, serves to recruit new members to one's fandom, it would seem to follow that those scoring higher in commitment should also engage in more proselytizing, if only as a means of growing and strengthening their fandom. Less clear is the link between the asset dimension and proselytizing, however. One possibility is that those who are able to recruit more potential fans might also be able to benefit from those new fans (e.g., sell them merchandise, earn status within the community). Testing such explanations remains a topic for future research.

Emotional Response to Fan Content

In addition to looking at specific behaviors fan engage in, we can also assess the extent to which the CAPE dimensions predict fans' emotional response to their interest. For example, in an undergraduate sample we asked participants to complete a measure assessing the extent to which they experienced strong emotional responses to content related to their fan interest. Commitment ($b = .330$, $SE = .051$, $p < .001$) and presence ($b = .218$, $SE = .046$, $p < .001$) emerged as positive predictors of emotional responsiveness while, unexpectedly, expression emerged as negatively associated with responsiveness ($b = -.111$, $SE = .046$, $p = .016$; asset: $b = .091$, $SE = .053$, $p = .088$). On the one hand, commitment, given its tie to the sheer magnitude of one's interest, would seem to be associated with emotional responsiveness insofar as the positive emotions tied to one's interest would be expected to fuel greater consumption. Likewise, the same fans looking for a moment of distraction from daily life or to regulate their mood here and now should also be more likely to be emotionally responsive to content which can fulfill these functions.

It seems strange, however, that those who draw the most significance from their fan interest would also be less likely to respond emotionally to it. Nevertheless, other studies have shown that this is far from a coincidence. In our 2019 brony study, for example, we asked participants to indicate their feelings of angst, threat, and nostalgia at the thought that the show in which they were a fan, *My Little Pony: Friendship is Magic*, was just weeks away from coming to an end after nearly a decade. When it came to feelings of angst, expression was again found to be uniquely negatively associated with such feelings ($b = -.140$, $SE = .060$, $p = .020$) while presence was again positively associated with the feelings (b = .097, SE = .048, p = .044; all other ps > .348). The same was also true for feeling threatened by the end of the show, with expression again significantly negatively associated with such feelings (b = -.210, SE = .085, p = .014) and presence positively associated with them (b = .173, SE = .068, p = .012; all other ps > .812). The only exception to this trend could be found with respect to feelings of nostalgia, where commitment was the only significant predictor (b = .280, SE = .080, p < .001; all other ps > .079).

As with many of the phenomena in this chapter, the surprising nature of this finding both illustrates the importance of assessing relevant fan outcomes with respect to the CAPE model and the need to delve more fully into understanding the mechanisms underlying these associations.

Fan Entitlement and Gatekeeping

Among the important fan-related attitudes and behaviors we've assessed with respect to their association with the CAPE model are feelings of entitlement and elitism among fans and the gatekeeping that such feelings are associated with (e.g., Plante et al., 2020). Insofar as fandoms rely on a steady influx of new members to sustain an interest over time and keep it vibrant, fandoms have a vested interest in ensuring that members of a fan group treat new fans well and avoid erecting unnecessary barriers to entry.

To this end, we asked undergraduate fans to indicate the extent to which they experienced a sense of entitlement as a fan—that is, an elevated sense of worth or elitism that leads to expectations of special treatment and which may lead to negative treatment or condescension toward other, newer fans. In this assessment, we found that only the CAPE asset dimension was significantly positively associated with feelings of entitlement (b = .293, SE = .054, p < .001; all other ps > .461). To put it another way, according to the CAPE model, it's fans who stand to personally benefit the most from their fan interest that are the most likely to feel a sense of entitlement, rather than the fans who most strongly identity with their fan interest, those who engage most frequently in fan activities, or those who find deeper significance and meaning in the activity itself.

Continuing this line of inquiry, we asked furries, anime fans, and a 2018 sample of bronies to indicate the extent to which they personally endorsed gatekeeping-related beliefs—that is, beliefs that only certain people, namely those satisfying criteria determined by the participant, should be permitted in their fandom. Consistent with the findings on entitlement, asset was the only CAPE dimension significantly associated with gatekeeping among furries (b = .068, SE = .034, p = .047; all other ps > .099) and among bronies (asset: b = .167, SE = .076, p = .029; all other ps > .127). Asset was also significantly positively associated with gatekeeping among anime fans ($b = .214$, $SE = .029$, $p < .001$), although not uniquely so, as commitment was also positively associated ($b = .115$, $SE = .025$, $p < .001$) and presence was negatively associated with gatekeeping ($b = -.060$, $SE = .023$, $p = .010$; expression: $b = -.053$, $SE = .029$, $p = .064$).

Having observed a fairly consistent association between the CAPE asset dimension and gatekeeping, it's worth noting that gatekeeping doesn't necessarily mean shutting off one's fandom to new fans. For one thing, fans may gatekeep to restrict fan membership to fans who might be harmful or deleterious to the fan community (e.g., fandoms banning extremists or violent members), which most would consider to be desirable. As such, we went one step further and assessed fans' negatively specifically toward new fans. In contrast to the previous findings on gatekeeping, presence was positively associated with negativity toward new fans ($b = .083$, $SE = .027$, $p = .002$) while expression was negatively associated with it ($b = -.090$, $SE = .030$, $p = .003$; neither commitment nor asset was associated with negativity toward new fans, $ps > .289$). However, in a sample of anime fans, asset was again the variable most strongly associated with negativity toward new fans ($b = .113$, $SE = .028$, $p < .001$), although it was not unique in this regard (expression: $b = -.110$, $SE = .028$, $p < .001$; presence: $b = -.141$, $SE = .023$, $p < .001$; commitment: $b = .008$, $SE = .025$, $p = .738$).

Taken together, these results suggest that asset is the variable most strongly tied to feelings of entitlement and negativity toward new fans. It remains to be seen why this is the case, though one possibility is that those who benefit significantly from their fandom involvement may perceive new fans as a possible threat to that benefit—either as possible competition for scarce resources (e.g., other possible vendors) or as people who may tarnish or harm their fandom's reputation, which would make the fandom itself less useful as a source of self-esteem.

Giving Help

In stark contrast to the antipathy observed the previous section, we've also assessed prosocial fan behavior. Specifically, we asked furries, anime fans, and a 2018 sample of bronies to indicate the extent to which they found themselves giving help—financial, emotional, or otherwise—to others in their fan community. For furries, commitment ($b = .171$, $SE = .028$, $p < .001$), asset ($b = .117$, $SE = .028$, $p < .001$), and presence ($b = .057$, $SE = .026$, $p = .028$) were all positively associated with helping behavior, while expression was the only dimension not associated with helping other fans ($b = .008$, $SE = .030$, $p = .795$). A similar pattern of results emerged in anime fans, with commitment ($b = .090$,

SE = .021, *p* < .001) and asset (*b* = .120, *SE* = .025, *p* < .001) positively associated with giving help. Unlike furries, however, expression was also associated with helping (*b* = .101, *SE* = .024, *p* < .001), while presence was not (*b* = .025, *SE* = .020, *p* = .211). Simplifying the story, in our brony sample commitment again emerged as a significant predictor of helping behavior (*b* = .206, *SE* = .080, *p* = .011), while none of the other dimensions were significant predictors (*ps* > .247). In short, commitment, unlike the other CAPE dimensions, is a robust predictor of intrafandom helping, likely due to its fairly unique association with feelings of connection to, and identification with, other fans.

Subgroup Identification

Fandoms, and indeed social groups in general, are far from homogeneous entities. They often involve a complex intermixing of people whose specific preferences with respect to the same fan interest may differ. For example, it's not unheard of for fans to divide themselves based on their favorite character, their favorite generation or season of a show, or based on their opinions regarding fan-created, non-canon content (e.g., Edwards et al., 2019). For this reason, researchers studying fans from a social identity perspective may find it helpful to assess not only fans' shared identity with other fans, but also their identification with specific subgroups within their fandom.

To test this possibility we asked *Star Wars* fans to indicate the extent to which they identified with several subgroups within the broader *Star Wars* fandom (e.g., based on their favorite trilogy of films, their favorite characters, their tendency to ship characters in fanfiction, etc.). The results revealed that commitment (*b* = .249, *SE* = .028, *p* < .001), expression (*b* = .082, *SE* = .036, *p* = .021), and presence (*b* = .234, *SE* = .028, *p* < .001) were all positively associated with subgroup identification while the asset dimension was not (*b* = .002, *SE* = .036, *p* = .957).

In another example of subgroup identification, we asked anime fans to indicate whether or not they identified as otaku—that is, a subgroup of anime fans distinguished by the seriousness with which they take their interest in anime (Reysen, Plante, Chadborn et al., 2021; see Table 31.5). The results revealed, in line with findings from the *Star Wars* fandom, that commitment was, again, among the strongest CAPE predictors of identification with a particular subgroup in the fandom.

Table 31.5

CAPE Variables in Otaku and Non-Otaku Anime Fans

Dimension	Group	Mean	SD	t(df)	p-Value
Commitment	Otaku	4.66	1.16	t(2230) = 20.865	< .001
	Non-Otaku	3.54	1.20		
Asset	Otaku	2.88	1.18	t(1301.048) = 13.067	< .001
	Non-Otaku	2.20	1.09		
Presence	Otaku	4.96	1.18	t(2230) = 10.400	< .001
	Non-Otaku	4.38	1.24		
Expression	Otaku	4.39	1.23	t(2230) = 14.894	< .001
	Non-Otaku	3.56	1.23		

Moving beyond subgroup identification in general, we also assessed another important question from social identity theory: Which fans are the most biased toward their own subgroup? Analyses of *Star Wars* fans revealed a similar tendency for commitment ($b = .080$, $SE = .040$, $p = .045$) and presence ($b = .083$, $SE = .040$, $p = .040$) to predict subgroup bias while expression was unrelated ($b = -.056$, $SE = .052$, $p = .282$). More importantly, however, asset, which was unrelated to the overall tendency to identify with a subgroup, was the dimension most strongly associated with bias toward one's own subgroup ($b = .281$, $SE = .052$, $p < .001$). Or, to put it another way: In line with the social identity perspective, which posits that people are motivated to bolster the groups to which they belong to while derogating those to which they don't belong to in service of their self-esteem (e.g., Tajfel & Turner, 1979; Turner et al., 1987), those who benefit most from their fan activities are the most likely to be biased in favor of their subgroup over others, even within the same fandom. Such findings illustrate the relevance of the CAPE model for questions derived from other theoretical perspectives (e.g., social identity theory).

Entitativity

As a final look at fan attitudes and beliefs we turn to another question from the literature on a social identity perspective: Do fans believe that their fan group is a well-defined entity that's categorically distinct from other groups—

known as entitativity—or do they see their fan group as a loosely-defined category with fuzzy and permeable boundaries between it and other fan groups?

In a 2019 study of bronies we asked participants to complete a measure of the perceived entitativity of the brony fandom. Expression was the CAPE dimension most strongly associated with perceived entitativity ($b = .268$, $SE = .061$, $p < .001$), although commitment scores were also modestly associated ($b = .108$, $SE = .055$, $p = .049$; all other $ps > .080$).

In a similar vein, we asked the same participants to also complete a measure of the extent to which they believed the boundary between being a brony or not was a highly permeable one—that is, the idea that a fan can easily go from being a brony to not being a brony, an idea at odds with entitativity. As you would expect from the previous findings, expression ($b = -.196$, $SE = .077$, $p = .012$) and commitment ($b = -.354$, $SE = .069$, $p < .001$) were both significantly negatively associated with perceived permeability (other $ps > .231$).

As one might have predicted, fans who are both more committed and for whom their fan interest represents something more meaningful and significant than the content itself are more likely to perceive their fandoms as distinct and impermeable categories. Committed fans for whom their fan interest expresses something deep and significant for them aren't necessarily opposed to the influx of new fans into their fandom either; rather, it seems that they may be more likely to believe that only certain types of people are fans and that this may be an immutable part of who they are. It remains for future research to suss out the mechanisms underlying these associations, suggesting yet again that the CAPE dimensions may be able to shed light on questions posed to fan researchers by other, non-fan theoretical perspectives.

Psychological Variables

Moving on from measures of fan-specific attitudes, beliefs, and behaviors, we can also assess the utility of the CAPE model when applied to broad psychological constructs (e.g., well-being, personality traits) and to more specific psychological variables (e.g., perceived stigma).

Well-Being

We've spoken earlier in this book about the fact that well-being is complex multifaceted construct. Because of this, across our various studies of fans we have measured well-being in a variety of different ways—both as a way of obtaining converging evidence for observed associations but also to assess the nuances and distinctions between different facets of fan activities and different facets of well-being.

Holistic Well-Being

Perhaps the most holistic way we've assessed well-being is through the use of scales which assess and compile several dimensions of well-being (i.e., physical well-being, psychological well-being, and social well-being). Using such a measure in a sample of furries, we find that the CAPE dimension of commitment is the only variable positively associated with omnibus well-being ($b = .190$, $SE = .026$, $p < .001$), while presence is negatively associated with well-being ($b = -.076$, $SE = .024$, $p = .002$; all other $ps > .698$). Of particular note, the asset dimension was not significantly associated with well-being as one might have anticipated, suggesting that those who benefit from their fan activities may not necessarily benefit in ways related to their well-being per se, but rather in more tangible, immediate, or specific ways. This same trend continues throughout the rest of this section.

Physical Health

In two studies of undergraduate fans we assessed the extent to which the CAPE dimensions predict physical well-being—that is, the quality of a person's physical health. In our first undergraduate sample, none of the four CAPE dimensions were significantly associated with participants' physical well-being (all $ps > .168$). Our second sample yielded contradictory results, however, with commitment positively associated with physical health ($b = .151$, $SE = .045$, $p = .001$) and expression was negatively associated with physical health ($b = -.127$, $p = .042$, $p = .003$; all other $ps > .680$). These findings speak to the relative weakness of being able to predict fans' physical health on the basis of fan-related variables from the CAPE model.

Psychological Well-Being

In the same two studies of undergraduate fans we also assessed the link between the CAPE dimensions and fans' psychological well-being. As was the case with measures of physical health, the first study revealed a lack of any relation between the CAPE dimensions and psychological well-being (all $ps > .062$). Also like the results for physical well-being, the second study revealed somewhat contradictory results: Commitment was again positively associated with psychological well-being ($b = .167$, $SE = .046$, $p < .001$) while expression was again negatively associated with psychological well-being ($b = -.114$, $SE = .043$, $p = .009$; all other $ps > .742$).

Despite this evidence seeming to suggest that, like physical well-being, there is little to no link between the COPE dimensions and fans' psychological well-being, follow-up studies looking at specific measures of psychological well-being (or lack thereof) offer some important nuance to the story. For example, across three different samples we assessed the extent to which participants experienced feelings of depressed mood. In *Star Wars* and anime fans, the results largely echoed the sentiments of the second undergraduate study. For *Star Wars* fans, commitment was negatively associated with feelings of depression (b = -.284, *SE* = .041, p < .001) whereas expression (b = .134, *SE* = .053, p = .012) and presence (b = .245, *SE* = .041, p < .001) were both positively associated with depression (asset: b = -.073, *SE* = .054, p = .172). Anime fans similarly showed a significant negative relation between commitment and depression (b = -.163, *SE* = .044, p < .001) and a positive association between depression and both expression (b = .175, *SE* = .050, p < .001) and presence (b = .223, SE = .040, p<.001; asset: b = -.054, *SE* = .050, p = .282). In a 2019 study of bronies, however, only presence was associated with depression (b = .407, *SE* = .079, p < .001; all other ps > .263).

The same studies also assessed another measure of reduced psychological well-being: A tendency for participants to experience feelings of anxiety. The results of these studies show trends similar to those for depression. Among *Star Wars* fans, commitment was negatively associated with anxiety (b = -.229, *SE* = .041, p < .001) and presence was positively associated with anxiety (b = -.306, *SE* = .042, p < .001) while asset and expression were not (ps > .411). For anime fans, commitment was similarly associated with lower anxiety (b = -.164, *SE* = .044, p < .001) and both expression (b = .178, *SE* = .050, p <.001) and presence (b = .214, *SE* = .040, p < .001) were associated with higher anxiety, while asset was again unrelated (b = -.018, *SE* = .051, p = .729). Finally, in a 2019 sample of bronies, only presence was associated with anxiety (b = .360, *SE* = 080, p < .001; all other ps > .086).

In a final measure of well-being, we asked participants in two studies to indicate, on a Likert-type scale, the extent to which they were satisfied with their life. While such a measure can be critiqued as overly simplistic and lacking in the nuance of some of our other measures of psychological well-being, it has the benefit of being a fairly face-valid measure of hedonic well-being.

In our sample of *Star Wars* fans we once again found evidence that commitment was positively associated with life satisfaction (b = .277, *SE* = .037, p < .001) whereas presence was negatively associated with life satisfaction (b = -.207, *SE* = .037, p < .001; all other ps > .112). The same trend was observed in a sample of anime fans, as both commitment (b = .237, *SE* = .040, p < .001) and, to a lesser extent, asset (b = .091, *SE* = .046, p = .049) were associated with greater life satisfaction while presence was associated with lower life satisfaction (b = -.104, *SE* = .037, p = .004; Expression: b = -.055, *SE* = .045, p = .222).

Taken together, these studies tell a rather messy story about the association between the CAPE dimensions and psychological well-being. In general, it seems that commitment is the CAPE dimension most strongly positively associated with psychological well-being while presence and, to a lesser extent, expression are associated negatively with psychological well-being. It's important to note, however, that the cross-sectional nature of this research precludes statements about causal direction between these variables. It may be tempting to suggest that being a certain kind of fan (e.g., one for whom their fan interest is significant and who obtain hedonic enjoyment from their interest) may lead to better or worse psychological well-being, and this would certainly be in-line with a lay perception of some fans as eccentric, excessive, and maladjusted.

An alternative explanation, however, points to the associated CAPE dimensions (e.g., expression and asset) as a symptom of, rather than the cause of, reduced psychological well-being. For example, those with the financial means and free time to commit to their fan activities may well be able to do so precisely because they're not presently dealing with mental health concerns. It may also be the case that those experiencing the biggest mental health problems—and, indeed, who struggle the most with day-to-day life—may be motivated to use fandom for escapist reasons—a finding consistent with research on other recreational activities (e.g., Plante, Gentile et al., 2019). Finally, those experiencing mental health problems may be searching for meaning, guidance, significance, and expression through their fan interest—a finding also consistent with research on the use of fan interests in restorative ways (Roberts et al., 2015). In short, until longitudinal or experimental studies can be conducted on these topics, our understanding of these associations may, at best, remain muddled and lacking in explanations.

Relationship Well-Being

Given the popular characterization of fans as lonely, isolated, and engaging in fan activities on their own, we also assessed the quality of fans' relationships in several of our samples. As a start, we found, in an undergraduate sample of fans, little evidence linking any of the CAPE dimensions to whether or not fans were currently in a relationship or not (all $ps > .157$). In other words, the nature of the fan, as assessed by the CAPE scale, says little about whether or not they are in a romantic relationship.

Delving deeper into the question, we asked a sample of bronies to indicate the frequency with which they felt lonely. The results revealed, in line with our findings from the above section on psychological well-being, that presence was uniquely associated with feelings of loneliness ($b = .182$, $SE = .062$, $p = .003$; all other *ps* > .168). So while the nature of the fan in question may say little about whether they happen to be in a relationship, fans characterized by especially high presence scores may nevertheless feel lonelier than other fans.

Asking more directly about the quality of fans' current relationships—including both romantic and platonic relationships—an undergraduate sample (all *ps* > .151) and a sample of bronies (all *ps* > .342) both found little evidence linking CAPE dimensions to relationship well-being. It was only in a second sample of undergraduates that we found a modest association between both commitment (*b* = .098, *SE* = .049, *p* = .045) and expression (*b* = -.155, *SE* = .046, *p* = .001) and relationship well-being (all other *ps* > .254).

In short, unlike the research on psychological well-being, which provides some evidence linking the CAPE dimensions to psychological well-being, there is little evidence concretely linking the CAPE dimensions to the quality of a fan's social life. At very least, however, the weakness of this association does suggest that popular portrayals of fans as solitary or maladaptive in their relationships are largely unsupported.

Individual Differences

The Big Five

If one's goal is to assess important individual differences between people, you would be hard-pressed to find a more famous and well-studied set of traits than the Big Five personality traits (Goldberg, 1993). While we, the authors, seldom find occasion to study these traits in our own work, which tends to focus primarily on self and identity processes in a social psychological context, we nevertheless recognize the importance of the Big Five personality traits to personality psychologists specifically and as potential moderator variables in other studies.

As such, we administered a measure of the Big Five traits to a sample of furries to assess the extent to which the CAPE dimensions predict, or perhaps even represent stand-ins for, these traits. With respect to extraversion scores, commitment (*b* = .129, *SE* = .025, *p* < .001) and asset (*b* = .067, *SE* = .024, *p* = .006) were both positively associated with extraversion scores (other *ps* > .077). Commitment was also positively associated with agreeableness scores (*b* = .093, *SE* = .018, *p* < .001), as was expression (*b* = .054, *SE* = .019, *p* = .004), whereas presence was negatively associated with agreeableness (*b* = -.058, *SE* = .016, *p* < .001; asset: *b* = -.006, *SE* = .017, *p* = .708). When it comes to conscientiousness, commitment (*b* = .117, *SE* = .019, *p* < .001) was positively associated while presence was again negatively associated (*b* = -.093, *SE* = .018, *p* < .001; all other *ps* > .622). Neuroticism scores were negatively associated with commitment (*b* = -.132, *SE* = .026, *p* < .001) and were positively associated with both expression (b = .054, SE = .027, p = .045) and presence (b = .095, SE = .024, p <.001; asset: b = .016, SE = .025, p = .511). Finally, when it comes to openness scores, commitment (b = .069, SE = .018, p < .001), expression (b = .069, SE = .018, p < .001) and presence (b = .036, SE = .016, p = .028) were all positively associated, with asset again emerging as the only exception (b = .000, SE = .017, p = .999).

As a single sample, it's hard to know precisely how to interpret these findings, as it's entirely possible that the observed relations are an idiosyncrasy of furries and don't generalize to other fan groups. Given the association of furries with the values of acceptance, tolerance, openness, and creativity (e.g., Reysen, 2015a), it is possible that the association of commitment to the furry fandom with the dimensions of agreeableness and openness to experience is a product of these norms. It is worth noting that commitment was consistently a significant predictor across all five of the personality traits, while each of the other CAPE dimensions varied with respect to which of the dimensions they were associated with, suggesting both that group norms cannot fully explain the association between commitment and Big Five scores and that the CAPE dimensions do differently predict Big Five scores, meaning they are not all measuring the same underlying dimension. Future research will be needed to both test the robustness of these findings in other contexts and to explain the nature of these relations (e.g., the association between asset and extraversion or between expression and agreeableness).

Empathy

Given that many fan groups center around media, and given the importance of empathy for the impact of media and its effects on viewers (e.g., Hall & Bracken, 2011; Plante, Chadborn, Groves, & Reysen, 2018), we tested whether the CAPE dimensions were associated with measures of trait empathy in two samples of media fans: bronies and *Star Wars* fans. In our 2018 brony sample, expression emerged as the sole significant predictor of trait empathy (b = .241, SE = .081, p = .003; all other ps > .063). Replicating the effect in a sample of *Star Wars* fans, expression was the dimension most strongly positively associated with empathy (b = .246, SE = .033, p < .001), although asset was also negatively associated with empathy scores (b = -.207, SE = .034, p < .001), while commitment and presence were not (ps > .074).

Across the two samples, the association between expression and trait empathy appears to be robust. It remains for future research to test the nature of this association, although we speculate that those who find significance, deeper meaning, and creativity in their fan interest (especially in media-based fandoms) may do so precisely because they find it easier to relate to and be emotionally affected by media, making it especially impactful and significant to them.

Maturity

In some of our most recent research we have begun to assess the role of maturity as a predictor of both specific fan behaviors and well-being in fan groups, given that perceived immaturity among fans may contribute to experienced stigma (e.g., Reysen & Plante, 2017; Reysen, Plante, Lam et al., 2020). As such, we assessed whether the CAPE dimensions were associated with self-rated maturity among fans.

In a first sample of undergraduate fans, presence was positively associated with self-rated maturity ($b = .173$, $SE = .046$, $p < .001$) while asset was negatively associated with self-rated maturity ($b = -.197$, $SE = .053$, $p < .001$; all other $ps > .261$). Presence was also positively associated with maturity ($b = .114$, $SE = .048$, $p = .020$), as was commitment ($b = .120$, $SE = .052$, $p = .021$) in a subsequent sample of undergraduate fans (all other $ps > .206$). In contrast, however, in a sample of *Star Wars* fans, commitment ($b = .087$, $SE = .027$, $p = .001$) and expression ($b = .097$, $SE = .035$, $p = .005$), but neither asset nor presence, were associated with maturity (all other $ps > .428$).

Together, the findings suggest that across fan groups, presence is consistently associated with maturity, a finding which flies in the face of lay theory suggesting that person who engage in more escapism or who pursue fan interests "merely" for hedonic pleasure are superficial and immature. A couple of important caveats to these results warrant further study. First, the contradictory findings from *Star Wars* fans suggest that these results may vary considerably depending on the specific fan interest being studied. Second, the measure employed was a self-report measure of maturity. As such, those who score high in presence may simply be unaware of their own immaturity or may be prone to overestimating their maturity if one supposes that levels of maturity are, in reality, normally distributed across fans regardless of their presence scores.

Nerdiness

Recent research has revealed what decades of science fiction, fantasy, and comic book fans have long known: Those who engage in these particular fan activities are commonly labeled as geeks or nerds. And while this label has, historically, been used in a derogatory way to demean members of non-mainstream (and often cerebral) fan interests, labels such as "geek" and "nerd" are more frequently being reclaimed by fans and seen in a less-negative, more neutral light.

With this in mind, we sought to test whether the CAPE scale could predict the extent to which a fan of any given interest would self-identify as a nerd in a pair of undergraduate samples. Our first sample revealed that expression was significantly positively associated with being a nerd ($b = .333$, $SE = .079$, $p < .001$), as was presence ($b = .193$, $SE = .080$, $p = .016$; all other ps $> .343$). A second study replicated the main finding, with expression again being positively associated with being a nerd ($b = .363$, $SE = .073$, $p < .001$) and, in a surprising twist, commitment negatively predicting nerdiness ($b = -.172$, $SE = .078$, $p = .028$; all other ps $> .129$).

These findings illustrate that those for whom their fan interest is significant, meaningful, and inspiring to them are more likely to identify as nerds. This makes sense, given that, for many people, a nerd or geek could be defined as a person who takes a hobby or piece of media "too seriously." That said, it is surprising to find that commitment seems to have relatively little to do with one's identification as a nerd and, if anything, may even be negatively associated with being a nerd. This hints at the tantalizing possibility that being a nerd is more about the significance one attributes to an interest more than the time or money spent on the interest itself. Alternatively, it may also be the case that the fandom component of the commitment dimension may undermine the perception of being a nerd or geek: Insofar as nerds or geeks are seen as pursuing their interests in a solitary fashion, the social component of fandom may undermine this categorization. It remains for future research to assess the plausibility of these and other possible explanations

Felt Stigma and Fan Identity Disclosure

Many fans—especially those who belong to fandoms whose interests are non-prototypical or non-mainstream (Reysen & Shaw, 2016)—are stigmatized by the general public. Research on specific fandoms provides converging evidence for this phenomenon (Edwards et al., 2019; Reysen, Plante, Chadborn et al., 2021) and has suggested that the stigma experienced by fans can not only be harmful to their well-being, but may also affect fans' willingness to disclose their fan identity (e.g., Mock et al., 2013). However, research also illustrates the importance of distinguishing between personal discrimination—being the direct target of discrimination – and group discrimination—being aware that members of one's group experience discrimination (Leshner et al., 2018). To address these issues pertaining to stigma and fans, we tested the association between the CAPE dimensions and these stigma-related variables.

To begin, we assessed the extent to which two different undergraduate samples perceived stigma toward their particular fan group. In the first sample, asset scores were significantly associated with perceived stigma toward their fan group ($b = .336$, $SE = .074$, $p < .001$) as were, to a lesser extent, commitment scores ($b = .187$, $SE = .074$, $p = .012$; other ps $> .900$). The finding was largely replicated in a second undergraduate sample, where asset was the only CAPE dimension which predicted felt stigma toward one's fan group (b = .231, SE = .077, p = .003; other ps > .07).

We also asked the same two samples of fans to indicate whether they had personally experienced stigma as a result of being a fan. The results of these findings were virtually identical to the results for group stigma: In the first sample, both asset (b = .390, SE = .074, p < .001) and commitment (b = .221, SE = .075, p = .003) were associated with experienced stigma (other ps > .614) while, in the second sample, asset was again the only dimension to significantly predict experienced stigma (b = .287, SE = .078, p < .001; other ps > .103).

As a further test of this association, we asked both an undergraduate sample and a sample of bronies to indicate the extent to which they would expect to be treated worse by people when those people discovered their fan interest. The undergraduate sample again showed a significant association solely between asset and expectations of negative treatment (b = .229, SE = .067, p = .001; all other ps > .227). The results were somewhat different in the 2018 sample of bronies however: Commitment was negatively associated with expected negativity (b = -.305, SE = .137, p = .027) and expression was positively associated with expected negativity (b = .318, SE = .154, p = .041), while neither presence nor asset were significantly related (ps > .145).

Taken together, these results overwhelmingly suggest, perhaps somewhat paradoxically, that fans characterized by a tendency to benefit from their fan interest are also those who both expect and experience the most stigma as a result of their fan interest. Due to the cross-sectional nature of the research, it is impossible to infer the causal direction of this association. One possibility is that fans who benefit from their fan interest (rather than merely being passive consumers of it) may be especially salient targets for stigmatization. Another possibility is that these fans, while not necessarily being more stigmatized, may be more aware of the stigma which does exist due to the importance of their fan interest to them because of the benefits it confers. A final possibility is that the stigma itself may contribute to the perceived benefits of the fan interest—a phenomenon not wholly without precedent, with prior research on stigmatized groups suggesting that members of these groups may, paradoxically, benefit from developing closer bonds and identifying more strongly with their group in response to the stigma experienced by group members (e.g., Bourguignon et al., 2020).

As a final, related measure, we asked a sample of furries to indicate the extent to which they disclosed their fan identity to others (e.g., friends, family, co-workers), with the presumption that those who experienced more stigma would also be more hesitant to disclose their fan identity to others. The results showed, as one might expect, that commitment scores were positively associated with fan identity disclosure ($b = .301$, $SE = .029$, $p < .001$) and that presence was negatively associated with identity disclosure ($b = -.097$, $SE = .027$, $p < .001$; expression: $b = -.007$, $SE = .031$, $p = .817$). Rather unexpectedly, however, asset scores were also positively associated with identity disclosure ($b = .156$, $SE = .029$, $p < .001$).

As a whole, the findings make it clear that there needs to be more research on this subject to help clarify the discrepancy that fans who benefit from their fan interest are, on the one hand, especially prone to the stigma of group membership while, on the other hand, also being more open to disclosing their identity to others, potentially making themselves a target for future stigma.

Demographics

In this final section we consider the potential association between the CAPE dimensions and several important demographic variables. Knowing how or whether the CAPE dimensions are associated with variables such as age or socioeconomic status (SES) can not only help us to better predict which people are the most likely to be which sort of fan, but they may also shed light on plausible moderator variables for future studies using the CAPE model.

Age

Age is an especially important demographic variable to consider when studying fans, for several reasons. For one thing, specific fan content may be appropriate or appealing to different age groups, yielding differences in the average age of two different fan groups (e.g., cartoons versus professional sports). Another important reason may stem from the perceived appropriateness of certain fan activities with age, something which may conceptually overlap with perceived maturity. For example, while it might be seen as appropriate for a 20-year-old to partake in cosplay, people may have reservations about a 45-year-old cosplayer. Finally, age brings with it other important demographic changes, including being more likely to have an established career, to be educated, or to be married and have children—all of which may influence the nature of a person's fan activities.

In a sample of undergraduate fans, the CAPE dimensions were not found to be significantly associated with age (all $ps > .102$), although this is just as likely to be an issue of range restriction than a lack of genuine association between the CAPE dimensions and age. Two other samples however, a 2018 brony study (all $ps > .073$) and a sample of *Star Wars* fans (all $ps > .078$), similarly found no relation between age and the CAPE dimensions.

Other samples do find a link between age and the CAPE dimensions, however. In furries, for example, commitment was positively associated with age ($b = .795$, $SE = .229$, $p = .001$) while presence was negatively associated with age ($b = -.431$, $SE = .208$, $p = .039$; other $ps > .680$). The same pattern of results was found in a sample of anime fans, with commitment being positively associated with age ($b = .522$, $SE = .142$, $p < .001$) and both presence ($b = -.302$, $SE = .131$, $p = .021$) and asset ($b = -.365$, $SE = .164$, $p = .026$; expression: $b = -.136$, $SE = .162$, $p = .401$) being negatively associated with age. In direct opposition to these findings, however, a sample of bronies revealed that only expression was associated with age ($b = -1.345$, $SE = .416$, $p = .001$; all other $ps > .167$).

Taken together, the findings suggest that age is not especially likely to be systematically associated with the CAPE dimensions across fandoms. It is possible that within specific fandoms there may idiosyncrasies wherein older and younger fans differ in the way their interests manifest or in the nature of their fan activities (e.g., generational differences in content or norms). But, across fan interests, trends seem to be weak or inconsistent. This lack of consistent, systematic associations also demonstrates, in a finding that will resonate throughout the rest of this section, that the CAPE dimensions are not simply proxy measures for fan demographics.

Gender

The topic of gender is a complex and multifaceted one, and we have, over the years, endeavored to measure gender in nuanced ways that takes into account the full range of gender expression. However, across our samples, the number of participants identifying as non-binary, transgender, genderqueer, agender, or in other ways tends to be fairly small, making their inclusion in quantitative analyses difficult—in part because it leads to very few participants being used to represent certain populations. For this reason, we restrict the following analyses to a comparison between people who identified (among other things) as men and people who identified (among other things) as women. We recognize that this is far from a complete analysis on the subject of gender and we look to future research on this subject to more fully detail the accounts and experiences of people of all genders in fan spaces beyond the brief overview provided here.

We looked at gender data across five different studies (see Tables 31.6 to 31.10 for statistics) to assess whether men and women consistently differed with respect to the CAPE dimensions. In the two samples of bronies, men and women did not differ significantly on any of the CAPE dimensions. In contrast, in the anime sample, women scored higher than men on all of the CAPE dimensions. Finally, in the two undergraduate samples, men scored higher on measures of commitment and asset and, in one of the samples, also on expression and presence. When taken as a whole, however, the findings are fairly inconsistent, and may differ too much from fandom to fandom to be able to discern conclusively whether any systematic association exists. The closest we come to such a test across fan interests, the undergraduate samples, does suggest that, across fan interests, men may score a bit higher than women with respect to the commitment and asset dimensions, although it remains to be seen how robust this association is and, if shown to be present, what drives it.

Table 31.6

CAPE Variables in Undergraduate Men and Women, Study 1

Dimension	Group	Mean	SD	t(df)	p-Value
Commitment	Men	5.03	1.36	$t(417) = 4.12$	< .001
	Women	4.48	1.33		
Asset	Men	3.16	1.42	$t(416) = 2.33$	.020
	Women	2.83	1.38		
Presence	Men	4.50	1.37	$t(417) = 1.37$	.172
	Women	4.68	1.37		
Expression	Men	3.74	1.51	$t(416) = .133$	.894
	Women	3.76	1.60		

Table 31.7

CAPE Variables in Undergraduate Men and Women, Study 2

Dimension	Group	Mean	SD	t(df)	p-Value
Commitment	Men	5.12	1.22	t(353) = 5.826	< .001
	Women	4.29	1.43		
Asset	Men	3.32	1.30	t(353) = 4.266	< .001
	Women	2.73	1.33		
Presence	Men	4.88	1.37	t(353) = 2.470	.014
	Women	4.51	1.45		
Expression	Men	4.14	1.57	t(353) = 2.433	.015
	Women	3.73	1.63		

Table 31.8

CAPE Variables in Anime Fans—Men and Women

Dimension	Group	Mean	SD	t(df)	p-Value
Commitment	Men	3.87	1.29	t(2109) = 2.265	.024
	Women	4.02	1.30		
Asset	Men	2.35	1.14	t(2109) = 4.018	< .001
	Women	2.59	1.15		
Presence	Men	4.53	1.24	t(2109) = 3.130	.002
	Women	4.73	1.25		
Expression	Men	3.71	1.25	t(2109) = 7.211	< .001
	Women	4.17	1.31		

Table 31.9

CAPE Variables in Brony Men and Women—2018

Dimension	Group	Mean	SD	t(df)	p-Value
Commitment	Men	4.83	1.17	t(199) = 1.747	.082
	Women	4.35	1.21		
Asset	Men	3.20	1.25	t(199) = 1.024	.307
	Women	2.90	1.14		
Presence	Men	4.57	1.01	t(199) = .407	.685
	Women	4.48	1.15		
Expression	Men	4.72	1.28	t(199) = .737	.462
	Women	4.50	1.21		

Table 31.10

CAPE Variables in Brony Men and Women—2019

Dimension	Group	Mean	SD	t(df)	p-Value
Commitment	Men	3.92	1.43	t(150) = .477	.634
	Women	4.05	1.43		
Asset	Men	2.71	1.22	t(150) = .513	.609
	Women	2.84	1.28		
Presence	Men	4.24	1.44	t(150) = 1.04	.300
	Women	4.55	1.21		
Expression	Men	4.24	1.46	t(150) = .437	.662
	Women	4.11	1.55		

Socioeconomic Status

Given that a fan's SES may impact their ability to engage in various fan activities (e.g., being able to afford to go to a convention, buy season tickets, or take time off work to travel), we assessed subjective SES in three different samples of fans to see whether they would be significantly predicted by the CAPE dimensions.

In a sample of undergraduate fans, expression was negatively associated with SES ($b = -.247$, $SE = .070$, $p < .001$) whereas asset was positively associated with SES ($b = .169$, $SE = .074$, $p = .024$; other $ps > .326$). These results differed from studies of specific fan groups, however: Among furries, commitment was the only dimension associated with SES ($b = .130$, $SE = .051$, $p = .012$; all other $ps > .056$), while the same was true among bronies in a 2018 sample (commitment: $b = .471$, $SE = .144$, $p = .001$; all other $ps > .065$). As with our previous findings regarding the link between the CAPE dimensions and demographic variables, these data suggest that any associations may differ from fandom to fandom, although other measures related to SES (e.g., education) were found to be non-significantly associated with the CAPE dimensions (e.g., furries, all $ps > .227$).

Political Orientation

As a final demographic measure, we asked participants across several studies to indicate their political orientation, as political leanings may both preclude fans from particular fan interests (e.g., conservatives may prefer sports over anime) and may influence the sorts of fan activities fans want to engage in (e.g., liberals may prefer to cosplay more than conservatives do).

In a sample of undergraduate fans we asked participants to indicate how conservative or liberal they felt along a single dimension. Liberalism was found to be positively associated with expression ($b = .245$, $SE = .071$, $p = .001$) and negatively associated with asset ($b = -.150$, $SE = .075$, $p = .046$; other $ps > .156$). This pattern of results was replicated in a sample of *Star Wars* fans, with expression again being positively associated with liberalism ($b = .170$, $SE = .046$, $p < .001$) and asset again being significantly negatively associated with liberalism ($b = -.163$, $SE = .047$, $p < .001$). In addition, however, presence was also positively associated with liberalism ($b = .093$, $SE = .036$, $p = .010$) while commitment was negatively associated with liberalism ($b = -.141$, $SE = .036$, $p < .001$).

In a follow-up study, we distinguished between social and economic conservatism and liberalism in response to feedback from participants who sometimes felt conflicted with respect to endorsing more conservative economic beliefs but more liberal social policies. Despite making this distinction in a sample of anime fans, however, the results yielded the same pattern of results. With respect to social liberalism, asset was again negatively associated with liberalism ($b = -.137$, $SE = .036$, $p = .001$) and with commitment ($b = -.075$, $SE = .036$, $p = .035$) and was positively predicted by expression ($b = .181$, $SE = .040$, $p < .001$; presence: $b = .061$, $SE = .033$, $p = .061$). A similar, though slightly different trend was also found for economic liberalism, which was significantly negatively predicted by commitment ($b = -.075$, $SE = .036$, $p = .035$) and positively predicted by expression ($b = .153$, $SE = .040$, $p < .001$), but which was not associated with either presence or asset ($ps > .148$).

These findings hint at the possibility that conservative and liberal-minded people may differ in the way their fan interests manifest, with conservatives being more likely to see their fan interest as something they benefit from whereas liberals may find deeper meaning and significance through their fan interest. Whether these two groups differ with respect to the types of fan interests they prefer and whether these differences, in turn, lead to differences in how they approach their fan interests remains a subject for future research.

Conclusion

Throughout this chapter we've have seen numerous examples of the applicability of the CAPE model to various theoretically and practically important topics: From questions about specific fan attitudes and behaviors to assessing important personality, well being, and social identity variables to questions about the demographic composition of a given fan group. Of course, this chapter is not intended to be the final word on what subjects the CAPE model is and is not applicable to. Instead, it should be seen as a first step, illustrating some of the many fruitful directions research involving the CAPE model can be taken in. These topics, and a myriad of others like it, are currently being studied by scholars studying fans and fan cultures from a variety of different perspectives. By using the CAPE model more consistently in future research, we can begin to draw together some of these disparate lines of research and more systematically study topics which, for decades, have historically been on the fringe of academia and which have been studied sporadically in idiosyncratic ways.

Conclusion

As we come to the end of this book we stand in awe at the sheer number of giants whose shoulders we've stood upon to get to this point. Across 28 chapters we reviewed the work of hundreds of scholars who, across decades, have worked to better our understanding of the way fans think, feel, and behave. Despite our tireless efforts to scour the literature as thoroughly as possible, we'll reaffirm what we said at the very start, that this book should not be taken as a systematic look at all of the different ways scholars have studied fan groups. Instead, it's been our humble attempt to condense an incomprehensibly large body of work into a set of 28 constructs in service of an even more ambitious project: To develop a model which simultaneously takes all of this work into account and concisely assesses it in a measure that can be added to almost any study of any fan group.

You'll recall that when we set out to develop the CAPE model, we had three specific goals in mind:

> 1. To non-redundantly assess all relevant dimensions of fan identity in a manner that considers and accounts for conceptual overlap between dimensions
> 2. To reliably and concisely assess these dimensions in a fandom-general fashion —that is, using items that can be flexibly applied to fans of all interests
> 3. To predict outcomes both theoretically important to researchers and practically important to fans and those working with fans

Upon reflecting on these goals, we feel that we have been able to achieve these goals, albeit in a very preliminary manner. Speaking to the first goal, we've used factor analysis to reduce redundancy in our model while retaining a set of 18 subscales which fall into the 4 broad categories of commitment, asset, presence, and expression. We suggest that most fan researchers will be able to find the strands of their own work embedded within these dimensions. More importantly, by pulling the individual strands into this model, we hope these same researchers will start to see the connections between their own work and the work of others they may not have been aware of, or which they had not considered before.

With respect to our second goal, we've begun to hone the CAPE model and its associated CAPE scale across five studies of specific fan groups and two heterogeneous samples of fans of all manner of interests. From its very start, the CAPE scale was designed to be flexibly used in samples ranging from furries to NASCAR fans, from model train enthusiasts to Juggalos (fans of the Insane

Clown Posse). While we were limited by our own access to a small sample of fan groups (just as all fan researchers are), it is our hope that others will find the CAPE scale to be as easily applied to their own fandoms as it has been to our own and we look forward to seeing the generalizability of our findings to fandoms, contexts, and regions we never even imagined when putting together our own studies.

When it comes to our final goal, we've only been able to scratch the surface when it comes to assessing variables that fan researchers are interested in. In a domain as broad and interdisciplinary as fan studies which includes marketers, social psychologists, anthropologists, media researchers, and sociologists, we were bound to miss something. Even so, across our seven studies we attempted to cast as wide a net as possible and assess variables that scholars from all of these disciplines might find theoretically or practically useful. We realize that our own explanations for some of the findings may be ham-handed at best, and fully acknowledge that future scholars will almost certainly take our humble studies and do them far better than we ever could, drawing upon their own expertise and paradigms from their own fields that we, as social psychologists, are only barely aware of. In fact, we look forward to this possibility: We encourage scholars to take what we've done here and improve upon it, answering the questions we've been left scratching our heads over and shoring up our meager evidence with far stronger studies employing the CAPE scale.

Because, in the end, perhaps more than anything else, our goal in developing the CAPE model has been to draw the field of fandom scholars closer to discuss these issues. Far too often fan scholarship feels a bit like being set adrift, floating in the void between disciplines, desperately trying to find others with the same research interests, a common language with which to converse, common journals in which to publish, and common conventions in which to meet up to present and view innovations in this field. If we can provide some of the impetus for this uniting through various scholars placing their own work within the CAPE model or trying the CAPE scale out in their own research, then we'll consider our job done.

Appendix A

Measure	Source1	# Items	Format	Study
Fan Attitudes / Behavior				
Type of Fan	New Item	1	MC, 5 choices	GEN1/ GEN2
Please choose the category that BEST represents your favorite fan interest. (Sport / Music / Media / Hobby / Other)				
Subgroup Categorization	New Measure	Varied	Checkbox	B19/ Anime/ Fur/ SW
Are you a… (Select all that apply): Artist/ Writer/ Cosplayer/ Figure Collector/ Hentai Fan/ Otaku/ Original Trilogy Fan/ Prequel Trilogy Fan/ Sequel Trilogy Fan				
Other Fan Interests	New Measure	3	Likert, 7-point	B18/ Fur
Please list up to three non-brony fan interests you have. How strongly do you identify as a fan of them?				
Multiple Fan Interests	Wagoner et al. (2017); Haslam et al. (2008)	2	Likert, 7 point	B19
I am a member of many different fandoms.				
Exclusivity of Interest	New Measure	3	Likert, 7-point	GEN1
I have no other interests that even come close to how passionate I am about this interest.				
Active Participation in Fan Interest	New Measure	1	Likert, 7-point	GEN2
I am an active participant with this interest.				
Passive Fan Consumption	New Measure	1	Likert, 7-point	GEN2
I tend to sit back and watch while engaging with this interest.				
Producing Fan Content	New Measure	1	Likert, 7-point	GEN2
I make or produce things related to this interest.				
Not Producing Fan Content	New Measure	1	Likert, 7-point	GEN2
I do NOT make or produce things related to this interest.				
Fan Activity Engagement	New Measure	4, 14	Likert, 8 - point	Anime/ B18/ B19/ SW
This past year, how often did you… watch *My Little Pony* / talk to				

friends about *My Little Pony* / wear or display clothing or items associated with *My Little Pony*

Money Spent (Year)	New Measure	1	Numeric	GEN1
In the last year, how much money would you estimate that you have spent on this fan interest (e.g., events, merchandise)?				
Specific Spending	New Measure	6	Numeric	Anime/ Fur
In the last year, how much money have you spent on… Physical anime artwork or commissions / Digital anime artwork or commissions / Erotic anime content				
Willing to spend $250	New Measure	1	Likert, 7-point	GEN1/ Fur
How likely would you be to spend more than $250 on something related to this fan interest?				
Value of Collection	New Measure	1	Numeric	B19
Estimate the monetary value of everything you own MLP [My Little Pony] Related.				
Willing to Travel	New Measure	1	Likert, 7-point	GEN1
How likely would you be to fly to another city to take part in an activity related to this fan interest (e.g., to attend a concert or convention?)				
Furthest Travel	New Measure	1	Numeric	GEN1
What is the furthest (miles) you have traveled for this fan interest (e.g., to attend a concert or convention?				
Emotional Response	New Measure	10	Likert, 7-point	GEN1
Please indicate the extent to which you have experienced each of the following emotional reactions to content related to your fan interest… Sadness / Anger / Nervousness / Anticipation…				
Nostalgia	Smeekes et al. (2018)	4	Likert, 7-point	B19
I often think back about the good old days of the brony fandom.				
Angst at Show Ending	Wohl & Branscombe (2009)	5	Likert, 7-point	B19
I feel anxious about the future of the brony fandom.				
Show Ending Threat	New Measure	2	Likert, 7-point	B19
The ending of MLP:FiM [*My Little Pony*] may mean the end of the				

brony fandom.

Expected Engagement Post-Show End	New Measure	15	Likert, 7-point	B18

Indicate your degree of agreement with the following statements regarding how much you expect to engage with *My Little Pony* content in the years after the last episode has aired. / Show old episodes of *My Little Pony* to my friends.

Fan Entitlement	Shaw et al. (2016)	7	Likert, 7-point	GEN1

Please rate your agreement with the following items with regard to content creators or celebrities in your fandom… They should answer any emails they get from fans.

Fan-Related Dreams	New Measure	1	Likert, 10-point	Anime/ SW

What percentage of your dreams are anime-related?

Fandom-Themed Pornography Use	New Measure	2	Likert, 7-point	Anime

I often view anime-related pornographic material / I view more anime pornographic material than non-anime pornographic material.

Shipping Behavior	New Measure	1	Likert, 7-point	SW

How often do you engage in shipping Star Wars characters?

Self and Social

Fanship Scale	Reysen & Branscombe (2010)	1/3	Likert, 7-point	B18/ B19/ Anime/ Fur/ SW

I am emotionally connected to being a brony.

Fandom Scale	Reysen et al. (2013); Doosje et al. (1995)	1/3	Likert, 7-point	B18/ B19/ Anime/ Fur/ SW

I strongly identify with bronies in the brony community.

Shared Fan Engagement	New Measure	1	Likert, 7-point	GEN2

I often interact with others while engaging with this interest.

Entitativity	Wagoner et al. (2017); Castano et al. (2003)	3	Likert, 7-point	B19

The brony fandom is a cohesive group.

Fandom Permeability	Mummendey et al. (1999)	2	Likert, 7-point	B19
If I wanted to, it would not be a problem to move from the brony fan group to a non-brony group.				
Subgroup Identification	Reysen et al. (2013); Doosje et al. (1995)	3	Likert, 7-point	SW
I strongly identify with other fans in this subgroup community.				
Subgroup Ingroup Bias	Reysen et al. (2015b)	3	Likert, 7-point	SW
My subgroup is better than other subgroups in the *Star Wars* fandom.				
Group Stigma	New Measure	1	Likert, 7-point	GEN1/ GEN2
Fans of this interest are discriminated against.				
Personal Stigma	New Measure	1	Likert, 7-point	GEN1/ GEN2
I have felt discriminated against because I am a fan of this interest.				
Treated Worse as a Fan	Leshner et al. (2018)	1	Likert, 7-point	GEN1/ B18
I feel that I am treated differently (worse) when people know I am a fan of this interest.				
Fan Identity Disclosure	Mock et al. (2013)	3	Likert, 7-point	Fur
For each of the following, please indicate the degree to which the group of people know about your furry identity. / Your network of friends / Your family / People in your day-to-day life (work, school, community)				
Fursona as Ideal Self	New Measure	1	Likert, 7-point	Fur
My fursona represents who I would ideally like to be.				
Identifying with Fursona	Reysen & Branscombe (2010)	3	Likert, 7-point	Fur
I am emotionally connected to my fursona. / I strongly identify with my fursona.				
Fan Proselytizing	Plante, Chadborn, & Reysen (2018)	5	Likert, 7-point	GEN1
To what extent do you engage in the following fan-related behaviors?... Trying to get others interested in your fan interest.				

Measure	Source	Items	Scale	Block
Nerd Identification	New Measure	2	Likert, 7-point	GEN1/ GEN2
I consider myself a nerd. / I strongly identify with nerds.				
Intragroup Status	New Measure	3	Likert, 7-point	B18/ Anime/ Fur
Other bronies look up to me as an example of what a brony should be.				
Treatment of New Fans	New Measure	8	Likert, 7-point	Anime / Fur
New people coming into the fandom are changing it for the worse.				
Fan Elitism	Plante et al. (2020)	10	Likert, 7-point	B18/ Anime/ SW
My interpretations of *My Little Pony* are more sophisticated than most fans'.				
Gatekeeping	Plante et al. (2020)	18	Likert, 7-point	B18/ Anime / Fur
The brony fandom would be better if it were less accepting of new members.				
Giving / Getting Help Scale	New Measure	5/10	Likert, 7-point	B18/ Anime/ Fur
I have received financial help (e.g., money) from bronies when I asked for it.				
Turn to Fans for Help	New Measure	3	Likert, 7-point	GEN1
How likely would you be to turn to each of the following sources for help or advice if you were having a problem in your life?... Other fans in your fan interest community / Other fans on social media / Online fan message board				
Relationship Assessment Scale (RAS)	Hendrick (1988)	7	Likert, 7-point	B19
To what extent have your friendships met your original expectations?				
Revised UCLA Loneliness Scale	Russell et al. (1980); Hays & DiMatteo (1987)	6	Likert, 7-point	B19
I lack companionship. / I feel isolated from others.				
Parasocial Relationships	Adam & Sizemore	6	Likert, 7-point	GEN1

	(2013)			
	I think people related to my fan interest could be friends of mine.			

Individual Differences

Big Five Inventory	John & Srivastava (1999)	44	Likert, 5-point	Fur
	I am someone who… is talkative / is reserved / can be tense.			
Interpersonal Reactivity Index (Empathy)	Davis (1980, 1983)	14	Likert, 7-point	B18
	I often have tender, concerned feelings for people less fortunate than me.			
Maturity	New Measure	2	Likert, 7-point	GEN1/ GEN2/ SW
	I am a mature person / Other people would describe me as a mature person.			
Fantasy Engagement Scale	Plante, Reysen et al. (2017)	10	Likert, 7-point	GEN1/ SW
	My interest in this has caused problems with me and my family. / Fantasizing about this has had a positive effect on my life.			
Transportation Scale	Green & Brock (2000)	9	Likert, 7-point	GEN1
	When I read a story, I can easily picture the events in it taking place.			
Immersion	Reysen, Plante, Roberts, & Gerbasi (2019); Bahk (2008); Bjorner et al. (2016); Fornerino et al. (2008); Fu et al. (2009); IJsselsteijn et al. (2013); Jennett et al. (2008);	6	Likert, 7-point	B18/ Anime/ Fur

	Poncin et al. (2015)			
I feel completely immersed.				

Well-being

BBC Well-Being Scale	Pontin et al. (2013)	24	Likert, 7-point	GEN1/ GEN2/ Fur
I feel depressed or anxious. / I am satisfied with my physical health. / I feel able to ask someone for help with a problem if I needed to.				
Life Satisfaction	Reysen et al. (2018b)	1	Likert, 7-point	Anime/ SW
I am satisfied with my life.				
Depression	Reysen et al. (2018b)	1	Likert, 7-point	B19 / Anime/ SW
I often feel depressed.				
Anxiousness	New Measure	1	Likert, 7-point	B19 / Anime/ SW
I am often anxious.				
Rosenberg Self-Esteem Scale	Rosenberg (1965)	10	Likert, 7-point	B19
On the whole, I am satisfied with myself.				
Single-Item Self-Esteem Measure	Robins et al. (2001)	1	Likert, 7-point	B18 / Anime/ SW
I have high self-esteem.				
Meaning in Life Questionnaire	Steger et al. (2006)	10	Likert, 7-point	GEN1
I understand my life's meaning.				

Demographics

Political Liberalism	New Measure	1	Likert, 7-point	GEN2/ Anime/ SW
Politically, I would say I am… (Very Conservative / Very Liberal)				
Social Liberalism	New Measure	1	Likert, 7-point	Anime
Socially, I would say I am… (Very Conservative / Very Liberal)				
Economic Liberalism	New Measure	1	Likert, 7-point	Anime
Economically, I would say I am… (Very Conservative / Very Liberal)				
Subjective Socioeconomic	Adler & Stewart	1	MC, 10-point	GEN2/ B18/ Fur

Status   (2007)

Place an X on the rung where you think you stand in this time of your life, relative to other people in your country.

[1]Items either drawn directly from source or inspired by / modified from original items.

Appendix B: Full Initial Inventory

Subscale	#	Item	Original Source[1]
Magnitude	1	I love this interest.	Vinney et al. (2019)
Magnitude	2	This interest is important to me.	Funk & James (2001)
Magnitude[2]	3	I am one of the biggest fans of this interest.	Thorne & Bruner (2006)
Magnitude	4	I am the most enthusiastic supporter of this interest.	New Item
Participation	5	I often watch, read, and/or discuss this interest.	Wann (1995)
Participation	6	I go to conventions or gatherings related to this interest.	Vinney et al. (2019)
Participation[2]	7	I follow everything (e.g., media, news, events) related to this interest.	Gibson et al. (2003)
Participation	8	I actively participate in this interest.	New Item
Recreation	9	To me, this interest is simply a form of recreation.	Wann (1995)
Recreation	10	I enjoy this interest because of its entertainment value.	Wann (1995)
Recreation	11	This interest is entertaining.	Oliver & Bartsch (2010)
Recreation	12	This interest is a fun way to spend my free time.	Oliver & Bartsch (2010); Gibson et al. (2002)
Meaning-Making[2]	13	This interest gives me a sense of "meaning" in my life.	Vignoles et al. (2006)
Meaning-Making	14	This interest is meaningful to me.	Oliver & Bartsch (2010)
Meaning-Making	15	This interest makes my actions feel significant.	Vinney et al. (2019)
Meaning-Making	16	This interest helps me think about the things I value.	Oliver & Bartsch (2010)
Guidance	17	This interest provides me with a sense of direction.	Vinney et al. (2019)
Guidance	18	When I make decisions in my life, I think about this interest.	Cole & Leets (1999)
Guidance	19	I use lessons that I've learned from this interest to guide my	Edwards, Griffin, Chadborn, &

		actions in day-to-day life.	Redden (2014)
Guidance	20	This interest provides me with answers/information/guidance I need to face situations in my life.	Chadborn et al. (2017)
Growth[2]	21	This interest has helped me grow as a person.	Oliver & Bartsch (2010)
Growth	22	I have become the best me I can be because of this interest.	Gibson et al. (2002)
Growth	23	I have been enriched because of this interest.	Gibson et al. (2002)
Growth	24	This interest provides me with an opportunity to grow and discover more aspects about myself.	Chadborn et al. (2017)
Fandom	25	I would describe myself as a member of the fan community of this interest.	Doosje et al. (1995)
Fandom	26	I strongly identify with other fans in the fan community of this interest.	Reysen et al. (2013)
Fandom[2]	27	I see myself as a member of the fan community for this interest.	Doosje et al. (1995)
Fandom	28	I feel strong ties with other fans in the fan community of this interest.	Doosje et al. (1995)
Social Interaction	29	I like this interest because it gives me an opportunity to interact with other people.	Wann (1995)
Social Interaction	30	To me, this interest gives me an opportunity to socialize.	Gibson et al. (2003)
Social Interaction	31	I often email/text/private message with other fans about this interest.	Thorne & Bruner (2006)
Social Interaction	32	I enjoy getting to share my interest with my friends.	Funk, Ridinger, & Moorman (2004)
Sensory Novelty	33	This interest provides me with a novel way to experience the world.	Gibson et al. (2003)
Sensory Novelty	34	This interest allows me to live a variety of experiences.	Vallerand et al. (2003)
Sensory Novelty	35	The new things that I discover with this interest allow me to appreciate it even more.	Vallerand et al. (2003)
Sensory Novelty[2]	36	This interest exposes me to novel experiences.	New Item

Escapism	37	One of the main reasons that I watch, read, or experience this interest is that doing so gives me the opportunity to temporarily escape life's problems.	Wann (1995)
Escapism	38	This interest provides me with a break from life's stresses.	Chadborn et al. (2017)
Escapism[2]	39	I like this interest because it provides me with a distraction from daily life for awhile.	Funk, Ridinger, & Moorman (2004)
Escapism	40	This interest is a great change of pace from what I regularly do.	Trail & James (2001)
Eustress	41	I like the stimulation that I get from this interest.	Wann (1995)
Eustress	42	I like the excitement associated with this interest.	Funk, Ridinger, & Moorman (2004)
Eustress[2]	43	I am drawn to the emotional drama involved in this interest.	Funk, Ridinger, & Moorman (2004)
Eustress	44	This interest is more enjoyable to me when there is some exciting drama involved.	Trail & James (2001)
Emotion	45	I feel an emotional connection to this interest.	Reysen & Branscombe (2010)
Emotion	46	I am emotionally engaged with this interest.	Gau (2013)
Emotion	47	I am passionate about this interest.	Thorne & Bruner (2006)
Emotion	48	I am emotionally moved by this interest.	Oliver & Bartsch (2010)
Materialism	49	I like to buy objects or memorabilia related to this interest.	Vinney et al. (2019)
Materialism	50	I spend a considerable amount of money on this interest.	Reysen & Branscombe (2010)
Materialism	51	I like collecting material related to this interest.	Hanna et al. (2011)
Materialism[2]	52	I own a lot of stuff related to this interest.	Thorne & Bruner (2006)
Loyalty	53	No matter what happens, I will continue to be a fan of this interest.	Vinney et al. (2019)

Loyalty	54	I am a loyal supporter of this interest.	Vinney et al. (2019)
Loyalty[2]	55	I am committed to this interest.	New Item
Loyalty	56	I am devoted to this interest.	Vinney et al. (2019)
Fanship	57	This interest is a part of who I am.	Reysen & Branscombe (2010); Tapp (2004)
Fanship	58	Being a fan of it is important to my identity.	Vinney et al. (2019)
Fanship	59	I strongly identify with this interest.	Reysen & Branscombe (2010)
Fanship	60	This interest helps define who I am as a person.	Vinney et al. (2019)
Uniqueness	61	This interest gives me an opportunity to express my uniqueness.	Chadborn et al. (2017)
Uniqueness[2]	62	This interest makes me feel distinct and unique compared to other people.	Vignoles et al. (2006)
Uniqueness	63	I'm different from others because I like this interest.	New Item
Uniqueness	64	Being a fan of this interest makes me unique.	New Item
Creativity	65	This interest provides me with an outlet for my creativity.	Chadborn et al. (2017)
Creativity[2]	66	I am more creative because I am a fan of this interest.	New Item
Creativity	67	I often create things (e.g., fan fiction, art, videos, etc.) related to this interest.	Vinney et al. (2019); Hanna et al. (2011)
Creativity	68	This interest sparks my imagination.	New Item
Aesthetics[2]	69	One of the main reasons that I like this interest is for the artistic value.	Wann (1995)
Aesthetics	70	I enjoy this interest because to me it is a form of art.	Vinney et al. (2019)
Aesthetics	71	I appreciate the beauty inherent in this interest.	Trail & James (2001)

Aesthetics	72	This interest is artistically valuable.	Oliver & Bartsch (2010)
Knowledge	73	I enjoy this interest because I know a lot about it.	Funk, Ridinger, & Moorman (2004)
Knowledge[2]	74	I am an expert about this interest.	Vinney et al. (2019)
Knowledge	75	I regularly track trends and information about this interest.	Trail & James (2001)
Knowledge	76	I would consider myself to be an expert on this interest.	Thorne & Bruner (2006)
Self-Esteem	77	I enjoy this interest because it makes me feel good about being me.	Wann (1995)
Self-Esteem[2]	78	This interest gives me a sense of self-esteem.	Vignoles et al. (2006)
Self-Esteem	79	How I feel depends on how well things are going with this interest.	New Item
Self-Esteem	80	This interest affects my degree of self-esteem.	New Item
Desirability	81	Others have a positive view of this interest.	Dimmock & Grove (2006)
Desirability	82	Others respect this interest	Dimmock & Grove (2006)
Desirability	83	Overall, this interest is considered good by others.	Luhtanen & Crocker (1992)
Desirability	84	Society holds a positive view of this interest.	New Item
Economic[2]	85	One of the main reasons that I like this interest is so I can profit from it.	Wann (1995)
Economic	86	This interest is only enjoyable if you can profit from it.	Wann (1995)
Economic	87	Profiting from this interest is the most enjoyable aspect of it.	Wann (1995)
Economic	88	I am a fan of this interest for economic reasons.	New Item
Accomplishment	89	This interest provides me with a sense of accomplishment.	Gibson et al. (2002)
Accomplishment[2]	90	My actions as a fan of this interest make me feel like I've accomplished something.	Gibson et al. (2002)
Accomplishm	91	This interest gives me the feeling	Vignoles et al.

ent		of being a competent or capable person.	(2006)
Accomplishm ent	92	Being a fan of this interest makes me feel successful.	New Item
Exclusivity	93	I am NOT a fan of anything else to the same extent that I am of this interest.	Tapp (2004)
Exclusivity	94	This interest is my only fan interest.	New Item
Exclusivity	95	I only focus exclusively on this interest.	New Item
Exclusivity[2]	96	I spend most of my time focusing on this one fan interest while ignoring other fan interests.	New Item
Self-Disclosure	97	My friends know about my interest.	Mock et al. (2013)
Self-Disclosure	98	My family knows about my interest.	Mock et al. (2013)
Self-Disclosure	99	I often tell new acquaintances about my fan interest.	New Item
Self-Disclosure	100	I want everyone to know I am a fan of this interest.	Reysen & Branscombe (2010)
Physical Attraction	101	I am physically attracted to aspects of this interest.	New Item
Physical Attraction	102	The main reason that I like this interest is because I find certain aspects of it attractive.	Trail & James (2001)
Physical Attraction	103	Sex appeal is a big reason why I like this interest.	Trail & James (2001)
Physical Attraction	104	I am sexually aroused by aspects of this interest.	New Item
Pathological	105	I have frequent thoughts about this interest even when I don't want to.	McCutcheon et al. (2002)
Pathological	106	I cannot live without this interest.	Vallerand et al. (2003)
Pathological	107	I am obsessed with this interest.	McCutcheon et al. (2002)
Pathological	108	Others would say that my connection to this interest is almost pathological.	New Item

Special Bond	109	I have a special bond with my interest.	New Item
Special Bond	110	When I think about my interest it makes me feel comfortable, as if I am with friends.	Eyal & Cohen (2006)
Special Bond	111	I share with my favorite interest a special bond that cannot be described in words.	Maltby et al. (2005)
Special Bond	112	I have almost a psychic connection with my interest.	New Item

[1]Items either drawn directly from source or inspired by / modified from original item. [2]Item is part of the final 18-item CAPE scale.

Appendix C
Final CAPE Scale

Instructions: Please rate your degree of agreement with the following items regarding your favorite fan interest.

Strongly Disagree 1 2 3 4 5 6 7 Strongly Agree

1. I am committed to this interest.
2. I am an expert about this interest.
3. I am one of the biggest fans of this interest.
4. I follow everything (e.g., media, news, events) related to this interest.
5. I see myself as a member of the fan community for this interest.
6. I own a lot of stuff related to this interest.
7. One of the main reasons that I like this interest is so I can profit from it.
8. This interest gives me a sense of self-esteem.
9. My actions as a fan of this interest make me feel like I've accomplished something.
10. I spend most of my time focusing on this one fan interest while ignoring other fan interests.
11. I like this interest because it provides me with a distraction from daily life for awhile.
12. This interest exposes me to novel experiences.
13. I am drawn to the emotional drama involved in this interest.
14. One of the main reasons that I like this interest is for the artistic value.
15. This interest gives me a sense of "meaning" in my life.
16. This interest has helped me grow as a person.
17. This interest makes me feel distinct and unique compared to other people.
18. I am more creative because I am a fan of this interest.

Scoring
Commitment: average items 1, 2, 3, 4, 5, 6
Asset: average of items 7, 8, 9, 10
Presence: average of items 11, 12, 13
Expression: average of items 14, 15, 16, 17, 18

References

Abarbanel, B., Macey, J., Hamari, J., & Melton, R. (2020). Gamers who gamble: Examining the relationship between esports spectatorship and event wagering. *The Journal of Emerging Sport Studies, 3.* https://digitalcommons.library.tru.ca/jess/vol3/iss1/1

Abrams, D. (1994). Political distinctiveness: An identity optimizing approach. *European Journal of Social Psychology, 24,* 357-365.

Abrams, D. (2009). Social identity on a national scale: Optimal distinctiveness and young people's self-expression through musical preference. *Group Processes and Intergroup Relations, 12*(3), 303-317. https://doi.org/10.1177/1368430209102841

Adachi, P. J. C., Ryan, R. M., Frye, J., McClurg, D., & Rigby, C. S. (2018). "I can't wait for the next episode!" Investigating the motivational pull of television dramas through the lens of self-determination theory. *Motivation Science, 4*(1), 78-94. https://dx.doi.org/10.1037/mot0000063

Adam, A. (2019). Perceptions of infidelity: A comparison of sexual, emotional, cyber-, and parasocial behaviors. *Interpersona, 13*(2), 237-252. https://doi.org/10.5964/ijpr.v13i2.376

Adam, A., & Sizemore, B. (2013). Parasocial romance: A social exchange perspective. *Interpersona, 7*(1), 12-25. https://doi.org/10.5964/ijpr.v7i1.106

Adler, N. E., & Stewart, J. (2007) *The MacArthur scale of subjective social status.* MacArthur Research Network on SES & Health. Retrieved from http://www.macses.ucsf.edu/Research/Psychosocial/subjective.php

Ahn, T. (2010). *The effect of user motives and interactivity on attitude toward a sport website* (Publication No. 3415206) [Doctoral dissertation, Florida State University]. ProQuest Dissertations and Theses Global.

Aiken, K. D., & Campbell, R. M. (2005). An empirical examination of unusual fan behaviors: Basking in reflected failure and cutting off reflected success. *AMA Educators' Proceedings: Enhancing Knowledge Development in Marketing, 16,* 116-122.

Ajzen, I. (1985). From intentions to actions: A theory of planned behavior. In J. Kuhi & J. Beckmann (Eds.), *Action-control: From cognition to behavior* (pp. 11-39). Springer.

Ajzen, I. (1991). The theory of planned behavior. *Organizational Behavior and Human Decision Processes, 50*(2), 179-211. https://doi.org/10.1016/0749-5978(91)90020-T

Alexandris, K. (2012). Exploring the role of motivation on the development of sport involvement. *International Journal of Sport Management and Marketing, 12*(1/2), 57-72. https://doi.org/10.1504/IJSMM.2012.051252

Alonso, A. D., Sakellarios, N., & Cseh, L. (2015). The theory of planned behavior in the context of a food and drink event: A case study. *Journal of Convention and Event Tourism, 16*(3), 200-227. https://doi.org/10.1080/15470148.2015.1035822

Aluja-Fabregat, A. (2000). Personality and curiosity about TV and films violence in adolescents. *Personality and Individual Differences, 29*(2), 379-392. https://doi.org/10.1016/S0191-8869(99)00200-7

Anderson, D. J.-F. (2019). *Investigating fandom, motives, and consumption patterns of esport consumers* (Publication No. 27805522) [Master's thesis, Sam Houston State University]. ProQuest Dissertations and Theses Global.

Anderson, S. L. (2018). Extraludic narratives: Online communities and video games. *Transformative Works and Cultures, 28.* http://dx.doi.org/10.3983/twc.2018.1255

Anderton, C. (2016). Sonic artefacts: "Record collecting" in the digital age. *iaspm@journal, 6*(1), 85-103. https://doi.org/10.5429/2079-3871(2016)v6i1.6en

Andrijiw, A. M., & Hyatt, C. G. (2009). Using optimal distinctiveness theory to understand identification with a nonlocal professional hockey team. *Journal of Sport Management, 23*(2), 156-181. https://doi.org/10.1123/jsm.23.2.156

Apostolopoulou, A., & Papadimitriou, D. (2018). Examining the meanings and consumption of sport licensed products through team identification. *Journal of Brand Management, 25,* 536-548. https://dx.doi.org/10.1057/s41262-018-0102-8

Argan, M., Argan, M. T., & Kaya, S. (2018). The role of empathy and sympathy on team identification: The determinants of team-based approach. *Gazi Journal of Physical Education and Sport Sciences, 23*(2), 59-74. https://dergipark.org.tr/en/pub/gbesbd/issue/36374/411559

Arismendi, O. J. G. (2020). *Using the Minecraft affinity subspace "First Dimension" to negotiate information literacy* [Master's thesis, University of Alberta]. https://doi.org/10.7939/r3-z5nj-bv88

Arms, R. L., Russell, G. W., & Sandilands, M. L. (1979). Effects on the hostility of spectators of viewing aggressive sports. *Social Psychology Quarterly, 42*(3), 275-279. https://doi.org/10.2307/3033771

Arnold, M. B. (1960). *Emotion and personality.* Columbia University Press.

Aruguete, M., Griffith, J., Edman, J., Green, T., & Mccutcheon, L. (2014). Body image and celebrity worship. *Implicit Religion, 17*(2), 223-234. https://dx.doi.org/10.1558/imre.v17i2.223

Aruguete, M. S., Huynh, H., Collisson, B., McCutcheon, L., & Piotrowski, C. (2020). Stacking up with the stars: Relative deprivation and excessive admiration of celebrities. *Psychological Reports, 123*(3), 952-965. https://doi.org/10.1177/0033294119836765

Ashe, D. D., Maltby, J., & McCutcheon, L. E. (2005). Are celebrity-worshippers more prone to narcissism? A brief report. *North American Journal of Psychology, 7*(2), 239-246.

Ashe, D. D., & McCutcheon, L. E. (2001). Shyness, loneliness, and attitude toward celebrities. *Current Research in Social Psychology, 6*(9), 124-133.

Ashmore, R. D., Deaux, K., & McLaughlin-Volpe, T. (2004). An organizing framework for collective identity: Articulation and significance of multidimensionality. *Psychological Bulletin, 130*(1), 80-114. https://doi.org/10.1037/0033-2909.130.1.80

Atwell Seate, A., Ma, R., Cohen, E. L., & Iles, I. (2020). Help a fan out? Effects of fandom type and task type on people's behavioral intentions toward different types of fans in a collaborative effort. *Psychology of Popular Media, 9*(3), 380-391. https://doi.org/10.1037/ppm0000252

Ay, U., & Kaygan, H. (2021). Autonomy or loyalty? Community-within-community interactions of a local football fandom group. *Journal of Consumer Culture*. Advance online publication. https://doi.org/10.1177/1469540520982337

Aygün, M., & Demir, E. K. (2020). Analysing motivations for sports consumption of students at school of physical education and sports. *Asian Journal of Education and Training, 6*(2), 314-319. https://dx.doi.org/10.20448/journal.522.2020.62.314.319

Bacon-Smith, C. (1992). *Enterprising women: Television fandom and the creation of popular myth*. University of Pennsylvania Press.

Bahk, C. M. (2008). Reliance, immersion, and enjoyment: An exploratory socio-psychological analysis on internet involvement. *Communications of the IIMA, 8*(1), 59-66.

Bailey, J., & Harvey, B. (2019). 'That pony is real sexy': *My Little Pony* fans, sexual abjection, and the politics of masculinity online. *Sexualities, 22*(3), 325-342. https://doi.org/10.1177/1363460717731932

Bailey, E. J., & Ivory, J. D. (2018). The moods meaningful media create: Effects of hedonic and eudaimonic television clips on viewers' affective states and subsequent program selection. *Psychology of Popular Media Culture, 7*(2), 130-145. https://dx.doi.org/10.1037/ppm0000122

Ballouli, K., Trail, G. T., Koesters, T. C., & Bernthal, M. J. (2016). Differential effects of motives and points of attachment on conative loyalty of formula 1 U.S. grand prix attendees. *Sport Marketing Quarterly, 25*(3), 166-181.

Balsam, K. F., & Szymanski, D. M. (2005). Relationship quality and domestic violence in women's same-sex relationships: The role of minority stress. *Psychology of Women Quarterly, 29*(1), 258-269. http://doi.org/10.1111/j.1471-6402.2005.00220.x

Banister, E. N., & Hogg, M. K. (2004). Negative symbolic consumption and consumers' drive for self-esteem: The case of the fashion industry. *European Journal of Marketing, 38*(7), 850-868. https://doi.org/10.1108/03090560410539285

Banister, E., Hogg, M., Decrop, A., & Roux, D. (2005). Symbolic consumption: The interplay between distinction, distastes and degrees of rejection. *European Advances in Consumer Research, 7,* 453-456.

Bartsch, A., Kalch, A., & Oliver, M. B. (2014). The role of emotional media experiences in stimulating reflective thoughts. *Journal of Media Psychology, 26*(3), 125-140. https://doi.org/10.1027/1864-1105/a000118

Battista, M. E. (2011). *Does anyone really like horror movies? Personality and automatic affective reactions to frightening films* [Doctoral dissertation, University of Western Ontario]. https://ir.lib.uwo.ca/etd/116

Bauer, H. H., Stokburger-Sauer, N. E., & Exler, S. (2008). Brand image and fan loyalty in professional team sport: A refined model and empirical assessment. *Journal of Sport Management, 22*(2), 205-226. https://doi.org/10.1123/jsm.22.2.205

Baumesiter, R. F., & Leary, M. R. (1995). The need to belong: Desire for interpersonal attachments as a fundamental human motivation. *Psychological Bulletin, 117*(3), 497-529. https://dx.doi.org/10.1037/0033-2909.117.3.497

Beaton, A. A., Funk, D. C., Ridinger, L., & Jordan, J. (2011). Sport involvement: A conceptual and empirical analysis. *Sport Management Review, 14*(2), 126-140. https://doi.org/10.1016/j.smr.2010.07.002

Bee, C. C., & Havitz, M. E. (2010). Exploring the relationship between involvement, fan attraction, psychological commitment and behavioural loyalty in a sports spectator context. *International Journal of Sports Marketing and Sponsorship, 11*(2), 140-157. https://doi.org/10.1108/IJSMS-11-02-2010-B004

Benckendorff, P., & Pearce, P. (2012). The psychology of events. In S. J. Page & J. Connell (Eds.), *The Routledge handbook of events* (pp. 165-185). Taylor & Francis.

Bennett, G., Ferreira, M., Lee, J., & Polite, F. (2009). The role of involvement in sports and sport spectatorship in sponsor's brand use: The case of mountain dew and action sports sponsorship. *Sport Marketing Quarterly, 18*(1), 14-24.

Benzecry, C. E. (2009). Becoming a fan: On the seductions of opera. *Qualitative Sociology, 32*(2), 131-151. https://doi.org/10.1007/s11133-009-9123-7

Benzecry, C. E. (2012). Opera thugs and passionate fandom. *Contexts, 11*(3), 39-45. https://doi.org/10.1177/1536504212456181

Berdychevsky, L. (2018). "Risky" leisure research on sex and violence: Innovation, impact, and impediment. *Leisure Sciences, 40*(1-2), 9-18. https://doi.org/10.1080/01490400.2017.1376012

Berendt, J., Uhrich, S., & Thompson, S. A. (2018). Marketing, get ready to rumble—How rivalry promotes distinctiveness for brands and consumers. *Journal of Business Research, 88*(1), 161-172. https://doi.org/10.1016/j.jbusres.2018.03.015

Berger, R. T. (2008). *High-profile celebrity court cases: An investigation into audience usage, needs, and motivations* (Publication No. 3350584) [Doctoral dissertation, Fielding Graduate University]. ProQuest Dissertations and Theses Global.

Bernier, R. G., Crittendon, D., & Roberts, A. (2016). *Friends close, fandom closer: Terror management and parasocial support.* Murray State University. https://digitalcommons.murraystate.edu/scholarsweek/Fall2016/PsychPIP/6/

Berument, H., & Yucel, E. M. (2005). Long live Fenerbahçe: The production boosting effects of football. *Journal of Economic Psychology, 26*(6), 842-861. https://doi.org/10.1016/j.joep.2005.04.002

Berument, M. H., Ceylan, N. B., & Ogut-Eker, G. (2009). Soccer, stock returns and fanaticism: Evidence from Turkey. *The Social Science Journal, 46*(3), 594-600. https://doi.org/10.1016/j.soscij.2009.06.001

Berument, M. H., & Ceylan, N. B. (2012). Effects of soccer on stock markets: The return–volatility relationship. *The Social Science Journal, 49*(3), 368-374. https://doi.org/10.1016/j.soscij.2012.03.003

Billings, A. C., Qiao, F., Conlin, L., & Nie, T. (2017). Permanently desiring the temporary? Snapchat, social media, and the shifting motivations of sports fans. *Communication and Sport, 5*(1), 10-26. https://doi.org/10.1177/2167479515588760

Biscaia, R., Hedlund, D. P., Dickson, G., & Naylor, M. (2018). Conceptualising and measuring fan identity using stakeholder theory. *European Sport Management Quarterly, 18*(4), 459-481. https://doi.org/10.1080/16184742.2017.1413580

Bishop, R. (2001). Stealing the signs: A semiotic analysis of the changing nature of professional sports logos. *Social Semiotics, 11*(1), 23-41. http://doi.org/10.1080/10350330120010948

Bizman, A., & Yinon, Y. (2002). Engaging in distancing tactics among sport fans: Effects on self-esteem and emotional responses. *Journal of Social Psychology, 142*(3), 381-392. https://doi.org/10.1080/00224540209603906

Bjarkman, K. (2004). To have and to hold: The video collector's relationship with an ethereal medium. *Television and New Media, 5*(3), 217-246. http://doi.org/10.1177/1527476403254000

Bjørner, T., Magnusson, A., & Nielson, R. P. (2016). How to describe and measure obstacles of narrative immersion in a film? The wheel of immersion as a framework. *Nordicom Review, 37*(1), 1-118. https://doi.org/10.1515/nor-2016-0004

Blain, B. (2014). *A study of female sport fans with respect to fantasy sport participation* [Master's thesis, Brock University]. Brock University Repository. http://hdl.handle.net/10464/5527

Blight, M. G. (2016). *Relationships to video game streamers: Examining gratifications, parasocial relationships, fandom, and community affiliation online* (Publication No. 10169577) [Doctoral dissertation, University of Wisconsin-Milwaukee]. ProQuest Dissertations and Theses Global.

Bloch, P. H., Sherrell, D. L., & Ridgway, N. M. (1986). Consumer search: An extended framework. *Journal of Consumer Research, 13*(1), 119-126. https://doi.org/10.1086/209052

Bodet, G., & Bernache-Assollant, I. (2011). Consumer loyalty in sport spectatorship services: The relationships with consumer satisfaction and team identification. *Psychology and Marketing, 28*(8), 781-802. https://doi.org/10.1002/mar.20412

Bolderman, L., & Reijnders, S. (2017). Have you found what you're looking for? Analysing tourist experiences of Wagner's Bayreuth, ABBA's Stockholm and U2's Dublin. *Tourism Studies, 17*(2), 164-181. https://doi.org/10.1177/1468797616665757

Bonny, J. W., Castaneda, L. M., & Swanson, T. (2016). Using an international gaming tournament to study individual differences in MOBA expertise and cognitive skills. *CHI '16: Proceedings of the 2016 CHI Conference on Human Factors in Computing Systems.* (pp. 3473-3484). https://doi.org/10.1145/2858036.2858190

Booth, P., & Kelly, P. (2013). The changing faces of Doctor Who fandom: New fans, new technologies, old practices. *Participations, 10*(1), 56-72.

Borer, M. I. (2009). Negotiating the symbols of gendered sports fandom. *Social Psychology Quarterly, 72*(1), 1-4. https://doi.org/10.1177/019027250907200101

Borgstedt, S. (2008). *The music star: Comparative image analysis of Alfred Brendel, Stefanie Hertel and Robbie Williams.* Transcript Verlag.

Bourguignon, D., Teixeira, C. P., Koc, Y., Outten, H. R., Faniko, K., & Schmitt, M. T. (2020). On the protective role of identification with a stigmatized identity: Promoting engagement and discouraging disengagement coping strategies. *European Journal of Social Psychology, 50*(6), 1125-1142. https://doi.org/10.1002/ejsp.2703

Boyal, B. A., & Magnusson, P. (2007). Social identity and brand equity formation: A comparative study of collegiate sports fans. *Journal of Sport Management, 21*(1), 497-520. https://doi.org/10.1123/jsm.21.4.497

Boyle, B. A., & Magnusson, P. (2007). Social identity and brand equity formation: A comparative study of collegiate sports fans. *Journal of Sport Management, 21*(4), 497-520. https://doi.org/10.1123/jsm.21.4.497

Braaten, A., Huta, V., Tyrany, L., & Thompson, A. (2019). Hedonic and eudaimonic motives toward university studies: How they relate to each other and to well-being derived from school. *Journal of Positive School Psychology, 3*(2), 179-196. https://journalppw.com/index.php/JPPW/article/view/123

Branscombe, N. R., Schmitt, M. T., & Harvey, R. D. (1999). Perceiving pervasive discrimination among African Americans: Implications for group identification and well-being. *Journal of Personality and Social Psychology, 77*(1), 135-149. http://dx.doi.org/10.1037/0022-3514.77.1.135

Branscombe, N. R., & Wann, D. L. (1991). The positive social and self concept consequences of sports team identification. *Journal of Sport and Social Issues, 15*(2), 115-127. https://doi.org/10.1177/019372359101500202

Braverman, J., LaBrie, R. A., & Shaffer, H. J. (2011). A taxometric analysis of actual internet sports gambling behavior. *Psychological Assessment, 23*(1), 234-244. https://doi.org/10.1037/a0021404

Brett, G. (2017). Reframing the 'violence' of mixed martial arts: The art of the fight. *Poetics, 62*(1), 15-28. https://doi.org/10.1016/j.poetic.2017.03.002

Brewer, M. B. (1991). The social self: On being the same and different at the same time. *Personality and Social Psychology Bulletin, 17*(5), 475-482. https://doi.org/10.1177/0146167291175001

Brombley, K. (2017). A case study of early British Sherlockian fandom. *Transformative Works and Cultures, 23.* https://dx.doi.org/10.3983/twc.2017.0861

Brooks, S. K. (2021). FANactics: Systematic literature review of factors associated with celebrity worship, and suggested directions for future research. *Current Psychology, 40,* 864-886. https://doi.org/10.1007/s12144-018-9978-4

Brown, C. A., McGuire, F. A., & Voelkl, J. (2008). The link between successful aging and serious leisure. *The International Journal of Aging and Human Development, 66*(1), 73-95. https://doi.org/10.2190/AG.66.1.d

Brown-Devlin, N., & Devlin, M. B. (2020). Winning with personality: Underscoring antecedents for college students' motives for team identification. *Communication and Sport, 8*(3), 364-388. https://doi.org/10.1177/2167479519832017

Brown-Devlin, N., Devlin, M. B., & Vaughan, P. W. (2018). Why fans act that way: Using individual personality to predict BRIGing and CORFing behaviors. *Communication and Sport, 6*(4), 395-417. https://doi.org/10.1177/2167479517725011

Bruner, M. W., Balish, S. M., Forrest, C., Brown, S., Webber, K., Gray, E., McGuckin, M., Keats, M. R., Rehman, L., & Shields, C. A. (2017). Ties that bond: Youth sport as a vehicle for social identity and positive youth development. *Research Quarterly for Exercise and Sport, 88*(2), 209-214. https://doi.org/10.1080/02701367.2017.1296100

Bruner, M. W., Boardley, I. D., & Côté, J. (2014). Social identity and prosocial and antisocial behavior in youth sport. *Psychology of Sport and Exercise, 15*(1), 56-64. https://doi.org/10.1016/j.psychsport.2013.09.003

Bundy, A. (2004). *Australian and New Zealand information literacy framework: Principles, standards, and practice.* Australian and New Zealand Institute for Information Literacy.

Burke, B. L., Martnes, A., & Faucher, E. H. (2010). Two decades of terror management theory: A meta-analysis of mortality salience research. *Personality and Social Psychology Review, 14*(2), 155-195. https://doi.org/10.1177/1088868309352321

Cacioppo, J. T., & Petty, R. E. (1982). The need for cognition. *Journal of Personality and Social Psychology, 42*(1), 116-131. https://doi.org/10.1037/0022-3514.42.1.116

Çakici, A. C., & Harman, S. (2007). Leisure involvement of Turkish birdwatchers. *Anatoli, 18*(1), 153-160. https://doi.org/10.1080/13032917.2007.9687043

Campbell, J., Dandignac, M., Bankert, C., Hall, C., McArthur, K., Sessions, B., & Young, C. (2021). Die-hard fans: Selective self-presentation in newspaper obituaries. *Mortality, 26*(1), 112-123. https://doi.org/10.1080/13576275.2020.1784122

Campbell, R. M., Aiken, D., & Kent, A. (2004). Beyond BIRGing and CORFing: Continuing the exploration of fan behavior. *Sports Marketing Quarterly, 13*(2), 151-157.

Cantinotti, M., Landouceur, R., & Jacques, C. (2004). Sports betting: Can gamblers beat randomness? *Psychology of Addictive Behaviors, 18*(2), 143-147. https://doi.org/10.1037/0893-164X.18.2.143

Carden, A. R. (2006). Sign of the times: An examination of the self-concept and emotional motivation of travelers on route 66 (1926-Present). *Journal of Travel & Tourism Marketing, 20*(2), 51-61. https://doi.org/10.1300/J073v20n02_04

Carter, M., Gibbs, M., & Witkowski, E. (2017). Understanding eSports spectatorship: Players, fans, recruits. *AoIR Selected Papers of Internet Research.* https://spir.aoir.org/ojs/index.php/spir/article/view/10040

Castano, E., Yzerbyt, V., & Bourguignon, D. (2003). We are one and I like it: The impact of ingroup entitativity on ingroup identification. *European Journal of Social Psychology, 33*(6), 735-754. https://doi.org/10.1002/ejsp.175

Cartwright, R. D., Lloyd, S., Knight, S., & Trenholme, I. (1984). Broken dreams: A study of the effects of divorce and depression on dream content. *Psychiatry, 47*(3), 251-259. https://doi.org/10.1080/00332747.1984 11024246

Chadborn, D., Edwards, P., & Reysen, S. (2017). Displaying fan identity to make friends. *Intensities: The Journal of Cult Media, 9,* 87-97.

Chadborn, D., Edwards, P., & Reysen, S. (2018). Reexamining differences between fandom and local sense of community. *Psychology of Popular Media Culture, 7*(3), 241-249. https://doi.org/10.1037/ppm0000125

Chadborn, D. P., Plante, C. N., & Reysen, S. (2016). Perceived stigma, social identity, and group norms as predictors of prosocial giving in a fandom. *International Journal of Interactive Communication Systems and Technologies, 6*(1), 35-49.

Chan, C., Berger, J., & Boven, L. V. (2012). Identifiable but not identical: Combining social identity and uniqueness motives in choice. *Journal of Consumer Research, 39*(3), 561-573. https://doi.org/10.1086/664804

Chao, T.-H. (2010). *Motivation of sport fans on different channels of sport entertainments* (Publication No. 1490631) [Master's thesis, Purdue University]. ProQuest Dissertations and Theses Global.

Chatterjee, A. (2017). Orange is the new aesthetic. *Behavioral and Brain Science, 40.* https://doi.org/10.1017/S0140525X17001637

Chen, C.-C., & Liao, Y.-S. (2019). From satisfaction to satiation: The gradation model of satiation in casual leisure. *Annals of Leisure Research, 22*(2), 233-246. https://doi.org/10.1080/11745398.2018.1496462

Chen, P.-J. (2010). Differences between male and female sport event tourists: A qualitative study. *International Journal of Hospitality Management, 29*(2), 277-290. https://doi.org/10.1016/j.ijhm.2009.10.007

Chen, Y. C., Shen, Y. C., & Liao, S. (2009). An integrated model of customer loyalty: an empirical examination in retailing practice. *The Service Industries Journal, 29*(3), 267-280. https://doi.org/10.1080/02642060701842886

Chen, Z., & Liu, Y. (2020). The state of leisure life situation and the meaning of leisure education for college students in China. *International Journal of Educational Research, 102,* Article 101613. https://doi.org/10.1016/j.ijer.2020.101613

Cheng, E., & Pegg, S. (2016). "If I'm not gardening, I'm not at my happiest": Exploring the positive subjective experiences derived from serious leisure gardening by older adults. *World Leisure Journal, 58*(4), 285-297. https://doi.org/10.1080/16078055.2016.1228219

Cheng, S. (1997). Psychological determinants of idolatry in adolescents. *Adolescence, 127*(32), 687-692.

Cheung, C. K., & Yue, X. (2000). Idol worshipping for vain glory, illusory romance or intellectual learning: A study in Nanjing and Hong Kong. *International Journal of Adolescence and Youth, 8*(4), 299-317. https://doi.org/10.1080/02673843.2000.9747859

Cheung, C. K., & Yue, X. D. (2011). Pentangular dimensions of Chinese adolescents' idol worship. *International Journal of Adolescence and Youth, 16*(3), 225-244. https://doi.org/10.1080/02673843.2011.9748058

Cheung, C. K., & Yue, X. D. (2019). Idols as sunshine or road signs: Comparing absorption-addiction idolatry with identification-emulation idolatry. *Psychological Reports, 122*(2), 411-432. https://doi.org/10.1177/0033294118758903

Chia, S. C., & Poo, Y. L. (2009). Media, celebrities, and fans: An examination of adolescents' media usage and involvement with entertainment celebrities. *Journalism and Mass Communication Quarterly, 86*(1), 23-44. https://doi.org/10.1177/107769900908600103

Chiou, J. S., Huang, C. Y., & Chuang, M. C. (2005). Antecedents of Taiwanese adolescents' purchase intention toward the merchandise of a celebrity: The moderating effect of celebrity adoration. *The Journal of Social Psychology, 145*(3), 317-334. https://doi.org/10.3200/SOCP.145.3.317-334

Cho, H., Joo, D., & Chi, C. G. (2019). Examining nostalgia in sport tourism: The case of US college football fans. *Tourism Management Perspectives, 29*(1), 97-104. https://doi.org/10.1016/j.tmp.2018.11.002

Chorbajian, L. (1978). The social psychology of American males and spectator sports. *International Journal of Sport Psychology, 9*(3), 165-175.

Cialdini, R. B., Borden, R. J., Thorne, A., Walker, M. R., Freeman, S. & Sloan, L. R. (1976). Basking in reflected glory: Three (football) field studies. *Journal of Personality and Social Psychology, 34*(3), 366-375. https://doi.org/10.1037/0022-3514.34.3.366

Cianfrone, B. A., Zhang, J. J., & Ko, Y. J. (2011). Dimensions of motivation associated with playing sport video games. *Sport, Business and Management: An International Journal, 1*(2), 172-189. https://doi.org/10.1108/20426781111146763

Cleland, J., Doidge, M., Millward, P., & Widdop, P. (2018). *Collective action and football fandom: A relational sociological approach.* Springer.

Clément, T. (2019). Fans as the researcher's unwitting collaborators: A few notes on Disney theme parks, fandom, and data collection. *Journal of Festive Studies, 1*(1), 52-77. https://doi.org/10.33823/jfs.2019.1.1.22

Clements, J. (2018). *Anime: A history.* Bloomsbury.

Click, M. A., Lee, H., & Holladay, H. W. (2013). Making monsters: Lady Gaga, fan identification, and social media. *Popular Music and Society, 36*(3), 360-379. https://doi.org/10.1080/03007766.2013.798546

Clopton, A. W. (2005). *Sport and community: Exploring the relationship between fan identification and sense of community on selected NCAA Division IA campuses* (Publication No. 3190405) [Doctoral dissertation, University of Kansas]. ProQuest Dissertations and Theses Global.

Coakley, J. (2003). *Sport in society: Issues & controversies* (8th ed.). McGraw Hill Publishers.

Coffin, P. (2018). *Custom reality and you* [Self published monograph].

Cohen, A. (2017). Fans' identification with teams: A field study of Israeli soccer fans. *Cogent Social Sciences, 3*(1). https://doi.org/10.1080/23311886.2017.1375062

Cohen, E. L. (2016). Enjoyment of a counter-hedonic serious digital game: Determinants and effects on learning and self-efficacy. *Psychology of Popular Media Culture, 5*(2), 157-170. https://doi.org/10.1037/ppm0000052

Cohen, E. L., Seate, A. A., Anderson, S. M., & Tindage, M. F. (2017). Sport fans and sci-fi fanatics: The social stigma of popular media fandom. *Psychology of Popular Media Culture, 6*(3), 193-207. http://dx.doi.org/10.1037/ppm0000095

Cohen, S. (1972). *Folk devils and moral panics: The creation of the mods and rockers*. Routledge.

Cohrdes, C., & Kopiez, R. (2015). Optimal distinctiveness as adolescent music appreciation: Development of music and image related typicality scales. *Psychology of Music, 43*(4), 578-595. https://doi.org/10.1177/0305735614520851

Cole, T., & Leets, L. (1999). Attachment styles and intimate television viewing: Insecurely forming relationships in a parasocial way. *Journal of Social and Personal Relationships, 16*(4), 495-511. https:doi.org/10.1177/0265407599164005

Collins, N., & Murphy, J. (2018). Segmenting fan communities: Toward a taxonomy for researchers and industry. In C. L. Wang (Ed.), *Exploring the rise of fandom in contemporary consumer culture* (pp. 1-17). IGI Global. https://doi.org/10.4018/978-1-5225-3220-0.ch001

Compton, W. C., Smith, M. L., Cornish, K. A., & Qualls, D. L. (1996). Factor structure of mental health measures. *Journal of Personality and Social Psychology, 71*(2), 406-413. https://doi.org/10.1037/0022-3514.71.2.406

Cottingham, M., Carroll, M. S., Phillips, D., Karadakis, K., Gearity, B. T., & Drane, D. (2014). Development and validation of the motivation scale for disability sport consumption. *Sport Management Review, 17*(1), 49-64. https://doi.org/10.1016/j.smr.2013.11.001

Cottingham, M., Phillips, D., Hall, S. A., Gearity, B. T., & Carroll, M. S. (2014). Application of the motivation scale for disability sport consumption: An examination of intended future consumption behavior of collegiate wheelchair basketball spectators. *Journal of Sport Behavior, 37*(2), 117-133.

Courtney, J. J., & Wann, D. L. (2010). The relationship between sport fan dysfunction and bullying behaviors. *North American Journal of Psychology, 12*(1), 191-198.

Crawford, G. (2004). Consuming sport: fans, sport and culture. *International Journal of Sports Marketing & Sponsorship, 6*(2), 47-62. https://doi.org/10.1108/IJSMS-06-02-2004-B007

Crome, A. (2014). Reconsidering religion and fandom: Christian fan works in My Little Pony fandom. *Culture and Religion, 15*(4), 399-418. https://doi.org/10.1080/14755610.2014.984234

Cronin, J., & Cocker, H. L. (2019). Managing collective effervescence: 'Zomsumption' and postemotional fandom. *Marketing Theory, 19*(3), 281-299. https://doi.org/10.1177/1470593118787589

Cunningham, G. B., & Kwon, H. (2003). The theory of planned behaviour and intentions to attend a sport event. *Sport Management Review, 6*(2), 127-145. https://doi.org/10.1016/S1441-3523(03)70056-4

Cusack, M., Jack, G., & Kavanagh, D. (2003). Dancing with discrimination: Managing stigma and identity. *Culture and Organization, 9*(4), 295-310. https://doi.org/10.1080/1475955042000195409

Cushen, P. J., Rife, S. C., & Wann, D. L. (2019). The emergence of a new type of sport fan: Comparing the fandom, motivational profiles, and identification of electronic and traditional sport fans. *Journal of Sport Behavior, 42*(2), 127-141.

Cuthbert, R., Turkey, S., & Brown, R. (2019). The effects of customisation on player experiences and motivation in a virtual reality game. *OZCHI'19: Proceedings of the 31st Australian Conference on Human-Computer-Interaction* (pp. 221-232). https://doi.org/10.1145/3369457.3369475

D'Adamo, A. (2019). Is Bowie our Kierkegaard?: A theory of agency in fandom. *Celebrity Studies, 10*(1), 60-74. https://doi.org/10.1080/19392397.2018.1559085

Daniels, M. J., & Norman, W. C. (2005). Motivations of equestrian tourists: An analysis of the colonial cup races. *Journal of Sport Tourism, 10*(3), 201-210. https://doi.org/10.1080/14775080500422494

Davidson, S. (2018). *A multi-dimensional model of enjoyment: Development and validation of an enjoyment scale (Enjoy)* (Publication No. 10791550) [Doctoral dissertation, Embry-Riddle Aeronautical University]. ProQuest Dissertations and Theses Global.

Davis, M. H. (1980). A multidimensional approach to individual differences in empathy. *JSAS Catalog of Selected Documents in Psychology, 10*, 85.

Davis, M. H. (1983). Measuring individual differences in empathy: Evidence for a multidimensional approach. *Journal of Personality and Social Psychology, 44*, 113-126. https://doi.org/10.1037/0022-3514.44.1.113

Debord, G. (1970). *Society of the spectacle.* Black & Red.

De Carlo, C. F. (2000). *What content makes people want to use sports website?* [Master's thesis, Louisiana State University]. LSU Digital Commons.

Deci, E. L. (1980). *The psychology of self-determination.* Lexington Books.

Deci, E. L., & Ryan, R. M. (1980). The empirical exploration of intrinsic motivational processes. In L. Berkowitz (Ed.), *Advances in experimental social psychology* (Vol. 13, pp. 39-80). Academic. https://doi.org/10.1016/S0065-2601(08)60130-6

Deci, E. L., & Ryan, R. M. (2000). The "what" and "why" of goal pursuits: Human needs and the self-determination of behavior. *Psychological Inquiry, 11*(4), 227-268. https://doi.org/10.1207/S15327965PLI1104_01

DeJordy, R. (2008). Just passing through: Stigma, passing, and identity decoupling in the work place. *Group and Organizational Management, 33*(5), 504-531. https://doi.org/10.1177%2F1059601108324879

Delia, E. B. (2015). The exclusiveness of group identity in celebrations of team success. *Sport Management Review, 18*(3), 396-406. https://doi.org/10.1016/j.smr.2014.10.006

Delmar, J. L., Plaza, J. F., & Sánchez, M. (2020). An approach to defining the identity of a media fan. *Palabra Clave, 23*(2). Article e2323. https://doi.org/10.5294/pacla.2020.23.2.3

Delmar, J. L., Sánchez-Martín, M., & Velázquez, J. A. M. (2018). To be a fan is to be happier: Using the eudaimonic spectator questionnaire to measure eudaimonic motivations in Spanish fans. *Journal of Happiness Studies, 19*(1), 257-276. https://doi.org/10.1007/s10902-016-9819-9

DeLuca, K. (2018). Shared passions, shared compositions: Online fandom communities and affinity groups as sites for public writing pedagogy. *Computers and Composition, 47*(1), 75-92. https://doi.org/10.1016/j.compcom.2017.12.003

Demasson, A., Partridge, H., & Bruce, C. (2016). Information literacy and the serious leisure participant: Variation in the experience of using information to learn. *Information Research, 21*(2). http://InformationR.net/ir/21-2/paper711.html

Denoo, M., Bibert, N., & Zaman, B. (2021). Disentangling the motivational pathways of recreational esports gamblers: A laddering study. *CHI Conference on Human Factors in Computing Systems (CHI 2021).* Yokohama, Japan. https://doi.org/10.1145/3411764.3445287

Derbiax, C., Decrop, A., & Cabossart, O. (2002). Colors and scarves: the symbolic consumption of material possessions by soccer fans. *Advances in Consumer Research, 29*(1), 511-518. http://hdl.handle.net/2078/20197

Derom, I., & Taks, M. (2011). Participants' experiences in two types of sporting events: A quest for evidence of the SL-CL continuum. *Journal of Leisure Research, 43*(3), 383-402. https://doi.org/10.1080/00222216.2011.11950242

Desai, M. (2017). *Analysing the loyalty levels displayed by football fans: A case study on Cape Town City Football Club* [Master's thesis, University of Cape Town]. http://hdl.handle.net/11427/27106

Dick, A. S., & Basu, K. (1994). Customer loyalty: toward an integrated conceptual framework. *Journal of the Academy of Marketing Science, 22*(2), 99-113. https://doi.org/10.1177/0092070394222001

Diener, E. (1984). Subjective well-being. *Psychological Bulletin, 95*(3), 542-575. https://doi.org/10.1037/0033-2909.95.3.542

Dietl, H. M., Özdemir, A., & Rendall, A. (2018). The role of physical attractiveness in tennis TV-viewership. *UZH Business Working Paper Series.* Article 376. https://dx.doi.org/10.2139/ssrn.3232811

Dietz, P. E., Matthews, D. B., Van Duyne, C., Martell, D. A., Parry, C. D., Stewart, T., & Crowder, J. D. (1991). Threatening and otherwise inappropriate letters to Hollywood celebrities. *Journal of Forensic Science, 36*(1), 185-209. https://doi.org/10.1520/JFS13019J

Dill-Shackleford, K. E., Vinney, C., & Hopper-Losenicky, K. (2016). Connecting the dots between fantasy and reality: The social psychology of our engagement with fictional narrative and its functional value. *Social and Personality Psychology Compass, 10*(11), 634-646. https://doi.org/10.1111/spc3.12274

Dimmock, J. A. & Grove, J. R. (2006). Identification with sport teams as a function of the search for certainty. *Journal of Sports Sciences, 24*(11), 1203-1211. https://doi.org/10.1080/02640410500497626

Dimmock, J. A., Grove, J. R., & Eklund, R. C. (2005). Reconceptualizing team identification: New dimensions and their relationship to intergroup bias. *Group Dynamics: Theory, Research, and Practice, 9*(2), 75-86. https://doi.org/10.1037/1089-2699.9.2.75

Dimmock, J. A., & Gucciardi, D. F. (2008). The utility of modern theories of intergroup bias for research on antecedents to team identification. *Psychology of Sport and Exercise, 9*(3), 284-300. https://doi.org/10.1016/j.psychsport.2007.04.001

Djikic, M., Oatley, K., & Carland, M. (2012). Genre or artistic merit?: The effect of literature on personality. *Scientific Study of Literature, 2*(1), 25-36. https://doi.org/10.1075/ssol.2.1.02dji

Dodson, J. (2020). Furry fandom as folk culture. The *Phoenix Papers, 4*(2), 93-103. http://dio.org/10.17605/OSF.IO/MXSZ3

Donahue, T., & Wann, D. L. (2009). Perceptions of the appropriateness of sport fan physical and verbal aggression: Potential influences of team identification and fan dysfunction. *North American Journal of Psychology, 11*(3), 419-428.

Donald, M. N., & Havighurst, R. J. (1959). The meanings of leisure. *Social Forces, 37*(4), 355-360. https://doi.org/10.2307/2574185

Doosje, B., Ellemers, N., & Spears, R. (1995). Perceived intragroup variability as a function of group status and identification. *Journal of Experimental Social Psychology, 31*(5), 410-436. https://doi.org/10.1006/jesp.1995.1018

Doyle, D. M., & Molix, L. (2014) How does stigma spoil relationships? Evidence that perceived discrimination harms romantic relationship quality through impaired self-image. *Journal of Applied Social Psychology, 44*(9), 600-610. http://doi.org/10.1111/jasp.12252

Drazen, P. (2014). *Anime explosion!: The what? Why? And wow! Of Japanese animation.* Stone Bridge Press.

Dreisinger, O. (2017). *Gimp Sue gets the girl: Disability, desirability, and the Twilight fanfiction* (Publication No. 28249641) [Master's thesis, McGill University]. Proquest Theses and Dissertations.

Drozda, C. (2006). Juveniles performing auto theft: An exploratory study into a deviant leisure lifestyle. *Leisure/Loisir, 30*(1), 111-132. https://doi.org/10.1080/14927713.2006.9651344

Duchesne, S. (2005). Little reckonings in great room: The performance of 'cosplay'. *Canadian Theatre Review, 121*, 17-26.

Dwyer, B. (2011). Divided loyalty? An analysis of fantasy football involvement and fan loyalty to individual national football league (NFL) teams. *Journal of Sport Management, 25*(5), 445-457. https://doi.org/10.1123/jsm.25.5.445

Dy, M. R., Iyer, J. S., & Mehta, R. (2020). Doing business with wizards, Spider-Men, and Jedi knights: Managing intellectual property and fandom in the experience economy. *Copyright Reporter,* 1-53. http://dx.doi.org/10.2139/ssrn.3639092

Edwards, P., Chadborn, D. P., Plante, C., Reysen, S., & Redden, M. H. (2019). *Meet the bronies: The psychology of adult* My Little Pony *fandom.* McFarland & Company.

Edwards, P. W., Griffin, J., Chadborn, D., & Redden, M. H. (2014, March 5-8). *Fan typology: "Who are the Bronies? Are they all alike?"* [Poster presentation]. Annual meeting of the Southeast Psychological Association Conference, San Antonio, TX.

Edwards, P., Griffin, J., & Redden, M. (2014, February 17). *The brony study.* Retrieved from https://sites.google.com/view/bronystudyresearch/home

Eerola, T., Vuoskoski, J. K., & Kautianinen, H. (2016). Being moved by unfamiliar sad music is associated with high empathy. *Frontiers in Psychology: Auditory Cognitive Neuroscience.* https://doi.org/10.3389/fpsyg.2016.01176

Elias, N., & Dunnung, E. (1970) The quest for excitement in unexciting societies. In G. Lüschen (Ed.), *The cross-cultural analysis of sport and games* (pp. 31-51). Stipes.

Ellemers, N., Kortekaas, P., & Ouwerkerk, J. W. (1999). Self-categorisation, commitment to the group and group self-esteem as related but distinct aspects of social identity. *European Journal of Social Psychology, 29*(2-3), 371-389. https://doi.org/10.1002/(SICI)1099-0992(199903/05)29:2/3%3C371::AID-EJSP932%3E3.0.CO;2-U

Elliott, D. J. (2020). Eudaimonia and well-doing. In G. D. Smith & M. Silverman (Eds.), *Eudaimonia: Perspectives for music learning* (pp. 107-120). Routledge.

Ellis, B. (2015). What bronies see when they brohoof: Queering animation on the dark and evil internet. *The Journal of American Folklore, 128*(2), 298-314. https://doi.org/10.5406/jamerfolk.128.509.0298

Engle, Y., & Kasser, T. (2005). Why do adolescent girls idolize male celebrities? *Journal of Adolescent Research, 20*(2), 263-283. https://doi.org/10.1177%2F0743558404273117

Ericsson, K. A. (2014). Adaptive expertise and cognitive readiness: A perspective from the expert-performance approach. In H. F. O'Neil, R. S. Perez, & E. L. Baker (Eds.), *Teaching and measuring cognitive readiness* (pp. 179-197). Springer.

Ericsson, K. A., Krampe, R. T., & Tesch-Romer, C. (1993). The role of deliberate practice in acquisition of expert performance. *Psychological Review, 100,* 363-406. https://doi.org/10.1037/0033-295X.100.3.363

Erickson, S. E., & Dal Cin, S. (2018). Romantic parasocial attachments and the development of romantic scripts, schemas and beliefs among adolescents. *Media Psychology, 21*(1), 111-136. https://doi.org/10.1080/15213269.2017.1305281

Erickson, S. E., Harrison, K., & Dal Cin, S. (2018). Toward a multi-dimensional model of adolescent romantic parasocial attachment. *Communication Theory, 28*(3), 376-399. https://doi.org/10.1093/ct/qtx006

Eyal, K., & Cohen, J. (2006). When good friends say goodbye: A parasocial breakup study. *Journal of Broadcasting and Electronic Media, 50*(3), 502-523. https://doi.org/10.1207/s15506878jobem5003_9

Eyal, K., & Rubin, A. M. (2003). Viewer aggression and homophily, identification, and parasocial relationships with television characters. Journal of Broadcasting and Electronic Media, 47(1), 77-98. https://doi.org/10.1207/s15506878jobem4701_5

Fairley, S., Green, B. C., & Chalip, L. (2014). The effects of commitment and identification on consumption. *Journal of Sport and Tourism, 19*(1), 55-78. https://doi.org/10.1080/14775085.2015.1005118

Fan, Y., Jiang, J., & Hu, Z. (2020). Abandoning distinctiveness: The influence of nostalgia on consumer choice. *Psychology of Marketing, 37*(10), 1342-1351. https://doi.org/10.1002/mar.21370

Fantasy Sports & Gaming Association. (2021). *Industry demographics.* https://thefsga.org/industry-demographics/

Farber, M. E., & Hall, T. E. (2007). Emotion and environment: Visitors' extraordinary experiences along the Dalton Highway in Alaska. *Journal of Leisure Research, 39*(2), 248-270. https://doi.org/10.1080/00222216.2007.11950107

Ferencz, K. (2013). *"I'm your biggest fan, I'll follow you…" Lady Gaga, little monsters and the religious dimension of fandom in pop music* [Master's thesis, Brock University]. Brock University.

Fink, J. S., Trail, G. T., & Anderson, D. F. (2002). An examination of team identification: Which motives are most salient to its existence? *International Sports Journal, 6*(2), 195-207.

Fiske, J. (1992). The cultural economy of fandom. In L. A. Lewis (ed.), *The adoring audience: Fan cultural and popular media* (pp. 30-49). Routledge.

Flanigan, M. (2014). *How fantasy sport participation affects fan loyalty* [Undergraduate project, St. John Fisher College]. Fisher Digital Publications. https://fisherpub.sjfc.edu/sport_undergrad/50

Fleischer, R. (2015). Towards a postdigital sensibility: How to get moved by too much music. *Culture Unbound: Journal of Current Cultural Research, 7*(2), 255-269. https://doi.org/10.3384/cu.2000.1525.1572255

Fornerino, M., Helme-Guizon, A., & Gotteland, D. (2008). Movie consumption experience and immersion: Impact on satisfaction. *Recherche et Applications en Marketing, 23*(3): 93-109. https://doi.org/10.1177/205157070802300306

Frable, D. E., Blackstone, T., & Scherbaum, C. (1990). Marginal and mindful: Deviants in social interactions. *Journal of Personality and Social Psychology, 59*(1), 140-149. https://doi.org/10.1037/0022-3514.59.1.140

Friedman, T., & Rapoport, T. (2020). How children become fans: Learning fandom via the body. In Rapoport T. (Ed.), *Doing fandom* (pp. 35-57). Palgrave Macmillan, Cham. https://doi.org/10.1007/978-3-030-46870-5_2

Fry, R. W. (2014). Becoming a "true blues fan": Blues tourism and the performances of the King Biscuit Blues Festival. *Tourism Studies, 14*(1), 66-85. https://doi.org/10.1177/1468797613511686

Fu, F.-L., Su, R.-C., & Yu, S.-C. (2009). EGameflow: A scale to measure learners' enjoyment of e-learning games. *Computers & Education, 52,* 101-112. https://doi.org/10.1016/j.compedu.2008.07.004

Funk, D. C., Filo, K., Beaton, A. A., & Pritchard, M. (2009). Measuring the motives of sport event attendance: Bridging the academic-practitioner divide to understanding behavior. *Sport Marketing Quarterly, 18*(3), 126-138.

Funk, D. C., Haugtvedt, C. P., & Howard, D. R. (2000). Contemporary attitude theory in sport: Theoretical considerations and implications. *Sport Management Review, 3*(2), 125-144. https://doi.org/10.1016/S1441-3523(00)70082-9

Funk, D. C., James, J. (2001). The psychological continuum model: A conceptual framework for understanding an individual's psychological connection to sport. *Sport Management Review, 4*(2), 119-150. https://doi.org/10.1016/S1441-3523(01)70072-1

Funk, D. C., & James, J. D. (2004). The fan attitude network (FAN) model: Exploring attitude formation and change among sport consumers. *Sport Management Review, 7*(1), 1-26. https://doi.org/10.1016/S1441-3523(04)70043-1

Funk, D. C., Ridinger, L. L., & Moorman, A. M. (2003). Understanding consumer support: Extending the sport interest inventory (SII) to examine individual differences among women's professional sport consumers. *Sport Management Review, 6*(1), 1-32. https://doi.org/10.1016/S1441-3523(03)70051-5

Funk, D. C., Ridinger, L. L., & Moorman, A. M. (2004). Exploring origins of involvement: understanding the relationship between consumer motives and involvement with professional sport teams. *Leisure Sciences, 26*(1), 35-61. https://doi.org/10.1080/01490400490272440

Galloway, G. (2002). Psychographic segmentation of park visitor markets: Evidence for the utility of sensation seeking. *Tourism Management, 23*(6), 581-596. https://doi.org/10.1016/S0261-5177(02)00025-0

Galloway, G., Mitchell, R., Getz, D., Crouch, G., & Ong, B. (2008). Sensation seeking and the prediction of attitudes and behaviours of wine tourists. *Tourism Management, 29*(5), 950-966. https://doi.org/10.1016/j.tourman.2007.11.006

Gantz, W. (1981). An exploration of viewing motives and behaviors associated with television sports. *Journal of Broadcasting and Electronic Media, 25*(3), 263-275. https://doi.org/10.1080/08838158109386450

Gantz, W., Wang, Z., Paul, B., & Potter, R. F. (2006). Sports versus all comers: Comparing TV sports fans with fans of other programming genres. *Journal of*

Broadcasting and Electronic Media, 50(1), 95-118.
https://doi.org/10.1207/s15506878jobem5001_6

Gantz, W., & Wenner, L. A. (1995). Fanship and the television sports viewing experience. *Sociology of Sport Journal, 12*(1), 56-74.
https://doi.org/10.1123/ssj.12.1.56

Garon, J. (2017). *Pop culture business handbook for cons and festivals.* Maneglare Publications.

Gau, L.-S. (2013). Development of a model connecting self-directive value and satisfaction of sociability needs in sport spectators. *Social Behavior and Personality, 41*(5), 795-804. https://dx.doi.org/10.2224/sbp.2013.41.5.795

Gau, L.-S., Huang, J.-C., Chen, M.-I., & Naylor, M. (2019). Team social responsibility embedded in correlates of universalism values, sport involvement, and team identification for sustainable management in sporting settings. *Sustainability, 11.* Article 5416. https://doi.org/10.3390/su11195416

Geiger, A., & Davis, L. (2019, July 12). A growing number of American teenagers - particularly girls - are facing depression. *Pew Research Center.* https://www.pewresearch.org/fact-tank/2019/07/12/a-growing-number-of-american-teenagers-particularly-girls-are-facing-depression/

Geraghty, L. (2014). *Cult collectors: Nostalgia, fandom and collecting popular culture.* Routledge.

Gerrig, R. J. (1993). *Experiencing narrative worlds: On the psychological activities of reading.* Yale University Press.

Giamo, L. S., Schmitt, M. T., & Outten, H. R. (2012). Perceived discrimination, group identification, and life satisfaction among multiracial people: A test of the rejection-identification model. *Cultural Diversity and Ethnic Minority Psychology, 18*(4), 319-328. https://doi.org/doi/10.1037/a0029729

Gibson, H., Willming, C., & Holdnak, A. (2003). Small-scale event sport tourism: Fans as tourists. *Tourism Management, 24*(2), 181-190.
https://doi.org/10.1016/S0261-5177(02)00058-4

Gibson, H., Willming, C., & Holdnak, A. (2002). "We're gators… not just gator fans": Serious leisure and University of Florida football. *Journal of Leisure Research, 34*(4), 397-425. https://doi.org/10.1080/00222216.2002.11949979

Giles, D. C., & Maltby, J. (2004). The role of media figures in adolescent development: Relations between autonomy, attachment, and interest in celebrities. *Personality and Individual Differences, 36*(4), 813-822.
https://doi.org/10.1016/S0191-8869(03)00154-5

Gkorezis, P., Bellou, V., Xanthopoulou, D., Bakker, A. B., & Tsiftsis, A. (2016). Linking football team performance to fans' work engagement and job performance: Test of a spillover model. *Journal of Occupational and*

Organizational Psychology, 89(4), 791-812.
https://doi.org/10.1111/joop.12155

Gladden, J. M., & Funk, D. C. (2001). Understanding brand loyalty in professional sport: Examining the link between brand associations and brand loyalty. *International Journal of Sports Marketing and Sponsorship, 3*(1), 54-81. https://doi.org/10.1108/IJSMS-03-01-2001-B006

Gladden, J. M., & Funk, D. C. (2002). Developing an understanding of brand associations in team sport: Empirical evidence from consumers of professional sport. *Journal of Sport Management, 16*(1), 54-81. https://doi.org/10.1123/jsm.16.1.54

Godbey, G., & Graefe, A. (1991). Repeat tourism, play, and monetary spending. *Annals of Tourism Research, 18*(2), 213-225. https://doi.org/10.1016/0160-7383(91)90005-V

Godwin, V. L. (2016). Fan pleasure and profit: Use-value, exchange-value, and one-sixth scale action figure customization. *Journal of Fandom Studies, 4*(1), 37-54. http://doi.org/10.1386/jfs.4.1.37_1

Goldberg, L. R. (1993). The structure of phenotypic personality traits. *The American Psychologist, 48*(1), 26-34. https://doi.org/10.1037//0003-066x.48.1.26

Goldman, M. M. (2014). *The function of sport fan identity in seeking optimal psychological distinctiveness* (Doctoral dissertation, University of Pretoria). UPSpace Institutional Repository. http://hdl.handle.net/2263/42047

Goldman, M. M., Chadwick, S., Funk, D. C., & Wocke, A. (2016). I am distinctive when I belong: Meeting the need for optimal distinctiveness through team identification. *International Journal of Sport Management and Marketing, 16*(3/4/5/6), 198-220. https://doi.org/10.1504/IJSMM.2016.077930

Goldsmith, A. L., & Walker, M. (2015). The NASCAR experience: Examining the influence of fantasy sport participation on 'non-fans.' *Sport Management Review, 18*(2), 231-243. https://dx.doi.org/10.1016/j.smr.2014.06.001

Goodwin, R. D., Weinberger, A. H., Kim, J. H., Wu, M., & Galea, S. (2020). Trends in anxiety among adults in the United States, 2008–2018: Rapid increases among young adults. *Journal of Psychiatric Research, 130*(1), 441-446. https://doi.org/10.1016/j.jpsychires.2020.08.014

Gordon, B. S., Yoshida, M., Nakazawa, M., & Bass, J. (2021). The role of pride feelings in the team and fan community identification process: An empirical examination in professional sport. *Corporate Reputation Review, 24,* 76-94. https://doi.org/10.1057/s41299-019-00092-y

Gordon, W. R., & Caltabiano, M. L. (1996). Urban-rural differences in adolescent self-esteem, leisure boredom, and sensation-seeking as predictors of leisure-time usage and satisfaction. *Adolescence, 31*(124), 883-901.

Grau, S. L., Roselli, G., & Taylor, C. R. (2007). Where's Tamika Catchings? A content analysis of female athlete endorsers in magazine advertisements. *Journal of Current Issues and Research in Advertising, 29*(1), 55-65. https://doi.org/10.1080/10641734.2007.10505208

Gray, G. T., & Wert-Gray, S. (2012). Customer retention in sports organization marketing: Examining the impact of team identification and satisfaction with team performance. *International Journal of Consumer Studies, 36*(3), 275-281. https://doi.org/10.1111/j.1470-6431.2011.00999.x

Gray, J. (2003). New audiences, new textualities: Anti-fans and non-fans. *International Journal of Cultural Studies, 6*(1), 64-81. https://doi.org/10.1177/1367877903006001004

Green, M. C., & Brock, T. C. (2000). The role of transportation in the persuasiveness of public narratives. *Journal of Personality and Social Psychology, 79*(5), 701-721. https://doi.org/10.1037/0022-3514.79.5.701

Green, T., Griffith, J., Aruguete, M. S., Edman, J., & McCutcheon, L. E. (2014). Materialism and the tendency to worship celebrities. *North American Journal of Psychology, 16*(1), 33-42.

Greenwell, T. C., Simmons, J. M., Hancock, M., Shreffler, M., & Thorn, D. (2017). The effects of sexualized and violent presentations of women in combat sport. *Journal of Sport Management, 31*(6), 533-545. https://doi.org/10.1123/jsm.2016-0333

Greenwood, D., McCutcheon, L. E., Collisson, B., & Wong, M. (2018). What's fame got to do with it? Clarifying links among celebrity attitudes, fame appeal, and narcissistic subtypes. *Personality and Individual Differences, 131*(1), 238-243. https://doi.org/10.1016/j.paid.2018.04.032

Greenwood, P. B. (2001). *Sport fan team identification in a professional expansion setting* (Publication No. 1412471) [Master's thesis, North Carolina State University]. ProQuest Dissertations and Theses Global.

Griffith, J., Aruguete, M., Edman, J., Green, T., & McCutcheon, L. (2013). The temporal stability of the tendency to worship celebrities. *SAGE Open, 3*(2). https://doi.org/10.1177/2158244013494221

Grimm, C., Kemp, S., & Jose, P. E. (2015). Orientations to happiness and the experience of everyday activities. *The Journal of Positive Psychology, 10*(3), 207-218. https://doi.org/10.1080/17439760.2014.941382

Grossberg, L. (1992). Is there a fan in the house? The affective sensibility of fandom. In L. A. Lewis (Eds.) *The adoring audience* (pp. 50-65). Routledge.

Gunderman, H. C. (2018). *Popular geopolitics, empathy, and cultural-media geographies in Doctor Who fandom* [Doctoral dissertation, University of Tennessee]. https://trace.tennessee.edu/utk_graddiss/4994

Gunderman, H. C., & Harty, J. P. (2016). "The music never stopped": Naming businesses as a method for remembering the Grateful Dead. *Journal of Cultural Geography, 34*(3), 373-395. https://doi.org/10.1080/08873631.2016.1264073

Gupta, A. (2019). *Meaningful consumption: A eudaimonic perspective on the consumer pursuit of happiness and well-being* (Publication No. 13860940) [Doctoral dissertation, The University of Nebraska-Lincoln]. ProQuest Dissertations and Theses Global.

Gwinner, K., & Swanson, S. R. (2003). A model of fan identification: Antecedents and sponsorship outcomes. *Journal of Services Marketing, 17*(3), 275-294. https://doi.org/10.1108/08876040310474828

Hagtvedt, H., & Vohs, K. D. (2017). Art enhances meaning by stimulating integrative complexity and aesthetic interest. *Behavioral and Brain Science, 40*(1), 30-31. https://doi.org/10.1017/S0140525X17001728

Häkkänen-Nyholm, H. (2020). Bruce Springsteen fan behavior and identification. *Psychology of Music, 49*(4), 691-703. https://doi.org/10.1177/0305735619891774

Hall, A. E. (2015). Entertainment-oriented gratifications of sports media: Contributors to suspense, hedonic enjoyment, and appreciation. *Journal of Broadcasting and Electronic Media, 59*(2), 259-277. https://doi.org/10.1080/08838151.2015.1029124

Hall, A. E., & Bracken, C. C. (2011). "I really liked that movie": Testing the relationship between trait empathy, transportation, perceived realism, and movie enjoyment. *Journal of Media Psychology: Theories, Methods, and Applications, 23*(2), 90-99. https://doi.org/10.1027/1864-1105/a000036

Hall, C. M. (1989). The definition and analysis of hallmark tourist events. *GeoJournal, 19*(3), 263-268. https://doi.org/10.1007/BF00454570

Hall, M., & Zeppel, H. (1990). Cultural and heritage tourism: The new grand tour. *Historic Environment, 7*(3/4), 86-98.

Hanna, R., Rohm, A., & Crittenden, V. L. (2011). We're all connected: The power of the social media ecosystem. *Business Horizons, 54*(3), 265-273. https://doi.org/10.1016/j.bushor.2011.01.007

Hargrove, K. L. (2011). *Becoming an outdoors-woman: Relationships among frequency of participation in BOW programs, enduring involvement, and leisure satisfaction* (Publication No. 3464534) [Doctoral dissertation, Middle Tennessee State University]. ProQuest Dissertations and Theses Global.

Harrington, C. L. (2018). Creativity and ageing in fandom. *Celebrity Studies, 9*(2), 231-243. https://doi.org/10.1080/19392397.2018.1465295

Harrison-Walker, L. J. (2001). The measurement of word-of-mouth communication and an investigation of service quality and customer commitment as potential antecedents. *Journal of Service Research, 4*(1), 60-75. https://doi.org/10.1177/109467050141006

Harrolle, M., Trail, G., Rodriguez, A., & Jordan, J. (2010). Conative loyalty of Latino and non-Latino professional baseball fans. *Journal of Sport Management, 24*(4), 456-471. https://doi.org/10.1123/jsm.24.4.456

Havard, C. T. (2014). Glory out of reflected failure: The examination of how rivalry affects sport fans. *Sport Management Review, 17*(3), 243-253. https://doi.org/10.1016/j.smr.2013.09.002

Havard, C. T., Grieve, F. G., & Lomenick, M. E. (2020). Marvel, DC, and sport: Investigating rivalry in the sport and comic setting. *Social Science Quarterly, 101*(3), 1075-1089. https://doi.org/10.1111/ssqu.12792

Havard, C. T., Inoue, Y., & Ryan, T. D. (2019). Celebrating out-group failure: Investigating the presence of glory out of reflected failure against rival groups. *Journal of Cultural Marketing Strategy, 3*(2), 172-183.

Havard, C. T., Wann, D. L., Grieve, F. G., & Collins, B. (2020). *Tales from Cinderella's castle: Examining fandom and rivalry within Disney.* Manuscript submitted for publication.

Havard, C. T., Wann, D. L., & Ryan, T. D. (2018). I love to see them lose: Investigating fan perceptions and behaviors toward rival teams. In C. L. Wang (Ed.), *Exploring the rise of fandom in contemporary consumer culture* (pp. 102-125). IGI Global. https://doi.org/10.4018/978-1-5225-3220-0.ch006

Haslam, C., Holme, A., Haslam, S. A., Iyer, A., Jetten, J., & Williams, W. H. (2008). Maintaining group memberships: Social identity continuity predicts well-being after stroke. *Neuropsychological Rehabilitation, 18*(5-6), 671-691. https://doi.org/10.1080/09602010701643449

Haugh, B. R., & Watkins, B. (2016). Tag me, tweet me if you want to reach me: An investigation into how sports fans use social media. *International Journal of Sport Communication, 9*(3), 278-293. https://doi.org/10.1123/ijsc.2016-0044

Havitz, M. E., & Howard, D. R. (1995). How enduring is enduring involvement? A seasonal examination of three recreational activities. *Journal of Consumer Psychology, 4*(3) 255-276. https://doi.org/10.1207/s15327663jcp0403_03

Havitz, M. E., & Mannell, R. C. (2005). Enduring involvement, situational involvement, and flow in leisure and non-leisure activities. *Journal of Leisure Research, 37*(2), 152-177. https://doi.org/10.1080/00222216.2005.11950048

Hays, R. D., & DiMatteo, M. R. (1987). A short-form measure of loneliness. *Journal of Personality Assessment, 51*(1), 69-81. https://doi.org/10.1207/s15327752jpa5101_6

Heath, Y., & Gifford, R. (2002). Extending the theory of planned behavior: Predicting the use of public transportation. *Journal of Applied Social Psychology, 32*(10), 2154-2189. https://doi.org/10.1111/j.1559-1816.2002.tb02068.x

Hedlund, D. P. (2014). Creating value through membership and participation in sport fan consumption communities. *European Sport Management Quarterly, 14*(1), 50-71. https://doi.org/10.1080/16184742.2013.865775

Hedlund, D. P., Biscaia, R., & Leal, M. C. (2018). Those who rarely attend alone: Tribal sport fans. In C. L. Wang (Ed.), *Exploring the rise of fandom in contemporary consumer culture* (pp. 71-101). IGI Global. https://dx.doi.org/10.4018/978-1-5225-3220-0.ch005

Hedlund, D. P., Biscaia, R., & Leal, M. D. (2019). Classifying sport consumers: From casual to tribal fans. In C. L. Wang (Ed.), *Handbook of research on the impact of fandom in society and consumerism* (pp. 323-356). IGI Global. https://dx.doi.org/10.4018/978-1-7998-1048-3.ch016

Hedlund, D. P., & Naylor, M. E. (2020). Determinants impacting why college sports fans purchase merchandise. *Journal of Contemporary Athletics, 14*(1), 17-35. http://www.novapublishers.org/catalog/product_info.php?products_id=66250

Heere, B., & James, J. D. (2007). Stepping outside the lines: Developing a multi-dimensional team identity scale based on social identity theory. *Sport Management Review, 10*(1), 65-91. https://doi.org/10.1016/S1441-3523(07)70004-9

Heere, B., Walker, M., Yoshida, M., Ko, Y. J., Jordan, J. S., & James, J. D. (2011). Brand community development through associated communities: Grounding community measurement within social identity theory. *Journal of Marketing Theory and Practice, 19*(4), 407-422. https://dx.doi.org/10.2753/MTP1069-6679190404

Henderson, C. W. (2020). *Pleasurable labors: activist fandom, sport communities, and the performance of place* (Publication No. 28028105) [Doctoral dissertation, University of Iowa]. ProQuest Dissertations and Theses Global.

Hendrick, S. S. (1988). A generic measure of relationship satisfaction. *Journal of Marriage and the Family, 50,* 93-98. https://doi.org/10.2307/352430

Heo, J., Lee, I. H., Kim, J., & Stebbins, R. A. (2012). Understanding the relationships among central characteristics of serious leisure: An empirical study of older adults in competitive sports. *Journal of Leisure Research, 44*(4), 450-462. https://doi.org/10.1080/00222216.2012.11950273

Heuser, L. (2005). We're not too old to play sports: The career of women lawn bowlers. *Leisure Studies, 24*(1), 45-60. https://doi.org/10.1080/0201436042000250131

Higie, R. A., & Feick, L. F. (1989). Enduring involvement: Conceptual and measurement issues. *Advances in Consumer Research, 16*(1), 690-696.

Hill, B., & Green, B. C. (2000). Repeat attendance as a function of involvement, loyalty, and the sportscape across three football contexts. *Sport Management Review, 3*(2), 145-162. https://doi.org/10.1016/S1441-3523(00)70083-0

Hillman, S., Procyk, J., & Neustaedter, C. (2014). 'alksjdf; Lksfd' tumblr and the fandom user experience. *Proceedings of the 2014 Conference on Designing Interactive Systems* (pp. 775-784). Association for Computing Machinery. https://doi.org/10.1145/2598510.2600887

Hills, M. (2014). From Dalek half halls to Daft Punk helmets: Mimetic fandom and the crafting of replicas. *Transformative Works and Cultures, 16*. https://doi.org/10.3983/twc.2014.0531

Hills, M. (2015). The expertise of digital fandom as a 'community of practice': Exploring the narrative universe of Doctor Who. *Convergence: The International Journal of Research into New Media Technologies, 21*(3), 360-374. https://doi.org/10.1177/1354856515579844

Hines, C. (2020). Cosplaying while black: The transgressive pleasure of blacktivism. *Journal of Cultural Research in Art Education, 37,* 219-230.

Hing, N., Russell, A. M. T., Vitartas, P., & Lamont, M. (2015). Demographic, behavioural and normative risk factors for gambling problems amongst sports bettors. *Journal of Gambling Studies, 32*(1), 625-641. https://doi.org/10.1007/s10899-015-9571-9

Hobson, W. (2015, February 27). Sports gambling in U.S.: Too prevalent to remain illegal? *The Washington Post.* https://www.washingtonpost.com/sports/sports-gambling-inus-too-prevalent-to-remain-illegal/2015/02/27/f1088e4c-b7d3-11e4-9423-f3d0a1ec335c_story.html?utm_term=.df4e8e4b275e

Hofer, M., Allemand, M., & Martin, M. (2014). Age differences in nonhedonic entertainment experiences. *Journal of Communication, 64*(1), 61-81. https://doi.org/10.1111/jcom.12074

Holt, D. B. (1995). How consumers consume: A typology of consumption practice. *Journal of Consumer Research, 22*(1), 1-16. https://www.jstor.org/stable/2489696

Holt-Lunstad, J. (2017). The potential public health relevance of social isolation and loneliness: Prevalence, epidemiology, and risk factors. *Public Policy and Aging Report, 27*(4), 127-130. https://doi.org/10.1093/ppar/prx030

Hong, M., & Raney, A. (2007). Online sports fans' motive research: Does interactivity lead motives or follow them. *NCA 93rd Annual Convention,* Chicago, IL.

Horng, J. S., Su, C. S., & So, S. I. A. (2013). Segmenting food festival visitors: Applying the theory of planned behavior and lifestyle. *Journal of Convention and Event Tourism, 14*(3), 193-216. https://doi.org/10.1080/15470148.2013.814038

Hornsey, M. J., & Hogg, M. A. (1999). Subgroup differentiation as a response to an overly-inclusive group: A test of optimal distinctiveness theory. *European Journal of Social Psychology, 29*(6), 543-550. https://doi.org/10.1002/(SICI)1099-0992(199906)29:4<543::AID-EJSP945>3.0.CO;2-A

Houghton, D. M., Nowlin, E. L., & Walker, D. (2019). From fantasy to reality: The role of fantasy sports in sports betting and online gambling. *Journal of Public Policy and Marketing, 38*(3), 332-353. https://doi.org/10.1177/0743915619841365

Houran, J., Navik, S., & Zerrusen, K. (2005). Boundary functioning in celebrity worshippers. *Personality and Individual Differences, 38*(1), 237-248. https://doi.org/10.1016/j.paid.2004.04.014

Hoverd, W. J., Atkinson, Q. D., & Sibley, C. G. (2012). Group size and the trajectory of religious identification. *Journal for the Scientific Study of Religion, 51*, 286-303.

Hoye, R., & Lillis, K. (2008). Travel motivations of Australian football league fans: An exploratory study. *Managing Leisure, 13*(1), 13-22. https://doi.org/10.1080/13606710701751369

Hoyle, R. H., Kernis, M. H., Leary, M. R., & Baldwin, M. W. (1999). *Selfhood: Identity, esteem, regulation.* Westview Press.

Hu, A. W.-L., & Tang, L.-R. (2010). Factors motivating sports broadcast viewership with fan identification as a mediator. *Social Behavior and Personality, 38*(5), 681-690. https://doi.org/10.2224/sbp.2010.38.5.681

Hughes, M. J. (2018). What motivates the authors of video game walkthroughs and FAQs? A study of six GameFAQs contributors. *First Monday, 23*(1), 1-13. https://dx.doi.org/10.5210/fm.v23i1.7925

Humphries, Z. J. (2020). *Investigating the impact of daily fantasy sports participation on sports fandom: A performative sport fandom perspective*

[Doctoral dissertation, Kent State University].
http://rave.ohiolink.edu/etdc/view?acc_num=kent1596618008798408

Hunt, K. A., Bristol, T., & Bashaw, R. E. (1999). A conceptual approach to classifying sports fans. *Journal of Services Marketing, 13*(6), 439-452. https://doi.org/10.1108/08876049910298720

Hur, Y., Ko, Y. J., & Valacich, J. (2007). Motivation and concerns for online sport consumption. *Journal of Sport Management, 21*(4), 521-539. https://doi.org/10.1123/jsm.21.4.521

Huynh, H., & McCutcheon, L. E. (2021). Humility is inversely related to celebrity interest and admiration. *North American Journal of Psychology, 23*(1), 95-104.

Igartua, J. J., & Barrios, I. (2013). Hedonic and eudaimonic motives for watching feature films. Validation of the Spanish version of Oliver & Raney's scale. *Communications, 38*(4), 411-431. https://doi.org/10.1515/commun-2013-0024

IJsselsteijn, W. A., de Kort, Y. A. W., & Poels, K. (2013). *The game experience questionnaire.* Einhoven, Netherlands: Technische Universiteit Eindhoven.

Ilicic, J., Baxter, S. M., & Kulczynski, A. (2016). The impact of age on consumer attachment to celebrities and endorsed brand attachment. *Journal of Brand Management, 23*(3), 273-288. https://doi.org/10.1057/bm.2016.5

IMDbPro. (2020, March 19). *Star Wars, Episode IX – The Rise of Skywalker.* Box Office Mojo. https://www.boxofficemojo.com/release/rl3305145857/

Iso-Ahola, S. E. (1980). Attributional determinants of decisions to attend football games. *Scandanavian Journal of Sports Science, 50*(1), 511-513.

Iso-Ahola, S. E., & Crowley, E. D. (1991). Adolescent substance abuse and leisure boredom. *Journal of Leisure Research, 23*(3), 260-271. https://doi.org/10.1080/00222216.1991.11969857

Iwasaki, Y. (2008). Pathways to meaning-making through leisure-like pursuits in global contexts. *Journal of Leisure Research, 40*(2), 231-249. https://doi.org/10.1080/00222216.2008.11950139

Iwasaki, Y. (2007). Leisure and quality of life in an international and multicultural context: What are major pathways linking leisure to quality of life? *Social Indicators Research, 82*(2), 233-264. https://doi.org/10.1007/s11205-006-9032-z

Iwasaki, Y., & Havitz, M. E. (1998). A path analytic model of the relationship between involvement, psychological commitment, and loyalty. *Journal of Leisure Research, 30*(2), 256-280. https://doi.org/10.1080/00222216.1998.11949829

Iwasaki, Y., & Havitz, M. E. (2004). Examining relationships between leisure involvement, psychological commitment and loyalty to a recreation agency. *Journal of Leisure Research, 36*(1), 45-72. https://doi.org/10.1080/00222216.2004.11950010

Jacoby, J., & Chestnut, R.W. (1978). *Brand loyalty: Measurement and management.* Wiley.

James, J. D., Fujimoto, J., Ross, S. D., & Matsuoka, H. (2009). Motives of United States and Japanese professional baseball consumers and level of team identification. *International Journal of Sport Management and Marketing, 6*(4), 351-366. https://doi.org/10.1504/IJSMM.2009.029299

James, J. D., Kolbe, R. H., & Trail, G. T. (2002). Psychological connection to a new sport team: Building or maintaining the consumer base? *Sport Marketing Quarterly, 11*(4), 215-225.

James, J. D., & Ross, S. D. (2004). Comparing sport consumer motivations across multiple sports. *Sport Marketing Quarterly, 13*(1), 17-25.

Jamrozy, U., Backman, S. J., & Backman, K. F. (1996). Involvement and opinion leadership in tourism. *Annals of Tourism Research, 23*(4), 908-924. https://doi.org/10.1016/0160-7383(96)00022-9

Jansen, D. (2018). A universe divided: Texts vs. games in The Elder Scrolls. *Proceedings of the 2018 International DiGRA Nordic Conference.* http://www.digra.org/digital-library/publications/a-universe-divided-texts-vs-games-in-the-elder-scrolls.

Jenkins, H. (1992). *Textual poachers: Television fans and participatory culture.* Routledge.

Jenkins, H. (2018). Fandom, negotiation, and participatory culture. In P. Booth (Ed.) *A companion to media fandom and fan studies* (pp. 11-26). Wiley.

Jennett. C., Cox, A. L., Cairns, P., Dhoparee, S., Epps, A., Tijs, T., & Walton, A. (2008). Measuring and defining the experience of immersion in games. *International Journal of Human-Computer Studies, 66*(9), 641-661. https://doi.org/10.1016/j.ijhcs.2008.04.004

Jenol, N. A. M., & Pazil, N. H. A. (2020). Escapism and motivation: Understanding K-pop fans well-being and identity. *Geografia-Malaysian Journal of Society and Space, 16*(4), 336-347. https://ejournal.ukm.my/gmjss/article/view/44476

Jensen, T. (2017). On the importance of presence within fandom spaces. *The Journal of Fandom Studies, 5*(2), 141-155. https://doi.org/10.1386/jfs.5.2.141_1

Jensen, J. A., Greenwell, C., Coleman, C., Stitsinger, M., & Andrew, D. (2018). From BIRFing to BIRGing: A 10-year study of the psychology of Cubs fans. *Sport Marketing Quarterly, 27*(4), 236-249.

Jensen, J. A., Turner, B. A., James, J., McEvoy, C., Seifried, C., Delia, E., Greenwell, T. C., Ross, S., & Walsh, P. (2016). Forty years of BRIGing: New perspectives on Cialdini's seminal studies. *Journal of Sport Management, 30*(2), 149-161. http://dx.doi.org/10.1123/jsm.2015-0340

Jenson, J. (1992). Fandom as pathology: The consequences of characterization. In L. A. Lewis (Ed.), *The adoring audience: Fan culture and popular media* (pp. 9-29). Routledge.

Jia, X., Hung, K., & Zhang, K. (2018). Diversity of fans on social media: The case of entertainment celebrity in China. In C. L. Wang (Ed.), *Exploring the rise of fandom in contemporary consumer culture* (pp. 163-184). IGI Global. https://dx.doi.org/10.4018/978-1-5225-3220-0.ch009

John, O. P., & Srivastava, S. (1999). The big-five trait taxonomy: History, measurement, and theoretical perspectives. In L. A. Pervin & O. P. John (Eds.), *Handbook of personality: Theory and research* (Vol 2., pp. 102-138). Guilford Press.

Jones, B. (2014). Written on the body: Experiencing affect and identity in my fannish tattoos. *Transformative Works and Cultures, 16.* https://doi.org/10.3983/twc.2014.0527

Jones, B. (2015). Fannish tattooing and sacred identity. *Transformative Works and Cultures*, 18. http://dx.doi.org/10.3983/twc.2015.0626

Kahle, L. R., Kambara, K. M., & Rose, G. M. (1996). A functional model of fan attendance motivations for college football. *Sport Marketing Quarterly, 5*(4), 51-60.

Kane, L. E. (2017). *Why cosplay? Motivations behind participation and use of social media among cosplayers who maintain Facebook artist pages* [Doctoral dissertation, Oregon State University]. ScholarsArchive@OSU. https://ir.library.oregonstate.edu/concern/graduate_thesis_or_dissertations/j0 98zd59k

Kane, M. J., & Zink, R. (2004). Package adventure tours: Markers in serious leisure careers. *Leisure Studies, 23*(4), 329-345. https://doi.org/10.1080/0261436042000231655

Kang, C., Lee, J., & Bennett, G. (2014). Comparative analysis of sport consumer motivation affecting sport consumption behavior between American and Asian international students. *International Journal of Sport Management, 15,* 286-310.

Kang, S. (2015). The mobile phone and professional sports: Fans' use of mobile content for loyalty, identification, and fandom. *International Journal of Sport Communication, 8*(4), 452-476. https://doi.org/10.1123/ijsc.2015-0098

Kang, S. J., Ha, J.-P., & Hambrick, M. E. (2015). A mixed-method approach to exploring the motives of sport-related mobile applications among college students. *Journal of Sport Management, 29*(3), 272-290. https://dx.doi.org/10.1123/jsm.2013-0065

Kashdan, T. B., Rose, P., & Fincham, F. D. (2004). Curiosity and exploration: Facilitating positive subjective experiences and personal growth opportunities. *Journal of Personality Assessment, 82*(3), 291-305. https://doi.org/10.1207/s15327752jpa8203_05

Katsumata, S., & Ichikohji, T. (2014). The growth of end user innovators and changing precedent factors: A case study of the comics industry. *Faculty of Economics, Nagasaki University Discussion Paper Series, 3*, 1-22.

Katz, E., & Foulkes, D. (1962). On the use of the mass media as "escape": Clarification of a concept. *Public Opinion Quarterly, 26*(3), 377-388. https://doi.org/10.1086/267111

Katz, M., & Heere, B. (2016). New team, new fans: A longitudinal examination of team identification as a driver of university identification. *Journal of Sport Management, 30*(2), 135-148. https://doi.org/10.1123/jsm.2014-0258

Katz, M., Ward, R. M., & Heere, B. (2018). Explaining attendance through the brand community triad: Integrating network theory and team identification. *Sport Management Review, 21*(2), 176-188. https://doi.org/10.1016/j.smr.2017.06.004

Kaynak, E., Salman, G. G., & Tatoglu, E. (2008). An integrative framework linking brand associations and brand loyalty in professional sports. *Journal of Brand Management, 15*(5), 336-357. https://doi.org/10.1057/palgrave.bm.2550117

Keaton, S. A. (2013). *Sport team fandom, arousal, and communication: A multimethod comparison of sport team identification with psychological, cognitive, behavioral, affective, and physiological measures* (Publication No. 2155) [Doctoral dissertation, Louisiana State University]. LSU Doctoral Dissertations. https://digitalcommons.lsu.edu/gradschool_dissertations/2155

Keaton, S. A., & Gearhart, C. C. (2014). Identity formation, identity strength, and self-categorization as predictors of affective and psychological outcomes: A model reflecting sport team fans' responses to highlights and lowlights of a college football season. *Communication and Sport, 2*(4), 363-385. https://doi.org/10.1177/2167479513498077

Kenworthy, J. B., Marusich, L. R., Paulus, P. B., Abellanoza, A., & Bakdash, J. Z. (2020). The impact of top performers in creative groups. *Psychology of Aesthetics, Creativity, and the Arts*. Advance online publication. https://doi.org/10.1037/aca0000365

Kerins, A. J., Scott, D., & Shafer, C. S. (2007). Evaluating the efficacy of a self-classification measure of recreation specialization in the context of ultimate Frisbee. *Journal of Park and Recreation Administration, 25*(3), 1-22.

Kerstetter, D. L., & Kovich, G. M. (1997). An involvement profile of Division I women's basketball spectators. *Journal of Sport Management, 11*(3), 234-249. https://doi.org/10.1123/jsm.11.3.234

Keyes, C. L. M., Shmotkin, D., & Ryff, C. D. (2002). Optimizing well-being: The empirical encounter of two traditions. *Journal of Personality and Social Psychology, 82*(6), 1007-1022. https://doi.org/10.1037/0022-3514.82.6.1007

Khazaal, Y., Chatton, A., Billieux, J., Bizzini, L., Monney, G., Fresard, E., Thorens, G., Bondolfi, G., El-Guebaly, N., Zullino, D., & Khan, R. (2012). Effects of expertise on football betting. *Substance Abuse Treatment, Prevention, and Policy, 7*. https://doi.org/10.1186/1747-597X-7-18

Kim, A., Qian, T. Y., Lee, H.-W., Mastromartino, B., & Zhang, J. J. (2020). Growth in sport media and the rise of new sport fandom. In S. L. Young (Ed.), *Multidisciplinary perspectives on media fandom* (pp. 150-171). IGI Global. https://doi.org/10.4018/978-1-7998-3323-9.ch009

Kim, A.-R. (2003). *Development and validation of instruments for assessing sport spectator involvement and factors affecting sport spectator involvement* (Publication No. 3093048) [Doctoral dissertation, University of New Mexico]. ProQuest Dissertations and Theses Global.

Kim, H. (2020). Unpacking unboxing video-viewing motivations: The uses and gratifications perspective and the mediating role of parasocial interaction on purchase intent. *Journal of Interactive Advertising, 20*(3), 196-208. https://doi.org/10.1080/15252019.2020.1828202

Kim, H. S., & Kim, M. (2020). Viewing sports online together? Psychological consequences on social live streaming service usage. *Sport Management Review, 23*(5), 869-882. https://doi.org/10.1016/j.smr.2019.12.007

Kim, J., & James, J. D. (2019). Sport and happiness: Understanding the relations among sport consumption activities, long- and short-term subjective well-being, and psychological need fulfillment. *Journal of Sport Management, 33*(2), 119-132. https://doi.org/10.1123/jsm.2018-0071

Kim, J., & Oliver, M. B. (2013). How do we regulate sadness through entertainment messages? Exploring three predictions. *Journal of*

Broadcasting and Electronic Media, 57(3), 374-391.
https://doi.org/10.1080/08838151.2013.816708

Kim, M. J., & Mao, L. L. (2021). Sport consumers motivation for live attendance and mediated sports consumption: A qualitative analysis. *Sport in Society: Cultures, Commerce, Media, Politics, 24*(4), 515-533.
https://doi.org/10.1080/17430437.2019.1679769

Kim, S., Greenwell, T. C., Andrew, D. P., Lee, J., & Mahony, D. F. (2008). An analysis of spectator motives in an individual combat sport: A study of mixed martial arts fans. *Sport Marketing Quarterly, 17*(2), 109-119.
https://oaks.kent.edu/flapubs/17

Kim, S., Morgan, A., & Assaker, G. (2021). Examining the relationship between sport spectator motivation, involvement, and loyalty: A structural model in the context of Australian rules football. *Sport in Society, 24*(6), 1006-1032.
https://doi.org/10.1080/17430437.2020.1720658

Kim, S.-K., Byon, K. K., Yu, J.-G., Zhang, J. J., & Kim, C. (2013). Social motivations and consumption behavior of spectators attending a formula one motor-racing event. *Social Behavior and Personality, 41*(8), 1359-1378.
https://dx.doi.org/10.2224/sbp.2013.41.8.1359

Kim, S.-S., Scott, D., & Crompton, J. L. (1997). An exploration of the relationships among social psychological involvement, behavioral involvement, commitment, and future intentions in the context of birdwatching. *Journal of Leisure Research, 29*(3), 320-341.
https://doi.org/10.1080/00222216.1997.11949799

Kim, Y., Magnusen, M., Kim, M., & Lee, H.-W. (2019). Meta-analytic review of sport consumption: Factors affecting attendance to sporting events. *Sport Marketing Quarterly, 28*(3), 117-134.
https://doi.org/10.32731/SMQ.283.092019.01

Kim, Y. K., Trail, G. T., & Magnusen, M. J. (2013). Transition from motivation to behaviour: examining the moderating role of identification (ID) on the relationship between motives and attendance. *International Journal of Sports Marketing and Sponsorship, 14*(3), 35-56. https://doi.org/10.1108/IJSMS-14-03-2013-B004

Knobloch-Westerwick, S. (2006). Mood management theory, evidence, and advancements. In J. Bryant & P. Vorderer (Eds.), *Psychology of entertainment* (pp. 239-254). Lawrence Erlbaum.

Knoop, C. A., Wagner, V., Jacobsen, T., & Menninghaus, W. (2016). Paining the aesthetic space of literature "from below". *Poetics, 56*(1), 35-49.
https://doi.org/10.1016/j.poetic.2016.02.001

Koenig-Lewis, N., Asaad, Y., & Palmer, A. (2018). Sports events and interaction among spectators: Examining antecedents of spectators' value creation. *European Sport Management Quarterly, 18*(2), 193-215. https://doi.org/10.1080/16184742.2017.1361459

Kokkinakis, A. V., Cowling, P. I., & Wade, A. R. (2017). Exploring the relationship between video game expertise and fluid intelligence. *PLoS ONE, 12*(11). https://doi.org/10.1371/journal.pone.0186621

Kolbe, R. H., & James, J. D. (2003). The internalization process among team followers: Implications for team loyalty. *International Journal of Sport Management, 4*(1), 25-43.

Koo, G.-Y., Andrew, D. P. S., & Kim, S. (2008). Mediated relationships between the constituents of service quality and behavioural intentions: A study of women's college basketball fans. *International Journal of Sport Management and Marketing, 4*(4), 390-411. https://doi.org/10.1504/IJSMM.2008.022378

Koo, G.-Y., & Hardin, R. (2008). Difference in interrelationship between spectators' motives and behavioral intentions based on emotional attachment. *Sport Marketing Quarterly, 17*(1), 30-43.

Kowal, M., Toth, A. J., Exton, C., & Campbell, M. J. (2018). Different cognitive abilities displayed by action video gamers and non-gamers. *Computers in Human Behavior, 88,* 255-262. https://doi.org/10.1016/j.chb.2018.07.010

Kraxenberger, M., & Menninghaus, W. (2017). Affinity for poetry and aesthetic appreciation of joyful and sad poems. *Frontiers in Psychology: Theoretical and Philosophical Psychology.* https://doi.org/10.3389/fpsyg.2016.02051

Kremar, M., & Greene, K. (1999). Predicting exposure to and uses of violent television. *Journal of Communication, 49*(3), 25-45. https://doi.org/10.1111/j.1460-2466.1999.tb02803.x

Krier, D. H. (2017). *Sports media involvement via team identity and antecedent motivations for the prediction of total daily sports media consumption* (Publication No. 10281043) [Doctoral dissertation, Michigan State University]. ProQuest Dissertations and Theses Global.

Krohn, F. B., & Clarke, M. (1998). Psychological and sociological influences on attendance at... *College Student Journal, 32*(2), 277-288.

Krupa, J., & Nawrocka, E. (2020). Fan tourism and fan tourists: Discussion on definitions and research issues. *Tourism, 30*(2), 27-33. http://dx.doi.org/10.18778/0867-5856.30.2.18

Kubey, R. W. (1986). Television use in everyday life: Coping with unstructured time. *Journal of Communication, 36*(3), 108-123. https://doi.org/10.1111/j.1460-2466.1986.tb01441.x

Kulczynski, A. (2014). *Concert attendee behavior: The influence of motivations, fan identification and product involvement* [Doctoral dissertation, University of Newcastle]. University of Newcastle.

Kulczynski, A., Baxter, S., & Young, T. (2016). Measuring motivations for popular music concert attendance. *Event Management, 20*(2), 239-254. https://dx.doi.org/10.3727/152599516X14643674421816

Kwon, H. H., & Armstrong, K. L. (2004). An exploration of the construct of psychological attachment to a sport team among college students: A multidimensional approach. *Sport Marketing Quarterly, 13*(2), 94-103.

Kwon, H. H., & Armstrong, K. L. (2006). Impulse purchases of sport team licensed merchandise: What matters? *Journal of Sport Management, 20*(1), 101-119. https://doi.org/10.1123/jsm.20.1.101

Kwon, H., & Trail, G. (2001). Sport fan motivation: A comparison of American students and international students. *Sport Marketing Quarterly, 10*(2), 147-155.

Kwon, H., & Trail, G. (2005). The feasibility of single-item measures in sport loyalty research. *Sport Management Review, 8*(1), 69-89. https://doi.org/10.1016/S1441-3523(05)70033-4

Kwon, H. H., Trail, G. T., Anderson, D. F. (2005). Are multiple points of attachment necessary to predict cognitive, affective, conative, or behavioral loyalty? *Sport Management Review, 8*(3), 255-270 https://doi org/10.1016/S1441-3523(05)70041-3

Kwon, H. H., Trail, G., & James, J. D. (2007). The mediating role of perceived value: Team identification and purchase intention of team-licensed apparel. *Journal of Sport Management, 21*(4), 540-554. https://doi.org/10.1123/jsm.21.4.540

Kwon, H. H., Trail, G. T., & Lee, D. (2008). The effects of vicarious achievement and team identification on BIRGing and CORFing. *Sport Marketing Quarterly, 17*(4), 209-217.

Kyle, G., Absher, J., Norman, W., Hammitt, W., & Jodice, L. (2007). A modified involvement scale. *Leisure Studies, 26*(4), 399-427. https://doi.org/10.1080/02614360600896668

Kyle, G., Graefe, A., Manning, R., & Bacon, J. (2003). An examination of the relationship between leisure activity involvement and place attachment among hikers along the Appalachian trail. *Journal of Leisure Research, 35*(3), 249-273. https://doi.org/10.1080/00222216.2003.11949993

Kyle, G. T., Kerstetter, D. L., & Guadagnolo, F. B. (2002). Market segmentation using participant involvement profiles. *Journal of Park and Recreation Administration, 20*(1), 1-21.

Kyle, G. T., & Mowen, A. J. (2005). An examination of the leisure involvement—agency commitment relationship. *Journal of Leisure Research, 37*(3), 342-363. https://doi.org/10.1080/00222216.2005.11950057

Laffan, D. A. (2020). Positive psychosocial outcomes and fanship in K-Pop fans: A social identity perspective. *Psychological Reports.* Advance online publication. https://doi.org/10.1177/0033294120961524

Lamerichs, N. (2015). Express yourself: An affective analysis of game cosplayers. In J. Enevold & E. MacCallum-Steward (Eds.), *Game love: Essays on play and affection* (pp. 125-154). McFarland & Company.

Landouceur, R., Giroux, I., & Jacques, C. (1998). Wining on the horses: How much strategy and knowledge are needed? *The Journal of Psychology, 132*(2), 133-142. https://doi.org/10.1080/00223989809599154

Lane, J. D., & Wegner, D. M. (1995). The cognitive consequences of secrecy. *Journal of Personality and Social Psychology, 69*(2), 237-253. https://doi.org/10.1037/0022-3514.69.2.237

Larkin, B. (2017). *Exploring the role of collective narcissism in sport team identification* [Doctoral dissertation, University of Massachusetts Amherst]. ScholarWorks@UMASS Amherst. https://doi.org/10.7275/9976870.0

Larkin, B., & Fink, J. S. (2019). Toward a better understanding of fan aggression and dysfunction: The moderating role of collective narcissism. *Journal of Sport Management, 33*, 69-78. https://doi.org/10.1123/jsm.2018-0012

Larkin, B. A., & Fink, J. S. (2016). Fantasy sport, FoMO, and traditional fandom: How second-screen use of social media allows fans to accommodate multiple identities. *Journal of Sport Management, 30*(6), 643-655. https://doi.org/10.1123/jsm.2015-0344

Laurent, G., & Kapferer, J.-N. (1985). Measuring consumer involvement profiles. *Journal of Marketing Research, 22*(1), 41-53. https://doi.org/10.1177/002224378502200104

Laverie, D. A., & Arnett, D. B. (2000). Factors affecting fan attendance: The influence of identity salience and satisfaction. *Journal of Leisure Research, 32*(2), 225-246. https://doi.org/10.1080/00222216.2000.11949915

Lazarus, R. S. (1982). Thoughts on the relations between emotion and cognition. *American Psychologist, 37*(9), 1019-1024. https://doi.org/10.1037/0003-066X.37.9.1019

Leach, C. W., Van Zomeren, M., Zebel, S., Vliek, M. L., Pennekamp, S. F., Doosje, B., Ouwerkerk, J. W., & Spears, R. (2008). Group-level self-definition and self-investment: a hierarchical (multicomponent) model of ingroup identification. *Journal of Personality and Social Psychology, 95*(1), 144-165. https://doi.org/10.1037/0022-3514.95.1.144

Leary, M. R., & Kowalski, R. M. (1990). Impression management: A literature review and two-component model. *Psychological Bulletin, 107*(1), 34-47.

Leder, H., & Nadal, M. (2014). Ten years of a model of aesthetic appreciation and aesthetic judgment: The aesthetic episode – Development and the challenges in empirical aesthetics. *British Journal of Psychology, 105*(4), 443-464. https://doi.org/10.1111/bjop.12084

Lee, C., Kim, C., & Song, W. (2005). Lived experience of Taekwondo training as serious leisure for female college student. *Journal of Leisure and Recreation Studies, 29,* 261-270.

Lee, E., Lee, J. A., Moon, J. H., & Sung, Y. (2015). Pictures speak louder than words: Motivations for using Instagram. *Cyberpsychology, Behavior, and Social Networking, 18,* 552-556. https://doi. org/10.1089/cyber.2015.0157

Lee, G., Pae, T.-I., & Bendle, L. J. (2016). The role of identity salience in the leisure behavior of film festival participants. *Journal of Leisure Research, 48*(2), 156-177. https://doi.org/10.18666/jlr-2016-v48-i2-4687

Lee, J. Ruihley, B. J., Brown, N., & Billings, A. C. (2013). The effects of fantasy football participation on team identification, team loyalty and NFL fandom. *Journal of Sports Media, 8*(1), 207-227. http://doi.org/10.1353/jsm.2013.0008

Lee, K. (2013). *An examination on the motivations of serious leisure in rock climbing: A structural equation modeling study* (Publication No. 3587739) [Doctoral dissertation, Indiana University]. ProQuest Dissertations and Theses Global.

Lee, K., Bentley, J., & Hsu, H. Y. M. (2017). Using characteristics of serious leisure to classify rock climbers: A latent profile analysis. *Journal of Sport & Tourism, 21*(4), 245-262. https://doi.org/10.1080/14775085.2017.1327369

Lee, K., & Ewert, A. (2019). Understanding the motivations of serious leisure participation: A self-determination approach. *Annals of Leisure Research, 22*(1), 76-96. https://doi.org/10.1080/11745398.2018.1469420

Lee, K., Gould, J., & Hsu, H. Y. M. (2017). Analysis of paddlesport commitment and multiple outcomes: A serious leisure perspective. *Cogent Social Sciences, 3*(1), Article 1325055. https://doi.org/10.1080/23311886.2017.1325055

Lee, S., & Bai, B. (2016). Influence of popular culture on special interest tourists' destination image. *Tourism Management, 52,* 161-169. https://doi.org/10.1016/j.tourman.2015.06.019

Lee, S., Bai, B., & Busser, J. A. (2019). Pop star fan tourists: An application of self-expansion theory. *Tourism Management, 72,* 270-280. https://doi.org/10.1016/j.tourman.2018.12.006

Lee, S., Busser, J. A., & Park, E. (2019). The influence of self-expansion on pop-star fans' leisure constraints, commitment, involvement and future intention. *Leisure/Loisir, 43*(1), 79-101. https://doi.org/10.1080/14927713.2019.1583074

Lee, S., In, S., & Seo, W. J. (2015). Repeat attendance as a function of liminality, communitas, and team identification. South African *Journal for Research in Sport, Physical Education and Recreation, 37*(1), 59-76. https://hdl.handle.net/10520/EJC170286

Lee, S., McMahan, K., & Scott, D. (2015). The gendered nature of serious birdwatching. *Human Dimensions of Wildlife, 20*(1), 47-64. https://doi.org/10.1080/10871209.2015.956375

Lee, S., Scott, D., & Kim, H. (2008). Celebrity fan involvement and destination perceptions. *Annals of Tourism Research, 35*(3), 809-832. https://doi.org/10.1016/j.annals.2008.06.003

Lee, S. H., & Jung, K. S. (2018). Loyal customer behaviors: Identifying brand fans. *Social Behavior and Personality, 46*(8), 1285-1304. https://doi.org/10.2224/sbp.6482

Lee, W., Kwak, D. H., Lim, C., Pedersen, P. M., & Miloch, K. S. (2011). Effects of personality and gender on fantasy sports game participation: The moderating role of perceived knowledge. *Journal of Gambling Studies, 27*(3), 427-441. http://doi.org/ 10.1007/s10899-010-9218-9

Lee, Y. H., & Smith, T. G. (2007). Why are Americans addicted to baseball? An empirical analysis of fandom in Korea and the United States. *Contemporary Economic Policy, 26*(1), 32-48. https://doi.org/10.1111/j.1465-7287.2007.00052.x

Leonardelli, G. J., Pickett, C., & Brewer, M. B. (2010). Optimal distinctiveness theory: A framework for social identity, social cognition, and intergroup relations. *Advances in Experimental Social Psychology, 43*(1), 63-113. https://doi.org/10.1016/S0065-2601(10)43002-6

Leshner, C., Reysen, S., Plante, C. N., Roberts, S. E., & Gerbasi, K. C. (2018). "My group is discriminated against but I'm not": Denial of personal discrimination in furry, brony, anime, and general interest fan groups. *The Phoenix Papers, 4*(1), 130-142. https://doi.org/10.31234/osf.io/8xvzr

Lever, J., & Wheeler, S. (1984). The Chicago tribune sports page, 1900-1975. *Sociology of Sport Journal, 1*(4), 299-313. https://doi.org/10.1123/ssj.1.4.299

Levine, M., Prosser, A., Evans, D., & Reicher, S. (2005). Identity and emergency intervention: How social group membership and inclusiveness of group boundaries shape helping behavior. *Personality and Social Psychology Bulletin, 31*(4), 443-453. https://doi.org/10.1177/0146167204271651

Lewandowski, G. W., Jr., Aron, A., Bassis, S., & Kunak, J. (2006). Losing a self-expanding relationship: Implications for the self-concept. *Personal Relationships, 13*(3), 317-331. https://doi.org/10.1111/j.1475-6811.2006.00120.x

Li, B., Dittmore, S. W., Scott, O. K. M., Lo, W., & Stokowski, S. (2019). Why we follow: Examining motivational differences in following sport organizations on Twitter and Weibo. *Sport Management Review, 22*(3), 335-347. https://doi.org/10.1016/j.smr.2018.04.006

Li, D., Liau, A., & Khoo, A. (2011). Examining the influence of actual-ideal self-discrepancies, depression, and escapism, on pathological gaming among massively multiplayer online adolescent gamers. *Cyberpsychology, Behavior, and Social Networking, 14,* 535-539. https://doi.org/10.1089/cyber.2010.0463

Li, X., Huang, L., Li, B., Wang, H., & Han, C. (2020). Time for a true display of skill: Top players in League of Legends have better executive control. *Acta Psychologica, 204.* https://doi.org/10.1016/j.actpsy.2020.103007

Lian, B., Aruguete, M. S., Huynh, H., McCutcheon, L. E., & Murtagh, M. P. (2019). Is gambling addiction related to celebrity addiction? *SIS Journal of Projective Psychology and Mental Health, 26*(2), 87-96.

Lianopoulos, Y., Theodorakis, N. D., Tsigilis, N., Gardikiotis, A., & Koustelios, A. (2020). Elevating self-esteem through sport team identification: A study about local and distant sport teams. *International Journal of Sports Marketing and Sponsorship, 21*(4), 695-718. https://doi.org/10.1108/IJSMS-10-2019-0115

Liebers, N., & Schramm, H. (2017). Friends in books: The influence of character attributes and the reading experience on parasocial relationships and romances. *Poetics, 65,* 12-23. https://doi.org/10.1016/j.poetic.2017.10.001

Liebers, N., & Schramm, H. (2019). Parasocial interactions and relationships with media characters–an inventory of 60 years of research. *Communication Research Trends, 38*(2), 4-31.

Liebers, N., & Straub, R. (2020). Fantastic relationships and where to find them: Fantasy and its impact on romantic parasocial phenomena with media characters. *Poetics, 83,* Article 101481. https://doi.org/10.1016/j.poetic.2020.101481

Lin, S. S., & Tsai, C. C. (2002). Sensation seeking and internet dependence of Taiwanese high school adolescents. *Computers in Human Behavior, 18*(4), 411-426. https://doi.org/10.1016/S0747-5632(01)00056-5

Linn, E. S. (2013). *Women who pursue contact with male celebrities: Attachment styles, fantasy content, and attitudes* (Publication No. 3562000) [Doctoral dissertation, Alliant International University]. ProQuest Dissertations and Theses Global.

Linton, M.-J., Dieppe, P., & Medina-Lara, A. (2016). Review of 99 self-report measures for assessing well-being in adults: Exploring dimensions of well-being and developments over time. *BMJ Open, 6*, e010641. https://doi.org/10.1136/bmjopen-2015-010641

Liu, J. K. K. (2013). *Idol worship, religiosity, and self-esteem among university and secondary students in Hong Kong* [Honors thesis in psychology, City University of Hong Kong]. CityU Institutional Repository. http://dspace.cityu.edu.hk/handle/2031/7134

Lock, D., Funk, D. C., Doyle, J. P., & McDonald, H. (2014). Examining the longitudinal structure, stability, and dimensional interrelationships of team identification. *Journal of Sport Management, 28*(2), 119-135. https://dx.doi.org/10.1123/jsm.2012-0191

Lock, D., & Heere, B. (2017). Identity crisis: A theoretical analysis of 'team identification' research. *European Sport Management Quarterly, 17*(4), 413-435. https://doi.org/10.1080/16184742.2017.1306872

Lohse, K. R., Boyd, L. A., & Hodges, N. J. (2016). Engaging environments enhance motor skill learning in a computer gaming task. *Journal of Motor Behavior, 48*(2), 172-182. https://doi.org/10.1080/00222895.2015.1068158

Lome, J. K. (2016). The creative empowerment of body positivity in the cosplay community. *Transformative Works and Cultures, 22*. http://dx.doi.org/10.3983/twc.2016.0712

Lopes, P. (2006). Culture and stigma: Popular culture and the case of comic books. *Sociological Forum, 21*(3), 387-414. https://doi.org/10.1007/s11206-006-9022-6

Lopez-Gonzalez, H., Griffiths, M. D., & Estévez, A. (2020). In-play betting, sport broadcasts, and gambling severity: A survey study of Spanish sports bettors on the risks of betting on sport while watching it. *Communication and Sport, 8*(1), 50-71. https://doi.org/10.1177/2167479518816338

Lotecki, A. (2012). *Cosplay culture: The development of interactive and living art through play* [Master's thesis, Ryerson University]. Ryerson University Digital Repository. https://digital.library.ryerson.ca/islandora/object/RULA%3A1176

Lu, W. C., Lin, S. H., & Cheng, C. F. (2011). Sports spectator behavior: A test of the theory of planned behavior. *Perceptual and Motor Skills, 113*(3), 1017-1026. https://doi.org/10.2466/05.17.PMS.113.6.1017-1026

Luhtanen, R., & Crocker, J. (1992). A collective self-esteem scale: Self-evaluation of one's social identity. *Personality and Social Psychology Bulletin, 18*(3), 302-318. https://doi.org/10.1177/0146167292183006

Lundberg, C., & Lexhagen, M. (2014). Pop culture tourism: A research model. In A. Chauvel, N. Lamerichs, & J. Seymour (Eds.) *Fan studies: Research popular audiences* (pp. 13-34). Inter-Disciplinary Press.

Luo, J. M., Lam, C. F., & Fan, D. X. (2020). The development of measurement scale for entertainment tourism experience: A case study in Macau. *Current Issues in Tourism, 23*(7), 852-866. https://doi.org/10.1080/13683500.2018.1556251

Lyu, S. O., & Oh, C. O. (2015). Bridging the conceptual frameworks of constraints negotiation and serious leisure to understand leisure benefit realization. *Leisure Sciences, 37*(2), 176-193. https://doi.org/10.1080/01490400.2014.952461

Macey, J., Tyrväinen, V., Pirkkalainen, H., & Hamari, J. (2020). Does esports spectating influence game consumption? *Behaviour and Information Technology*. Advance online publication. https://doi.org/10.1080/0144929X.2020.1797876

Mackellar, J. (2006). Fanatics, fans or just good fun? Travel behaviours and motivations of the fanatic. *Journal of Vacation Marketing, 12*(3), 195-127. https://doi.org/10.1177/1356766706064622

Mackellar, J. (2009). Dabblers, fans and fanatics: Exploring behavioural segmentation at a special-interest event. *Journal of Vacation Marketing, 15*(1), 5-24. https://doi.org/10.1177/1356766708098168

MacLeod, N., Shelley, J., & Morrison, A. M. (2018). The touring reader: Understanding the bibliophile's experience of literary tourism. *Tourism Management, 67*(1), 388-398. https://doi.org/10.1016/j.tourman.2018.02.006

Madill, A., & Zhao, Y. (2021) Engagement with female-oriented male-male erotica in Mainland China and Hong Kong: Fandom intensity, social outlook, and region. *Participations: Journal of Audience and Reception Studies, 18*(1), 111-131.

Madrigal, R. (1995). Cognitive and affective determinants of fan satisfaction with sporting event attendance. *Journal of Leisure Research, 27*(3), 205-227. https://doi.org/10.1080/00222216.1995.11949745

Madrigal, R. (2000). The influence of social alliances with sports teams on intentions to purchase corporate sponsors' products. *Journal of Advertising, 4*(1), 13-24. https://doi.org/10.1080/00913367.2000.10673621

Madrigal, R. (2006). Measuring the multidimensional nature of sporting event performance consumption. *Journal of Leisure Research, 38*(3), 267-292. https://doi.org/10.1080/00222216.2006.11950079

Mael, F., & Ashforth, B. E. (1992). Alumni and their alma mater: A partial test of the reformulated model of organizational identification. *Journal of Organizational Behavior, 13*(2), 103-123. https://doi.org/10.1002/job.4030130202

Maguire, E. A., Gadian, D. G., Johnsrude, I. S., Good, C. D., Ashburner, J., Frackowiak, R. S. J., & Frith, C. D. (2000). Navigation-related structural change in the hippocampi of taxi drivers. *Proceedings of the National Academy of Sciences of the United States of America, 97*, 4398-4403.

Mahan, J. E., Drayer, J., & Sparvero, E. (2012). Gambling and fantasy: An examination of the influence of money on fan attitudes and behaviors. *Sport Marketing Quarterly, 21*(3), 159-169. https://ssrn.com/abstract=2457128

Mahar, C., & Weeks, C. (2013). *Examining fan attitudes toward sponsor brans using social identity frameworks.* Paper presented at ANZMAC, Auckland, New Zealand.

Malchrowicz-Mosko, E., & Chlebosz, K. (2019). Sport spectator consumption and sustainable management of sport event tourism; fan motivation in high performance sport and non-elite sport. A case study of horseback riding and running: A comparative analysis. *Sustainability, 11*(1). https://dx.doi.org/10.3390/su11072178

Maltby, J., & Day, L. (2011). Celebrity worship and incidence of elective cosmetic surgery: Evidence of a link among young adults. *Journal of Adolescent Health, 49*(5), 483-489. https://doi.org/10.1016/j.jadohealth.2010.12.014

Maltby, J., & Day, L. (2017). Regulatory motivations in celebrity interest: Self-suppression and self-expansion. *Psychology of Popular Media Culture, 6*(2), 103-112. https://doi.org/10.1037/ppm0000087

Maltby, J., Day, L., McCutcheon, L. E., Gillett, R., Houran, J., & Ashe, D. D. (2004). Personality and coping: A context for examining celebrity worship and mental health. *British Journal of Psychology, 95*(4), 411-428. https://doi.org/10.1348/0007126042369794

Maltby, J., Day, L., McCutcheon, L. E., Houran, J., & Ashe, D. (2006). Extreme celebrity worship, fantasy proneness and dissociation: Developing the measurement and understanding of celebrity worship within a clinical personality context. *Personality and Individual Differences, 40*(2), 273-283. https://doi.org/10.1016/j.paid.2005.07.004

Maltby, J., Day, L., McCutcheon, L. E., Martin, M. M., & Cayanus, J. L. (2004). Celebrity worship, cognitive flexibility, and social complexity. *Personality and Individual Differences, 37*(7), 1475-1482. https://doi.org/10.1016/j.paid.2004.02.004

Maltby, J., Giles, D. C., Barber, L., & McCutcheon, L. E. (2005). Intense-personal celebrity worship and body image: Evidence of a link among female adolescents. *British Journal of Health Psychology, 10*(1), 17-32. https://doi.org/10.1348/135910704X15257

Maltby, J., Houran, J., Lange, R., Ashe, D., & McCutcheon, L. E. (2002). Thou shalt worship no other gods – unless they are celebrities: The relationship between celebrity worship and religious orientation. *Personality and Individual Differences, 32*(7), 1157-1172. https://doi.org/10.1016/S0191-8869(01)00059-9

Maltby, J., Houran, J., & McCutcheon, L. E. (2003). A clinical interpretation of attitudes and behaviors associated with celebrity worship. *The Journal of Nervous and Mental Disease, 191*(1), 25-29. https://doi.org/10.1097/00005053-200301000-00005

Maltby, J., McCutcheon, L. E., Ashe, D. D., & Houran, J. (2001). The self-reported psychological well-being of celebrity worshippers. *North American Journal of Psychology, 3*(3), 441-452.

Maltby, J., McCutcheon, L. E., & Lowinger, R. J. (2011). Brief report: Celebrity worshipers and the five-factor model of personality. *North American Journal of Psychology, 13*(2), 343-348.

Manfredo, M. J., Driver, B. L., & Tarrant, M. A. (1996). Measuring leisure motivation: A meta-analysis of the recreation experience preference scales. *Journal of Leisure Research, 28*(3), 188-213. https://doi.org/10.1080/00222216.1996.11949770

Martin, C., Anton, G., Ochsner, A., Elmergreen, J., & Steinkuehler, C. (2012). Information literacy and online reading comprehension in WoW and school. *Proceedings of the 8th Annual Games+Learning+Society Conference, 2,* 209-216.

Martin, C., & Steinkuehler, C. (2010). Collective information literacy in massively multiplayer online games. *E-Learning and Digital Media, 7*(4), 355-365. http://dx.doi.org/10.2304/elea.2010.7.4.355

Martin, R. J., Kozel, K. G., Sewell, K. B., Coghill, J. G., & Lee, J. G. L. (2020). A systematic review of motivations for fantasy sport participants. *Journal of*

Sport Behavior, 43(3), 352-375. http://doi.org/
10.1080/16184742.2017.1347192

Maslow, A. H. (1943). A theory of human motivation. *Psychological Review, 50*(4), 370-396. https://doi.org/10.1037/h0054346

Maslow, A. H. (1981). *Motivation and personality*. Prabhat Prakashan.

Matsuoka, H., Chelladurai, P., & Harada, M. (2003). Direct and interaction effects of team identification and satisfaction on intention to attend games. *Sport Marketing Quarterly, 12*(4), 244-253.

Maxton, B. (2019). *Understanding sports fan motivation: A study into fan involvement, satisfaction and loyalty* [Doctoral dissertation, University of Pretoria]. http://hdl.handle.net/2263/71722

McConnel, J. (2019). Fan spaces as third spaces: Tapping into the creative community of fandom. *Urbana, 109*(1), 45-51.

McCutcheon, L. E. (2002). Are parasocial relationship styles reflected in love styles? *Current Research in Social Psychology, 7*(6), 82-94.

McCutcheon, L. E., & Aruguete, M. S. (2021). Is celebrity worship increasing over time? *Journal of Studies in Social Sciences and Humanities, 7*(1), 66-75.

McCutcheon, L. E., Aruguete, M., McCarley, N. G., & Jenkins, W. J. (2016). Further validation of an indirect measure of celebrity stalking. *Journal of Studies in Social Sciences, 14*(1), 75-91.

McCutcheon, L. E., Ashe, D. D., Houran, J., & Maltby, J. (2003). A cognitive profile of individuals who tend to worship celebrities. *The Journal of Psychology, 137*(4), 309-322. https://doi.org/10.1080/00223980309600616

McCutcheon, L. E., Gillen, M. M., Browne, B. L., Murtagh, M. P., & Collisson, B. (2016). Intimate relationships and attitudes toward celebrities. *Interpersona, 10*(1), 77-89. https://doi.org/10.5964/ijpr.v10i1.208

McCutcheon, L. E., Griffith, J. D., Aruguete, M. S., & Haight, E. (2012). Cognitive ability and celebrity worship revisited. *North American Journal of Psychology, 14*(2), 383-392.

McCutcheon, L. E., Lange, R., & Houran, J. (2002). Conceptualization and measurement of celebrity worship. *British Journal of Psychology, 93*(1), 67-87. https://doi.org/10.1348/000712602162454

McDaniel, S. R. (2003). Reconsidering the relationship between sensation seeking and audience preferences for viewing televised sports. *Journal of Sport Management, 17*(1), 13-36. https://doi.org/10.1123/jsm.17.1.13

McDonald, H., Leckie, C., Karg, A., Zubebcevic-Basic, N., & Lock, D. (2016). Segmenting initial fans of a new team: A taxonomy of sport early adopters. *Journal of Consumer Behaviour, 15*(2), 136-148. https://doi.org/10.1002/cb.1558

McDonald, R. E., Wagner, T., & Minor, M. S. (2008). Cheers! A means-end chain analysis of college students' bar-choice motivations. *Annals of Leisure Research, 11*(3-4), 386-403. https://doi.org/10.1080/11745398.2008.9686804

McGuire, J. (2002). Selective perception and its impact on the evaluation of radio sports play-by-play announcers. *Journal of Radio Studies, 9*(1), 51-64. https://doi.org/10.1207/s15506843jrs0901_6

McIlwraith, R. D. (1998). "I'm addicted to television": The personality, imagination, and TV watching patterns of self-identified TV addicts. *Journal of Broadcasting & Electronic Media, 42*(3), 371-386. https://doi.org/10.1080/08838159809364456

McInroy, L. B. (2020). Building connections and slaying basilisks: fostering support, resilience, and positive adjustment for sexual and gender minority youth in online fandom communities. *Information, Communication and Society, 23*(13), 1874-1891. https://doi.org/10.1080/1369118X.2019.1623902

McIntyre, N., & Pigram, J. J. (1992). Recreation specialization reexamined: The case of vehicle-based campers. *Leisure Sciences, 14*(1), 3-15. https://doi.org/10.1080/01490409209513153

McMillan, D. W., & Chavis, D. M. (1986). Sense of community: A definition and theory. *Journal of Community Psychology, 14*(1), 6-23. https://doi.org/10.1002/1520-6629(198601)14:1<6::AID-JCOP2290140103>3.0.CO;2-I

McMullen, A. (2018) *'They're like cool librarians': Investigating the information behaviour of pop music fans* [Doctoral dissertation, University College London]. https://hcommons.org/deposits/item/hc:21933

McPherson, B. D. (1975). Past, present and future perspectives for research in sport sociology. *International Review of Sport Sociology, 10*(1), 55-72. https://doi.org/10.1177/101269027501000104

Menninghaus, W., Wagner, V., Wassiliwizky, E., Jacobsen, T., & Keep, C. A. (2017). The emotional and aesthetic powers of parallelistic diction. *Poetics, 63*(1), 47-59. https://doi.org/10.1016/j.poetic.2016.12.001

Menninghaus, W., Wagner, V., Wassiliwizky, E., Schindler, I., Hanich, J., Jacobsen, T., & Koelsch, S. (2019). What are aesthetic emotions? *Psychological Review, 126*(2), 171-195. http://dx.doi.org/10.1037/rev0000135

Mercier, J., Sevigny, S., Jacques, C., Goulet, A., Cantinotti, M., & Giroux, I. (2018). Sports bettors: A systematic review. *Journal of Gambling Issues, 38*(1), 203-236. http://dx.doi.org/10.4309/jgi.2018.38.11

Metzger, M. J. (2002). When no news is good news: Inferring closure for news issues. *Journalism & Mass Communication Quarterly, 77*(4), 760-787. https://doi.org/10.1177/107769900007700404

Meyer, I. H. (2003). Prejudice, social stress, and mental health in lesbian, gay, and bisexual populations: Conceptual issues and research evidence. *Psychological Bulletin, 129*(5), 674-697. http://doi.org/10.1037/0033-2909.129.5.674

Miller, C. B. (2009). Yes we did! Basking in the reflected glory and cutting off reflected failure in the 2008 presidential election. *Analyses of Social Issues and Public Policy, 9*(1), 283-296. https://doi.org/10.1111/j.1530-2415.2009.01194.x

Miller, S. (2018). Rebooting ponies and men: Discordant masculinity and the Brony fandom. *The Journal of Men's Studies, 26*(3), 327-345. https://doi.org/10.1177/1060826518773468

Milne, G. R., & McDonald, M. A. (1999). *Sport marketing: Managing the exchange process*. Jones and Bartlett Publishers.

Min, J. H. (2019). *The impact of college football tourists' personality and motivation on their destination and team loyalty* [Doctoral dissertation, Texas Tech University]. https://hdl.handle.net/2346/85353

Miranda, J., & Storms, M. (1989). Psychological adjustment of lesbians and gay men. *Journal of Counseling and Development, 68*(1), 41-45. https://doi.org/10.1002/j.1556-6676.1989.tb02490.x

Mlicki, P. P., & Ellemers, N. (1996). Being different or being better? National stereotypes and identifications of Polish and Dutch students. *European Journal of Social Psychology, 16*(1), 97-114. https://doi.org/10.1002/(SICI)1099-0992(199601)26:1%3C97::AID-EJSP739%3E3.0.CO;2-F

Mock, S. E., Plante, C., Reysen, S., & Gerbasi, K. C. (2013). Deeper leisure involvement as a coping resource in a stigmatized leisure context. *Leisure/Loisir, 37*, 111-126. https://doi.org/10.1080/14927713.2013.801152

Moody, K. A. (2014). *Modders: Changing the game through user-generated content and online communities* (Publication No. 3628417) [Doctoral dissertation, University of Iowa]. ProQuest Dissertations and Theses Global.

Moor, L. (2006). "The buzz of dressing": Commodity culture, fraternity, and football fandom. *South Atlantic Quarterly, 105*(2), 327-347. https://doi.org/10.1215/00382876-105-2-327

Morgan, M. (1984). Heavy television viewing and perceived quality of life. *Journalism Quarterly, 61*(3), 499-740. https://doi.org/10.1177/107769908406100303

Morgan, M. L. (2015). *Developing 21st century skills through gameplay: To what extent are young people who play the online computer game Minecraft acquiring and developing media literacy and the Four Cs skills?*(Publication No. 10020378) [Doctoral dissertation, New England College]. ProQuest Theses and Dissertations.

Morrison, K. A., Misener, K. E., & Mock, S. E. (2020). The influence of corporate social responsibility and team identification on spectator behavior in major junior hockey. *Leisure Sciences, 42*(2), 133-151. https://doi.org/10.1080/01490400.2017.1408511

Mowen, J. C., Fang, X., & Scott, K. (2009). A hierarchical model approach for identifying the trait antecedents of general gambling propensity and of four gambling-related genres. *Journal of Business Research, 62*(1), 1262-1268. https://doi.org/10.1016/j.jbusres.2008.11.007

Moyer-Gusé, E., Chung, A. H., & Jain, P. (2011). Identification with characters and discussion of taboo topics after exposure to an entertainment narrative about sexual health. *Journal of Communication, 61*(3), 387-406. https://doi.org/10.1111/j.1460-2466.2011.01551.x

Mummendey, A., Klink, A., Mielke, R., Wenzel, M., & Blanz, M. (1999). Socio-structural characteristics of intergroup relations and identity management strategies: Results from a field study in East Germany. *European Journal of Social Psychology, 29,* 259-285. https://doi.org/10.1002/(SICI)1099-0992(199903/05)29:2/3%3C259::AID-EJSP927%3E3.0.CO;2-F

Murrell, A. J., & Dietz, B. (1992). Fan support of sport teams: The effect of a common group identity. *Journal of Sport and Exercise Psychology, 14*(1), 28-39. https://doi.org/10.1123/jsep.14.1.28

Mustonen, A., Arms, R. L., & Russell, G. W. (1996). Predictors of sports spectators' proclivity for riotous behaviour in Finland and Canada. *Personality and Individual Differences, 21*(4), 519-525. https://doi.org/10.1016/0191-8869(96)00089-X

Mutz, M., & Meier, H. E. (2016). Successful, sexy, popular: Athletic performance and physical attractiveness as determinants of public interest in male and female soccer players. *International Review for the Sociology of Sport, 51*(5), 567-580. https://doi.org/10.1177/1012690214545900

Na, S., Su, Y., & Kunkel, T. (2019). Do not bet on your favourite football team: The influence of fan identity-based biases and sport context knowledge on game prediction accuracy. *European Sport Management Quarterly, 19*(3), 398-418. https://doi.org/10.1080/16184742.2018.1530689

Nabi, R. L., & Wirth, W. (2008). Exploring the role of emotion in media effects: An introduction to the special issue. *Media Psychology, 11*(1), 1-6. https://doi.org/10.1080/15213260701852940

Napier, S. J. (2005). *Anime: From* Akira *to* Howl's Moving Castle. Palgrave MacMillan.

Nassis, P., Theodorakis, N. D., Afthinos, Y., & Kolybalis, H. (2014). The effect of fans' attitudes on sponsorship outcomes: Evidence from an exploratory study in Greece. *Journal of Applied Sport Management, 6*(1), 48-71.

Nassis, P., Theodorakis, N. D., Alexandris, K., Tsellou, A., & Afthinos, Y. (2012). Testing the role of team identification on the relationship between sport involvement and sponsorship outcomes in the context of professional soccer. *International Journal of Sport Management, 13,* 1-17.

Neale, L., & Funk, D. (2006). Investigating motivation, attitudinal loyalty and attendance behavior with fans of Australian football. *International Journal of Sports Marketing and Sponsorship, 7*(4), 307-317.

Neus, F. (2020). *Event marketing in the context of higher education marketing and digital environments.* Springer. https://doi.org/10.1007/978-3-658-29262-1_6

Newman, D. B., Tay, L., & Diener, E. (2014). Leisure and subjective well-being: A model of psychological mechanisms as mediating factors. *Journal of Happiness Studies, 15*(3), 555-578. https://doi.org/10.1007/s10902-013-9435-x

Noppe, N. (2011). Why we should talk about commodifying fan work. *Transformative Works and Culture, 8.* https://doi.org/10.3983/twc.2011.0369

North, A. C., & Hargreaves, D. J. (1999). Music and adolescent identity. *Music Education Research, 1*(1), 75-92.

North, A. C., & Hargreaves, D. J. (2007). Lifestyle correlates of musical preference: Relationships, living arrangements, beliefs and crime. *Psychology of Music, 35*(1), 325-344.

North, A. C., Sheridan, L., Maltby, J., & Gillett, R. (2007). Attributional style, self-esteem, and celebrity worship. *Media Psychology, 9*(2), 291-308. https://doi.org/10.1080/15213260701285975

Oakes, S. (2010). Profiling the jazz festival audience. *International Journal of Event and Festival Management, 1*(2), 110-119. https://doi.org/10.1108/17852951011056892

Obiegbu, C. J., Larsen, G., Ellis, N., & O'Reilly, D. (2019). Co-constructing loyalty in an era of digital music fandom: An experiential-discursive perspective. *European Journal of Marketing, 53*(3), 463-482. https://doi.org/10.1108/EJM-10-2017-0754

Obst, P., Zinkiewicz, L., & Smith, S. G. (2002a). Sense of community in science fiction fandom, part 1: Understanding sense of community in an international community of interest. *Journal of Community Psychology, 30*(1), 87-103. https://doi.org/10.1002/jcop.1052

Obst, P., Zinkiewicz, L., & Smith, S. G. (2002b). Sense of community in science fiction fandom, part 2: Comparing neighborhood and interest group sense of community. *Journal of Community Psychology, 30*(1), 105-117. https://doi.org/10.1002/jcop.1053

Odağ, Ö., Hofer, M., Schneider, F. M., & Knop, K. (2016). Testing measurement equivalence of eudaimonic and hedonic entertainment motivations in a cross-cultural comparison. *Journal of Intercultural Communication Research, 45*(2), 108-125. https://doi.org/10.1080/17475759.2015.1108216

Oetting, E. R., & Donnermeyer, J. F. (1998). Primary socialization theory: The etiology of drug use and deviance. I. *Substance Use & Misuse, 33*(4), 995-1026. https://doi.org/10.3109/10826089809056252

Oliver, M. B., & Bartsch, A. (2010). Appreciation as audience response: Exploring entertainment gratifications beyond hedonism. *Human Communication Research, 36*(1), 53-81. https://doi.org/10.1111/j.1468-2958.2009.01368.x

Oliver, M. B., & Bartsch, A. (2011) Appreciation of entertainment: The importance of meaningfulness via virtue and wisdom. *Journal of Media Psychology, 23*(1), 29-33. https://doi.org/10.1027/1864-1105/a000029

Oliver, M. B., Bowman, N. D., Woolley, J. K., Rodgers, R., Sherrick, B. I., & Chung, M. (2015). Video games as meaningful entertainment experiences. *Psychology of Popular Media Culture, 5*(4), 390-405. http://dx.doi.org/10.1037/ppm0000066

Oliver, M. B., Hartmann, T., & Woolley, J. K. (2012). Elevation in response to entertainment portrayals of moral virtue. *Human Communication Research, 38*(3), 360-378. https://doi.org/10.1111/j.1468-2958.2012.01427.x

Oliver, M. B., & Raney, A. A. (2011). Entertainment as pleasurable and meaningful: Identifying hedonic and eudaimonic motivations for entertainment consumption. *Journal of Communication, 61*(5), 984-1004. https://dx.doi.org/10.1111/j.1460-2466.2011.01585.x

Oliver, R. L. (1999). Whence consumer loyalty? *Journal of Marketing, 63*(4), 33-44. https://doi.org/10.1177/00222429990634s105

Olsen, S. O. (2007). Repurchase loyalty: The role of involvement and satisfaction. *Psychology and Marketing, 24*(4), 315-341. https://doi.org/10.1002/mar.20163

Otmazgin, N. (2016). A new cultural geography of East Asia: Imagining a 'region' though popular culture. *The Asia-Pacific Journal, 14*(7). Article 4879.

Pachankis, J. E. (2007). The psychological implications of concealing a stigma: a cognitive-affective-behavioral model. *Psychological Bulletin, 133*(2), 328-345. https://psycnet.apa.org/doi/10.1037/0033-2909.133.2.328

Pan, S.-L., Wu, H. C., Morrison, A. M., Huang, M.-T., & Huang, W.-S. (2018). The relationships among leisure involvement, organizational commitment and well-being: Viewpoints from sport fans in Asia. *Sustainability, 10*(3), Article 740. https://doi.org/10.3390/su10030740

Pandelaere, M. (2016). Materialism and well-being: the role of consumption. *Current Opinion in Psychology, 10,* 33-38. https://doi.org/10.1016/j.copsyc.2015.10.027

Papyrina, V. (2012). If you want to like me, should I be like you or unlike you? The effect of prior positive interactions with the group on conformity and distinctiveness in consumer decision making. *Journal of Consumer Behavior, 11,* 467-476.

Park, J., Suh, Y. I., & Pedersen, P. M. (2016). Examining spectator motivations in major league baseball: A comparison between senior and non-senior consumers. *Choregia: Sport Management International Journal, 12*(2), 13-36. https://doi.org/10.4127/ch.2016.0110

Park, S. B., Ok, C. M., & Chae, B. K. (2016). Using Twitter data for cruise tourism marketing and research. *Journal of Travel and Tourism Marketing, 33*(6), 885-898. https://doi.org/10.1080/10548408.2015.1071688

Parry, K. D., Jones, I., & Wann, D. L. (2014). An examination of sport fandom in the United Kingdom: A comparative analysis of fan behaviors, socialization processes, and team identification. *Journal of Sport Behavior, 37*(3), 251-267. https://doi.org/10.1177/1012690210380582

Pearce, J. M. (1987). A model for stimulus generalization in Pavlovian conditioning. *Psychological Review, 94*(1), 61-73. https://doi.org/10.1037/0033-295X.94.1.61

Pease, D. G., & Zhang, J. J. (2001). Socio-motivational factors affecting spectator attendance at professional basketball games. *International Journal of Sport Management, 2*(1), 31-59.

Peaslee, R. M., El-Khoury, J., & Liles, A. (2014). The media festival volunteer: Connecting online and on-ground fan labor. *Transformative Works and Cultures, 15.* https://doi.org/10.3983/twc.2014.0502

Pentecost, R. (2009). Assessing the role of passion as a mediator of consumer intentions to attend a motor sports event. *Anais da ANZMAC: Australian & New Zealand Marketing Academy Annual Conference.* Melbourne, Australia.

Pentecost, R., & Andrews, L. (2010). Fashion retailing and the bottom line: The effects of generational cohorts, gender, fashion fanship, and attitudes and impulse buying on fashion expenditure. *Journal of Retailing and Consumer Services, 17*(1), 43-52. https://doi.org/10.1016/j.jretconser.2009.09.003

Perse, E. M. (1990). Audience selectivity and involvement in the newer media environment. *Communication Research, 17*(5), 675-697. https://doi.org/10.1177/009365090017005005

Peterson, C., & Seligman, M. E. (2004). *Character strengths and virtues: A handbook and classification* (Vol. 1). Oxford University Press.

Pham, M. T. (1992). Effects of involvement, arousal, and pleasure on the recognition of sponsorship stimuli. In J. F. Sherry & B. Sternthal (Eds.), *Advances in consumer research* (Vol. 19, pp. 85-93). Association for Consumer Research.

Phillips, T. (2013). *Fandom and beyond: Online community, culture and Kevin Smith fandom* (Publication No. 10058372) [Doctoral dissertation, University of East Anglia]. ProQuest Dissertations and Theses Global.

Pizzo, A. D., Bakers, B. J., Na, S., Lee, M. A., Kim, D., & Funk, D. C. (2018). eSport vs. sport: A comparison of spectator motives. *Sport Marketing Quarterly, 27*(2), 108-123.

Plante, C., Anderson, C. A., Allen, J. J., Groves, C. L., & Gentile, D. (2019). *Game on!: Sensible answers about video games and media violence.* ZenGen: Ames, IA.

Plante, C., Chadborn, D., Groves, C., & Reysen, S. (2018). Letters from Equestria: Prosocial media, helping, and empathy in fans of My Little Pony. *Communication and Culture Online, 9,* 206-220. https://doi.org/10.18485/kkonline.2018.9.9.11

Plante, C. N., Chadborn, D., & Reysen, S. (2018). 'When entertaining isn't enough': Fan motivation and word of mouth spreading of fan interests. *Journal of Digital and Social Media Marketing, 6,* 168-180.

Plante, C. N., Gentile, D. A., Groves, C. L., Modlin, A., & Blanco-Herrera, J. (2019). Video games as coping mechanisms in the etiology of video game addiction. *Psychology of Popular Media Culture, 8*(4), 385-394. https://doi.org/10.1037/ppm0000186

Plante, C. N., Reysen, S., Chadborn, D., Roberts, S. E., & Gerbasi, K. C. (2020). 'Get out of my fandom newbie': A cross-fandom study of elitism and gatekeeping in fans. *Journal of Fandom Studies, 8*(2), 123-146. https://doi.org/10.1386/jfs_00013_1

Plante, C. N., Reysen, S., Groves, C. L., Roberts, S. E., & Gerbasi, K. (2017). The fantasy engagement scale: A flexible measure of positive and negative fantasy engagement. *Basic and Applied Social Psychology, 39*(3), 127-152. https://doi.org/10.1080/01973533.2017.1293538

Plante, C. N., Roberts, S., Reysen, S., & Gerbasi, K. (2014a). Interaction of socio-structural characteristics predicts identity concealment and self-esteem in stigmatized minority group members. *Current Psychology, 33,* 3-19. https://doi.org/10.1007/s12144-013-9189-y

Plante, C. N., Roberts, S., Reysen, S., & Gerbasi, K. (2014b). "One of us": Engagement with fandoms and global citizenship identification. *Psychology of Popular Media Culture, 3,* 49-64. https://doi.org/10.1037/ppm0000008

Plante, C. N., Roberts, S. E., Reysen, S., & Gerbasi, K. C. (2015). "By the numbers": Comparing furries and related fandoms. In T. Howl (Ed.), *Furries among us: Essays on furries by the most prominent members of the fandom* (pp. 106-126). Thurston Howl Publications.

Plante, C. N., Roberts, S. E., Reysen, S., & Gerbasi, K. C. (2017). "Say it ain't so": Addressing and dispelling misconceptions about furries. In T. Howl (Ed.), *Furries among us 2: More essays on furries by furries* (pp. 142-161). Thurston Howl Publications.

Plante, C. N., Roberts, S. E., Snider, J. S., Schroy, C., Reysen, S., & Gerbasi, K. (2015). 'More than skin-deep': Biological essentialism in response to a distinctiveness threat in a stigmatized fan community. *British Journal of Social Psychology, 54*(2), 359-370. https://doi.org/10.1111/bjso.12079

Poncin, I., Garnier, M., & Maille, V. (2015). A merchant virtual universe as an innovative retail setting: A dynamic perspective on the immersion process. In E. Pantano (Ed.), *Successful technological integration for competitive advantage in retail settings* (pp. 43-75). IGI Global.

Pons, F., Mourali, M., & Nyeck, S. (2006). Consumer orientation toward sporting events: Scale development and validation. *Journal of Service Research, 8*(3), 276-287. https://doi.org/10.1177/1094670505283931

Pontin, E., Schwannauer, M., Tai, S., & Kinderman, P. (2013). A UK validation of a general measure of subjective well-being: The modified BBC subjective well-being scale (BBC-SWB). *Health and Quality of Life Outcomes, 11,* Article 150. https://doi.org/10.1186/1477-7525-11-150

Poor, N. (2014). Computer game modders' motivations and sense of community: A mixed-methods approach. *New Media and Society, 16*(8), 1249-1267. https://doi.org/10.1177/1461444813504266

Porter, H., Iwasaki, Y., & Shank, J. (2010). Conceptualizing meaning-making through leisure experiences. *Loisir Et Société/Society and Leisure, 33*(2), 167-194. https://doi.org/10.1080/07053436.2010.10707808

Postmes, T., Haslam, S. A., & Jans, L. (2013). A single-item measure of social identification: Reliability, validity, and utility. *British Journal of Social Psychology, 52*(4), 597-617. https://doi.org/10.1111/bjso.12006

Pramaggiore, M. (2015). The taming of the bronies: Animals, autism and fandom as therapeutic performance. *Alphaville: Journal of Film and Screen Media, 9.* http://www.alphavillejournal.com/Issue9/HTML/ArticlePramaggiore.html

Proudfoot, S. T., Plante, C. N., & Reysen, S. (2019). Why we put on the sorting hat: Motivations to take fan personality tests. *Current Issues in Personality Psychology, 7*(4), 265-273. https://doi.org/10.5114/cipp.2020.91473

Pugh, A. S., Grieve, F. G., Derryberry, W. P., & Clayton, K. (2019). What motivates sport fans to attend minor league baseball and roller derby events? *Journal of Contemporary Athletics, 13*(4), 265-280.

Pyszczynski, T., Solomon, S., & Greenberg, J. (2015). Thirty years of terror management theory: From genesis to revelation. *Advances in Experimental Social Psychology, 52,* 1-70. http://dx.doi.org/10.1016/bs.aesp.2015.03.001

Qian, T. Y., Wang, J. J., Zhang, J. J., & Hulland, J. (2020). Fulfilling the basic psychological needs of esports fans: A self-determination theory approach. *Communication and Sport.* Advance online publication. https://doi.org/10.1177/2167479520943875

Quinn, D. M., & Chaudoir, S. R. (2009). Living with a concealable stigmatized identity: the impact of anticipated stigma, centrality, salience, and cultural stigma on psychological distress and health. *Journal of Personality and Social Psychology, 97*(4), 634-651. https://doi.org/10.1037/a0015815

Rahman, O., Wing-Sun, L., & Cheung, B. H.-M. (2012). "Cosplay": Imaginative self and performing identity. *Fashion Theory, 16*(3), 317-341. https://doi.org/10.2752/175174112X13340749707204

Raney, A. A. (2006). Why we watch and enjoy mediated sports. In A. A. Raney & J. Bryant (Eds.), *Handbook of sports and media* (pp. 313-329). Lawrence Erlbaum.

Raney, A. A. (2013). Reflections on communication and sport: On enjoyment and disposition. *Communication and Sport, 1*(1-2), 164-175. https://doi.org/10.1177/2167479512467979

Raney, A. A., Janicke, S. H., Oliver, M. B., Dale, K. R., Jones, R. P., & Cox, D. (2018). Profiling the audience for self-transcendent media: A national survey.

Mass Communication and Society, 21(3), 296-319.
https://doi.org/10.1080/15205436.2017.1413195

Ray, A., Plante, C. N., Reysen, S., Roberts, S. E., & Gerbasi, K. C. (2017). Psychological needs predict fanship and fandom in anime fans. *The Phoenix Papers, 3*(1), 56-68.

Raymen, T. W. (2016). *The paradox of parkour: An exploration of the deviant-leisure nexus in late-capitalist urban space* [Doctoral dissertation, Durham University]. Durham E-Theses Online. http://etheses.dur.ac.uk/12255/

Raymen, T., & Smith, O. (2019). Deviant leisure: A critical criminological perspective for the twenty-first century. *Critical Criminology, 27*(1), 115-130. https://doi.org/10.1007/s10612-019-09435-x

Read, S. E. (1980). A prime force in the expansion of tourism in the next decade: special interest travel. In D. E. Hawkins, E. L. Shafer, & J. M. Rovelstad (Eds.), *Tourism marketing and management issues* (pp. 193-202). George Washington University.

Rees, T., Haslam, S. A., Coffee, P., & Lavallee, D. (2015). A social identity approach to sport psychology: Principles, practice, and prospects. *Sports Medicine, 45,* 1083-1096. https://doi.org/10.1007/s40279-015-0345-4

Reeves, R. A., Baker, G. A., & Truluck, C. S. (2012). Celebrity worship, materialism, compulsive buying, and the empty self. *Psychology and Marketing, 29*(9), 674-679. https://doi.org/10.1002/mar.20553

Reichenberger, I., & Smith, K. A. (2020). Co-creating communities: Fandoms in tourism spaces. *Tourist Studies, 20*(2), 166-181. https://doi.org/10.1177/1468797619874504

Reichheld, F. F., & Schefter, P. (2000). E-loyalty: your secret weapon on the web. *Harvard Business Review, 78*(4), 105-113.

Reunders, S., Waysdorf, A., Zwaan, K., & Duits, L. (2017). Fandom and fan fiction. In R. Possler, C. A. Hoffner, & L. van Loonen (Eds.), *The international encyclopedia of media effects* (pp. 1-12). John Wiley & Sons. https://doi.org/10.1002/9781118783764.wbieme0176

Reysen, S. (2006). Secular versus religious fans: Are they different?: An empirical examination. *Journal of Religion and Popular Culture, 12.* https://doi.org/10.3138/jrpc.12.1.001

Reysen, S., & Branscombe, N. R. (2010). Fanship and fandom: Comparisons between sport fans and non-sport fans. *Journal of Sport Behavior, 33*(2), 176-193.

Reysen, S., Chadborn, D., & Plante, C. N. (2018). Theory of planned behavior and intention to attend a fan convention. *Journal of Convention and Event Tourism, 19*(3), 204-218. https://doi.org/10.1080/15470148.2017.1419153

Reysen, S., Katzarska-Miller, I., Nesbit, S. M., & Pierce, L. (2013). Further validation of a single-item measure of social identification. *European Journal of Social Psychology, 43*(6), 463-470. https://doi.org/10.1002/ejsp.1973

Reysen, S., Katzarska-Miller, I., Plante, C. N., Roberts, S. E., Gerbasi, K. C., Brooks, T. R., & Tague, A. M. (2020). Anime and global citizenship identification. *The Phoenix Papers, 4*(2), 48-61.

Reysen, S., & Plante, C. N. (2017). Fans, perceived maturity, and willingness to form a romantic relationship: Application of a short maturity measure. *Communication and Culture Online, 8*(1), 154-173. https://doi.org/10.18485/kkonline.2017.8.8.8

Reysen, S., Plante, C. N., & Chadborn, D. (2017). Better together: Social connections mediate the relationship between fandom and well-being. *AASCIT Journal of Health, 4*(6), 68-73.

Reysen, S., Plante, C. N., & Chadborn, D. (2021). *Permeability of group boundaries as a mediator between belonging to multiple fandoms and loneliness.* Manuscript submitted for publication.

Reysen, S., Plante, C. N., Chadborn, D., Roberts, S. E., & Gerbasi, K. C. (2021). *Transported to another world: The psychology of anime fans.* International Anime Research Project.

Reysen, S., Plante, C. N., Lam, T. Q., Kamble, S. V., Katzarska-Miller, I., Assis, N., Packard, G., & Moretti, E. G. (2020). Maturity and well-being: Consistent associations across samples and measures. *Journal of Wellness, 2*(2), Article 10, 1-8. https://doi.org/10.18297/jwellness/vol2/iss2/10

Reysen, S., Plante, C. N., Roberts, S. E., & Gerbasi, K. C. (2015a). A social identity perspective of personality differences between fan and non-fan identities. *World Journal of Social Science Research, 2,* 91-103. https://doi.org/10.22158/wjssr.v2n1p91

Reysen, S., Plante, C. N., Roberts, S. E., & Gerbasi, K. C. (2015b). Ingroup bias and ingroup projection in the furry fandom. *International Journal of Psychological Studies, 7*(4), 49-58. https://doi.org/10.5539/ijps.v7n4p49

Reysen, S., Plante, C. N., Roberts, S. E., & Gerbasi, K. C. (2016). Optimal distinctiveness and identification with the furry fandom. *Current Psychology, 35,* 638-642. https://doi.org/10.1007/s12144-015-9331-0

Reysen, S., Plante, C. N., Roberts, S. E., & Gerbasi, K. C. (2017a). Anime fans to the
rescue: Evidence of Daniel Wann's team identification-social psychological health model. *The Phoenix Papers, 3*(1), 237-247.

Reysen, S., Plante, C. N., Roberts, S. E., & Gerbasi, K. C. (2017b). Optimal distinctiveness needs as predictors of identification in the anime fandom. *The*

Phoenix Papers, 3(1), 25-32.

Reysen, S., Plante, C. N., Roberts, S. E., & Gerbasi, K. C. (2017c). "It just clicked": Discovering furry identity and motivations to participate in the fandom. In T. Howl (Ed.), *Furries among us 2: More essays on furries by furries* (pp. 111-128). Thurston Howl Publications.

Reysen, S., Plante, C. N., Roberts, S. E., & Gerbasi, K. C. (2018a). Motivations of cosplayers to participate in the anime fandom. *The Phoenix Papers, 4*(1), 29-40. https://doi.org/10.17605/OSF.IO/UT4FB

Reysen, S., Plante, C. N., Roberts, S. E., & Gerbasi, K. C. (2018b). "Coming out" as an anime fan: Cosplayers in the anime fandom, fan disclosure, and well-being. *The Phoenix Papers, 4*(1), 1-9. https://doi.org/10.31235/osf.io/hujgs

Reysen, S., Plante, C. N., Roberts, S. E., & Gerbasi, K. C. (2018c). Anime fans to the rescue: Evidence of Daniel Wann's team identification-social psychological health model. *The Phoenix Papers, 3*(1), 237-247.

Reysen, S., Plante, C. N., Roberts, S. E., & Gerbasi, K. C. (2019). Initial validation and reliability of the single-item measure of immersion. *Creative Industries Journal, 12*(3), 272-283. https://doi.org/10.1080/17510694.2019.1621586

Reysen, S., Plante, C. N., Roberts, S. E., & Gerbasi, K. C. (2020a). My animal self: The importance of preserving fantasy-themed identity uniqueness. *Identity, 20*(1), 1-8. https://doi.org/10.1080/15283488.2019.1676245

Reysen, S., Plante, C. N., Roberts, S. E., & Gerbasi, K. C. (2020b). Psychology and fursonas in the furry fandom. In T. Howl (Ed.), *Furries among us 3: Essays by furries about furries* (pp. 86-104). Thurston Howl Publications.

Reysen, S., Plante, C. N., Roberts, S. E., & Gerbasi, K. C. (2021). *Social activities mediate the relation between fandom identification and psychological well-being*. Manuscript submitted for publication.

Reysen, S., Plante, C. N., Roberts, S. E., Gerbasi, K. C., Mohebpour, I., & Gamboa, A. (2016). Pale and geeky: Prevailing stereotypes of anime fans. *The Phoenix Papers, 2*(1), 78-103.

Reysen, S., Plante, C. N., Roberts, S. E., Gerbasi, K. C., & Shaw, J. (2016). An examination of anime fan stereotypes. *The Phoenix Papers, 2*(2), 90-117.

Reysen, S., & Shaw, J. (2016). Sport fan as the default fan: Why non-sport fans are stigmatized. *The Phoenix Papers, 2*(2), 234-252.

Reysen, S., Snider, J. S., & Branscombe, N. R. (2012). Corporate renaming of stadiums, team identification, and threat to distinctiveness. *Journal of Sport Management, 26*, 350-357. https://doi.org/10.1123/jsm.26.4.350

Rhein, S. (2000). "Being a fan is more than that": Fan-specific involvement with music. *The World of Music, 42*(1), 95-109. https://www.jstor.org/stable/41699316

Richardson, B., Turley, D. (2006). Support your local team: resistance, subculture and the desire for distinction. *Advances in Consumer Research, 33,* 175-180.

Ricks, T., & Wiley, J. (2010). Do baseball fans experience the fan effect? *Proceedings of the Annual Meeting of the Cognitive Science Society, 32*(32), 2176-2181. https://escholarship.org/uc/item/59b863m4

Rieger, D., Frischlich, L., & Oliver, M. B. (2018). Meaningful entertainment experiences and self-transcendence: Cultural variations shape elevation, values, and moral intentions. *International Communication Gazette, 80*(7), 658-676. https://doi.org/10.1177/1748048518802218

Roberts, S. E., Plante, C., Gerbasi, K., & Reysen, S. (2015). Clinical interaction with anthropomorphic phenomenon: Notes for health professionals about interacting with clients who possess this unusual identity. *Health & Social Work, 40,* e42-e50. https://doi.org/10.1093/hsw/hlv020

Robins, R. W., Hendin, H. M., & Trzesniewski, K. H. (2001). Measuring global self-esteem: Construct validation of a single-item measure and the Rosenberg self-esteem scale. *Personality and Social Psychology Bulletin, 27*(2), 151-161. https://doi.org/10.1177/0146167201272002

Robinson, M. J., & Trail, G. T. (2005). Relationships among spectator gender, motives, points of attachment, and sport preference. *Journal of Sport Management, 19*(1), 58-80. https://doi.org/10.1123/jsm.19.1.58

Robinson, M. J., Trail, G. T., Dick, R. J., & Gillentine, A. J. (2005). Fans vs. spectators: an analysis of those who attend intercollegiate football games. *Sport Marketing Quarterly, 14*(1), 43-53.

Robinson, M. J., Trail, G. T., & Kwon, H. (2004). Motives and points of attachment of professional golf spectators. *Sport Management Review, 7*(2), 167-192. https://doi.org/10.1016/S1441-3523(04)70049-2

Röhlcke, S., Bäcklund, C., Sörman, D. E., & Jonsson, B. (2018). Time on task matters most in video game expertise. *PLoS ONE, 13*(10). https://doi.org/10.1371/journal.pone.0206555

Rosenberg, M. (1965). *Rosenberg and the adolescent self-image.* Princeton, NJ: Princeton University Press.

Rosenberger P. J., III, Yun, J. H., Rahman, M. M., Köcher, S., & de Oliveira, M. J. (2019). Gooool: Motivation drivers of attitudinal and behavioral fan loyalty in Brazil. *Revista Brasileira de Marketing, 18*(4), 116-136. https://doi.org/10.5585/remark.v18i4.16386

Roy, D. P., & Goss, B. D. (2007). A conceptual framework of influences on fantasy sports consumption. *The Marketing Management Journal, 17*(2), 96-108.

Rubin, A. M. (1981). An examination of television viewing motivations. *Communication Research, 8*(2), 141-165. https://doi.org/10.1177/009365028100800201

Rubin, A. M. (1983). Television uses and gratifications: The interactions of viewing patterns and motivations. *Journal of Broadcasting, 27*(1), 37-51. https://dx.doi.org/10.1080/08838158309386471

Rubin, A. M. (1984). Ritualized and instrumental television viewing. *Journal of Communication. 34*(3), 67-77. https://doi.org/10.1111/j.1460-2466.1984.tb02174.x

Ruggeri, G. (2020, June 8). *The allocation of time in America, 2003 and 2018.* Retrieved September 15, 2020, from https://ssrn.com/abstract=3622724

Ruihley, B. J., & Billings, A. C. (2012). Infiltrating the boys' club: Motivations for women's fantasy sport participation. *International Review for the Sociology of Sport, 48*(4), 435-452. https://doi.org/10.1177/1012690212443440

Runco, M. A., & Jaeger, G. J. (2012). The standard definition of creativity. *Creativity Research Journal, 24*(1), 92-96. https://doi.org/10.1080/10400419.2012.650092

Russell, D., Peplau, L. A., & Cutrona, C. E. (1980). The revised UCLA loneliness scale: Concurrent and discriminant validity evidence. *Journal of Personality and Social Psychology, 39,* 472-480. https://doi.org/10.1037/0022-3514.39.3.472

Ryan, R. M., & Deci, E. L. (2001). On happiness and human potentials: A review of research on hedonic and eudaimonic well-being. *Annual Review of Psychology, 52*(1), 141-166. https://doi.org/10.1146/annurev.psych.52.1.141

Ryan, R. M., Rigby, C. S., & Przybylski, A. (2006). The motivational pull of video games: A self-determination theory approach. *Motivation and Emotion, 30,* 347-363. https://doi.org/10.1007/s11031-006-9051-8

Ryff, C. D. (1989). Happiness is everything, or is it? Explorations on the meaning of psychological well-being. *Journal of Personality and Social Psychology, 57*(6), 1069-1081. https://doi.org/10.1037/0022-3514.57.6.1069

Ryu, J., & Heo, J. (2016). Relaxation and watching televised sports among older adults. *Educational Gerontology, 42*(2), 71-78. https://dx.doi.org/10.1080/03601277.2015.1071596

Samra, B., & Wos, A. (2014). Consumer in sports: Fan typology analysis. *Journal of Intercultural Management, 6*(4), 263-288. https://doi.org/10.2478/joim-2014-0050

Sandvoss, C. (2005). *Fans: The mirror of consumption.* Polity.

Santos, K. M. L. (2020). The bitches of boys love comics: The pornographic response of Japan's rotten women. *Porn Studies, 7*(3), 279-290. https://doi.org/10.1080/23268743.2020.1726204

Sari, I., Eskiler, E., & Soyer, F. (2011). Does psychological commitment to team enhance self-esteem? An easy way to raise self-esteem. *International Journal of Humantities and Social Science, 19*(1), 187-196.

Savit, L. (2020). Examining the fan labor of episodic TV podcast hosts. *Transformative Works and Cultures, 34.* https://doi.org/10.3983/twc.2020.1721

Scanlan, T. K., Carpenter, P. J., Simons, J. P., Schmidt, G. W., & Keeler, B. (1993). An introduction to the sport commitment model. *Journal of Sport and Exercise Psychology, 15*(1), 1-15. https://doi.org/10.1123/jsep.15.1.1

Scaraboto, D., Ferreira, M. C., & Chung, E. (2017). Materials matter: An exploration of the curatorial practices of consumers as collectors. *Research in Consumer Behavior, 18*(1), 217-243. http://researchonline.ljmu.ac.uk/id/eprint/3884/

Schachter, S. (1964). The interaction of cognitive and physiological determinants of emotional state. *Advances in Experimental Social Psychology, 1,* 49-80. https://doi.org/10.1016/S0065-2601(08)60048-9

Scheff, T. J. (1979). *Catharsis in healing, ritual, and drama.* University of California Press.

Schenk, C. B. (2009). *Pornography as a leisure behavior: An investigation of pornography use and leisure boredom* [Master's thesis, Brigham Young University]. http://hdl.lib.byu.edu/1877/etd3191

Schlenker, B. R. (1980). *Impression management: The self-concept, social identity, and interpersonal research.* Brooks/Cole.

Schroy, C., Plante, C. N., Reysen, S., Roberts, S. E., & Gerbasi, K. C. (2016). Different motivations as predictors of psychological connection to fan interest and fan groups in anime, furry, and fantasy sport fandoms. *The Phoenix Papers, 2*(2), 148-167.

Schmitt, C. D. (2014). *An investigation of involvement in university-affiliated alumni sport fan clubs* (Publication No. 3634731) [Doctoral dissertation, University of Northern Colorado]. ProQuest Dissertations and Theses Global.

Schmitt, M. T., Branscombe, N. R., Postmes, T., & Garcia, A. (2014). The consequences of perceived discrimination for psychological well-being: A

meta-analytic review. *Psychological Bulletin, 140*(4), 921-948.
https://dx.doi.org/10.1037/a0035754

Schnarre, P., & Adam, A. (2018). Parasocial romances as infidelity: Comparing perceptions of real-life, online, and parasocial extradyadic relationships. *Journal of the Indiana Academy of the Social Sciences, 20*(1), 82-93. https://digitalcommons.butler.edu/jiass/vol20/iss1/24

Scroggs, B., & Vennum, A. (2021). Gender and sexual minority group identification as process of identity development during emerging adulthood. *Journal of LGBT Youth, 18*(3), 287-304. https://doi.org/10.1080/19361653.2020.1722780

Seate, A. A., Ma, R., Cohen, E. L., & Iles, I. (2020). Help a fan out? Effects of fandom type and task type on people's behavioral intentions toward different types of fans in a collaborative effort. *Scholarship and Professional Work-Communications,* 380-391. https://digitalcommons.butler.edu/ccom_papers/187

Sedikides, C., & Gregg, A. (2003). Portraits of the self. In M. A. Hogg & J. Cooper (Eds.), *Sage handbook of social psychology* (pp. 110-138). Sage.

Selfhout, M. H. W., Branjie, S. J. T., ter Bogt, T. F. M., & Meeus, W. H. J. (2009). The role of music preferences in early adolescents' friendship formation and stability. *Journal of Adolescence, 32*(1), 95-107. https://doi.org/10.1016/j.adolescence.2007.11.004

Seo, W. J., & Green, B. C. (2008). Development of the motivation scale for sport online consumption. *Journal of Sport Management, 22*(1), 82-109. https://doi.org/10.1123/jsm.22.1.82

Sereda, A. (2019). *"Dirty stories saved my life": Fanfiction as a source of emotional support* [Bachelor's thesis, Charles University]. Charles University Digital Repository. http://hdl.handle.net/20.500.11956/110315

Seungmo, K., Greenwell, T. C., Andrew, D. P. S., Lee, J., & Mahony, D. F. (2008). An analysis of spectator motives in an individual combat sport. A study of mixed martial arts fans. *Sport Marketing Quarterly, 17*(2), 109-119.

Shabahang, R., Bagheri Sheykhangafshe, F., Yousefi Siahkoucheh, A., Mokhtari Chirani, B., Mousavi, S. M., & Akhavan, M. (2020). Role of parasocial interaction with narcotic-addicted celebrities and worshiping them in the prediction of addiction potential. *International Journal of Psychology, 14*(1), 163-191. https://doi.org/10.24200/IJPB.2020.206719.1133

Shabazz, D. L. (2019). *An exploration of viewers' motivations and social interactions before, during and after watching the Super Bowl on television* (Publication No. 22617117) [Doctoral dissertation, Regent University]. ProQuest Dissertations and Theses Global.

Shank, M. D., & Beasley, F. M. (1998). Fan or fanatic: Refining a measure of sports involvement. *Journal of Sport Behavior, 21*(4), 435-443.

Shapiro, S. L., Ridinger, L. L., & Trail, G. T. (2013). An analysis of multiple spectator consumption behaviors, identification, and future behavioral intentions within the context of a new college football program. *Journal of Sport Management, 27*(2), 130-145. https://doi.org/10.1123/jsm.27.2.130

Shaw, J., Plante, C. N., Reysen, S., Roberts, S. E., & Gerbasi, K. C. (2016). Predictors of fan entitlement in three fandoms. *The Phoenix Papers, 2*(2), 203-219.

Shen, X. S., & Yarnal, C. (2010). Blowing open the serious leisure-casual leisure dichotomy: What's in there? *Leisure Sciences, 32*(2), 162-179. https://doi.org/10.1080/01490400903547179

Sheridan, L., Maltby, J., & Gillett, R. (2006). Pathological public figure preoccupation: Its relationship with dissociation and absorption. *Personality and Individual Differences, 41*(3), 525-535. https://doi.org/10.1016/j.paid.2006.02.010

Sherif, M., & Cantril, H. (1947). *The psychology of ego-involvements: Social attitudes and identifications.* John Wiley & Sons.

Sherry, J. L. (2004). Flow and media enjoyment. *Communication Theory, 14*(4), 328-347. https://doi.org/10.1111/j.1468-2885.2004.tb00318.x

Sherry, J. L., Lucas, K., Greenberg, B. S., & Lachlan, K. (2006). Video game uses and gratifications as predictors of use and game preference. In P. Vorderer & J. Bryant (Eds.), *Playing video games: Motives, responses, and consequences* (pp. 213-224). Lawrence Erlbaum.

Shim, H., & Kim, K. J. (2018). An exploration of the motivations for binge-watching and the role of individual differences. *Computers in Human Behavior, 82,* 94-100. https://doi.org/10.1016/j.chb.2017.12.032

Shinew, K. J., & Parry, D. C. (2005). Examining college students' participation in the leisure pursuits of drinking and illegal drug use. *Journal of Leisure Research, 37*(3), 364-386. https://doi.org/10.1080/00222216.2005.11950058

Shipway, R., & Jones, I. (2008). A running commentary: Participant experiences at international distance running events. In J. Ali-Knight, M. Robertson, A. Fyall, & A. Ladkin (Eds.), *International perspectives on festivals and events: Advances in tourism research series* (pp. 173-186). Elsevier Butterworth-Heinemann.

Shore, L. M., Randel, A. E., Chung, B. G., Dean, M. A., Ehrhart, K. H., & Singh, G. (2011). Inclusion and diversity in work groups: A review and model for future research. *Journal of Management, 37,* 1262-1289.

Shuv-Ami, A., & Alon, A. T. (2020). How do you categorize yourself as a sports fan?: A new scale of sports fan social-personal identity salience (FSPIS) and its consequences. *Communication and Sport.* Advance online publication. https://doi.org/10.1177/2167479520967278

Shuv-Ami, A., Alon, A. T., Loureiro, S. M. C., & Kaufmann, H. R. (2020). A new love-hate scale for sports fans. *International Journal of Sports Marketing and Sponsorship, 21*(3), 543-560. https://doi.org/10.1108/IJSMS-11-2019-0122

Shuv-Ami, A., Thrassou, A., & Vrontis, D. (2015). Fans' brand commitment to basketball teams: Establishing the validity and reliability of a new multidimensional scale. *Journal of Customer Behavior, 14*(4), 311-329. https://doi.org/10.1362/147539215X14503490289341

Sidani, A. (2019). *"You're on one side or the other. You're either a Leafs fan or a Sabres fan". An interpretive study of Buffalo Sabres and Toronto Maple Leafs fans in Fort Erie, Ontario* [Master's thesis, Brock University]. http://hdl.handle.net/10464/14592

Sierra, J. J., Taute, H. A., Heiser, R. S. (2012). Explaining NFL fans' purchase intentions for revered and reviled teams: A dual-process perspective. *Journal of Retail and Consumer Services, 19*(3), 332-342. https://doi.org/10.1016/j.jretconser.2012.03.007

Silveira, M. P., Cardoso, M. V., & Quevedo-Silva, F. (2019). Factors influencing attendance at stadiums and arenas. *Marketing Intelligence and Planning, 37*(1), 50-65. https://doi.org/10.1108/MIP-02-2018-0048

Silver, N., & Slater, M. D. (2019). A safe space for self-expansion: Attachment and motivation to engage and interact with the story world. *Journal of Social and Personal Relationships, 36*(11-12), 3492-3514. https://doi.org/10.1177/0265407519826345

Silvia, P. J., Fayn, K., Nusbaum, E. C., & Beaty, R. E. (2015). Openness to experience and awe in response to nature and music: Personality and profound aesthetic experiences. *Psychology of Aesthetics, Creativity, and the Arts, 9*(4), 376-384. https://doi.org/10.1037/aca0000028

Singh, R. P., & Banerjee, N. (2019). Exploring the influence of celebrity worship on brand attitude, advertisement attitude, and purchase intention. *Journal of Promotion Management, 25*(2), 225-251. https://doi.org/10.1080/10496491.2018.1443311

Sivan, A., Tam, V., Siu, G., & Stebbins, R. (2019). Adolescents' choice and pursuit of their most important and interesting leisure activities. *Leisure Studies, 38*(1), 98-113. https://doi.org/10.1080/02614367.2018.1539867

Sjöblom, M., Macey, J., & Hamari, J. (2020). Digital athletics in analogue stadiums: Comparing gratifications for engagement between live attendance and online esports spectating. *Internet Research, 30*(3), 713-735. https://doi.org/10.1108/INTR-07-2018-0304

Skov, M., & Nadal, M. (2020). There are no aesthetic emotions: Comment on Menninghaus et al. (2019). *Psychological Review, 127*(4), 640-649. httpS://dx.doi.org/10.1037/rev0000187

Sloan, L. R. (1989). The motives of sports fans. In J. H. Goldstein (Ed.), *Sports, games, and play: Social and psychological viewpoints* (pp. 175-240). Psychology Press.

Slotter, E. B., Duffy, C. W., & Gardner, W. L. (2014). Balancing the need to be me with the need to be we: Applying optimal distinctiveness theory to the understanding of multiple motivates within romantic relationships. *Journal of Experimental Social Psychology, 52*, 71-81.

Smart, L., & Wegner, D. M. (1999). Covering up what can't be seen: Concealable stigma and mental control. *Journal of Personality and Social Psychology, 77*(3), 474-486. https://doi.org/10.1037/0022-3514.77.3.474

Smeekes, A., Jetten, J., Verkuyten, M., Wohl, M.J.A., Jasinskaja-Lahti, I., Ariyanto, A... van der Bles, A. M. (2018). Regaining in-group continuity in times of anxiety about the group's future: A study on the role of collective nostalgia across 27 countries. *Social Psychology, 49*(6), 311-329. https://doi.org/10.1027/1864-9335/a000350

Smith, G. J. (1988). The noble sports fan. *Journal of Sport and Social Issues, 12*(1), 54-65. https://doi.org/10.1177/019372358801200105

Smith, J. F., & Abt, V. (1984). Gambling as play. *The Annals of the American Academy of Political and Social Science, 474*(1), 122-132. https://www.jstor.org/stable/1044369

Smith, S., Fisher, D., & Cole, S. J. (2007). The lived meanings of fanaticism: Understanding the complex role of labels and categories in defining the self in consumer culture. *Consumption, Markets and Culture, 10*(2), 77-94. https://doi.org/10.1080/10253860701256125

Snyder, C. R., & Fromkin, H. L. (1980). *Uniqueness: The human pursuit of difference*. Plenum Press.

Snyder, C. R., Lassegard, M., & Ford, C. E. (1986). Distancing after group success and failure: Basking in reflected glory and cutting off reflected failure. *Journal of Personality and Social Psychology, 51*(2), 382-388. https://doi.org/10.1037/0022-3514.51.2.382

Snyder, M., & Swann, W. (1976). When actions reflect attitudes: The politics of impression management. *Journal of Personality and Social Psychology, 34*(5), 1034-1042.

Song, W., & Fox, J. (2016). Playing for love in a romantic video game: Avatar identification, parasocial relationships, and Chinese women's romantic beliefs. *Mass Communication and Society, 19*(2), 197-215. https://doi.org/10.1080/15205436.2015.1077972

Sotomayor, S., & Barbieri, C. (2016). An exploratory examination of serious surfers: Implications for the surf tourism industry. *International Journal of Tourism Research, 18*(1), 62-73. https://doi.org/10.1002/jtr.2033

Spinda, J. S. W., Earnheardt, A. C., & Hugenberg, L. W. (2009). Checkered flags and mediated friendships: Parasocial interaction among NASCAR fans. *Journal of Sports Media, 4*(2), 31-55. https://doi.org/10.1353/jsm.0.0041

Springer, K. W., & Hauser, R. M. (2006). An assessment of the construct validity of Ryff's scales of psychological well-being: Method, mode, and measurement effects. *Social Science Research, 35*(4), 1080-1102. https://doi.org/10.1016/j.ssresearch.2005.07.004

Staiger, J. (2005). Cabinets of transgression: Collecting and arranging Hollywood images. *Participations, 1*(5). https://www.participations.org/volume%201/issue%203/1_03_staiger_article.htm

Stebbins, R. A. (1982). Serious leisure: A conceptual statement. *Pacific Sociological Review, 25*(2), 251-272. https://doi.org/10.2307/1388726

Stebbins, R. A. (1992). *Amateurs, professionals, and serious leisure*. Montreal, QC: McGill-Queen's University Press.

Stebbins, R. A. (1997). Casual leisure: a conceptual statement. *Leisure Studies, 16*(1), 17-25. https://doi.org/10.1080/026143697375485

Stebbins, R. A. (2001). Serious leisure. *Society, 38*(4), 53-57. https://doi.org/10.1007/s12115-001-1023-8

Stebbins, R. A. (2007). *Serious leisure. A perspective for our time*. Transaction Publishers.

Stebbins, R. A., Rojek, C., & Sullivan, A. M. (2006). Deviant leisure. *Leisure/Loisir, 30*(1), 3-5.

Steenkamp, E. (2018). *"Don't forget to be awesome". The role of social learning as a component of belonging in virtual communities: A case study of the Youtube fan community "Nerdighteria"* [Master's thesis, Rhodes University]. http://hdl.handle.net/10962/63753

Steger, M. F., Frazier, P., Oishi, S., & Kaler, M. (2006). The meaning in life questionnaire: Assessing the presence of and search for meaning in life.

Journal of Counseling Psychology, 53(1), 80-93.
https://doi.org/10.1037/0022-0167.53.1.80

Sternberg, R. J. (2006). The nature of creativity. *Creativity Research Journal, 18*(1), 87-98. https://doi.org/10.1207/s15326934crj1801_10

Stevens, S., & Rosenberger, P. J. (2012). The influence of involvement, following sport and fan identification on fan loyalty: An Australian perspective. *International Journal of Sports Marketing and Sponsorship, 13*(3), 221-235. https://doi.org/10.1108/IJSMS-13-03-2012-B006

Stever, G. S. (1991). The celebrity appeal questionnaire. *Psychological Reports, 68*(3), 859-866. https://doi.org/10.2466/pr0.1991.68.3.859

Stever, G. S. (2008). The celebrity appeal questionnaire: Sex, entertainment, or leadership. *Psychological Reports, 103*(1), 113-120.
https://doi.org/10.2466/pr0.103.1.113-120

Stock, M. L., Peterson, L. M., Molloy, B. K., & Lambert, S. F. (2017). Past racial discrimination exacerbates the effects of racial exclusion on negative affect, perceived control, and alcohol-risk cognitions among black young adults. *Journal of Behavioral Medicine, 40,* 377-391.
http://dx.doi.org/10.1007/s10865-016-9793-z

Sung, J., Son, J., & Choi, Y. (2017). Relationship between motivational factors of online sport consumption and future behavioral intentions among Korean college sport fans. *Journal of Physical Education and Sport, 17*(1), 269-277.
https://doi.org/10.7752/jpes.2017.01040

Surratt, B. (2021). *Visiting Jane: Jane Austen, fan culture, and literary tourism* [Senior thesis, University of South Carolina]. Scholar Commons.
https://scholarcommons.sc.edu/senior_theses/393

Sutton, W. A., McDonald, M. A., Milne, G. R., & Cimperman, J. (1997). Creating and fostering fan identification in professional sports. *Sport Marketing Quarterly, 6*(1), 15-22.

Swami, V., Taylor, R., & Carvalho, C. (2009). Acceptance of cosmetic surgery and celebrity worship: Evidence of associations among female undergraduates. *Personality and Individual Differences, 47*(8), 869-872.
https://doi.org/10.1016/j.paid.2009.07.006

Swami, V., Taylor, R., & Carvalho, C. (2011). Body dissatisfaction assessed by the Photographic Figure Rating Scale is associated with sociocultural, personality, and media influences. *Scandinavian Journal of Psychology, 52*(1), 57-63. https://doi.org/10.1111/j.1467-9450.2010.00836.x

Swanson, S., & Kent, A. (2015). Fandom in the workplace: Multi-target identification in professional team sports. *Journal of Sport Management, 29*(4), 461-477. https://dx.doi.org/10.1123/JSM.2014-0132

Swanson, S. R., Davis, J. C., & Zhao, Y. (2008). Art for art's sake? An examination of motives for arts performance attendance. *Nonprofit and Voluntary Sector Quarterly, 37*(2), 300-323. https://doi.org/10.1177/0899764007310418

Tabata, R. (1989). Implications of special interest tourism for interpretation and resource conservation. In D. Uzzell (Ed.), *Heritage interpretation* (pp. 68-77). Belhaven Press.

Tabbah, R., Chung, J. J., & Miranda, A. H. (2016). Ethnic identity and discrimination: An exploration of the rejection-identification model in Arab American adolescents. *Identity, 16*(4), 319-334. https://doi.org/10.1080/15283488.2016.1231609

Tachis, S., & Tzetzis, G. (2015). The relationship among fans' involvement, psychological commitment, and loyalty in professional sport teams. *International Journal of Sport Management Recreation and Tourism, 18,* 1-25. https://www.ijsmart.eu/onlinepic/vol18_a_Tachis%20Stavros.pdf

Tacon, R., & Vainker, S. (2017). Fantasy sport: A systematic review and new research directions. *European Sport Management Quarterly, 17*(5), 558-589. https://doi.org/10.1080/16184742.2017.1347192

Tague, A. M., Reysen, S., & Plante, C. (2020). Belongingness as a mediator of the relationship between felt stigma and identification in fans. *The Journal of Social Psychology, 160*(3), 324-331. https://doi.org/10.1080/00224545.2019.1667748

Tajfel, H., Billig, M. G., Bundy, R. P., & Flament, C. (1971). Social cagetorization and intergroup behavior. *European Journal of Social Psychology, 1*(2), 149-178.

Tajfel, H., & Turner, J. C. (1979). An integrative theory of intergroup conflict. In W.Austin & S. Worchel (Eds.), *The social psychology of intergroup relations* (pp. 33-47). Brooks/Cole.

Tan, E. S.-H. (2008). Entertainment is emotion: The functional architecture of the entertainment experience. *Media Psychology, 11*(1), 28-51. https://doi.org/10.1080/15213260701853161

Tapp, A. (2004). The loyalty of football fans – we'll support you evermore? *Database Marketing and Customer Strategy Management, 11*(3), 203-215. https://doi.org/10.1057/palgrave.dbm.3240221

Tapp, A., & Clowes, J. (2002). From "carefree casuals" to "professional wanderers": Segmentation possibilities for football supporters. *European Journal of Marketing 36*(11/12), 1248-1269. https://doi.org/10.1108/03090560210445164

Taylor, L. D. (2021). Eudaimonia, hedonia, and fan behavior: Examining the motives of fans of fictional texts. *Psychology of Aesthetics, Creativity, and the Arts, 15*(2), 264-271. https://dx.doi.org/10.1037/aca0000270

Taylor, L. D., & Gil-Lopez, T. (2020). Personality traits and fans' motives for attention to fictional narratives. In R. A. Dunn (Ed.), *Multidisciplinary perspectives on media fandom* (pp. 20-36). IGI Global. https://dx.doi.org/10.4018/978-1-7998-3323-9.ch002

Taylor, N. (2019). *The fantasy of embodiment: Afrofuturism, cosplay and the Afrodiaspora* [Master's thesis, Concordia University]. Unpublished master's thesis. https://spectrum.library.concordia.ca/985846/9/Taylor_MA_F2019.pdf

Theodorakis, N. D., Alexandris, K., Tsigilis, N., & Karvounis, S. (2013). Predicting spectators' behavioural intentions in professional football: The role of satisfaction and service quality. *Sport Management Review, 16*(1), 85-96. https://doi.org/10.1016/j.smr.2012.05.004

Theodorakis, N. D., Dimmock, J., Wann, D., & Barlas, A. (2010). Psychometric evaluation of the team identification scale among Greek sport fans: A cross-validation approach. *European Sport Management Quarterly, 10*(3), 289-305. https://doi.org/10.1080/16184741003770180

Thompson, C. J., Rindfleisch, A., & Arsel, Z. (2006). Emotional branding and the strategic value of the doppelgänger brand image. *Journal of Marketing, 70*(1), 50-64. https://doi.org/10.1509/jmkg.70.1.050.qxd

Thomson, M. (2006). Human brands: Investigating antecedents to consumers' strong attachments to celebrities. *Journal of Marketing, 70*(3), 104-119. https://doi.org/10.1509/jmkg.70.3.104

Thorne, S., & Bruner, G. C. (2006). An exploratory investigation of the characteristics of consumer fanaticism. *Qualitative Market Research, 9*(1), 51-72. https://doi.org/10.1108/13522750610640558

Tian, K. T., Bearden, W. O., & Hunter, G. L. (2001). Consumers' need for uniqueness: Scale development and validation. *Journal of Consumer Research, 28*(1), 50-66. https://doi.org/10.1086/321947

Tinson, J., Sinclair, G., & Kolyperas, D. (2017). Sport fandom and parenthood. *European Sport Management Quarterly, 17*(3), 370-391. https://doi.org/10.1080/16184742.2017.1280068

Tobacyk, J. J., Myers, H., & Bailey, L. (1981). Field-dependence, sensation-seeking, and preference of paintings. *Journal of Personality Assessment, 45*(3), 270-277. https://doi.org/10.1207/s15327752jpa4503_8

Todd, B. M., & Soule, C. A. A. (2018). Fans and brands: Delineating between fandoms, brand communities, and brand publics. In C. L. Wang (Ed.),

Exploring the rise of fandom in contemporary consumer culture (pp. 18-34). IGI Global. https://doi.org/10.4018/978-1-5225-9282-2.ch033

Todd, C. (2008, May 17). *Thank you. Posting to improv everywhere homepage.* Retrieved May 21, 2008, from http://improveverywhere.com

Toder-Alon, A., & Brunel, F. F. (2018). Peer-to-peer word-of-mouth: word-of-mouth extended to group online exchange. *Online Information Review, 42*(2), 176-190. https://doi.org/10.1108/OIR-09-2016-0290

Toh, W. (2016). Gamers and their weapons: An appraisal perspective on weapons manipulation in video games. In S. Y. Tettegah & W. D. Huang (Eds.), *Emotions, technology, and digital games: A volume in emotions and technology* (pp. 83-113). Elsevier. https://doi.org/10.1016/B978-0-12-801738-8.00005-1

Tokuyama, S., & Greenwell, T. C. (2011). Examining similarities and differences in consumer motivation for playing and watching soccer. *Sport Marketing Quarterly, 20*(3), 148-156.

Tomasino, B., Guatto, E., Rumiati, R. I., & Fabbro, F. (2012). The role of volleyball expertise in motor simulation. *Acta Psychologica, 139*(1), 1-6. https://doi.org/10.1016/j.actpsy.2011.11.006

Tosenberger, C. (2008). "Oh my god, the fanfiction!": Dumbledore's outing and the online Harry Potter fandom. *Children's Literature Association Quarterly, 33*(2), 200-206. https://doi.org/10.1353/chq.0.0015

Trail, G. T., Anderson, D. F., & Fink, J. (2000). A theoretical model of sport spectator consumption behavior. *International Journal of Sport Management, 1,* 154-180.

Trail, G. T., Anderson, D. F., & Lee, D. (2017). A longitudinal study of team-fan role identity on self-reported attendance behavior and future intentions. *Journal of Amateur Sport, 3*(1), 27-49. https://doi.org/10.17161/jas.v0i0.5712

Trail, G. T., Fink, J. S., & Anderson, D. F. (2003). Sport spectator consumption behavior. *Sport Marketing Quarterly, 12*(1), 8-17.

Trail, G. T., & James, J. D. (2001). The motivation scale for sport consumption: Assessment of the scale's psychometric properties. *Journal of Sport Behavior, 24*(1), 108-127.

Trail, G. T., Kim, Y., Kwon, H. H., Harrolle, M. G., Braunstein-Minkove, J. R., & Dick, R. (2012). The effects of vicarious achievement on BIRGing and CORFing: Testing moderating and mediating effects of team identification. *Sport Management Review, 15*(3), 345-354. https://doi.org/10.1016/j.smr.2011.11.002

Trail, G. T., Robinson, M. J., Dick, R. J., & Gillentine, A. J. (2003). Motives and points of attachment: Fans versus spectators in intercollegiate athletics. *Sport Marketing Quarterly, 12*(4), 217-227.

Tropp, L. R., & Wright, S. C. (2001). Ingroup identification as the inclusion of ingroup in the self. *Personality and Social Psychology Bulletin, 27*(5), 585-600. https://doi.org/10.1177/0146167201275007

Trzcińska, J. (2018). *Polish k-pop fandom: phenomenon, structure & communication.* The Association of Pop Culture Researchers and Pop-cultural Education. https://depot.ceon.pl/handle/123456789/17059

Tsaur, S.-H., & Huang, C.-C. (2020). Serious tourists or casual tourist? Development and validation of a scale to measure tourists' serious/casual participation. *Current Issues in Tourism, 23*(2), 217-232. https://doi.org/10.1080/13683500.2018.1495697

Tsay-Vogel, M., & Krakowiak, M. (2016). Effects of hedonic and eudaimonic motivations on film enjoyment through moral disengagement. *Communication Research Reports, 33*(1), 54-60. https://doi.org/10.1080/08824096.2015.1117443

Tsay-Vogel, M., & Sanders, M. S. (2017). Fandom and the search for meaning: Examining communal involvement with popular media beyond pleasure. *Psychology of Popular Media Culture, 6*(1), 32-47. https://doi.org/10.1037/ppm0000085

Tsiotsou, R. (2010). An empirical analysis of the brand personality effects on brand involvement. *Academic Public Administration Studies Archive.* http://www.apas.admpubl.snspa.ro/handle/2010/223

Tsiotsou, R. H. (2017). Predicting sport team loyalty: High and low scenarios. In C. L. Campbell (Ed.), *The customer is NOT always right? Marketing orientations in a dynamic business world* (pp. 200-204). Springer.

Tuffiash, M., Roring, R. W., & Ericsson, K. A. (2007). Expert performance in SCRABBLE: Implications for the study of the structure and acquisition of complex skills. *Journal of Experimental Psychology: Applied, 13,* 124-134. https://doi.org/10.1037/1076-898X.13.3.124

Tukachinsky, R. (2010). Para-romantic love and para-friendships: Development and assessment of a multiple-parasocial relationships scale. *American Journal of Media Psychology, 3*(1/2), 73-94.

Tukachinsky, R., & Stever, G. (2019). Theorizing development of parasocial engagement. *Communication Theory, 29*(3), 297-318. https://doi.org/10.1093/ct/qty032

Turner, J. C., Hogg, M. A., Oakes, P. J., Reicher, S. D., & Wetherell, M. (1987). *Rediscovering the social group: A self-categorization theory.* Blackwell.

Ulker-Demirel, E., & Ciftci, G. (2020). A systematic literature review of the theory of planned behavior in tourism, leisure and hospitality management research. *Journal of Hospitality and Tourism Management, 43,* 209-219. https://doi.org/10.1016/j.jhtm.2020.04.003

Underwood, M. (2017). Exploring the social lives of image and performance enhancing drugs: An online ethnography of the Zyzz fandom of recreational bodybuilders. *International Journal of Drug Policy, 39,* 78-85. https://doi.org/10.1016/j.drugpo.2016.08.012

Underwood, M., & Olson, R. (2019). 'Manly tears exploded from my eyes, lets feel together brahs': Emotion and masculinity within an online body building community. *Journal of Sociology, 55*(1), 90-107. https://doi.org/10.1177/1440783318766610

Unruh, D. R. (1980). The nature of social worlds. *Sociological Perspectives, 23*(3), 271-296. https://doi.org/10.2307/1388823

Unsworth, K. (2001). Unpacking creativity. *Academy of Management Review, 26*(2), 289-297. https://doi.org/10.5465/amr.2001.4378025

Uvinha, R. R., Chan, C., Man, C., & Marafa, L. M. (2018). Sport tourism: A comparative analysis of residents from Brazil and Hong Kong. *Revista Brasileira de Pesquisa em Turismo, 12*(1). https://doi.org/10.7784/rbtur.v12i1.1374

Uysal, M., & Jurowski, C. (1994). Testing the push and pull factors. *Annals of Tourism Research, 21*(4), 844-846. https://doi.org/10.1016/0160-7383(94)90091-4

Valkenburg, P. M., & Peter, J. (2006). Fantasy and imagination. In J. Bryant & P.

Vorderer (Eds.), *Psychology of entertainment* (pp. 105-117). Lawrence Erlbaum.

Vallerand, R. J. (1983). The effect of differential amounts of positive verbal feedback on the intrinsic motivation of male hockey players. *Journal of Sport and Exercise Psychology, 5*(1), 100-107. https://doi.org/10.1123/jsp.5.1.100

Vallerand, R. J., Blanchard, C., Mageau, G. A., Koestner, R., Ratelle, C., Gangné, M., & Marsolais, J. (2003). Les passions de l'âme: On obsessive and harmonious passion. *Journal of Personality and Social Psychology, 85*(4), 756-767. https://doi.org/10.1037/0022-3514.85.4.756

Vally, Z., Moussa, D., Khalil, E., Al Fahel, A., Al Azry, N., & Jafar, N. (2021). Celebrity worship in the United Arab Emirates: An examination of its association with problematic internet use, maladaptive daydreaming, and desire for fame. *Psychology of Popular Media, 10*(1), 124-134. https://doi.org/10.1037/ppm0000276

van Zyl, L. E., & Rothmann, S. (2014). Towards happiness interventions: Construct clarification and intervention methodologies. *Journal of Psychology in Africa, 24*(4), 327-341. https://doi.org/10.1080/14330237.2014.980621

Vardell, E., Thomas, P., & Wang, T. (2020). Information seeking behavior of cosplayers. *Professional Association for Information Science & Technology, 57.* https://doi.org/10.1002/pra2.401

Vigil, J. D. (1988). Group processes and street identity: Adolescent Chicano gang members. *Journal of the Society for Psychological Anthropology, 15*(4), 421-445. https://doi.org/10.1525/eth.1988.16.4.02a00040

Vignoles, V. L., Regalia, C., Manzi, C., Golledge, J., & Scabini, E. (2006). Beyond self-esteem: Influence of multiple motives on identity construction. *Journal of Personality and Social Psychology, 90*(2), 308-333. https://doi.org/10.1037/0022-3514.90.2.308

Vinney, C., Dill-Shackleford, K. E., Plante, C. N., & Bartsch, A. (2019). Development and validation of a measure of popular media fan identity and its relationship to well-being. *Psychology of Popular Media Culture, 8*(3), 296-307. https://doi.org/10.1037/ppm0000188

Vorderer, P. (2011). What's next? Remarks on the current vitalization of entertainment theory. *Journal of Media Psychology, 23*(1), 60-63. https://doi.org/10.1027/1864-1105/a000034

Vorderer, P., & Groeben, N. (1992). Audience research: What the humanistic and the social science approaches could learn from each other. *Poetics, 21,* 361-376. https://doi.org/10.1016/0304-422X(92)90014-T

Vorderer, P., & Knolbloch, S. (2000). Conflict and suspense in drama. In D. Zillman & P. Vorderer (Eds.), *Media entertainment: The psychology of its appeal* (pp. 59-72). Lawrence Erlbaum.

Vorderer, P., & Reinecke, L. (2015). From mood to meaning: The changing model of the user in entertainment research. *Communication Theory, 25*(4), 447-453. https://doi.org/10.1111/comt.12082

Wagoner, J., Belavadi, S., & Jung, J. (2017). Social identity uncertainty: Conceptualization, measurement, and construct validity. *Self and Identity, 16*(5), 505-530. https://doi.org/10.1080/15298868.2016.1275762

Wakefield, K. L., & Wann, D. L. (2006). An examination of dysfunctional sport fans: Method of classification and relationships with problem behaviors. *Journal of Leisure Research, 38*(3), 168-186.

Wallace, E., Buil, I., de Chernatony, L., & Hogan, M. (2014). Who "likes" you... and why? A typology of Facebook fans. *Journal of Advertising Research, 54*(1), 92-109. https://doi.org/10.2501/JAR-54-1-092-109

Walsh, D. W., Green, B. C., & Cottingham, M. (2017). Exploring the efficacy of youth sport camps to build customer relationships. *Leisure Studies, 36*(5), 657-669. https://doi.org/10.1080/02614367.2016.1240222

Wang, B. (2019). *Entertainment enjoyment as social: Identifying relatedness enjoyment in entertainment consumption* (Publication No. 13896577) [Doctoral dissertation, University of California, Davis]. ProQuest Dissertations and Theses Global.

Wang, P.-T. (2010). *Affective otaku labor: The circulation and modulation of affect in the anime industry* (Publication No. 3426892) [Doctoral dissertation, City University of New York]. ProQuest Dissertations and Theses Global.

Wang, R. T., Zhang, J. J., & Tsuji, Y. (2011). Examining fan motives and loyalty for the Chinese professional baseball league in Taiwan. *Sport Management Review, 14*(4), 347-360. https://doi.org/10.1016/j.smr.2010.12.001

Wang, T. R., Min, S. D., & Kim, S. K. (2013). Fulfillment of sport spectator motives: The mediation effect of well-being. *Social Behavior and Personality, 41*(9), 1421-1434. http://dx.doi.org/10.2224/sbp.2013.41.9.1421

Wang, W. (2019). *Is binge watching bad for you? Escapism, stress, self-control and gratifications?* [Master's thesis, Brigham Young University]. https://scholarsarchive.byu.edu/etd/7757

Wann, D. L. (1993). Aggression among highly identified spectators as a function of their need to maintain positive social identity. *Journal of Sport and Social Issues, 17*(2), 134-143. https://doi.org/10.1177/019372359301700207

Wann, D. L. (1994). The "noble" sports fan: The relationships between team identification, self-esteem, and aggression. *Perceptual and Motor Skills, 78*(3), 864-866. https://doi.org/10.1177/003151259407800337

Wann, D. L. (1995). Preliminary validation of the sport fan motivation scale. *Journal of Sport and Social Issues, 19*(4), 377-396. https://doi.org/10.1177/019372395019004004

Wann, D. L. (2005). Essay: Aggression in sport. *The Lancet, 366,* s31-s32. https://doi.org/10.1016/S0140-6736(05)67837-3

Wann, D. L. (2006a). Understanding the positive social psychological benefits of sport team identification: The team identification—social psychological health model. *Group Dynamics: Theory, Research, and Practice, 10*(4), 272-296. https://doi.org/10.1037/1089-2699.10.4.272

Wann, D. L. (2006b). Examining the potential causal relationship between sport team identification and psychological well-being. *Journal of Sport Behavior, 29*(1), 79-95.

Wann, D. L., Allen, B., & Rochelle, A. R. (2004). Using sport fandom as an escape: Searching for relief from under-stimulation and over-stimulation. *International Sports Journal, 8*(1), 104-113.

Wann, D. L., Bayens, C., & Driver, A. (2004). Likelihood of attending a sporting event as a function of ticket scarcity and team identification. *Sport Marketing Quarterly, 13*(4), 209-215.

Wann, D. L., Brame, E., Clarkson, M., Brooks, D., & Waddill, P. J. (2008). College student attendance at sporting events and the relationship between sport team identification and social psychological health. *Journal of Intercollegiate Sport, 1*(2), 242–254. https://doi.org/10.1123/jis.1.2.242

Wann, D. L., & Branscombe, N. R. (1990). Die-hard and fair-weather fans: Effects of identification on BIRGing and CORFing tendencies. *Journal of Sport and Social issues, 14*(2), 103-117. https://doi.org/10.1177/019372359001400203

Wann, D. L., & Branscombe, N. R. (1993). Sports fans: Measuring degree of identification with their team. *International Journal of Sport Psychology, 24*(1), 1-17.

Wann, D. L., Brewer, K. R., & Royalty, J. L. (1999). Sport fan motivation: Relationships with team identification and emotional reactions to sporting events. *International Sports Journal, 3*(2), 8-18.

Wann, D. L., Carlson, J. D., & Schrader, M. P. (1999). The impact of team identification on the hostile and instrumental verbal aggression of sport spectators. *Journal of Social Behavior and Personality, 14*(2), 279-286.

Wann, D. L., Culver, Z., Akanda, R., Daglar, M., De Divitiis, C., & Smith, A. (2005). The effects of team identification and game outcome on willingness to consider anonymous acts of hostile aggression. *Journal of Sport Behavior, 28*(3), 282–294.

Wann, D. L., Dimmock, J. A., & Grove, J. R. (2003). Generalizing the team identification-psychological health model to a different sport and culture: The case of Australian rules football. *Group Dynamics, Theory, Research, and Practice, 7*(4), 289-296. https://doi.org/10.1037/1089-2699.7.4.289

Wann, D. L., Dolan, T. J., McGeorge, K. K., & Allison, J. A. (1994). Relationships between spectator identification and spectators' perceptions of influence, spectators' emotions, and competition outcome. *Journal of Sport and Exercise Psychology, 16*(4), 347-364. https://dx.doi.org/10.1123/jsep.16.4.347

Wann, D. L., Dunham, M. D., Byrd, M. L., & Keenan, B. L. (2004). The five-factor model of personality and the psychological health of highly identified sport fans. *International Sports Journal, 8*(2), 28-36.

Wann, D. L., & Ensor, C. L. (2001). The psychological health of "joiners". *Psychological Reports, 89*(1), 122-122. https://doi.org/10.2466/pr0.2001.89.1.122

Wann, D. L., Fahl, C. L., Erdmann, J. B., & Littleton, J. D. (1999). Relationship between identification with the role of sport fan and trait aggression. *Perceptual and Motor Control, 88*(3), 1296-1298. https://doi.org/10.2466%2Fpms.1999.88.3c.1296

Wann, D. L., Grieve, F. G., Zapalac, R. K., & Pease, D. G. (2008). Motivational profiles of sport fans of different sports. *Sport Marketing Quarterly, 17*(1), 6-19.

Wann, D. L., Hackathorn, J., & Sherman, M. R. (2017). Testing the team identification–social psychological health model: Mediational relationships among team identification, sport fandom, sense of belonging, and meaning in life. *Group Dynamics: Theory, Research, and Practice, 21*(2), 94-107. https://doi.org/10.1037/gdn0000066

Wann, D. L., Hunter, J. L., Ryan, J. A., & Wright, L. A. (2001). The relationship between team identification and willingness of sport fans to consider illegally assisting their team. *Social Behavior and Personality, 29*(6), 531-536. https://doi.org/10.2224/sbp.2001.29.6.531

Wann, D. L., & James, J. D. (2019). *Sport fans: The psychology and social impact of fandom*. Routledge.

Wann, D. L., Keenan, B., & Page, L. (2009). Testing the team identification-social psychological health Model: Examining non-marquee sports, seasonal differences, and multiple teams. *Journal of Sport Behavior, 32*(1), 112-124.

Wann, D. L., Martin, J., Grieve, F. G., & Gardner, L. (2008). Social connections at sporting events: Attendance and its positive relationship with state social psychological well-being. *North American Journal of Psychology, 10*(2), 229-238.

Wann, D. L., Metcalf, L. A., Adcock, M. L., Choi, C.-C., Dallas, M. B., & Slaton, E. (1997). Language of sport fans: Sportugese revisited. *Perceptual and Motor Skills, 85*(3), 1107-1110. https://doi.org/10.2466/pms.1997.85.3.1107

Wann, D. L., Peterson, R. R., Cothran, C., & Dykes, M. (1999). Sport fan aggression and anonymity: The importance of team identification. *Social Behavior and Personality, 27*(6), 597-602. https://doi.org/10.2224/sbp.1999.27.6.597

Wann, D. L., & Pierce, S. (2003). Measuring sport team identification and commitment: An empirical comparison of the sport spectator identification scale and the psychological commitment to team scale. *North American Journal of Psychology, 5,* 365-372.

Wann, D. L., & Polk, J. (2007). The positive relationship between sport team identification and belief in the trustworthiness of others. *North American Journal of Psychology, 9*(3), 251-256.

Wann, D. L., & Schrader, M. P. (1997). Team identification and the enjoyment of watching a sporting event. *Perceptual and Motor Skills, 84*(3), 954-954. https://doi.org/10.2466/pms.1997.84.3.954

Wann, D. L., Schrader, M. P., & Carlson, J. D. (2000). The verbal aggression of sport spectator: A comparison of hostile and instrumental motives. *International Sports Journal, 4,* 56-63.

Wann, D. L., Schrader, M. P., & Wilson, A. M. (1999). Sport fan motivation: Questionnarie validation, comparisons by sport, and relationship to athletic motivation. *Journal of Sport Behavior, 22*(1), 114-139.

Wann, D. L., Shelton, S., Smith, T., & Walker, R. (2002). Relationship between team identification and trait aggression: A replication. *Perceptual and Motor Skills, 94*(2), 595-598. https://doi.org/10.2466%2Fpms.2002.94.2.595

Wann, D. L., Waddill, P. J., Bono, D., Scheuchner, H., Ruga, K. (2017). Sport spectator verbal aggression: The impact of team identification and fan dysfunction on fans' abuse of opponents and officials. *Journal of Sport Behavior, 40*(4), 423-443.

Wann, D. L., Walker, R. G., Cygan, J., Kawase, I., & Ryan, J. (2005). Further replication of the relationship between team identification and social psychological well-being: Examining non-classroom settings. *North American Journal of Psychology, 7*(3), 361-365.

Wann, D. L., & Weaver, S. (2009). Understanding the relationship between sport team identification and dimensions of social well-being. *North American Journal of Psychology, 11*(2), 219-230.

Wann, D. L., & Wilson, A. M. (1999). Relationship between aesthetic motivation and preferences for aggressive and nonaggressive sports. *Perceptual and Motor Skills, 89*(3), 931-934. https://doi.org/10.2466/pms.1999.89.3.931

Ward, R. E. (2002). Fan violence: Social problem or moral panic? *Aggression and Violent Behavior, 7*(5), 543-475. https://doi.org/10.1016/S1359-1789(01)00075-1

Wasserberg, M. (2009). Understanding sports spectator's motives for attending live events: a study of darts fans in the UK. *Birkerbeck Sport Business Centre Research Paper Series, 2*(3), 2-79.

Watkins, M. (1999, April). *Ways of experiencing leisure* [Paper presentation]. ANZALS Conference, University of Waitkato Hamilton, New Zealand.

Weiner, B. (1981). The role of affect in sport psychology. In G. Roberts & D. Landers (Eds.), *Psychology of motor behavior and sport-1980*. Human Kinetics.

Wenger, E. (1998). *Communities of practice: Learning, meaning, and identity*. Cambridge University Press. https://doi.org/10.1017/CBO9780511803932

Wenner, L. A., & Gantz, W. (1989). The audience experience with sports on television. In L. A. Wenner (Ed.), *Media, sports, & society* (pp. 241-269). Sage.

Wiid, J. A., & Cant, M. C. (2015). Sport fan motivation: Are you going to the game? *International Journal of Academic Research in Business and Social Sciences, 5*(1), 383-398. https://EconPapers.repec.org/RePEc:hur:ijarbs:v:5:y:2015:i:1:p:383-398

Wiley, J., George, T., & Rayner, K. (2018). Baseball fans don't like lumpy batters: Influence of domain knowledge on the access of subordinate meanings. *Quarterly Journal of Experimental Psychology, 71*(1), 93-102. https://doi.org/10.1080/17470218.2016.1251470

Williams, D. J. (2008). Contemporary vampires and (blood-red) leisure: Should we be afraid of the dark? *Leisure/Loisir, 32*(2), 513-539. https://doi.org/10.1080/14927713.2008.9651420

Williams, D. J. (2009). Deviant leisure: Rethinking "the good, the bad, and the ugly". *Leisure Sciences, 31*(2), 207-213. https://doi.org/10.1080/01490400802686110

Williams, K. L. (2006). *The impact of popular culture fandom on perceptions of Japanese language and culture learning: The case of student anime fans* (Publication No. 3245796) [Doctoral dissertation, University of Texas at Austin]. ProQuest Dissertations and Theses Global.

Wills, T. A. (1981). Downward comparison principles in social psychology. *Psychological Bulletin, 90*(2), 245-271. https://doi.org/10.1037/0033-2909.90.2.245

Winge, T. (2006). Costuming the imagination: Origins of anime and manga cosplay. *Mechademia, 1*(1), 65-76. https://doi.org/10.1353/mec.0.0084

Winter, R., Salter, A., & Stanfill, M. (2021). Communities of making: Exploring parallels between fandom and open source. *First Monday, 26*(2). https://dx.doi.org/10.5210/fm.v26i2.10870

Wirth, W., Hofer, M., & Schramm, H. (2012). Beyond pleasure: Exploring the eudaimonic entertainment experience. *Human Communication Research, 38*(4), 406-428. https://doi.org/10.1111/j.1468-2958.2012.01434.x

Wohl, M. J. A. & Branscombe, N. R. (2009). Group threat, collective angst, and ingroup forgiveness for the war in Iraq. *Political Psychology, 30*(2), 193-217. https://doi.org/10.1111/j.1467-9221.2008.00688.x

Won, J., & Kitamura, K. (2006). Motivational factors affecting sports consumption behavior of K-league and J-league spectators. *International Journal of Sport and Health Sciences, 4,* 233-251. https://doi.org/10.5432/ijshs.4.233

Wong, M., Goodboy, A. K., Murtagh, M. P., Hackney, A. A., & McCutcheon, L. E. (2010). Are celebrities charged with murder likely to be acquitted? *North American Journal of Psychology, 12*(3), 625-636.

Woo, B., Trail, G. T., Kwon, H. H., & Anderson, D. (2009). Testing models of motives and points of attachment among spectators in college football. *Sport Marketing Quarterly, 18*(1), 38-53.

Wu, R., Wang, C. L., Hao, W. (2018). A hero who never dies: Steve Jobs in his fans' minds. In C. L. Wang (Ed.), *Exploring the rise of fandom in contemporary consumer culture* (pp. 35-51). IGI Global. https://doi.org/10.4018/978-1-5225-3220-0.ch003

Wu, S.-H., Tsai, C.-Y., & Hung, C.-C. (2012). Toward team or player? How trust, vicarious achievement motive, and identification affect fan loyalty. *Journal of Sport Management, 26*(2), 177-191. https://doi.org/10.1123/jsm.26.2.177

Wundt, W. M. (1893). *Grundzuge der physiologischem psychologie.* Engleman.

Xiao, M. (2020). Factors influencing esports viewership: An approach based on the theory of reasoned action. *Communication and Sport, 8*(1), 92-122. https://doi.org/10.1177/2167479518819482

Xu, H., & Yan, R.-N. (2011). Feeling connected via television viewing: Exploring the scale and its correlates. *Communication Studies, 62*(2), 186-206. https://doi.org/10.1080/10510974.2010.550380

Yamato, E. (2016). 'Growing as a person': experiences at anime, comics, and games fan events in Malaysia. *Journal of Youth Studies, 19*(6), 743-759. https://doi.org/10.1080/13676261.2015.1098769

Yang, L. (2009). All for love: The Corn fandom, prosumers, and the Chinese way of creating a superstar. *International Journal of Cultural Studies, 12*(5), 527-543. https://doi.org/10.1177/1367877909337863

Yannopoulos, P. (2017). Segmenting the Greek football market. *Would Journal of Management, 8*(1), 122-133.

Yen, C.-H., & Teng, H.-Y. (2015). Celebrity involvement, perceived value, and behavioral intentions in popular media-induced tourism. *Journal of*

Hospitality and Tourism Research, 39(2), 225-244.
https://doi.org/10.1177/1096348012471382

Yenilmez, M. I., Ersöz, G., Çınarlı, S., & Sarı, I. (2020). Examination of the psychometric properties of the sport interest inventory in a sample of Turkish football spectators. *Managing Sport and Leisure, 25*(4), 246-258. https://dx.doi.org/10.1080/23750472.2019.1708208

Yoon, Y., & Uysal, M. (2005). An examination of the effects of motivation and satisfaction on destination loyalty: a structural model. *Tourism Management, 26*(1), 45-56. https://doi.org/10.1016/j.tourman.2003.08.016

Yoshida, M., Gordon, B., Heere, B., & James, J. D. (2015). Fan community identification: An empirical examination of its outcomes in Japanese professional sport. *Sport Marketing Quarterly, 24*(2), 105-119.

Yoshida, M., Heere, B., & Gordon, B. (2015). Predicting behavioral loyalty through community: Why other fans are more important than own intentions, our satisfaction, and the team itself. *Journal of Sport Management, 29*(3), 318-333. https://doi.org/10.1123/jsm.2013-0306

Yousaf, A., Bashir, M., & Amin, I. (2015). Youth motivations to watch sports in Indian context: Exploring cross-nationality and cross-gender differences. *Management & Marketing, 10*(4), 330-340.

Yousaf, A., Gupta, A., & Mishra, A. (2017). Sport team brand-equity index: A new measurement. *Journal of Indian Business Research, 9*(2), 169-188. https://doi.org/10.1108/JIBR-07-2016-0069

Young, R. A., & Crandall, R. (1984). Wilderness use and self-actualization. *Journal of Leisure Research, 16*(2), 149-160. https://doi.org/10.1080/00222216.1984.11969582

Yue, X., & Cheung, C. (2019). *Idol worship in Chinese society: A psychological approach*. Routledge.

Yue, X. D., & Cheung, C. K. (2000). Selection of favourite idols and models among Chinese young people: A comparative study in Hong Kong and Nanjing. *International Journal of Behavioral Development, 24*(1), 91-98. https://doi.org/10.1080/016502500383511

Yue, X. D., Cheung, C. K., & Wong, D. S. W. (2010). From glamour-oriented idolatry to achievement-oriented idolatry: A framing experiment among adolescents in Hong Kong and Shenzhen. *Asian Journal of Social Psychology, 13*(1), 1-8. https://doi.org/10.1111/j.1467-839X.2010.01295.x

Yun, J. H., Rosenberger, P. J., & Sweeney, K. (2020). Drivers of soccer fan loyalty: Australian evidence on the influence of team brand image, fan engagement, satisfaction and enduring involvement. *Asia Pacific Journal of*

Marketing and Logistics, 33(3), 755-782. https://doi.org/10.1108/APJML-07-2019-0444

Yun-Tsan, L. (2017). Influence of spectator motivation and team identification on team loyalty and switching intentions of sports fans. *Advances in Management, 10*(4), 7-17.

Zaichkowsky, J. L. (1985). Measuring the involvement construct. *Journal of Consumer Research, 12*(3), 341-352. https://doi.org/10.1086/208520

Zaichkowsky, J. L. (1994). The personal involvement inventory: Reduction, revision, and application to advertising. *Journal of Advertising, 23*(4), 59-70. https://doi.org/10.1080/00913367.1943.10673459

Zaleski, Z. (1984). Sensation seeking and preferences for emotional visual stimuli. *Personality and Individual Differences, 5*(5), 609-611. https://doi.org/10.1016/0191-8869(84)90040-0

Zani, B., & Kirchler, E. (1991). When violence overshadows the spirit of sporting competition: Italian football fans and their clubs. *Journal of Community and Applied Social Psychology, 1*(1), 5-21. https://doi.org/10.1002/casp.2450010103

Zetou, E., Kouli, O., Psarras, A., Tzetzis, G., & Michalopoulou, M. (2013). The role of involvement in the loyalty of sport fans in professional volleyball. *International Journal of Sport Management Recreation and Tourism, 12*, 1-16. http://www.ijsmart.eu/onlinepic/vol12_a%20Eleni%20Zetou.pdf

Zhang, J. J., Lam, E. T. C., Connaughton, D. P., Bennett, G., Pease, D. G., Pham, U. L., Killion, L. E., Ocker, L. B., & Duley, A. R. (2004). Variables affecting spectator enjoyment of minor league hockey games. *International Journal of Sport Management, 5*, 157-182.

Zhang, J. J., Pease, D. G., & Lam, E. T. (2001). Sociomotivational factors affecting spectator attendance at minor league hockey games. *Sport Marketing Quarterly, 10*(1), 43-54.

Zhang, Y. (2017). *National basketball association fandom in China: A comparative analysis of fan behaviors, fan motivation, and team identification* [Master's thesis, University of Texas at Austin]. University of Texas at Austin. http://hdl.handle.net/2152/60434

Zhao, Z. (2020). *Effects of inspirational media experiences in instagram on visit intention: The role of subjective and eudaimonic well-being* [Master's thesis, University of Guelph]. https://hdl.handle.net/10214/21260

Zheng, Y., Ma, Y., Guo, L., Cheng, J., & Zhang, Y. (2018). Prediction of Chinese drivers' intentions to park illegally in emergency lanes: An application of the theory of planned behavior. *Traffic Injury Prevention, 19*(6), 629-636. https://doi.org/10.1080/15389588.2018.1479062

Zillman, D. (2000). The coming of media entertainment. In D. Zillman & P. Vorderer (Eds.), *Media entertainment: The psychology of its appeal* (pp. 1-20). Lawrence Erlbaum Associates.

Zillmann, D., & Vorderer, P. (Eds.). (2000). *Media entertainment: The psychology of its appeal*. Routledge.

Zsila, Á., Orosz, G., McCutcheon, L. E., & Demetrovics, Z. (2020). A lethal imitation game? Exploring links among psychoactive substance use, self-harming behaviors and celebrity worship. *Addictive Behaviors Reports, 12*. Article 100319. https://doi.org/10.1016/j.abrep.2020.100319

Zubeck, J. P. (1969). *Sensory deprivation: Fifteen years of research*. Appleton-Century-Crofts.

Zuckerman, M. (1979). *Sensation seeking: Beyond the optimal level of arousal*. Lawrence Erlbaum.

Zuckerman, H. (1988). The sociology of science. In N. J. Smelser (Ed.), *Handbook of sociology* (pp. 511-574). Sage.

Zuckerman, M. (1994). *Behavioral expressions and biosocial bases of sensation seeking*. Cambridge University Press.

Zuckerman, M. (2008). Personality and sensation seeking. In G. Boyle, G. Matthews, & D. Saklofske (Eds.), *The SAGE handbook of personality theory and assessment: Personality theories and models* (Vol. 1, pp. 379-398). Sage.

Zuckerman, E. (2014). New media, new civics? *Policy and Internet, 6*(2), 151-168. https://doi.org/10.1002/1944-2866.POI360

Zuckerman, M., Bone, R. N., Neary, R., Mangelsdorff, D., & Brustman, B. (1972). What is the sensation seeker? Personality trait and experience correlates of the sensation-seeking scales. *Journal of Consulting and Clinical Psychology, 39*(2), 308-321. https://doi.org/10.1037/h0033398

Made in the USA
Monee, IL
01 April 2022